YEAR A ▪ 2002

workbook
FOR LECTORS AND GOSPEL READERS

Aelred R. Rosser

LITURGY
TRAINING
PUBLICATIONS

WORKBOOK FOR LECTORS AND GOSPEL READERS 2002, UNITED STATES EDITION © 2001 Archdiocese of Chicago. All rights reserved.

Liturgy Training Publications
1800 North Hermitage Avenue
Chicago, IL 60622-1101
1-800-933-1800
fax 1-800-933-7094
orders@ltp.org
www.ltp.org

Editor: David A. Lysik
Production editor: Bryan M. Cones
Typesetter: Jim Mellody-Pizzato
Original book design: Jill Smith
Revised design: Anna Manhart and Jim Mellody-Pizzato
Cover art: Barbara Simcoe
Interior art: Steve Erspamer, SM

Printed in the United States of America by Von Hoffmann Graphics, Inc.

ISBN 1-56854-372-7
WL02

CONTENTS

The Author

Aelred Rosser was born and reared in an evangelical tradition of Christianity that has always centered its religious experience on the Bible, the word of God. Since becoming a Catholic at the age of 20, he has spent 40 years promoting the best of both religious traditions—a profound love for scripture expressed in a nourishing liturgical celebration of the sacraments. Aelred holds degrees in philosophy, religion and theology, and a doctorate in rhetoric, linguistics and literature from the University of Southern California. He is also certified as a teacher of English as a foreign language (TEFL). Aelred has conducted lector workshops and preaching seminars nationwide. His other writings on the ministry of proclamation are among the resource works listed at the end of the introduction.

Dedication

This book is affectionately dedicated to Monsignor Thomas P. Leonard, pastor of Holy Trinity Parish, New York City, whose great heart and sense of humor showed me how joyful Christian ministry can be. And to my fellow writer, Padre Mizael Roa Cardenas of Bogota, Colombia, whose Latino zest for life doubled the size of my world.

INTRODUCTION

Those who proclaim God's word in the liturgy are ministers. When you answer the call to be a minister of the word, you enter a deeper relationship with God revealed in sacred scripture. You take upon yourself the awesome duty and privilege of bringing the printed word to life, making it flesh. Your proclamation enables God's word to achieve the purpose for which it was sent. In short, you become a prophet, one who speaks for God. John the Baptist is your model, preparing the way of the Lord, making crooked paths straight and rough places smooth. You cry out with every breath, "See, there is the Lamb of God!" Finally, you join yourself to the Jewish tradition, which sees prayerful study of God's word as the worthiest of all endeavors. And as a Christian you believe that God's words find their fullest expression in that one perfect Word—Jesus, the Word made flesh.

The Word

"The Word of God" means more to us than a simple "word." It means "all the words of God." Or perhaps it means "the Bible." And certainly for Christians it means Jesus Christ, "the Word made flesh," the "incarnate Word." The familiar liturgical proclamation that follows every reading, "The word of the Lord," and the response to it, "Thanks be to God," have a formative influence on us over time. It creates in our hearts and minds an association between the words of the reading and the benevolent actions of the God who revealed them.

That association is even more vivid in the languages in which the words of God were originally written. The Hebrew word for "word" is *dabar*, and it means "deed" (an action) as well as "word." In this definition, words are not merely sounds or symbols that describe deeds; they are themselves deeds. Contemporary language scholars have formulated a similar view. They argue that words are not always

just sounds or written symbols that *refer* to something, as in "There is the house where I live." In some usage, words actually *do* something. In these cases they are called "performative speech acts." For example, the words "I baptize you" or "I forgive you" or (at the eucharist) "this is my body" do not simply refer to an action; they actually accomplish the action.

We understand the words of liturgical proclamation more accurately when we view them as "performative," as accomplishing the work of salvation they describe even as the reader proclaims them. The word of God is not a history lesson, though there is history in it. It is not a story, though it is full of stories. It is not a set of rules to live by, though there is much in it to guide our choices. No, the word of God is a living and dynamic presence, achieving the salvation it describes, even as the reader proclaims it. The church's own teaching expresses this view: "[Christ] is present in his word, since it is he himself who speaks when the holy scriptures are read in church"; and, again, "[I]n the liturgy God is speaking to his people and Christ is still proclaiming his gospel" (Second Vatican Council, *Constitution on the Liturgy*, 7, 33).

The Words of the Word

All of sacred scripture is written in exalted language because its writers were always engaged in communicating something more than their actual words. Even what appears to be the most straightforward narrative has a deeper purpose. The deeper purpose explains, in part, why the gospel narratives of Matthew, Mark and Luke differ so much from each other. Each writer had a governing purpose, not only in recording events in the life of Jesus but in recording them *in a certain way*. And the gospel of John is radically different from the other three. In John's account of the passion, for example, Jesus is very much in control of the situation. He is not victim; he is king and ruler. A loyal band of followers stands at the foot of his cross. In the other accounts, a mocking crowd witnesses Jesus' death. John's purpose is different, so he portrays the passion of Jesus differently. Such controlling themes elevate

prose far beyond the merely literal and project it into the realm of the figurative, even the poetic.

The point is that casual attempts to "translate" scripture into colloquial, informal or even "everyday" expressions reveal a lack of understanding of scripture and the subtleties of its original forms. More serious still is the effect of such attempts, no matter how well-intentioned or motivated: They invariably and inevitably trivialize sacred scripture. They also underestimate the sensitivities of the hearers and emphasize the proclaimer at the expense of the word of God.

The Shapes of the Word

The Bible is a collection of many different kinds of literature: narratives (stories), poetry, sermons, hymns, and so on. Your instincts will tell you that different kinds of literature require different treatments. Trust your instincts, but avoid stereotypes. There is no reason to imitate bad Shakespearean actors when reading poetry, or Mother Goose when reading a story.

There is an important reason for recognizing and respecting the different literary styles in the Bible, and it has been alluded to above. The writer's message is told in a particular way (literary form) because the writer is making a particular point or appealing to the audience in a particular way. The choice of style is not arbitrary. A poetic account of the creation story, for example, may not be in accord with what science has shown to be factual. The writers of the Bible were seldom concerned with scientific data. The author of Genesis has but one point: to demonstrate that the Creator God is responsible for all that is. The facts of the case are beside that point—presenting a problem for those who like their logic tight. But poetry is usually not the style of choice for logicians.

Readers who have studied literature in high school and college should not hesitate to approach the Bible as a collection of literature written in a variety of genres. Concepts such as metaphor, simile, narrative, plot and denouement (resolution) all apply to scripture. Understanding poetic structure, word order, alliteration and onomatopoeia can be helpful when studying biblical poetry. Yes, many poetic elements such as these are lost in translation, but the better translations today have tried to preserve them.

The point here is that readers often bring to the ministry of proclamation a wealth of experience that should be capitalized upon, not tossed aside in the mistaken notion that the literature of the Bible—and effective proclamation of it—is so rarefied that it requires a whole new frame of reference.

The Proclaimer

The reader proclaims God's word to the assembled faith community. It's that simple and that sublime. Although the ministry is a simple one, that does not mean it's easy to do well or requires little energy or effort. Simplicity refers to the mode of the ministry, the reader's ability to proclaim the word transparently, which allows the word itself, and not the proclaimer, to take center stage. Simplicity does not, however, refer to the reader's task, for the task itself is quite challenging. Not everyone is equal to it.

But there is an element of the sublime in the work of the reader as well. To be chosen to proclaim God's word to one's fellow believers is to participate in the mystery and struggle of their individual journeys of faith. There can be no more sublime ministry than that. And there can be no more humbling responsibility, for the quality of the reader's proclamation determines whether his or her service will help or hinder the hearers.

Women and men who take on the ministry of reader are presumed to be of good faith, eager to serve their fellow Christians, and willing to engage in ongoing formation for effective service. But it is not presumed that they are particularly holy, exceptionally gifted, or highly skilled in communication techniques. Basic abilities are required, and these are the subject of part of this book. Highly developed communication skills related to certain professions (public speaking, broadcasting and acting, for example) must be developed by the reader, but they do not in themselves render a person capable of effective liturgical proclamation. The purpose of liturgical worship is different from the objectives we find in the work of professional communicators: conveying information, entertaining, persuading to action, and so forth. The liturgy may do all of these things, of course, but they are not its purpose, which is to celebrate the faith shared by the worshipers.

Finally, the mere wish or willingness to serve as reader does not qualify one for the ministry. This statement sounds harsh. No one wants to discourage a volunteer. But the fact remains that the ministry of reader is a charism for the building up of the community. It requires certain native abilities that some do not have, such as an adequate vocal instrument, for example. It also requires self-possession and confidence, maturity, poise and sensitivity to diversity in one's audience. Such qualities can be enhanced in a formation program, but should already be present to a significant degree in the potential reader.

Like all ministries in the church, liturgical proclamation of the word is an awesome responsibility to which one is called and into which one is formed. Fifteen hundred years ago, Saint Benedict wrote in his *Rule:* "They should not presume to read who by mere chance take up the book. . . . Only those are to discharge these duties who can do so to the edification of the hearers."

The Proclaimer's Book

As a proclaimer of God's word, you know that your best friend is a book called the lectionary (from the Latin word *lectio*, which means "reading" or "lesson"). It is a collection of Bible texts arranged for proclamation according to the church's liturgical calendar. Seasoned lectors and gospel readers should have a thorough knowledge of the lectionary and be able to use it with ease. More than that, the committed proclaimer respects this holy book as the medium through which God's word is lavished upon the people of God for their comfort and inspiration, and as an invitation to respond to God's love more fully.

When the Second Vatican Council insisted that the riches of sacred scripture be opened more lavishly for the faithful, we had lived for centuries with one set of Bible readings that were the same each year and for every day of the year. The lectionary compiled after Vatican II nearly tripled our exposure to the Bible during liturgical worship with a collection of readings covering a three-year cycle for the Sunday liturgy and a two-year cycle for weekdays.

In order to abide by the Council's directive, two major changes were made. The Sunday liturgy of the word was expanded from two readings (epistle and gospel) to include an additional selection, what we know now as the first reading, almost always from the Hebrew scriptures (the Old Testament) except during the Easter season, and chosen with the gospel of the day in mind. The second reading is taken from New Testament books other than the gospels. No particular relationship to the other readings guides its choice; it is often a *lectio continua*, which means that part of a New Testament book is proclaimed in sections in semi-continuous fashion over a number of weeks.

When the cycle of readings was expanded from one year to three (Years A, B and C), gospel readings from the three synoptic gospels—Matthew, Mark and Luke—were assigned for each year, respectively. These three evangelists write a kind of "synopsis" of Jesus' life and ministry, a more or less sequential narrative. The gospel of John, very different in character and purpose from the synoptics, fills in occasionally, but it is primarily reserved for the Easter season in all three years.

Part of the lectionary we have been using for the past 30 or so years has recently been revised (the part containing the readings for Sundays, solemnities and certain feasts). Even this, we hope, is not a final revision. We will continue to see improvements in the selection of scripture texts (and the way they are edited for public proclamation) for several more years to come. We will also see improved translations in the future, translations that take into even greater consideration such issues as inclusive language, oral presentation and other existing lectionaries.

The most obvious feature of the lectionary is its organization in accord with the liturgical calendar. There is a three-year cycle of readings for Sundays that begins with the seasons of Advent and Christmas, and continues with Lent, Easter and Pentecost. Between Christmas and Lent, and again between Pentecost and Advent, are the Sundays in Ordinary Time, divided into two parts. Incidentally, the word "ordinary" here does not mean "plain" or "common" or the opposite of "extraordinary." The root word involved is "ordinal" (as in the ordinal numbers) and indicates that Ordinary Time is composed of those Sundays we number consecutively from the Second Sunday in Ordinary Time (the "first" Sunday is the feast of the Lord's baptism, the last day of the Christmas season) to the Thirty-fourth Sunday in Ordinary Time, the solemnity of Christ the King.

Notice that each group of readings is numbered in the lectionary (and in *Workbook*) for easy reference. Thus, the First Sunday of Advent (Year A) is #1, the First Sunday of Advent (Year B) is #2, and so on. Readers who are unaware of how the lectionary is laid out run the risk of proclaiming the wrong reading (Year C instead of Year A, for example). If you are fortunate, however, your parish will have acquired the newly revised Sunday lectionary in a three-volume set (Year A, Year B, Year C), which makes the book much easier to use.

Clearly, the lector who knows the "why" and "how" of the lectionary is better equipped to perform the ministry of reader effectively. No reading is completely isolated from the others at a given celebration. Each is carefully chosen for its relevance to a particular season, its relationship to the other readings at the same celebration, or its appropriateness for a particular feast day. Lectors and gospel readers who are truly committed to their important ministry will take some time to learn more about how the church's book of readings is put together. Knowledge of the lectionary is nothing less than knowledge of the means by which God speaks to the Sunday assembly through your voice.

The Proclaimer's Instrument

Our personal experience is sufficient evidence for the power of the human speech. We know that it can heal, destroy, provoke to anger. We have used it to express love, hate, disgust, ecstasy, anger, joy—the full range of human emotions. We have heard others speak and have known that it can affect us quite profoundly, for good or ill. We have heard strong arguments spoken by trustworthy speakers who have changed our way of thinking and our choices. We have seen others swayed to poor choices by charlatans who have misused the power of speech.

In our ministry as readers we need to become more aware of the power of our speech. Our proclamation of the word is *never* without effect. The poorest proclamation, the mediocre proclamation, the most compelling proclamation—each affects the hearers. What is true of liturgical worship is true of proclamation during that worship: poor liturgy diminishes faith; good liturgy augments it. A time-proven Latin axiom sums it up best: *lex orandi, lex credendi*—as we pray, so we believe.

But it is the potential of our speech's power for good that we want to emphasize here. And to do that we need to consider another aspect of human speech as it applies to our ministry: *sacramentality*. The familiar definition of sacrament as "an outward sign of an inward reality" can help us appreciate why the church invests the proclamation of the word with such significance: "It is Christ himself who speaks." Christ's word is creative and causative. The water poured at baptism and the words that are spoken ("I baptize you in the name of . . .") are the outward sign of the sacrament of baptism. The inward reality is the incorporation of the newly baptized into the church, the Body of Christ. Similarly, when the reader proclaims the Good News in a liturgy, the word goes forth from the reader and is fulfilled in the hearing of the assembly. An action takes place. The "sign," the proclamation, is outward. The fulfillment of the word even as it is proclaimed is the "inward reality."

This is not to say that proclamation of the word is itself a sacrament. But it does have a sacramental character and effect, like the liturgy of which it is a part. In the words of the apostle Paul, "As often as you eat this bread and drink the cup, you proclaim the Lord's death until he comes" (1 Corinthians 11:26). The eucharist is more than a simple recollection of what Christ accomplished in his death and resurrection. It is a continuation of that accomplishment throughout history and into the future. Proclamation of the word is more than a retelling or rereading. It is a continuation of God's saving presence in human history.

Human speech is powerful. When employed in the proclamation of the word of God, it is sacramental. Proclaimers who recognize the power and responsibility with which they are entrusted will not take their charism lightly.

The Proclaimer's Tools

Many factors are involved in producing speech that meets the expectations of the hearers. They all add up to what communication specialists tell us is the single most important quality demanded by listeners: vocal variety. What listeners find most difficult to listen to is a voice that lacks color, variations of pitch, animation and warmth.

Vocal variety is an umbrella term that includes all the characteristics of speech discussed below. It includes melody (or modulation), rate, pause, volume and articulation—and this list is not exhaustive. Each term is elusive and imprecise. What is "too fast"? How loud is "too loud"? When does a pause become "dead space"? In our discussion of vocal variety, keep in mind that the complexities of human speech sounds do not fit into precise categories. Matters of taste, individual preference and many other considerations make the esthetics of speech an imprecise science! Nevertheless, we can certainly speak of what is effective and pleasant and generally considered "listenable." By the same token we can certainly identify undesirable characteristics: monotony, dullness, inaudibility, lack of clarity and "phoniness," to name a few.

As you experiment with the individual components of vocal variety, keep in mind that they are interdependent. After all, they cannot be considered or experienced in isolation. The melody of the passage will influence the rate at which it is proclaimed; effective pausing depends on how fast or slow the text is read, as does good articulation. Although the volume at which you read must always be adequate and appropriate, it should not always be the same. Melody, rate and articulation all affect considerations of loudness and softness.

The Listener

Both speaker and listener are constantly sending signals; the circular flow of information and feedback is constant. The difference between the two is that the communicator is ordinarily sending verbal signals, whereas the listener is sending nonverbal signals. The effective communicator must remain constantly alert to this feedback. We have all experienced readers in the liturgy who cannot be heard and yet seem unaware of it. They seem, in fact, to be oblivious to the fact

that they have an assembly of listeners. Such readers conceive of their task as one-sided. They send out signals but do not receive them. The communication act is incomplete.

As reader, you must remain aware of how your listeners are responding. Are they attentive? Are they distracted by something else? Are they nodding off? Are they finding seats because they came late? Are they searching in pamphlets to find the printed text of what they can't hear?

The reason contemporary listeners will not tolerate insufficient volume is that they ordinarily do not have to. In informal conversation they can ask their communication partner to speak up. Radios, televisions and other sound media have volume controls. If your reading is simply not loud enough, then something else is being perceived as louder. That could be crying infants, the air-conditioning system, a restless assembly, or the "inner noise" that we all have playing in our heads at every moment. The point is, if something is louder (let alone more interesting and commanding of attention), the reading will not be heard.

But sheer volume is not the answer. Indeed, excessive volume is more disagreeable than insufficient volume. The kind of volume required in public communication situations is more complex than turning a knob—either on the microphone system or in the human body! Just as important as volume is sound "height" and "weight," or pitch and projection. Depending on the environment in which your ministry is exercised (Gothic cathedral or tiny chapel), the

"height" or pitch of the voice must be elevated accordingly. And the voice must take on a proportionate degree of "weight" or strength of projection as well. Experimentation and feedback can help you find and discover the vocal tools that are best for you and your hearers.

Beyond the esthetics of a well-employed vocal instrument, there is another matter the proclaimer must take very much to heart: credibility with the listeners. Before they can believe in your proclamation, they must believe in you. And credibility with the members of the assembly is your responsibility alone. The assembly may owe you courtesy and attention, but you must earn the one and capture the other.

What is involved in building credibility with the assembly? Everything from your conduct as a member of the parish community to the way you arrange your hair. If either borders on the bizarre, your credibility will suffer. However, leaving most of the obvious things aside, consider some of the common problems that compromise the proclaimer's credibility—and therefore detract from the assembly's participation in the liturgy.

Mispronounced words, especially proper biblical names, are intolerable. You simply cannot stumble over these, even though some of them are quite foreign to the modern ear and difficult to pronounce. The instant you announce a reading from "Deuteromony" instead of "Deuteronomy," you will be branded inept. Even to stumble once during a list of place names (Cappadocia, Emmaus, Galatia, Thessalonica, Horeb, Caesarea and Philippi) is not acceptable. The point is made so strongly because the solution is so easy. Consult a dictionary or any of a dozen pronunciation guides available. *Pronunciation Guide for the Sunday Lectionary* by Susan E. Myers is a good reference tool, readily available from Liturgy Training Publications for a couple of dollars. If you underestimate the importance of this point, you are underestimating the members of your assembly and your power for good.

Overly dramatic (theatrical, gooey, self-centered or bombastic) proclamation is a severe disservice to the assembly and to God's word. Though you may be convinced of your power to instill joy or dread or comfort or obedience by means of a "powerful" presentation, you will have to lay aside such insensitive arrogance. In every assembly there are those who are sad, distraught, happy, excited, bored, weary, full of pep and grieving. How can you enable the word of

God to reach all of them? A degree of restraint and sincere involvement with the text will let it work on its own merits and allow all these various moods to hear God's message.

Excessive solemnity, dullness, monotonous delivery and inaudibility are perhaps even worse than showiness. They communicate a lack of care and involvement that will not be tolerated by a more or less captive listener. In some cases, dullness is the effect of stage fright. Our voice is as petrified as we are. Experience is the solution; stage fright itself is repressed energy that can be released through the proclamation, empowering both text and reader.

More obvious threats to the proclaimer's credibility need only be mentioned: gaudy or sloppy dress, poor posture, nonverbal noise (uhs, ahs, jingling pocket change, losing one's place, rushing to and from the ambo). Consider all these dangers, even the ones you think are not a problem for you.

If your response to these warnings is, "It's the assembly's problem if they are so picky and can't overlook a mistake or two," you are partially right. The assembly's members should not be so picky, and you will find that most are extraordinarily tolerant and forgiving. But consider this: Did the members of the assembly come to church to exercise tolerance of the proclaimer or to hear the word of God proclaimed in a way that will alter their lives for the good? Certainly, liturgical celebration is not an antiseptic experience. After all, it's done by human beings. But the better we do it the better it can work its miracle

of transforming individual lives to transform in turn the world we live in.

The Proclaimer's Dialogue with the Assembly

Liturgical dialogue is effective when the principle of "expected form" is observed: "The word of the Lord"; "Thanks be to God"; "A reading from the holy gospel according to Luke"; "The gospel of the Lord"; "Praise to you, Lord Jesus Christ." The dialogue loses its ritual power when the proclaimer departs from it for the misguided purpose of making it literal, relevant, "warm" or informative. Thus it is important that readers be faithful to the dialogue assigned to them, not embellishing or augmenting it in any way. Doing so destroys the appeal of liturgy and ritual as an expected form of worship. Ritual works its long-term and subtle effect on us precisely because of its repetition and predictability. The constant search for new and potentially disarming ways to alter liturgical dialogue violates liturgy's purpose and function.

In recent years, we have heard readers at pains to "refresh" liturgical dialogue by creating their own versions of it. "The word of the Lord" has seen such permutations as "And this, my brothers and sisters, is the word of the Lord." The content of the two statements is arguably the same, but the form, function and purpose are all radically different. Aside from the fact that the assembly will be caught off guard and so will be unable to respond with spontaneity, the casting of the dialogue in this literal and "informative" way misses the mark in at least two ways. First, it destroys the expectations with regard to "form" that are essential to ritual, and, second, it "tells" us something instead of "doing something."

It is only recently that the ritual form has been officially changed by the church. You may recall that at the end of the reading the reader used to say, "This is the word of the Lord." The formula was reduced to "The word of the Lord" not only in the interests of a better translation of the Latin *(Verbum Domini)*, as some have asserted, but to render it more appropriate to ritual (performative) and less referential (literal, informative). "This is . . ." clearly carries a feeling of the demonstrative, which explains in part the tendency of some readers to hold the lectionary aloft as they spoke the words. This practice confused things further by drawing attention to the book when the proper focus of the assembly's attention should have been the living proclamation of the word.

The fact that the shorter formula *is* closer to the Latin simply shows that the Latin carries the non-referential, non-demonstrative sense of a text that is more acclamation than explanation. The simple change has a subtle and important effect over time. It lessens our tendency to see the liturgy as a gathering in which we "learn" about our faith and intensifies our experience of the liturgy as a gathering in which we "celebrate" our faith.

A Word of Caution

You will notice that we have continued the practice of marking certain words in the scriptural text to help the proclaimer emphasize them in an attempt to communicate the overall context more effectively. We do so because experience has told us that users of the *Workbook* appreciate this aid. However, the markings are not to be taken slavishly or considered obligatory. Effective proclamation can never be quite so rigidly orchestrated. If the markings help you in the development of sensitive vocal variety, use them; if not, ignore them.

Pronunciation Key

Most consonants in the pronunciation key are straightforward: The letter B always represents the sound B and D is always D, and so on. Vowels are more complicated. Note that the long I sound (as in kite or ice) is represented by *ī*, while long A (skate, pray) is represented by *ay*. Long E (beam, marine) is represented by *ee*; long O (boat, coat) is represented by *oh*; long U (sure, secure) is represented by *oo* or *yoo*. Short A (cat), E (bed), I (slim) and O (dot) are represented by *a*, *e*, *i* and *o* except in an unstressed syllable, when E and I are signified by *eh* and *ih*. Short U (cup) is represented by *uh*. An asterisk (*) indicates the schwa

sound, as in the last syllable of the word "stable." The letters *oo* and *th* can each be pronounced in two ways (as in cool or book; thin or they); underlining differentiates between them. Stress is indicated by the capitalization of the stressed syllable in words of more than one syllable.

bait = bayt	thin = thin
cat = kat	vision = VIZH-*n
sang = sang	ship = ship
father = FAH-<u>th</u>er	sir = ser
care = kayr	gloat = gloht
paw = paw	cot = kot
jar = jahr	noise = noyz
easy = EE-zee	poison = POY-z*n
her = her	plow = plow
let = let	although = awl-<u>TH</u>OH
queen = kween	church = church
delude = deh-L<u>OO</u>D	fun = fuhn
when = hwen	fur = fer
ice = īs	flute = fl<u>oo</u>t
if = if	foot = foot
finesse = fih-NES	

Recommended Works

Guides for Proclaiming God's Word

Connell, Martin. *Guide to the Revised Lectionary.* Chicago, Illinois: Liturgy Training Publications, 1998.

Lector Training Program: This Is the Word of the Lord. Audio tapes and booklet. Chicago, Illinois: Liturgy Training Publications, 1988.

The Lector's Ministry: Your Guide to Proclaiming the Word. Mineola, New York: Resurrection Press, 1990.

Lee, Charlotte I., and Galati, Frank. *Oral Interpretation*, 9th ed. Boston, Massachusetts: Houghton Mifflin, 1997.

Myers, Susan E. *Pronunciation Guide for the Sunday Lectionary.* Chicago, Illinois: Liturgy Training Publications, 1998.

Proclaiming the Word: Formation for Readers in the Liturgy. Video. Chicago, Illinois: Liturgy Training Publications, 1994.

Rosser, Aelred R. *A Well-Trained Tongue: Formation in the Ministry of Reader.* Chicago, Illinois: Liturgy Training Publications, 1996.

———. *A Word That Will Rouse Them: Reflections on the Ministry of Reader.* Chicago, Illinois: Liturgy Training Publications, 1995.

———. *Guide for Lectors.* Chicago, Illinois: Liturgy Training Publications, 1998.

General Reference Works on the Bible

Boadt, Lawrence. *Reading the Old Testament: An Introduction.* New York, New York/Mahwah, New Jersey: Paulist Press, 1984.

Brown, Raymond E. *An Introduction to the New Testament* (The Anchor Bible Reference Library). New York, New York: Doubleday, 1997.

Collegeville Bible Commentary, Old Testament Series. Diane Bergant, general editor. Collegeville, Minnesota: The Liturgical Press, 1985.

Collegeville Bible Commentary, New Testament Series. Robert J. Karris, general editor. Collegeville, Minnesota: The Liturgical Press, 1991.

The Collegeville Pastoral Dictionary of Biblical Theology. Carroll Stuhlmueller, general editor. Collegeville, Minnesota: The Liturgical Press, 1996.

The New Jerome Biblical Commentary. Raymond E. Brown, Joseph Fitzmyer and Roland E. Murphy, editors. Englewood Cliffs, New Jersey: Prentice Hall, 1990.

New Testament Message: A Biblical-Theological Commentary. Wilfrid Harrington and Donald Senior, editors. Collegeville, Minnesota: The Liturgical Press, 1980.

The Women's Bible Commentary, expanded edition. Carol A. Newsom and Sharon H. Ringe, editors. Louisville, Kentucky: Westminster/John Knox Press, 1998.

Commentaries on the Gospel of Matthew

Harrington, Daniel. *The Gospel of Matthew* (Sacra Pagina). Collegeville, Minnesota: The Liturgical Press, 1991.

Meier, John P. *Matthew* (New Testament Message). Collegeville, Minnesota: The Liturgical Press, 1980.

Stock, Augustine. *The Method and Message of Matthew.* Collegeville, Minnesota: The Liturgical Press, 2000.

1st SUNDAY OF ADVENT

Lectionary #1

READING I   Isaiah 2:1–5

Always remember to look at the assembly
when you announce the reading. Then
pause slightly, look back at the book,
and begin.
Amoz = AY-muhz
The reading is poetry, not prose. An
exalted tone is appropriate.

A reading from the book of the prophet Isaiah

This is what *Isaiah*, son of *Amoz*,
saw concerning *Judah* and *Jerusalem*.

In days to *come*,
the mountain of the LORD's house
   shall be established as the *highest* mountain
   and raised above the *hills*.

All *nations* shall *stream* toward it;
   many *peoples* shall come and say:
"Come, let us climb the LORD's mountain,
   to the house of the God of *Jacob*,
that he may *instruct* us in his *ways*,
   and we may *walk* in his *paths*."

Make good use of the parallelism.
Almost every line has a "mate" in the
line that follows. Be sure this is clear
in your delivery.

For from *Zion* shall go forth *instruction*,
   and the word of the LORD from *Jerusalem*.
He shall *judge* between the *nations*,
   and impose *terms* on many *peoples*.
They shall beat their *swords* into *plowshares*
   and their *spears* into *pruning* hooks;
one nation shall *not* raise the *sword* against *another*,
   nor shall they train for *war* again.

The final two lines are a fervent plea.

O house of Jacob, *come*,
   let us walk in the *light* of the *Lord*!

READING I During these first few weeks of the new liturgical year we hear the good news proclaimed *as news!* It comes to us like a late-breaking story, and it has a feeling of immediacy and urgency we won't hear again until Easter. Many different voices—Isaiah in today's first reading, Paul in the second, and Jesus himself in the gospel—are in a rush to tell us that things are changing and that we need to get ready for the change.

But what is this good news? Is it that the world will be at peace in the reign of God (Isaiah's "plowshares and pruning hooks"),

or is it that the Lord will return suddenly, and so we must be prepared? It's both, of course. Advent has two faces, like the Roman god Janus, whose name graces the first month of our calendar. It looks back at the coming of Jesus in history, and it looks forward to the coming of Christ in mystery. It divides human history into two distinct periods: before and after the fulfillment of God's promise in the coming of the Messiah.

And in what way is the news good? There is no question about the first reading's picture of good. Can you imagine any greater good than a world without war? Isaiah says

that such a day will come when the Lord's mountain is the highest. In other words, only when all nations have adopted God's plan for the world shall we know peace. Isaiah did not see this day of fulfillment, but he was confident that God's vision for the world would be realized, sooner or later.

During Advent we remind ourselves frequently that God's plan is being worked out in Jesus. With his coming in history, his coming in mystery has already begun to happen. This is good news indeed! Spurred on by the guarantee that God's plan and will are inexorable, we might even hasten the

There is no scolding in this reading, only heartfelt encouragement. Let your voice be encouraging rather than challenging.

There should be no disdain or disgust in your voice when you name the deeds of darkness. These are facts of life, and nothing human is foreign to the Christian. Rather, communicate the joy and freedom (no smugness!) that comes from living honorably.

When Jesus speaks about the end of time, he is teaching, not threatening. Fill your voice with the dignity of a confident teacher.

READING II   Romans 13:11–14

A reading from the letter of Saint Paul to the Romans

Brothers and sisters:
You know the *time*;
    it is the hour *now* for you to *awake* from *sleep.*
For our *salvation* is *nearer* now than when we first *believed*;
    the night is *advanced,* the day is at *hand.*
Let us then *throw off* the works of *darkness*
        and put on the *armor* of *light;*
    let us *conduct* ourselves *properly* as in the *day,*
    not in *orgies* and *drunkenness,*
    not in *promiscuity* and *lust,*
    not in *rivalry* and *jealousy.*

But put on the *Lord* Jesus *Christ,*
    and make *no* provision for the *desires* of the *flesh.*

GOSPEL   Matthew 24:37–44

A reading from the holy gospel according to Matthew

Jesus said to his *disciples*:
"As it was in the days of *Noah,*
    so it will be at the *coming* of the Son of *Man.*
In *those* days before the *flood,*
    they were *eating* and *drinking,*
    marrying and *giving* in marriage,
    up to the day that Noah entered the *ark.*

Day of the Lord by behaving like optimistic inhabitants on the Lord's mountain. Proclaim Isaiah's vision with all the optimism and confidence you can muster. Proclaim it as the good news it is! It shows us how things will be—and how we can make them that way.

READING II Paul presumes that we can all sense how God's love is rushing upon us and that the world is dashing toward better days. There's no longing in Paul for the "good ol' days." The good days are now, and better days are coming. Imagine how our behavior would change

if we fully adopted Paul's view. And yet this is the basic Christian view of the church in the world. We're rushing toward God even as God rushes toward us. Faith tells us that God's redemptive plan is not to be thwarted—and that plan is eternal happiness for all humankind.

How do folks behave when they know all their dreams are about to come true? They watch with great energy and enthusiasm. They get ready for the great day by putting on their best behavior, embracing the light of day rather than the murkiness of

night, living honorably in selfless concern for one another.

Nowhere in his writing is Paul more excited than here. Communicate that optimistic energy to the members of your assembly, and enable them to begin Advent with the joy appropriate to the season.

GOSPEL There is a sense of dread in this gospel passage. After all, the flood that Noah survived devastated the earth and nearly all who dwelt upon it. But that's not Jesus' point here. Remember that God vowed after the flood never again

The mysteriousness of the examples ("one taken, another left") is intentional, not meant to be confusing. Tell it like it is.

They did not *know* until the *flood* came
      and carried them all *away*.
So will it be *also* at the *coming* of the Son of *Man*.
Two *men* will be out in the *field*;
      one will be *taken*, and *one* will be *left*.
Two *women* will be grinding at the *mill*;
      one will be *taken*, and one will be *left*.

"Therefore, stay *awake*!
For you do not *know* on which *day* your Lord will *come*.
Be sure of *this*: if the *master* of the *house*
      had known the *hour* of night when the *thief* was coming,
      he would have stayed *awake*
      and not let his house be *broken into*.
So *too*, you *also* must be prepared,
      for at an hour you do not *expect*, the Son of *Man* will *come*."

The last sentence is encouraging. Speak it to yourself, as well as to the members of the assembly, and you will adopt just the right tone.

to destroy the world; the rainbow was set in the sky as a reminder of that promise. The coming of the Son of Man is compared to the flood because people refused to heed Noah's warning and suffered the consequences. Jesus is telling us not to make the same mistake. God was the perpetrator of the tragedy of the flood, but we will be the perpetrators of our own destruction if we refuse to ready ourselves for the glory of the Lord's coming. In other words, the responsibility is ours. God is not threatening us. God is encouraging us to prepare ourselves for the glory to come. You wouldn't want to miss *this* event!

Here is an analogy that makes the point obvious. Imagine a robber sending a note ahead telling the homeowner the time of the intended break-in. There's no way the homeowner will be unprepared for the crime, and the robber doesn't stand a chance of staging a successful break-in. Although Jesus does not tell us precisely when, he tells us that he certainly will return—and we can depend on it! So, we know he's coming, but we don't know when. The only sensible thing to do is live in a state of readiness.

Does this approach seem a bit unlike our approach to other future events? No

doubt it does. If we have a procrastinating nature, it may even seem burdensome. We're tempted to say, "Just tell me when you're coming, so I can put off getting ready until I have to." The presumption underlying this view is that getting ready and being ready is tiresome, a nuisance and a burden. But here's the other point of Jesus' teaching: Being ready for the Lord's coming is a good way to live. It gives life purpose, meaning, impetus, force and dignity. And it makes us good company for our fellow travelers along the way.

IMMACULATE CONCEPTION

Lectionary #689

READING I   Genesis 3:9–15, 20

A reading from the book of Genesis

> The reading begins with a story. But the second half (except for the last sentence) is God's judgment on the situation. Prepare yourself for the change in tone.

After the man, *Adam*, had eaten of the *tree*,
 the LORD God *called* to the man and *asked* him,
  "Where *are* you?"
He answered, "I *heard* you in the garden;
 but I was *afraid*, because I was *naked*,
 so I *hid* myself."

Then he asked, "Who *told* you that you were *naked*?
You have *eaten*, then,
 from the *tree* of which I had *forbidden* you to eat!"
The man replied, "The *woman* whom you put here with me—
 she gave me *fruit* from the tree, and so I *ate* it."
The LORD God then asked the *woman*,
 "Why did you *do* such a thing?"
The woman answered, "The *serpent* tricked me *into* it,
  so I ate it."

> Allow for a significant pause before pronouncing the terrible sentence of exile and punishment.

Then the LORD God said to the *serpent*:
 "Because you have *done* this, you shall be *banned*
 from all the *animals*
 and from all the wild *creatures*;
 on your *belly* shall you crawl,
 and *dirt* shall you eat
 all the *days* of your *life*.

READING I The story of Adam and Eve and the ancient serpent is an unforgettable way of explaining how evil came to be in the world—and why it continues to this day. How should we approach such a story? How should we tell it? Well, first we should remember that it is hallowed by the ages, like all good stories that have stood the test of time. It should be told lovingly, with all the vigor necessary to enable the hearers to relish the familiarity—even

as they are encouraged to penetrate the meaning more deeply.

And what is the meaning of the story in the context of today's feast? It was chosen to be proclaimed today because of the symbolism of the relationship between Eve and Mary. As Eve was mother of all life, Mary becomes mother of Life itself in giving birth to Christ. Eve's offspring continue to battle

the serpent, and the serpent's attack upon the world continues today. Evil still strikes at the heels of Eve's offspring; we still keep our foot on its ugly head. Though evil has been cursed by God, we are still living under the collective curse of sin—banned like Adam and Eve from the garden of God's intimate presence. Mary opened the way back to the garden when she uttered her obedient *fiat*, which we hear in today's gospel: "Let it be done as you have said." Her obedience

I will put *enmity* between *you* and the *woman,*
and between *your* offspring and *hers;*
he will *strike* at your *head,*
while *you* strike at his *heel.*"

The man called his wife Eve,
because she became the mother of all the living.

Add another pause here before adding the final part of the narrative, which reminds us that we all share in the effect of the sin of disobedience.

READING II Ephesians 1:3–6, 11–12

A reading from the letter of Saint Paul to the Ephesians

Brothers and sisters:
Blessed be the *God* and *Father* of our Lord Jesus *Christ,*
who has *blessed* us in Christ
with every *spiritual* blessing in the *heavens,*
as he *chose* us in him, before the foundation of the *world,*
to be *holy* and without *blemish* before him.

In *love* he *destined* us for *adoption* to himself
through Jesus *Christ,*
in accord with the *favor* of his *will,*
for the *praise* of the *glory* of his *grace*
that he *granted* us in the *beloved.*

In *him* we were also *chosen,*
destined in accord with the *purpose* of the One
who accomplishes *all* things according to the intention
of his *will,*
so that we might *exist* for the praise of his *glory,*
we who *first hoped* in Christ.

Sustain the energy level throughout this brief hymn/poem—and take it slowly! Every line is loaded with good news.

Notice that the reading is composed of three long sentences. But, since it's poetry, let the sense of each line (not the punctuation) guide you.

"The word of the Lord" must always be preceded by a pause—especially after this reading—and then delivered with firmness and conviction while looking at the assembly.

cancels the disobedience of Eve and deals the death blow to our old enemy, sin.

It is a wonderful story you are proclaiming, full of familiar figures and phrases. But remember that it is as relevant today as ever. It packs a wallop, reminding us that obedience to the loving commands of God is the only effective antidote to the ills of our world.

READING II The Good News has never sounded better than in this exultant outburst of joy. What a revelation to discover that we have been chosen—from all eternity—to be holy and spotless! And what a challenge! Who can be holy and spotless? The answer is found in a deeper understanding of the text, and of the Good News itself. In Christ we have been given every spiritual blessing, and we have been *made* holy and spotless. Christianity is never so much about what we are supposed to do and be; it is always much more about who God is and what God has done for us. Just as Adam and Eve were created sinless, so we have been re-created sinless. And why has God done this? Pure love and gratuitous goodness are God's motives, and we exist in Christ to reflect that goodness.

This reading deserves a careful preparation and proclamation. Every word is precious and carefully chosen. Your best skills will be required to communicate the full meaning of this scriptural gem.

GOSPEL Luke 1:26–38

A reading from the holy gospel according to Luke

Avoid letting the familiarity of this story rob your voice of fresh energy. Proclaim it so that your hearers will be able to hear it with fresh ears—and hearts.

The angel *Gabriel* was sent from *God*
   to a town of *Galilee* called *Nazareth*,
   to a *virgin* betrothed to a man named *Joseph*,
   of the house of *David*,
   and the virgin's *name* was *Mary*.
And coming to her, he said,
   "*Hail*, full of *grace*! The *Lord* is with you."

The angel's greeting perplexes Mary. Here begins a pattern of conflict and resolution.

But she was greatly *troubled* at what was said
   and *pondered* what sort of greeting this might *be*.
Then the angel said to her,
   "Do not be *afraid*, *Mary*,
   for you have found *favor* with God.
Behold, you will conceive in your womb and bear a *son*,
   and you shall *name* him *Jesus*.
He will be *great* and will be called *Son* of the Most *High*,
   and the Lord God will give him the *throne* of *David* his *father*,
   and he will *rule* over the house of *Jacob forever*,
   and of *his* kingdom there will be *no end*."

Mary asks a second perplexing question: "How can this be?" The angel resolves the question.

But *Mary* said to the *angel*,
   "How can this *be*,
   since I have no *relations* with a *man*?"

GOSPEL   The stigma of evil in the Adam and Eve story is swept away in the gospel story. The good news summarized in the second reading is inaugurated and acted out in the gospel narrative. Imagine yourself to be a witness to this dialogue. Listen to the feeling and tone of the words as they are spoken by Mary and

the angel. You cannot help but sense the solemnity and gravity of the moment. Even Mary's question is an obligatory formula, not to be spoken lightly, as if Mary is just satisfying her curiosity.

Luke has structured the narrative with great genius. Notice that each pronouncement of the angel is followed by a sense of conflict that must be resolved. The angel greets Mary; she is troubled by the nature

of the greeting. The angel calms her and reveals her role in the redemption of the world; she is troubled by the obvious contradiction in conceiving a child without sex. The angel not only explains how this will be accomplished but offers Elizabeth's unlikely pregnancy as testimony to the inevitability of God's plan. Nothing as paltry as human

And the angel said to her in *reply*,
   "The Holy *Spirit* will come upon you,
   and the *power* of the Most *High* will *overshadow* you.
Therefore the *child* to be *born*
   will be called *holy*, the Son of *God*.
And *behold*, *Elizabeth*, your *relative*,
   has *also* conceived a son in her *old age*,
   and this is the sixth *month* for her who was called *barren*;
   for *nothing* will be *impossible* for *God*."

Mary said, "*Behold*, I am the *handmaid* of the *Lord*.
May it be *done* to me according to your *word*."
Then the angel *departed* from her.

You must emphasize "old age" more than "also." Otherwise it sounds like Mary is old as well.

Mary utters the words that resolve all conflict—and ushers in the messianic age. Let your voice communicate the import of her response. And be careful not to let the last sentence (the angel's departure) be too anti-climactic. If spoken as an afterthought, it can compromise what has gone before.

limitations or frailty can hinder God's loving will to redeem us.

The narrative structure of revelation, conflict and resolution should be clearly discernible in your proclamation. Then the final resolution—Mary's "may it be done"—will have its intended effect. It's all over in a moment. The angel comes, the angel leaves, and the world will never be the same. Let your listeners experience the full weight of the moment.

2ND SUNDAY OF ADVENT

Lectionary #4

READING I   Isaiah 11:1–10

A reading from the book of the prophet Isaiah

There are three parts to this reading: (1) a description of the king's virtues; (2) a description of how he reigns; and (3) a description of life in his kingdom. The last four lines predict the admiration of the nations. Let your proclamation make these divisions clear.

On that *day*, a *shoot* shall sprout from the stump of *Jesse*,
    and from his *roots* a *bud* shall blossom.
The spirit of the *Lord* shall *rest* upon him:
    a spirit of *wisdom* and of *understanding*,
a spirit of *counsel* and of *strength*,
    a spirit of *knowledge* and of fear of the *Lord*,
    and his *delight* shall be the fear of the *Lord*.

Not by *appearance* shall *he* judge,
    nor by *hearsay* shall *he* decide,
but *he* shall judge the *poor* with *justice*,
    and decide *aright* for the land's *afflicted*.
He shall strike the *ruthless* with the rod of his *mouth*,
    and with the breath of his *lips* he shall slay the *wicked*.
Justice shall be the *band* around his *waist*,
    and *faithfulness a belt* upon his *hips*.

The parallelism is relentless. Make sure you don't lapse into sing-song. Give each new image fresh presentation.

Then the *wolf* shall be a *guest* of the *lamb*,
    and the *leopard* shall lie *down* with the *kid*;
the *calf* and the young *lion* shall *browse* together,
    with a little *child* to guide them.

READING I The "stump of Jesse" refers to the lineage of King David, Jesse's son and the ancestor of Jesus. The traits of King David are the traits of a royal and exalted figure—one who is anointed by God for a special purpose. Notice where the characteristics of a mighty ruler all originate: "the spirit of the Lord shall rest upon him." Wisdom, understanding, counsel— these virtues are great because they are qualities of God and are by nature oriented toward protection of the meek and obliteration of injustice. When rulers see the world

through God's eyes, they rule with justice and mercy. Isaiah longs for the day when a monarch with that kind of vision is on the throne.

And what will that day be like? Isaiah's description has left us with some of the most memorable and beloved metaphors in all of scripture: lion and lamb lie down together, the child plays over the adder's lair, and so forth. It is an idyllic scene, and the words

are full of the peace they describe. An enormous affection for this text should be recognizable in your proclamation.

In the Christian tradition, of course, Isaiah's prophecy is fulfilled in the coming of Jesus (son of David, root of Jesse) and the establishment of the reign of God on earth. Although still "under construction," that reign will one day be complete. This reading encourages us to increase our longing for inner peace and our determination to help build the reign of God.

The *cow* and the *bear* shall be *neighbors*,
  together their *young* shall *rest*;
  the *lion* shall eat *hay* like the *ox*.
The *baby* shall *play* by the *cobra's* den,
  and the *child* lay his *hand* on the *adder's* lair.
There shall be no *harm* or *ruin* on *all* my holy mountain;
  for the earth shall be *filled* with *knowledge* of the *Lord*,
  as *water* covers the *sea*.

On *that* day, the root of *Jesse*,
  set up as a *signal* for the *nations*,
the *Gentiles* shall seek *out*,
  for his *dwelling* shall be *glorious*.

Though the last word is "glorious," end on a quiet note. As always, pause before "The word of the Lord."

READING II   Romans 15:4–9

A reading from the letter of Saint Paul to the Romans

Brothers and sisters:
Whatever was written *previously* was written for our *instruction*,
  that by *endurance* and by the encouragement of the *Scriptures*
  we might have *hope*.
May the *God* of endurance and encouragement
  grant you to think in *harmony* with one another,
  in keeping with Christ *Jesus*,
  that with *one accord* you may with *one voice*
  glorify the God and Father of our *Lord* Jesus *Christ*.

Notice that this reading is divided neatly into two equal parts. The second half begins with "Welcome" and implies that the admonition to welcome is a consequence of what went before. Paul then explains that our inclusiveness is an imitation of Christ's.

The reading utilizes one of the most characteristic devices of Hebrew poetry, parallelism, in which each line is followed by one or two lines that restate the message or refine the image of the first: "a shoot shall sprout/a bud shall blossom"; "not by appearance/nor by hearsay"; "strike the ruthless/slay the wicked."

READING II Paul had a terrible struggle trying to understand why his fellow Jews could not embrace the good news of Christ wholesale. But he never suggests that they have lost favor with God. How could that be, since we are all one in Christ, neither Jew nor Greek, male nor female? Paul states clearly that prejudice against or a feeling of superiority over people of a different race, religion or culture is

antithetical to Christ. Unfortunately, we have yet to embrace that message, for prejudice and social injustice still vitiate our society and our religion. (Notice the painful contrast with the images of unity portrayed in the first reading.)

Here is your chance to make a very strong plea for greater unity among your listeners. Beg them, as Paul does, to "live

Welcome one another, then, as *Christ* welcomed *you*,
   for the glory of *God*.
For I say that *Christ* became a minister of the *circumcised*
   to show God's *truthfulness*,
   to confirm the promises to the *patriarchs*,
   but so that the *Gentiles* might *glorify* God for his *mercy*.
As it is written:
   "Therefore, I will praise you among the *Gentiles*
   and sing *praises* to your *name*."

GOSPEL   Matthew 3:1–12

A reading from the holy gospel according to Matthew

John the *Baptist* appeared, preaching in the desert of *Judea*
   and saying, "*Repent*, for the kingdom of *heaven* is at *hand*!"
It was of *him* that the prophet *Isaiah* had spoken when he said:
   "A voice of one *crying out* in the desert,
   Prepare the way of the *Lord*,
   make straight his *paths*."

John wore *clothing* made of *camel's* hair
   and had a leather *belt* around his waist.
His *food* was *locusts* and wild *honey*.
At *that* time *Jerusalem*, all *Judea*,
   and the *whole region* around the *Jordan*
   were going *out* to him
   and were being *baptized* by him in the Jordan River
   as they *acknowledged* their *sins*.

The first half of the gospel introduces and describes John. The second half relates his message in his own words. Pause at the end of the first half, and begin the second half with a new tone of voice.

in harmony with one another" and glorify God with "one voice." Make the motive for such behavior clear: Christ showed no partiality but welcomed all. How can we treat each other with anything less noble than radical inclusiveness? There is even a hint of preposterousness in Paul's words: "Why, it's positively outrageous to think that we would dare to exclude someone on any grounds whatsoever when Christ himself has included all!" You needn't *sound* outraged, but it wouldn't hurt your proclamation to feel it a bit.

GOSPEL   The repentance John the Baptist preaches is not a lukewarm, fleeting sorrow for the sins of our past. No, what John calls for is life-shattering, life-altering, even life-threatening conversion! Matthew accords this eccentric prophet the weight of the Hebrew scriptures as back-up for his preaching: "This is the one Isaiah was talking about! He's out to change the world!" The very

appearance, clothing and diet of John put him in line with prophets of old and add to his credibility. (This reading is full of vivid images and strong language, but don't reenact the scene; that happens in the listener's mind and heart.)

And how do the people react to this wild man? Apparently, they're flocking to him in droves: from Jerusalem, all Judea and the Jordan region! There is a spirit of reformation in the air when John appears. The people are feeling the need for a more fervent expression of their faith in the God

Do not "become" John as you read his strong words. Liturgical proclamation is not reenactment. Let the members of your assembly re-create the scene in their hearts. Strong dialogue must be read energetically, but you are relating what happened, not acting it out.

Pause after "cut down and thrown into the fire," which concludes his admonition. The lines that follow introduce Christ and explain his mission.

When he saw many of the *Pharisees* and *Sadducees*
　　coming to his baptism, he said to them, "You brood of *vipers*!
Who *warned* you to flee from the coming *wrath*?

"Produce good *fruit* as *evidence* of your *repentance*.
And do not presume to say to yourselves,
　　'We have *Abraham* as our *father*.'
For I tell you,
　　God can raise up children to *Abraham* from these *stones*.
Even *now* the *ax* lies at the root of the *trees*.
Therefore every tree that does *not* bear *good* fruit
　　will be cut *down* and thrown into the *fire*.

"*I* am baptizing you with *water*, for *repentance*,
　　but the one who is coming *after* me is *mightier* than I.
I am not worthy to carry his *sandals*.
He will baptize you with the Holy *Spirit* and *fire*."
His *winnowing* fan is in his *hand*.
He will clear his *threshing* floor
　　and gather his *wheat* into his *barn*,
　　but the *chaff* he will *burn* with unquenchable *fire*."

who chose them. In other words, the time is ripe for John, and ripe for Jesus as well. John is striking while the iron is hot!

But the scene changes when John sees Pharisees and Sadducees approaching to be baptized. We must assume that they were doing so with impure motives, going through the motions, joining the crowd, doing the politically correct thing. John will brook no such phoniness. There are no shoo-ins in the reign of God. John calls for no less than a sincere conversion that produces the good fruit of a changed life.

Once John has made it clear what kind of baptism he is preaching, he points ahead to the ultimate baptism—with fire in the Holy Spirit. That's the baptism Jesus brings. It, too, demands sincere conversion. But it also brings the consuming love of God, which transforms us, incinerates our chaff and gathers up our wheat. John's baptism makes us ready for our complete makeover by Christ.

3RD SUNDAY OF ADVENT

Lectionary #7

READING I   Isaiah 35:1–6a, 10

A reading from the book of the prophet Isaiah

The text is pure poetry, and the images are rich and numerous. Proclaim it slowly, boldly and sensitively.
steppe = step

Carmel = KAHR-m*l
Sharon = SHAYR-uhn

Pause. The text changes here from description to exhortation.

Pause again. Now the text moves back to description.

The *desert* and the *parched* land will *exult*;
    the *steppe* will *rejoice* and *bloom*.
They will bloom with abundant *flowers*,
    and *rejoice* with joyful *song*.
The glory of *Lebanon* will be given to them,
    the splendor of *Carmel* and *Sharon*;
they will see the *glory* of the *Lord*,
    the *splendor* of our *God*.

Strengthen the hands that are *feeble*,
    make *firm* the knees that are *weak*,
say to those whose hearts are *frightened*:
    Be *strong*, fear *not*!
Here is your *God*,
    he comes with *vindication*;
with divine *recompense*
    he comes to *save* you.
Then will the eyes of the *blind* be *opened*,
    the ears of the *deaf* be *cleared*;
then will the *lame* leap like a *stag*,
    then the tongue of the *mute* will *sing*.

READING I The prophet Isaiah describes the immense joy of the Israelite people in being delivered from bondage and returned to their homeland from exile. Jesus in today's gospel proclaims some of the same signs that are listed here: the blind see, the lame walk, and so forth. For the Christian, deliverance from bondage and escape from exile is precisely what Christ brings by delivering us from eternal death and leading us into eternal life. Some of the signs of the renewed world Isaiah saw can be seen in the healing ministry of Jesus.

Do we see the same signs today? Of course we do. In the "miracles" of modern medicine we see relief from misery that no contemporary of Jesus could ever have imagined. Good works by good people around the world strengthen "feeble hands" and "weak knees." The point is that the risen Christ is very much in the business of transforming the world. And we must keep reminding ourselves to be alert to the signs of Christ's loving presence. Otherwise, the scriptures we read become either a history lesson or a fantasy about the future. But the word of God accomplishes the purpose for which it was sent—and it does so on a daily basis.

Let the assembly hear the matched pairs of sounds in "ransomed/return" and "Zion/singing."

Those whom the Lord has *ransomed* will *return*
> and enter Zion *singing*,
>> crowned with everlasting *joy*;
they will meet with *joy* and *gladness*,
> *sorrow* and *mourning* will *flee*.

READING II   James 5:7–10

A reading from the letter of Saint James

Be *patient*, brothers and sisters,
> until the *coming* of the *Lord*.
See how the *farmer* waits for the precious fruit of the *earth*,
> being *patient* with it
> until it receives the *early* and the *late* rains.
You *too* must be patient.
Make your hearts *firm*,
> because the coming of the *Lord* is at *hand*.

Do not *complain*, brothers and sisters, about one another,
> that you may not be *judged*.
Behold, the Judge is standing before the *gates*.
Take as an example of *hardship* and *patience*, brothers
>> and sisters,
> the *prophets* who spoke in the name of the *Lord*.

Remember to give the words "patient" and "patience" special emphasis.

There is more than pleading here. The threat of judgment makes that clear.

Clearly, patience involves hardship and suffering.

The abundant joy of this lovely passage is exceeded only by its comforting tone. It is not a giddy kind of exaltation we see here but a subdued awe.

READING II The words "patient" and "patience" appear a total of four times in this brief reading. Each time the members of your assembly hear one of these words, they should remember that they heard one of them earlier and that James is showing us how to exercise the virtue of patience. As you may know, the meaning of the word "patience" includes nuances of lengthy suffering and endurance in the face of trial or pain. Patience is not the passive, soft-spoken, milquetoast virtue it is often painted to be. Genuine patience involves some teeth-grinding and tongue-biting.

And what is the most obvious sign of impatience? Grumbling and complaining about the way things and people don't measure up to our demands or hopes certainly qualify. Saint Benedict, in his *Rule for Monasteries*, comes down hard on monks who grumble. "First and foremost," he writes, "there must be no word or sign of the evil of grumbling, no manifestation of it for any reason at all." In his wisdom, the saint knew, as James did, that grumbling in the Christian community is a sure sign that we are not preparing for Christ's coming.

GOSPEL Matthew 11:2–11

A reading from the holy gospel according to Matthew

When John the *Baptist* heard in *prison* of the works of the *Christ*,
   he sent his *disciples* to Jesus with this *question*,
   "Are *you* the one who is to *come*,
   or should we look for *another*?"
Jesus said to them in *reply*,
   "*Go* and tell John what you *hear* and *see*:
   the *blind* regain their *sight*,
   the *lame walk*,
   lepers are *cleansed*,
   the *deaf hear*,
   the *dead* are *raised*,
   and the *poor* have the good *news* proclaimed to them.
And *blessed* is the one who takes no *offense* at me."

Notice that the first half of the text is addressed to John's disciples, the second half to the crowds.

Take this slowly. Each "sign" should be given its due.

GOSPEL Three distinct kinds of literature appear in today's readings: the poem from Isaiah, the instruction or exhortation from James, and the narrative about John from Matthew. The one who proclaims the word of God should develop and refine a sensitivity to the genres of literature found in the Bible. Proclamation techniques and skills will then develop accordingly.

Jesus quotes Isaiah as he sends back a resounding "yes" to John in prison. "Yes, John, I am the one whose coming was foretold. And here's proof, just as the prophets predicted: The blind see, the lame walk, the deaf hear." With the coming of Jesus, the reign of God has begun. It will come to perfect fulfillment when Christ comes again at the end of time.

The second half of the gospel is different in tone. There is no reason to think that Jesus is scolding here. He is pointing out that the prophet and the prophet's message may be different from what we may expect. And the signs of the approaching reign of God are not all pretty. John is in prison and will be beheaded for criticizing the immoral behavior of an authority figure. That, too, is a sign of the reign of God. And the "way" John is commissioned to prepare for Jesus is strewn with similar difficulties.

Pause here. Raise your voice slightly when Jesus begins to speak. Avoid making the questions confrontational. Jesus is teaching, not scolding.

As they were going off,
　　Jesus began to speak to the crowds about *John*,
　　"What did you go out to the desert to *see*?
A *reed* swayed by the *wind*?
Then what *did* you go out to *see*?
Someone dressed in fine *clothing*?
Those who wear fine *clothing* are in royal *palaces*.
Then *why* did you go *out*? To see a *prophet*?
Yes, I tell you, and *more* than a prophet.
This is the one about whom it is *written*:
　　'*Behold*, I am sending my *messenger* ahead of you;
　　he will prepare your way before you.'

The final sentence is a solemn pronouncement—but a joyful one!

"*Amen*, I say to you,
　　among those born of *women*
　　there has been none *greater* than John the *Baptist*;
　　yet the *least* in the kingdom of *heaven* is *greater* than *he*."

　　The last words of Jesus in this gospel passage are more about the reign of God than they are about John. Though John's role on earth to "prepare the way" was unsurpassed in human history, his membership in the reign of God is far more significant. Jesus is saying it's the same for us. "Strive for true greatness: membership in the kingdom of heaven, where the least are greater than the greatest outside it."

　　All the words of Jesus here are of an exalted tone, even a bit mysterious. Proclaim them boldly, slowly, carefully. Give each image and metaphor time to sink in before going on to the next. The complexity and richness of the text can easily be lost if the passage is proclaimed too quickly or without sufficient understanding and care.

4TH SUNDAY OF ADVENT

Lectionary #10

READING I   Isaiah 7:10–14

A reading from the book of the prophet Isaiah

You are reporting a conversation among
three persons.
Ahaz = AY-haz

The LORD spoke to *Ahaz*, saying:
Ask for a *sign* from the LORD, your *God*;
   let it be *deep* as the *netherworld*, or *high* as the *sky*!
But *Ahaz answered*,
   "I will *not* ask! I will not *tempt* the LORD!"

Emphasize "not" rather than "ask," and
"tempt" rather than "Lord."

Then *Isaiah* said:
   Listen, O house of *David*!
Is it not *enough* for you to weary *people*,
   must you *also* weary my *God*?
Therefore the Lord *himself* will give you *this* sign:
   the *virgin* shall *conceive*, and bear a *son*,
   and shall *name* him *Emmanuel*.

Emphasize both "name" and "Emmanuel,"
not just the latter.
Emmanuel = ee-MAN-y<u>oo</u>-el

READING I   This brief reading is packed with challenges for the reader. Why doesn't Ahaz ask for a sign? Why is God asking him to ask? Why is Isaiah so upset with the house of David?

Though your hearers may not know this, Ahaz had been playing politics and going against the Lord's plan that a king be chosen from the house of David. This is the reason for his fawning response, "Oh, no, I really couldn't." The text was chosen because Christian tradition sees in the conception of Jesus in Mary's womb the fulfillment of the promised sign.

But beyond the meaning, there are challenges of delivery. In the space of a dozen lines you encounter three speakers: God, Ahaz and Isaiah. And there are three distinct sections: (1) the dialogue between God and Ahaz; (2) Isaiah's rebuke; and (3) the promise we've all been waiting for. With so much shifting in such a short passage, make a special effort to read carefully, distinctly and slowly.

READING II   Announce clearly, "A reading from the beginning of the letter of Saint Paul to the Romans," and then pause. This will give Paul's long salutation some context and make it more accessible. But it's still a challenge, with layer upon layer of subordinate clauses and no main verb. Obviously, it's a poetic formula and should be read like poetry, that is, letting each "spin-off" about the gospel and Paul's apostleship spiral up to the intended climax: "Jesus Christ our Lord."

READING II   Romans 1:1–7

A reading from the beginning of the letter of Saint Paul to the Romans

Paul, a slave of Christ *Jesus*,
    called to be an *apostle* and set apart for the *gospel* of *God*,
        which he promised *previously* through his *prophets*
            in the holy *Scriptures*,
the gospel about his *Son*, descended from *David*
        according to the *flesh*,
    but established as Son of *God* in *power*
    according to the Spirit of *holiness*
        through resurrection from the *dead*, Jesus *Christ* our *Lord.*

Through *him* we have received the grace of *apostleship*,
    to bring about the *obedience* of *faith*,
    for the sake of his *name*, among all the *Gentiles*,
        among whom are you *also*, who are called to *belong*
            to Jesus Christ;
    to all the beloved of God in *Rome*, called to be *holy.*

Grace to you and *peace* from God our *Father*
    and the Lord Jesus *Christ.*

The first paragraph is difficult. But if you avoid a repetitive downward movement of the voice, it won't sound like a list of clauses. The secret to doing this well is to study the reading carefully so you understand the relationship among the clauses and the gradual build toward "Jesus Christ our Lord."

I actually heard an assembly respond to the final sentence with "And also with you." You can avoid this robotic reaction by reading the last part at a dramatically slower pace.

The second half offers similar challenges. But it, too, builds toward the greeting in a slow steady climb. A reading like this must be rendered very carefully and slowly, letting the upward swing of the voice allow for what is to follow. A continual downward swing will separate the text into a series of unrelated clauses instead of a series of closely related ones.

Clearly the text was chosen because Paul not only summarizes the mission of Jesus and the apostles who follow him, but also because he mentions the attribute of Christ that is central to Advent: "descended from David according to the flesh." If you prepare this reading by closely examining all the fundamentals of our faith contained in it, you will do well.

GOSPEL   This reading is a discrete unit, a perfect short story, complete in every way. It sets the stage, introduces the problem, solves the problem in a way that gives the story purpose and meaning, and ends on a note of quiet resolution. In response to the structure of the passage, imagine a quiet (but easily heard!) beginning and a slow crescendo to the peak exactly halfway through: "Do not be afraid to take Mary . . ." From this point on there is a gradual downward movement (but no loss of energy) through the revelation of Jesus' destiny, the fulfillment of the prophet's words, and Joseph's humble obedience.

But no narrative in the gospels is simply an account of an occurrence in history. The story of how Jesus was born is no exception. The larger purpose here is to demonstrate in every detail how the intervention of God in human history is irresistible and

GOSPEL   Matthew 1:18–24

A reading from the holy gospel according to Matthew

This is how the *birth* of Jesus Christ came *about.*
When his mother *Mary* was betrothed to *Joseph,*
but before they *lived* together,
she was found with *child* through the Holy *Spirit.*

Joseph her *husband,* since he was a *righteous* man,
yet unwilling to expose her to *shame,*
decided to *divorce* her *quietly.*

Such was his *intention* when, *behold,*
the angel of the *Lord* appeared to him in a *dream* and said,
"*Joseph,* son of David,
do not be afraid to take *Mary* your wife into your *home.*
For it is through the Holy *Spirit*
that this child has been *conceived* in her.
She will bear a *son* and you are to name him *Jesus,*
because he will save his *people* from their *sins.*"

All this took *place* to fulfill what the Lord had said
through the *prophet:*
"*Behold,* the *virgin* shall conceive and bear a *son,*
and they shall *name* him *Emmanuel,*"
which means "*God* is with us."
When Joseph *awoke,*
he did as the angel of the Lord had *commanded* him
and *took* his wife into his *home.*

Begin with the energy of a real storyteller, making sure the text sounds fresh and new.

Emphasize Joseph's goodness here. It's quite beautiful.

There must be a pause here, even though the next line begins with "For."

Experiment with emphasizing "God" instead of "with."

Make sure not to downplay the final three lines too much. Pause before them, then give them the energy they deserve.

---

unstoppable. Encountering human obstacles at every turn, the irrevocable will of God to love the world into redemption nevertheless proceeds, undaunted and undiminished.

Think of how many hurdles have been bounded over so far: Mary's fear, her questions, her virginity, Elizabeth's old age, Joseph's shame, his painful decision to divorce Mary. And there are many more to come. What's the point? The point is that nothing will slow the onrush of God's love for

us, neither then nor now. We can all think of a thousand reasons why God might have qualms about loving us without reservation. Yet God's ways are not our ways. What we think should stop divine love in its tracks seems to accelerate God's movement toward us. It may be difficult to understand, maybe, but it is both comforting and encouraging.

Matthew begins his gospel with a genealogy of Jesus, demonstrating that Jesus has a human origin—and fulfills the prophecy that the Messiah will be of the

house and lineage of David. Matthew's purpose here is to demonstrate the fulfillment of Isaiah's prophecy of old and to show that Jesus has a divine origin. To bring this out, be sure to give special emphasis to the last part of the reading, beginning with "All this took place to fulfill . . ."

CHRISTMAS VIGIL

Lectionary #13

READING I   Isaiah 62:1–5

A reading from the book of the prophet Isaiah

For *Zion's* sake I will *not* be silent,
    for *Jerusalem's* sake I will not be *quiet,*
until her *vindication* shines *forth* like the *dawn*
    and her *victory* like a burning *torch.*

Nations shall *behold* your vindication,
    and all the kings your glory;
you shall be called by a *new* name
    pronounced by the mouth of the LORD.
You shall be a glorious *crown* in the hand of the LORD,
    a royal *diadem* held by your *God.*

No *more* shall people call you "*Forsaken,*"
    or your *land* "*Desolate,*"
but you shall be called "My *Delight,*"
    and your land "*Espoused.*"
For the LORD *delights* in you
    and makes your land his *spouse.*

As a young *man* marries a *virgin,*
    your *Builder* shall marry *you;*
and as a *bridegroom* rejoices in his *bride*
    so shall your *God* rejoice in *you.*

Notice the poetic device called parallelism. The thought of every line is echoed in the line that follows it. Let this poetic structure be heard, but avoid a repetitious pattern of intonation.

The text is clearly divided into four brief sections. Begin each section with new energy.

The word "you" must be emphasized above the rest, for that is the point.

READING I We have been hearing the songs of Isaiah all through Advent, and we continue to hear them at all four of the Masses of Christmas—vigil, midnight, dawn and day. Portions of these exultant canticles have been unforgettably set to music in Handel's *Messiah.* They all celebrate Israel's return from exile, the restoration of the holy city of Jerusalem, and a new intimate relationship with God.

To describe this new relationship adequately, Isaiah has to resort to metaphors that paint a picture of total intimacy: young lovers, bride and bridegroom, married couple. Such relationships are the only ones tender enough to describe God's loving care for Israel. And we still use this kind of language to describe our relationship with God. We speak of the marriage of heaven and earth at the incarnation, the church as bride and Christ as bridegroom at the resurrection, and the wedding banquet of heaven that awaits us.

The challenge of this reading is to find just the right combination of ecstatic joy and tenderness in your proclamation. A further challenge is to give each image its due; don't rush through the text, but give each line and its parallel restatement time to be absorbed before going on to the next. This does not mean the reading will be punctuated with lengthy pauses, but it will need breadth in proclamation, expansiveness in delivery and largeness in tone. In other words, share these words with the broadness and exultation the text clearly demands. Such readings are not for lightweights!

READING II   Acts 13:16–17, 22–25

A reading from the Acts of the Apostles

Antioch = AN-tee-ahk
Pisidia = pih-SID-ee-uh

When *Paul* reached *Antioch* in *Pisidia* and entered
    the *synagogue*,
he stood *up*, motioned with his *hand*, and said,

Pause after the first sentence, which
sets the scene, then launch into Paul's
exposition.

"Fellow *Israelites* and you *others* who are *God*-fearing, *listen*.
The God of this people *Israel* chose our *ancestors*
    and *exalted* the people during their *sojourn*
        in the land of *Egypt*.
With uplifted arm he led them out of it.

"Then he *removed Saul* and raised up *David* as king;
    of *him* he testified,
    'I have found *David*, son of *Jesse*, a man after my own *heart*;
    he will carry *out* my every *wish*.'

Come to a rest here before going on, then
renew the energy and let your voice carry
the conviction of the text.

"From *this* man's *descendants* God, according to his *promise*,
    has brought to *Israel* a *savior*, *Jesus*.
John heralded his *coming* by proclaiming a *baptism* of *repentance*
    to all the people of Israel;
    and as John was *completing* his course, he would say,
    'What do you suppose that I *am*? I am *not* he.
Behold, one is coming *after* me;
    I am not *worthy* to unfasten the *sandals* of his *feet*.'"

READING II   Paul is preaching to his fellow Jews, laying out a case for seeing in Jesus the Messiah foretold by the prophets, prefigured in historical events, and testified to by that latter-day prophet, John the Baptist. From a logical and scientific point of view, Paul's argument proves nothing, just as from that point of view we can prove nothing about our faith. That's the difference between faith and knowledge. Believing is not the same as knowing. We might say, "In my heart of hearts I *know* Jesus rose from the dead," but of course we don't *know* it; we believe it strongly and allow it to guide our lives accordingly.

Paul's audience probably didn't distinguish between believing and knowing as we do today. The ancient Near Eastern way of thinking was different from our own Western approach—more intuitive, less rationalistic—and we must remember this when we read the scriptures. Many came to believe in Jesus because of the strength of Paul's argument, but they weren't forced into belief by hard logic. The evidence presented to them in no way compelled them to draw Paul's conclusions.

Such is always the case with you as a proclaimer of the word. You invite your listeners over and over again to hear the evidence of God's love for us and respond to it. The invitation will be most effective when it comes from the heart of your own faith. It was probably Paul's fervent faith, as much as his so-called "argument," that won the people over.

GOSPEL   Matthew 1:1–25

A reading from the holy gospel according to Matthew

The *book* of the *genealogy* of *Jesus Christ,*
   the son of *David,* the son of *Abraham.*

Abraham became the father of *Isaac,*
   Isaac the father of *Jacob,*
   Jacob the father of *Judah* and his *brothers.*
Judah became the father of *Perez* and *Zerah,*
   whose mother was *Tamar.*
Perez became the father of *Hezron,*
   Hezron the father of *Ram,*
   Ram the father of *Amminadab.*
Amminadab became the father of *Nahshon,*
   Nahshon the father of *Salmon,*
   Salmon the father of *Boaz,*
   whose mother was *Rahab.*
Boaz became the father of *Obed,*
   whose mother was *Ruth.*
Obed became the father of *Jesse,*
   Jesse the father of *David* the *king.*

David became the father of *Solomon,*
   whose *mother* had been the wife of *Uriah.*
Solomon became the father of *Rehoboam,*
   Rehoboam the father of *Abijah,*
   Abijah the father of *Asaph.*
Asaph became the father of *Jehoshaphat,*
   Jehoshaphat the father of *Joram,*
   Joram the father of *Uzziah.*

If you decide to proclaim the genealogy, practice the names so that you can proclaim each one with ease, so the members of the assembly can relax and listen instead of rooting for you!

Perez = PAYR-ez

Zerah = ZEE-rah

Tamar = TAY-mahr

Hezron = HEZ-ruhn

Ram = ram

Amminadab = uh-MIN-uh-dab

Nahshon = NAH-shuhn

Salmon = SAL-muhn

Boaz = BOH-az

Rahab = RAY-hab

Obed = OH-bed

Uriah = yoo-RĪ-uh

Rehoboam = ree-huh-BOH-uhm

Abijah = uh-BĪ-juh

Asaph = AY-saf

Jehoshaphat = jeh-HOH-shuh-fat

Joram = JOHR-uhm

Uzziah = uh-ZĪ-uh

GOSPEL   Most will decide to take the shorter version of this gospel passage, choosing to leave the long list of Jesus' ancestors for silent meditation. And that's a good decision if the genealogy is read poorly. Only those who have mastered the reading's many names and have acquired a deep understanding of why Matthew included this genealogy in the first place should attempt to proclaim it! A sloppy stumbling through the names, or a bored and boring rattling off of them, will do more harm than omitting it altogether. In such a case, it is better to be content with proclaiming the last eight verses (the shorter version).

Having said that, let's consider what the genealogy can teach us when masterfully proclaimed and opened up a little by the homilist. First of all, the geneaology says, "If you want to know this Jesus, you have to know the Hebrew scriptures, the Old Testament, which is a record of the lives of his ancestors." Second, it makes specific mention of several women who played important roles in salvation history— something we can hear with great profit, given the patriarchal society of Jesus' fore-bears and our male-dominated notions about God and church. Third, it demonstrates, with that special kind of intuitive logic found in the second reading, that God's goodwill on our behalf is documented all the way back to Abraham. God's plan to save us has not, and will not, be thwarted.

Jotham = JOH-thuhm

Ahaz = AY-haz

Hezekiah = hez-eh-KĪ-uh

Manasseh = muh-NAS-uh

Amos = AY-m*s

Josiah = joh-SĪ-uh

Jechoniah = jek-oh-NĪ-uh

Shealtiel = shee-AL-tee-uhl

Zerubbabel = zuh-ROOB-uh-b*l

Abiud = uh-BĪ-uhd

Eliakim = ee-LĪ-uh-kim

Azor = AY-zohr

Zadok = ZAY-dok

Achim = AH-kim

Eliud = ee-LĪ-uhd

Eleazar = el-ee-AY-zer

Matthan = MATH-uhn

Uzziah became the father of *Jotham*,
  Jotham the father of *Ahaz*,
  Ahaz the father of *Hezekiah*.
Hezekiah became the father of *Manasseh*,
  Manasseh the father of *Amos*,
  Amos the father of *Josiah*.
Josiah became the father of *Jechoniah* and his *brothers*
  at the time of the *Babylonian* exile.

After the *Babylonian* exile,
  Jechoniah became the father of *Shealtiel*,
  Shealtiel the father of *Zerubbabel*,
  Zerubbabel the father of *Abiud*.
Abiud became the father of *Eliakim*,
  Eliakim the father of *Azor*,
  Azor the father of *Zadok*.
Zadok became the father of *Achim*,
  Achim the father of *Eliud*,
  Eliud the father of *Eleazar*.
Eleazar became the father of *Matthan*,
  Matthan the father of *Jacob*,
  Jacob the father of *Joseph*, the husband of *Mary*.
Of *her* was born *Jesus* who is called the *Christ*.

Thus the total number of *generations*
  from *Abraham* to *David*
  is *fourteen* generations;
  from *David* to the *Babylonian* exile,
  fourteen generations;
  from the *Babylonian* exile to the *Christ*,
  fourteen generations.

But many people on that list tried to thwart it! Here's something else we learn from the genealogy: There are some heavy-duty sinners among Jesus' ancestors. God works through human agents—even through their sinfulness. Here's the antidote to that recurring malady that makes us think only saints can be channels of grace, that seals up God's activity behind church walls and corrals divine wisdom into official pronouncements. God is at work, God's wisdom is to be found in the people of God, that motley crew of both saints and sinners that God dotes on as newlyweds dote on each other.

The story of how the birth of Jesus came about is presented here in an eight-verses mini-drama. The potentially idyllic scene of the young married couple is marred by the scandal of a pregnancy before marriage. But divine intervention brings a happy resolution, and Joseph's dilemma is solved. Proclaim this material as the story it is while remembering its solemn consequences for the future of all creation!

The break here is obvious, but connect it to what comes before by emphasizing the word "birth." Jesus has already been mentioned above, as have Mary and Joseph. The following story does not introduce them. If you begin here (taking the shorter version), then emphasize both "birth" and "Christ."

Now *this* is how the *birth* of Jesus Christ came *about*.
When his mother *Mary* was betrothed to *Joseph*,
    but before they *lived* together,
    she was found with *child* through the Holy *Spirit*.

Joseph her *husband*, since he was a *righteous* man,
    yet unwilling to expose her to *shame*,
    decided to *divorce* her *quietly*.
Such was his *intention* when, *behold*,
    the angel of the *Lord* appeared to him in a *dream* and said,
    "*Joseph*, son of David,
    do not be afraid to take *Mary* your wife into your *home*.
For it is through the Holy *Spirit*
    that this child has been *conceived* in her.
She will bear a *son* and you are to name him *Jesus*,
    because he will save his *people* from their *sins*."

The genealogy tells of Jesus' human origins. Now we hear of his divine origin as well.

All this took *place* to fulfill
    what the Lord had said through the *prophet*:
    "*Behold*, the *virgin* shall conceive and bear a *son*,
    and they shall *name* him *Emmanuel*,"
    which means "God is *with* us."

The final lines are filled with peaceful resolution. Matthew's remark about Mary and Joseph having no "relations" emphasizes his point that Jesus is of divine origin.

When Joseph *awoke*,
    he did as the angel of the Lord had *commanded* him
    and *took* his wife into his *home*.
He had no *relations* with her until she bore a *son*,
    and he *named* him *Jesus*.

[Shorter: Matthew 1:18–25]

CHRISTMAS MIDNIGHT

Lectionary #14

READING I   Isaiah 9:1–6

Pause before and after the announcement. You must have the assembly's attention.

A reading from the book of the prophet Isaiah

The people who walked in *darkness*
   have seen a great *light*;
upon those who dwelt in the land of *gloom*
   a *light* has shone.

Maintain an exalted tone throughout. This is poetry.

You have brought them abundant *joy*
   and great *rejoicing*,
as they *rejoice* before you as at the *harvest*,
   as people make *merry* when dividing *spoils*.

For the *yoke* that *burdened* them,
   the *pole* on their *shoulder*,
and the *rod* of their *taskmaster*
   you have *smashed*, as on the day of *Midian*.

For every *boot* that tramped in *battle*,
   every *cloak* rolled in *blood*,
   will be *burned* as *fuel* for *flames*.

Here are the words the assembly is waiting for. Make their delivery special.

For a *child* is born to us, a *son* is given us;
   upon his shoulder *dominion* rests.
They name him Wonder-*Counselor*, God-*Hero*,
   Father-*Forever*, Prince of *Peace*.
His dominion is *vast*
   and forever *peaceful*,

READING I Christmas Midnight Mass is special in Christian tradition. You will probably be proclaiming God's word to a church full of people whose attention is drawn by many things: the decorations, the children, the crèche, the special music. It is especially important that you begin in such a way that you capture the attention of those present. A strong announcement of the reading preceded and followed by a brief silence may do the trick. The text before you has been immortalized by writers, readers, composers and musicians. It deserves special treatment.

Isaiah writes about Israel's liberation from oppression through the ascendancy of King Hezekiah. The yoke, pole and rod of the oppressor all symbolize Assyria, and because God sides with Israel, the oppressor will be conquered. Hezekiah is supposed to bring to his reign a kind of justice that will make him truly great, a man after God's own heart. But the expectations of him are too high, and he doesn't live up to the prophecy.

There is one who does, however, and that is the Messiah-king whose birth we celebrate this night. The yoke, pole and rod of oppression that he will smash are the yoke of sin, the pole of punishment and the rod of death—the ultimate enemies of all humankind. The birth of Christ ushers in the messianic age, the age in which we live. The second coming of Christ will bring the fullness of that age—forever peaceful, ruled in justice, brought about by the zeal of the Lord of hosts. Here is the full meaning of Christmas. Import as much of it as possible into your proclamation.

from *David's* throne, and over his *kingdom*,
    which he *confirms* and *sustains*
by *judgment* and *justice*,
    both *now* and for*ever*.
The *zeal* of the LORD of *hosts* will *do* this!

READING II   Titus 2:11–14

A reading from the letter of Saint Paul to Titus

Beloved:
The grace of *God* has *appeared*, saving *all*
    and *training* us to reject *godless* ways and *worldly* desires
    and to live *temperately*, *justly*, and *devoutly* in this age,
    as we await the blessed *hope*,
    the *appearance* of the *glory* of our great *God*
    and *savior* Jesus *Christ*,
    who *gave* himself for us to *deliver* us from all *lawlessness*
    and to *cleanse* for himself a people as his *own*,
    eager to do what is *good*.

This reading is brief but packed with meaning. Do not rush. Be sure you understand the meaning of every phrase, and give each its proper weight. Punctuation is not your best guide here. The meaning of the text is.

GOSPEL   Luke 2:1–14

A reading from the holy gospel according to Luke

In *those* days a *decree* went out from Caesar *Augustus*
    that the whole *world* should be *enrolled*.
This was the *first* enrollment,
    when *Quirinius* was governor of *Syria*.

The gospel proclamation is particularly significant tonight. Bring that significance to your proclamation.

Quirinius = kwih-RIN-ee-uhs

READING II   The first reading and the gospel both celebrate the birth of a child. This brief passage from Titus identifies the child and looks far ahead—beyond the historical event itself—to the moment toward which all history is aimed: the appearance of the glory of God in the coming of Jesus Christ. Clearly we live between two singular events. The first has saved us and "trained" us how to live in expectation of the second. It's a wonderful way of looking at the grace of God, which trains us to live godly lives, to await the age

to come with eager longing, and meanwhile to be enthusiastic about doing good deeds.

The author of this passage has packed it with meaning. Because it is so brief, take great care lest it end before it has had a chance to work its intended effect. This is a thinking person's formulation of the Good News: Give the members of the assembly time to think, especially on this night when the spirit of the season makes us more receptive than ever.

GOSPEL   Perhaps the most familiar text of the entire Bible, this passage will be gratefully received simply because it is so beloved. But the danger for the reader is that familiarity will bring over-confidence. Strive for an energetic, fresh approach that makes the old story new. A deeper understanding of the text can help a reader achieve this.

Every single fact recounted here has a second level of meaning. Luke is not so much interested in history as in its interpretation. The significance of each event is more important than its historical accuracy.

A more inclusive rendering would be: "All went to their own towns to be enrolled." Please don't say "each to their own town."

So all went to be *enrolled*, each to his own *town*.
And *Joseph too* went up from *Galilee* from the town of *Nazareth*
    to *Judea*, to the city of *David* that is called *Bethlehem*,
    because he was of the *house* and *family* of David,
    to be enrolled with *Mary*, his *betrothed*, who was with *child*.

While they were there,
    the *time* came for her to *have* her *child*,
    and she gave *birth* to her firstborn *son*.
She wrapped him in *swaddling* clothes and laid him in a *manger*,
    because there was no *room* for them in the *inn*.

Pause. A new section begins here.

Now there were *shepherds* in that region living in the *fields*
    and keeping the *night* watch over their *flock*.
The angel of the *Lord* appeared to them
    and the *glory* of the Lord *shone* around them,
    and they were struck with great *fear*.
The angel *said* to them,
    "Do *not* be afraid;
    for *behold*, I proclaim to you *good news* of *great joy*
    that will be for *all* the *people*.
For *today* in the city of *David*
    a *savior* has been born for you who is *Christ* and *Lord*.
And this will be a *sign* for you:
    you will find an *infant* wrapped in *swaddling* clothes
    and lying in a *manger*."

Again, this is clearly a new section. Give it renewed energy.

And *suddenly* there was a multitude of the heavenly *host*
        with the angel,
    praising *God* and saying:
    "*Glory* to God in the *highest*
    and on earth *peace* to those on whom his *favor* rests."

Indeed, some of the facts are disputed. But this does not alter the meaning or significance one bit. For example, Caesar Augustus may or may not have ordered that a census be taken. There is no evidence from any other source that he did. But the meaning is that Caesar Augustus was known as a bringer of peace, and Luke wants to point out that the real bringer of peace is Jesus. There was no room for the Holy Family in the inn—a fitting and consistent circumstance for one who would be spurned, despised and rejected. Whether or not Jesus was laid in a manger, Luke means to say that this child is food for the world. Were the shepherds truly the first to hear of the birth of this lowly Messiah? The question misses the point. The point is that shepherds were part of the lowest social class of the time— the kind of people for whom this humble Messiah will show preference and special love. The wonderful events happened in Bethlehem because it is the "city of David," and all the prophets knew the Messiah would be born from that royal line.

You will be amazed by the change in your proclamation of this text when you are attentive to the significance of every detail, rather than to the detail itself. Simply holding in your mind the meaning of the events will affect your reading in a wonderful way. Above all else, read the passage lovingly, for this story reveals just how much God loves us.

CHRISTMAS DAWN

Lectionary #15

READING I Isaiah 62:11–12

A reading from the book of the prophet Isaiah

Notice that there are three levels here: (1) The Lord proclaims; (2) "Say to daughter Zion; (3) 'Your savior comes!'" Make sure this is clear.

Place stress on "reward" and "recompense," not on the prepositions "with" and "before."

"Frequented" is odd and weak. Give it special attention.

See, the LORD *proclaims*
    to the ends of the *earth*:
say to daughter *Zion*,
    your *savior* comes!
Here is his *reward* with him,
    his *recompense* before him.

They shall be called the *holy* people,
    the *redeemed* of the LORD,
and you shall be called *"Frequented,"*
    a city that is *not forsaken*.

READING I Notice how brief all three readings are for the Mass at dawn. And yet all the fundamental truths of our faith are proclaimed in them. Isaiah tells Zion, "Your savior has come, and you are made holy by this coming." Paul makes it clear that the Good News has nothing to do with commandments and laws. No, he says, "Not because of anything good we have done, but because of God's mercy are we saved." And Luke's image of the nativity says, in effect, "Seeing is believing"—not *knowing* but *believing*. It reminds us of John 3:16, "For God so loved the world that he gave his only Son, so that everyone who believes in him may not perish but have eternal life." That's it. There's nothing very complex about that. And yet it is so profound that, like Mary, we will spend the rest of our lives reflecting on it in our hearts.

Isaiah's context is the great Feast of Lights (Tabernacles), so it is appropriate that at dawn on the day we celebrate the birth of Christ, the light of the world, we should hear this lovely poetry. It must be read slowly, joyfully and with great dignity. The message is that the people of God ("daughter Zion") are made holy by God's presence in their midst. They are no longer to be considered "forsaken" or "abandoned," just the opposite. Emmanuel ("God-with-us") has pitched his tent among them. God has made of Zion a tabernacle, a dwelling place, and all the nations of the world will seek this holy place, filling it with eager pilgrims.

This is truly a Christmas message for those in the assembly who may feel abandoned or forsaken. For many, Christmas is a time when warm memories of better days make present difficulties all the more bitter. Comfort them with Isaiah's words.

In two sentences, Paul gives us a thumbnail sketch of the Good News. Be sure every phrase is carefully nuanced. There are no spare words here.

READING II   Titus 3:4–7

A reading from the letter of Saint Paul to Titus

Beloved:
When the *kindness* and generous *love*
    of God our *savior* appeared,
not because of any righteous deeds *we* had done
    but because of his *mercy*,
he *saved* us through the bath of *rebirth*
    and *renewal* by the Holy *Spirit*,
whom he richly *poured out* on us
    through Jesus *Christ* our *savior*,
so that we might be *justified* by his *grace*
    and become *heirs* in *hope* of eternal *life*.

READING II   If there is a "bottom line" in Christian faith, here it is. We believe that a God of infinite kindness and love lavished the Spirit upon us through Jesus Christ to open eternity and make us happy. God did not do this to reward us for a life of obedience and virtue, or to redeem us from the wicked things we have done, or even to obligate us to a life of good deeds. No, God offers this gift only out of pure kindness and love.

There is something in human nature that makes us skeptical of disinterested love, love that is offered without expectation of return, love that is totally gratuitous, spontaneous, given out of a pure heart. When we are told we are loved, we find ourselves trying to figure out a motive, a hidden agenda, a reason beyond the reason given. Or we consider how being loved like this may obligate us in some way, even limit our freedom.

Perhaps this explains why, in spite of Paul's clarity in this reading, Christianity appears to the world like a code of ethics and obligations rather than the Good News it is. Perhaps it explains why Christianity has, over and over again, turned itself into a "creed with consequences": I believe because if I don't, I'll be punished. The problem with the Good News for many people is that it's too good to be true. Where's the catch? And if no catch can be easily found, we'll invent one.

Well, those considerations are not in the spirit of the day at all! Let the Good News ring out, today at least, in all its blissful simplicity. God's loving kindness has appeared in Jesus Christ, lavished upon the creation that God looked upon when he made it and saw it was good. Redeemed in pure love, it is now even better.

GOSPEL   Luke 2:15–20

A reading from the holy gospel according to Luke

When the *angels* went *away* from them to *heaven*,
  the shepherds *said* to one another,
  "Let us *go*, then, to *Bethlehem*
  to *see* this thing that has taken place,
  which the *Lord* has made *known* to us."

So they went in *haste* and found *Mary* and *Joseph*,
  and the infant lying in the *manger*.
When they *saw* this,
  they made *known* the message
  that had been *told* them about this child.
All who *heard* it were *amazed*
  by what had been *told* them by the *shepherds*.

And *Mary kept* all these things,
  reflecting on them in her *heart*.
Then the shepherds *returned*,
  glorifying and *praising* God
  for all they had *heard* and *seen*,
  just as it had been *told* to them.

There is a trap here. Pause after the comma to avoid making it sound like Mary, Joseph and Jesus are all lying in the manger.

Pause here. Give special emphasis to Mary's response; it is different from that of the shepherds.

GOSPEL   Appropriately enough, this passage continues where the gospel left off at Midnight Mass. (Please see the commentary there.) In this brief gospel, pay particular attention to these words: "made known to us"; "they made known the message that had been told them"; "all they had heard and seen." Notice how much "hearing and telling" there is in this passage. The shepherds hear the Good News and immediately pass it on. Their response to it seems automatic, almost knee-jerk, certainly spontaneous. There is clearly no suggestion that this news should

be kept a secret. It's so wonderful that one's instant reaction is to tell others.

Notice, though, that Mary's response is different. She "kept" the news, "reflecting" on it. Hers is the contemplative response, and it shows us that not everyone reacts in the same way to the gospel. There are people whose nature practically compels them to shout out the good news of God's love for us. There are others whose natural response is to fall silent in the face of such news. Their inclination is to find a quiet place where they can think about what they have heard and plumb its depths.

The mature Christian probably does both, realizing that to share one's faith effectively, one must have done some serious reflection on it first. The gushy and wildly enthusiastic response to Christ in this passage is as yet untempered by the sobering realization that to follow Christ means to take up a cross. By emulating both the shepherds' enthusiasm and Mary's contemplation, we will find that brand of joy that has been called the surest sign of God's presence within us.

CHRISTMAS DAY

Lectionary #16

READING I   Isaiah 52:7–10

A reading from the book of the prophet Isaiah

Begin with strong conviction and a big voice. This text is not for the timid.

How *beautiful* upon the *mountains*
    are the *feet* of him who brings glad *tidings*,
announcing *peace*, bearing good *news*,
    announcing *salvation*, and saying to *Zion*,
    "Your God is *King*!"

Do not shout "Hark" or make it sound stern, but pause slightly before it.

Hark! Your *sentinels* raise a *cry*,
    together they shout for *joy*,
for they see *directly*, before their *eyes*,
    the LORD *restoring* Zion.

Break out together in *song*,
    O ruins of *Jerusalem*!
For the LORD *comforts* his people,
    he *redeems* Jerusalem.
The LORD has *bared* his holy *arm*
    in the sight of all the *nations*;
all the *ends* of the *earth* will *behold*
    the *salvation* of our *God*.

The last two lines are crucial; they express one of the major themes of Christmas.

READING I Does it seem odd to you that this reading begins by talking about "beautiful feet"? A special poetic device is being employed here. The feet of the messenger symbolize the whole experience of receiving glad tidings: expecting the message, seeing the messenger from afar, hearing the footsteps as the messenger draws closer. And that experience is surely beautiful.

The sentinels see the effect of the good news: The Lord is restoring Zion, comforting the people and demonstrating his power to save. And finally the whole people are encouraged to break out in song. Notice that this reading builds upon itself. The message gets bigger and bigger as more and more voices join in, until "all the ends of the earth" behold God's salvation.

If you are one of those lectors who feels inhibited by emotion-laden and poetic texts like this one, take comfort. You are not expected to dramatize or reenact the feelings expressed here. In fact, it would be a great mistake if you tried to. Liturgical proclamation is different from oral interpretation of literature or dramatic reading. The purpose of liturgical proclamation is to allow the power of God's word to do its work. You are involved, but you should be transparent. In dramatic reading, the text is interpreted in a certain way so that the actor and the text both become part of the audience's experience. The lector in the liturgy does not interpret but should remain objective and permit the text to have its intended effect. The text is always in the foreground; the proclaimer serves it in the background. This does not mean that the proclaimer is cold or that the proclamation is without feeling. It means that

READING II Hebrews 1:1–6

A reading from the letter to the Hebrews

Brothers and sisters:
In times *past*, God spoke in *partial* and *various* ways
    to our *ancestors* through the *prophets*;
        in these *last* days, he has spoken to us through the *Son*,
        whom he made *heir* of all things
        and *through* whom he created the *universe*,
        who is the refulgence of his *glory*,
        the very *imprint* of his *being*,
        and who *sustains* all things by his mighty *word*.

When he had accomplished *purification* from *sins*,
    he took his *seat* at the right hand of the *Majesty* on *high*,
        as far *superior* to the *angels*
        as the *name* he has inherited is more *excellent* than *theirs*.

For to which of the *angels* did God ever say:
    "You are my *son*; this day I have *begotten* you"?
Or again:
    "I will be a *father* to him, and he shall be a *son* to me"?
And again, when he leads the *firstborn* into the world, he says:
    "Let all the *angels* of God *worship* him."

Consider omitting "Brothers and sisters."
The author of the text did not begin
with this greeting, and it weakens a strong
opening phrase.

Be as precise and emphatic as the author
is here: This Son is the "refulgence" of
God's glory, the "very imprint" of God's
being. See how different translations try
to capture the writer's point.

Beware of a scoffing here; the mood is one
of wonder!

the reader serves the text's purpose rather than the text serving the reader's purpose. Take full charge of your ministry by letting the word of God take full charge of you.

READING II For the first time in this liturgical year we hear a reading from the letter to the Hebrews. The entire work is an *apologia*—that is, a demonstration that all the prophesies and hopes of the Hebrew scriptures have their fulfillment in

Jesus the Christ. The reading also shows us that the relationship of the Father and the Son has existed for all eternity—well before the Son took flesh and came to live among us. Clearly, this reading leads us to a fuller and richer meaning of the Christmas celebration.

This is not an easy reading, however. The sentences are long and layered with subordinate clauses. The text requires a great deal of study and preparation before justice can be done to it in proclamation, and it contains some semi-apocalyptic imagery that we may never fully understand. But once we have mastered its structure and glimpsed

the depth of its meaning, we can read it with the conviction and nobility the text demands.

One thing is quite clear. The author of the letter to the Hebrews was very much concerned with teaching us about the divinity of Jesus and his exalted origin as the Son of God. This is a dimension of Christmas that is often neglected but should not be. The "babe in the manger" is a compelling image, but remembering that this babe is the firstborn Son of the Father makes it all the more compelling.

This is a huge reading, laden with important truths of Christianity. Take great pains to help the assembly listen attentively. Communicate the uniqueness of this special text by making its message your own.

GOSPEL   John 1:1–18

A reading from the holy gospel according to John

In the *beginning* was the *Word*,
    and the Word was *with* God,
    and the Word *was* God.
He was in the *beginning* with God.
All things came to *be* through him,
    and *without* him *nothing* came to be.
What came to be through him was *life*,
    and this *life* was the *light* of the human *race*;
    the light *shines* in the *darkness*,
    and the *darkness* has *not* overcome it.

A man named *John* was *sent* from God.
He came for *testimony*, to testify to the *light*,
    so that *all* might *believe* through him.
He was *not* the light,
    but came to *testify* to the light.

The *true* light, which enlightens *everyone*,
        was coming into the *world*.
He was *in* the world,
    and the world came to *be* through him,
    but the world did not *know* him.
He came to what was his *own*,
    but his *own people* did not *accept* him.

GOSPEL   John opens his gospel with the same words that open the book of Genesis, the book of creation, thus putting Jesus Christ (the Word) in the context of eternity and revealing him as the one through whom all things came to be. Here again, as in today's second reading from Hebrews, we are jolted into an awareness of the full meaning of Christmas: The eternal Word that was *with* God and *is* God become flesh. Here is the awesome mystery of the incarnation: the divine becoming human.

As you might suspect after a close reading of this gospel passage, John has more to accomplish here than simple instruction. He strongly emphasizes Christ's divinity and his involvement in the creation of the world because there were schools of thought at the time of his writing that denied both. There were Christians who tried to reconcile an understanding of God as pure, perfect spirit and a material world that is flawed by evil by saying that the two had nothing to do with each other; God could not be associated with anything imperfect. There were other Christians who could not believe that

Christ, who is God, could really be mortal. They decided that the Jesus who walked the earth only appeared to be human—his body wasn't a real human body.

John is at pains to show Christ (the Word of God who is God) both deeply much involved with the creation of the world and, through the wonder of the incarnation, truly flesh and blood. Jesus Christ existed from all eternity as God and chose to become a human being at a particular moment in time.

But to those who *did* accept him
 he gave *power* to become children of *God*,
 to those who believe in his *name*,
 who were born not by *natural* generation
 nor by *human* choice nor by a *man's* decision
 but of *God*.

And the Word became *flesh*
 and made his *dwelling* among us,
 and we saw his *glory*,
 the glory as of the Father's only *Son*,
 full of *grace* and *truth*.

John *testified* to him and cried out, saying,
 "*This* was he of whom I said,
 'The one who is coming *after* me ranks *ahead* of me
 because he *existed* before me.'"

From his *fullness* we have all *received*,
 grace in place of *grace*,
 because while the *law* was given through *Moses*,
 grace and *truth* came through Jesus *Christ*.
No one has ever seen *God*.
The only *Son*, God, who is at the Father's *side*,
 has *revealed* him.

[Shorter: John 1:1–5, 9–14]

The closing lines, beginning with "No one has ever seen God," are important. They mean, "No one has ever seen God until *now!* The Son, who is God, has shown us God!"

But what's the motive for this divine being to become human? John gives us the answer: grace. The grace of God has appeared in Jesus Christ. We toss the word "grace" around a lot. But what does it mean? Synonyms for grace include kindness, decency, favor, mercy, mercifulness, charity, benevolence, clemency and leniency. I particularly like the last two: clemency and leniency. The grace of God is the face of God, seen in Jesus. No longer do we have to guess what God is like. Jesus shows us that the face of God is clement, lenient, merciful, benevolent, loving.

What about God as sometimes described in the Hebrew scriptures—vengeful, merciless, angry, even petulant? Of course, we no longer believe these traits describe God. But our understanding of God's nature has developed over time and was incomplete until Jesus appeared. It's not that the God of the Old Testament is supplanted by the God of the New Testament. It's the same God, and God does not change. But our notion of God has definitely changed across the centuries! The writers of the Hebrew scriptures wrote about God as they understood God to be. But as we heard in the second reading, in times past we knew God only partially and in various ways. Now the grace and the face of God have appeared in fullness and clarity in Jesus Christ. That's what we celebrate on Christmas Day.

HOLY FAMILY

Lectionary #17

READING I   Sirach 3:2–6, 12–14

Sirach = SEER-ak

Remember that you are reading a series of proverbs—related, of course, but not like a prose development of a theme. Take care that each kernel of insight and wisdom gets its due, and that the assembly gets enough time to let them sink in.

A reading from the book of Sirach

God sets a *father* in *honor* over his *children*;
    a *mother's authority* he *confirms* over her *sons*.
Whoever honors his *father* atones for *sins*,
    and *preserves* himself from them.
When he *prays*, he is *heard*;
    he stores up *riches* who reveres his *mother*.
Whoever honors his *father* is gladdened by *children*,
    and, when he *prays*, is *heard*.
Whoever reveres his *father* will live a long *life*;
    he who *obeys* his father brings *comfort* to his *mother*.

My son, take *care* of your father when he is *old*;
    grieve him *not* as long as he *lives*.
Even if his *mind* fail, be *considerate* of him;
    revile him *not* all the days of his *life*;
kindness to a *father* will not be *forgotten*,
    firmly *planted* against the debt of your *sins*
    —a house raised in *justice* to you.

READING I The book of Sirach is the work of a sage who had traveled widely and pondered the scriptures before setting down this collection of proverbs. The book is no longer included in the Hebrew scriptures, nor is it included in the canon of sacred writings recognized by Christian denominations other than Catholic. But we have always drawn extensively from Sirach in our liturgical texts and catechesis, so much so, in fact, that the book goes by another name: Ecclesiasticus (literally, the church book).

Sirach is a charming work, filled with timeless wisdom set down in the form of aphorisms—sayings, maxims, kernels of truth. One of my personal favorites has to do with the evil of gossip: "Let whatever you hear die within you," Sirach says, "Be assured it will not make you burst!"

Today's passage is clearly chosen for its observations about familial relationships, the mutual duties of children and parents—appropriate enough for the feast of the Holy Family. There is great poignancy in some of these lines, and harsh reality as well: "Take care of your parents when they are old; even

if their minds fail, be considerate of them." The author clearly knew some of the difficulties of family life.

Texts like this one call for a strong and exalted proclamation. Nothing offhand or casual will do. Equally inappropriate would be a haughty or distant rendition. Between those extremes is a noble and solid proclamation that gives the text its full weight and elicits thoughtful listening on the part of the members of the assembly.

READING II Colossians 3:12–21

A reading from the letter of Saint Paul to the Colossians

Brothers and sisters:
Put *on*, as God's *chosen* ones, *holy* and *beloved*,
    heartfelt *compassion*, *kindness*, *humility*, *gentleness*,
        and *patience*,
    bearing with one another and *forgiving* one another,
    if one has a *grievance* against another;
    as the Lord has forgiven *you*, so must you *also* do.
And over *all* these put on *love*,
    that is, the *bond* of *perfection*.
And let the *peace* of Christ *control* your hearts,
    the *peace* into which you were *also* called in one *body*.
And be *thankful*.

Let the *word* of Christ dwell in you *richly*,
    as in all *wisdom* you *teach* and *admonish* one another,
    singing *psalms*, *hymns*, and spiritual *songs*
    with *gratitude* in your hearts to *God*.
And *whatever* you do, in *word* or in *deed*,
    do *everything* in the name of the Lord *Jesus*,
    giving *thanks* to God the *Father* through *him*.

Wives, be *subordinate* to your husbands,
    as is *proper* in the Lord.
Husbands, *love* your wives,
    and avoid any *bitterness* toward them.

Pause here. This is a crucial point: Above all and over all and most important of all, put on love!

A new section begins here as Paul describes the virtues he has listed above with the example of married couples.

READING II Paul gives us in fewer than a dozen verses a fine recipe for living together in peace and harmony. One would think we could do much better than our record indicates. Surely nothing here is beyond human capacity—and certainly not beyond the ability of anyone who embraces Christian values: mercy, kindness, humility, patience, love, thankfulness. Paul even admits how difficult we can be for each other when he counsels us to bear with and forgive one another. He knows human nature well enough to presume the occasional necessity of putting up with each other—not the highest of virtues, of course, but as much as we can muster sometimes.

Imagine the family who adopted Paul's words as their charter for living! That would truly be a holy family—not a pietistic one but a real family who knows that the heat created by friction is better than the cold resulting from resentment.

Of course, it is genuine love that binds all our good efforts together and makes them one, and it is love that is the fruit of all those good works. But perhaps most striking here is the final admonition in Paul's list: "And be thankful." The grateful heart is the one that most spontaneously gives itself away. A thankful person is one of life's greatest gifts, a joy to be around, a ray of light on those darker days. Thankfulness is clearly the most appropriate mode of living for the Christian. We have a God who loves us exactly as we are, warts and all. Isn't that reason enough to live in thankfulness?

Children, obey your *parents* in *everything*,
    for this is *pleasing* to the Lord.
Fathers, do not *provoke* your children,
    so they may not become *discouraged*.

[Shorter: Colossians 3:12–17]

GOSPEL   Matthew 2:13–15, 19–23

A reading from the holy gospel according to Matthew

When the *magi* had *departed, behold,*
    the angel of the *Lord* appeared to *Joseph* in a *dream* and said,
      "*Rise*, take the *child* and his *mother; flee* to *Egypt,*
    and *stay* there until I *tell* you.
Herod is going to *search* for the child to *destroy* him."
Joseph *rose* and took the child and his mother by *night*
    and departed for *Egypt.*
He *stayed* there until the *death* of Herod,
    that what the Lord had said through the *prophet*
      might be *fulfilled,*
    "Out of *Egypt* I called my *son.*"

When Herod had *died, behold,*
    the angel of the *Lord* appeared in a *dream*
    to Joseph in *Egypt* and said,
      "*Rise*, take the *child* and his *mother* and
        go to the land of *Israel,*
    for those who sought the child's *life* are *dead.*"
He *rose*, took the *child* and his *mother,*
    and went to the land of *Israel.*

Consider beginning with the angel's appearance: "Behold . . ." The departure of the magi is a weak beginning.

Matthew's purpose is to show the fulfillment of two prophecies. Emphasize the first prophecy, which begins with "Out of Egypt . . ."

The last paragraph will rankle some hearers. It is hopelessly archaic and even inflammatory to speak of "subordinate" wives today, but it wasn't in Paul's time, and we need to keep that in mind. Paul's views, here and elsewhere, about the submission of wives to husbands spring from his culture, not from the mind of God. Things have changed a bit for the better—another reason to be thankful.

GOSPEL | This gospel reading begins better if you drop the initial clause about the magi. Try beginning simply with the statement about the angel appearing to Joseph. If the intention in beginning with the departure of the wise men is to connect the flight into Egypt with the Christmas story, the season itself will do that.

The connection between this reading and today's feast is a bit forced. Portrayal of a happy family in Nazareth is certainly not

Matthew's purpose in this passage. Such a scene is painted more vividly in Luke, after Jesus' worried parents find the twelve-year-old in the temple: "Jesus went down with them and came to Nazareth, and was obedient to them. His mother treasured all these things in her heart. And Jesus increased in wisdom and in years, and in divine and human favor" (Luke 2:51–52). The story of the flight into Egypt has another purpose, though

Archelaus = ahr-kih-LAY-uhs

But when he heard that *Archelaus* was ruling over *Judea*
    in place of his father *Herod,*
      he was afraid to go *back* there.
And because he had been *warned* in a *dream,*
    he departed for the region of *Galilee.*
He went and dwelt in a town called *Nazareth,*
    so that what had been spoken through the *prophets*
      might be *fulfilled,*
    "He shall be called a *Nazorean.*"

The second prophecy begins with "He shall be called . . ." Give it emphasis as well.
Nazorean = naz-uh-REE-uhn

it does, of course, continue the infancy narrative proper to the Christmas season.

We might get a fresh picture of what "family" entails if we look at the parallel that Matthew clearly draws between the exodus of the Hebrews from Egypt and the mission of Christ. The ultimate biblical symbol of deliverance is rescue from exile. The ultimate goal and purpose of this Nazarene child is to deliver us from the exile of sin and death—by becoming sin on our behalf and dying so we might live. "Out of Egypt I called my son"—Matthew is reminding us of Israel's deliverance from slavery in Egypt, when they were led to freedom by Moses. And since Matthew is preoccupied with showing Jesus as the fulfillment of every prophecy and promise, we, as the new Israel, are to be led out of slavery by Christ, the second Moses.

The effects of that deliverance bind us to one another with ties stronger than any blood relationship. Christian notions about "family" include recognition of the solidarity that binds all believers together. This is the picture of family that Matthew would draw from the story of the flight into Egypt. And it is probably the picture of family that should be in your mind as you proclaim this beautifully crafted story.

MARY, MOTHER OF GOD

Lectionary #18

READING I   Numbers 6:22–27

A reading from the book of Numbers

The LORD said to *Moses*:
"Speak to *Aaron* and his *sons* and tell them:
    This is how you shall *bless* the *Israelites*.

"Say to them:
    The LORD *bless* you and *keep* you!
    The LORD let his *face* shine upon you,
        and be *gracious* to you!
    The LORD look upon you *kindly*
        and give you *peace*!

"So shall they invoke my *name* upon the Israelites,
    and I will *bless* them."

With such a brief reading you need to be sure the assembly is listening before you begin. Pause after announcing the reading until silence prevails.

Give each invocation sufficient emphasis and time to sink in.

Pause slightly before and after the word "peace."

READING I   The purpose of the book of Numbers is to show that God never deserts Israel, even during the darkest days of exile. The familiar blessing that is the heart of this reading is a comfort to the assembly on this first day of a new year. Thought brief, the reading is a rich summary of God's attitude toward the people of the covenant. Keep in mind the following implications of this profound message as you proclaim it.

First, formal blessings are generally reserved to persons chosen for spiritual leadership. The descendants of Aaron were entrusted with this blessing to show how essential it is for the people's well-being.

Second, there are dark days in everyone's life, when it seems that the Lord's face is hidden. The blessing has this in mind when it asks that the Lord's face shine upon us.

Third, our word "peace" is a weak translation of *shalom*, a word that implies "every good thing in full measure." You can communicate something of the special character of this word by pausing slightly before and after saying the word "peace."

Finally, God's promise is irrevocable. When this blessing is invoked with sincerity and received gratefully, God says with utter certainty, "I will bless them." Pronounce the final words with great conviction, optimism and strength. This is wonderful to hear as we begin a new year.

READING II   Paul was a master at creating brief summaries of what Christians believe and should live by. This passage is such a text. The "fullness of time" implies the arrival of a pre-designated moment in history and reminds us that we are involved in a divine plan that stretches

READING II   Galatians 4:4–7

A reading from the letter of Saint Paul to the Galatians

Brothers and sisters:
When the *fullness* of *time* had *come*, God sent his *Son*,
    born of a *woman*, born under the *law*,
    to *ransom* those under the law,
    so that we might receive *adoption* as *sons*.

As *proof* that you are sons,
    God sent the *Spirit* of his Son into our *hearts*,
    crying out, "*Abba, Father*!"
So you are no longer a *slave* but a *son*,
    and if a *son* then also an *heir*, through *God*.

back into eternity. There is a mission implied in the words "God sent his Son." The Son did not appear arbitrarily, but came for a purpose. And this Son was born of a woman, that is, fully human, sharing completely in our weakness—as well as our subjection to the law.

Paul is playing with words here. It is ironic that Jesus had to be subject to the law so that he could liberate us from it. He participated in all that the law required (including the circumcision we read about in the gospel) so that he could show us he is master of all law and came to give us something beyond a law-based relationship with God. He transforms our legal relationship to God into a parent-child relationship. He comes to teach us to call God "Abba," an intimate term for father implying complete security, warmth, affection and strength.

Elevation from the rank of slave to the rank of child is a dramatic move indeed. And becoming an heir to the Father's riches is even more dramatic. There can be a note of disbelief in your proclamation of this text. It is as if you are saying, "I know this is hard to believe, but in Christ we see that God loves us as children and wants us to call out, 'Abba.'"

GOSPEL   You will recognize that this is the same gospel passage proclaimed at the Mass at dawn on Christmas Day. Since this is the octave day of Christmas, it seems appropriate. However, a final sentence has been added to show us that Jesus was circumcised in accordance with Mosaic law. It was important for Jesus to follow the law of Moses so that he would

GOSPEL   Luke 2:16–21

A reading from the holy gospel according to Luke

The *shepherds* went in *haste* to *Bethlehem*
        and found *Mary* and *Joseph*,
    and the *infant* lying in the *manger*.
When they *saw* this,
        they made *known* the message
        that had been *told* them about this child.
All who *heard* it were *amazed*
        by what had been *told* them by the *shepherds*.

And *Mary kept* all these things,
        reflecting on them in her *heart*.
Then the shepherds *returned*,
        glorifying and praising *God*
        for all they had *heard* and *seen*,
        just as it had been *told* to them.

When *eight days* were completed for his *circumcision*,
        he was named *Jesus*, the name given him by the *angel*
        before he was *conceived* in the *womb*.

Beware of a trap here that makes it sound like the entire Holy Family is in the manger! Pause after "Joseph," and do not pause after "infant."

Pause before this new section. Single out the words about Mary.

Emphasize that the name Jesus is of divine origin.

be credible when he revealed himself to be the fulfillment of it.

In the second reading, Paul notes the irony of Jesus being subjected to the law so that he could liberate us from it. The problem with law is that it tends to make life appear too easy. What could be clearer than a pre-scribed set of laws that, when followed to the letter, guarantees the reward it promises (whatever that reward might be). In Jesus' time, the Mosaic law had grown to an enor-mous size, governing every aspect of daily life. It was terribly complex and difficult to keep straight, but the extent to which it

was fulfilled indicated the goodness of a person. There is no clearer presentation of the folly of such thinking than the exchanges throughout the gospels between Jesus and the scribes and Pharisees.

Law can fool us by making it look easy to be good, but the problem is that law never made anybody good. The best thing about law is that it can, to some extent, protect us from those outside it. Even we who obey the law are no more than law-abiding citizens, which isn't a bad thing to be, but it certainly doesn't guarantee that we're good citizens. Jesus came to show us that God has called

us to far more noble tasks than obeying the law. Jesus enables us to become the kind of people for whom law is unnecessary.

Perhaps this is what Mary pondered, treasured and reflected on in her heart. Her life seems to indicate as much. Doing a lit-tle pondering on our own wouldn't be a bad way to begin a new year. We might become less like slaves to rules and more like chil-dren of the Ruler.

EPIPHANY OF THE LORD

Lectionary #20

READING I   Isaiah 60:1–6

A reading from the book of the prophet Isaiah

Be aware of the parallelism in this poetry. Almost every line is echoed, restated or developed in the line that follows it. You will avoid a sing-song effect if you relish each line of text and allow its unique meaning to shine through.

Rise up in *splendor, Jerusalem*! Your *light* has *come*,
  the *glory* of the LORD *shines* upon you.
See, darkness covers the earth,
  and thick *clouds* cover the *peoples;*
but upon *you* the LORD *shines*,
  and over *you* appears his *glory.*

A new but related section begins here. Pause slightly.

Nations shall *walk* by your *light*,
  and *kings* by your shining *radiance.*
Raise your *eyes* and look *about;*
  they all *gather* and *come* to you:
your *sons* come from *afar*,
  and your *daughters* in the arms of their *nurses.*

Another new section begins here.

Then you shall be *radiant* at what you see,
  your heart shall *throb* and *overflow*,
for the riches of the *sea* shall be emptied *out* before you,
  the wealth of *nations* shall be *brought* to you.
Caravans of *camels* shall fill you,
  dromedaries from *Midian* and *Ephah;*
all from *Sheba* shall come
  bearing *gold* and *frankincense,*
  and proclaiming the *praises* of the LORD.

Midian = MID-ee-uhn
Ephah = EE-fah
Sheba = SHEE-buh

READING I | Some years ago we started celebrating the feast of the Epiphany on the Sunday nearest January 6 rather than on that date itself. Today, happily, the two coincide, so we can actually celebrate the twelfth day of Christmas on the twelfth day of Christmas! But partridges and pear trees are not our concern here.

A beautiful text from the church's Evening Prayer summarizes today's feast: "Three mysteries mark this holy day: today the star leads the Magi to the infant Christ; today water is changed into wine for the wedding feast; today Christ wills to be baptized by John in the river Jordan to bring us salvation." Obviously, these three events did not occur on the same day. The point is that in all three events the divinity of Jesus was manifested to the world—and that's even what the word "epiphany" means.

Isaiah, too, is concerned with the epiphany (the showing forth) of God's glory, and wants to emphasize especially that God's glory shines upon Jerusalem (the chosen people) even when darkness and clouds cover it. The prophet encourages the people of Israel to see beyond appearances and glimpse the glory of God's action in their midst, guiding them through whatever difficulties threaten to blind them to God's favor. It is an exultant hymn that looks into the future and confidently announces that God will be faithful.

This, of course, is the message of Advent, Christmas and Epiphany. During Advent we remember the promises that foretell the coming of the Messiah. At Christmas we celebrate that coming in history. On Epiphany we stand in awe of the revealed mystery of the Word made flesh.

It is important that you build up to the dramatic statement that is the point of this reading. The buildup rises through "to his holy prophets and apostles by the Spirit," and then the climax reveals that the Gentiles are part of the plan!

READING II Ephesians 3:2–3a, 5–6

A reading from the letter of Saint Paul to the Ephesians

Brothers and sisters:
You have *heard* of the *stewardship* of God's *grace*
    that was given to *me* for your *benefit*,
    namely, that the mystery was made *known* to me
        by *revelation*.

It was *not* made known to people in *other* generations
    as it has *now* been revealed
    to his holy *apostles* and *prophets* by the *Spirit*:
    that the *Gentiles* are *coheirs*, members of the *same body*,
    and *copartners* in the promise in Christ *Jesus*
        through the *gospel*.

Every detail in this story is important. Tell it with great care.

GOSPEL Matthew 2:1–12

A reading from the holy gospel according to Matthew

When *Jesus* was *born* in *Bethlehem* of *Judea*,
    in the days of King *Herod*,
    behold, *magi* from the *east* arrived in Jerusalem, saying,
    "Where is the newborn *king* of the *Jews*?
We saw his *star* at its *rising*
    and have come to do him *homage*."

READING II It may be difficult for us to think of the message of Christ being limited to a certain people, and yet realizing that even Gentiles are included in God's plan of salvation was one of the earliest struggles faced by the church. In fact, it took some years before the universality of Christ's mission was fully understood. Remembering that the earliest Christians were mostly Jews, we can appreciate just how startling Paul's assertion in this reading really is: The Gentiles are coheirs, members of the body, sharers of the promise.

One of the great theme songs of the season of Christmas is "All the ends of the earth have seen the salvation of God." There can be no more appropriate day than Epiphany to sing this song, for this feast celebrates God's unlimited glory, shining from east to west, illuminating all of creation. With the manifestation of divinity through the humanity of Christ, every living thing appears in a different light.

Though the epistle writer speaks of God's secret plan, it was not God's intention to keep things secret. The point is that until Christ came we did not know God's plan. We had no idea how universal it was, nor did we fully know the nature of God until Christ revealed it in himself. In Christ, all the world has seen God, and all peoples have become coheirs of the ancient promises.

As you proclaim this message, imagine yourself sharing an ambassador's delight over a successful mission, an effort at reconciliation that has exceeded even the highest hopes. Groups with apparently irreconcilable differences have come together to embrace a common belief, reach for a common goal and share a wondrous destiny.

When King *Herod* heard this,
   he was greatly *troubled*,
   and all *Jerusalem with* him.
Assembling all the chief *priests* and the *scribes* of the people,
   he *inquired* of them where the *Christ* was to be born.
They said to him, "In *Bethlehem* of *Judea*,
   for thus it has been *written* through the *prophet*:
   'And *you*, Bethlehem, land of *Judah*,
   are by no means *least* among the *rulers* of Judah;
   since from *you* shall come a *ruler*,
   who is to *shepherd* my people *Israel*.'"

The conflict begins with Herod's hypocrisy.

Then Herod *called* the magi *secretly*
   and ascertained from them the *time* of the star's *appearance*.
He sent them to *Bethlehem* and said,
   "*Go* and search *diligently* for the child.
When you have *found* him, bring me *word*,
   that I *too* may go and do him *homage*."

After their *audience* with the *king* they set *out*.
And *behold*, the *star* that they had seen at its *rising*
      preceded them,
   until it came and *stopped* over the place where the *child* was.

The conflict recedes for a moment in the joy of finding the child.

They were *overjoyed* at seeing the star,
   and on entering the *house*
   they saw the *child* with Mary his *mother*.

They *prostrated* themselves and did him *homage*.
Then they opened their *treasures*
   and offered him *gifts* of *gold*, *frankincense*, and *myrrh*.

The conflict resumes and includes more than a hint of the troubles ahead.

And having been warned in a dream *not* to return to *Herod*,
   they departed for their *country* by another *way*.

GOSPEL | Matthew's purpose in telling this story is the same one that governs his entire gospel: to demonstrate that every prophecy and promise of old has come to fulfillment in Christ. Your objective is the same as Matthew's, namely, to show the members of the assembly that their faith in Christ is well placed.

As promised by the prophets, the humble town of Bethlehem (the city of King David's ancestor Ruth) has become the Messiah's birthplace. As promised, Gentile sages from foreign lands, guided by a miraculous star, have acknowledged Jesus' birth with gifts of gold, frankincense and myrrh. Although Matthew quotes the prophets for only one of these fulfilled promises, it is clear that he has many ancient texts in mind.

The rich splendor of "Herod's city" (Jerusalem) stands in sharp contrast to the lowliness of Bethlehem, just as Herod's jealousy is the opposite of the humility of the Gentile magi. And the joy of birth is more than a little diminished by the hint of danger and impending doom. The foreign visitors have to avoid the envious and hypocritical Herod.

Clearly, this child brings into the world a new dimension of the inevitable struggle between good and evil. When light shines out in the darkness, the darkness does not always flee willingly. When faced with news that seems too good to be true, some resist it. That resistance, too, is part of God's plan, since only the death of this Messiah will bring that plan to its mysterious fulfillment.

BAPTISM OF THE LORD

Lectionary #21

READING I   Isaiah 42:1–4, 6–7

A reading from the book of the prophet Isaiah

Some of Isaiah's most important poetry appears here. Let your voice signal its significance.

Thus says the LORD:
Here is my *servant* whom I *uphold*,
    my *chosen* one with whom I am *pleased*,
upon whom I have put my *spirit*;
    he shall bring forth *justice* to the nations,
not crying out, *not* shouting,
    not making his voice heard in the *street*.
A *bruised* reed he shall not *break*,
    and a smoldering *wick* he shall not *quench*,
until he establishes *justice* on the earth;
    the *coastlands* will *wait* for his *teaching*.

A new section begins here. Prepare for it with a pause.

I, the LORD, have *called* you for the victory of *justice*,
    I have grasped you by the *hand*;
I *formed* you, and set you
    as a *covenant* of the people,
    a *light* for the *nations*,
to open the eyes of the *blind*,

A quiet (not weak!) resolution seems appropriate here.

    to bring out *prisoners* from *confinement*,
    and from the *dungeon*, those who live in *darkness*.

READING I There are four sections in the book of Isaiah that are called the "suffering servant songs." They depict in poignant poetry a chosen servant who must suffer much because of fidelity to God. This reading is taken from the first of those songs. Isaiah describes the election, anointing and mission of the servant, as well as the way the servant will go about accomplishing the objectives set out by God.

Who was this servant? An individual person, or the personification of the whole people of Israel? Whatever the answer to these questions, the suffering servant songs have been applied to Jesus Christ from the beginning of his ministry, which we celebrate in today's feast. Authors and preachers from the first days of the Christian era have seen in Jesus the perfect image of the suffering servant. Indeed, Jesus himself quotes from the songs and sees himself as their fulfillment.

As you proclaim this reading, it should be easy for the assembly to recognize the kind of ministry Jesus undertook following his baptism, the inauguration of his mission on earth. But remember that you are reading a poetic text, not a literal or prosaic description. The tone is exalted throughout and each image deserves to be relished. Isaiah clearly did not formulate these lines without effort. They deserve your most careful preparation and energetic proclamation.

READING II This reading echoes the struggle referred to in last Sunday's second reading from Ephesians, the struggle involved in recognizing that God is not partial to any one people. Anyone who approaches God with a sincere heart is acceptable. More than that, God wills that

READING II   Acts 10:34–38

A reading from the Acts of the Apostles

Peter proceeded to speak to those gathered
in the house of *Cornelius*, saying:

In *truth*, I see that *God* shows no *partiality*.
Rather, in *every* nation whoever *fears* him and acts *uprightly*
is *acceptable* to him.
You *know* the word that he sent to the *Israelites*
as he proclaimed *peace* through Jesus *Christ*, who is Lord of *all*,
what has happened all over *Judea*,
beginning in *Galilee* after the baptism
that *John* preached,
how God anointed *Jesus* of *Nazareth*
with the Holy *Spirit* and *power*.
He went about doing *good*
and *healing* all those oppressed by the *devil*,
for *God* was with him."

Make Peter's words and convictions your own. Explain to the assembly this new insight.

A new section begins here, more conversational than before.

all the world hear the good news of his plan to save the world: Jew, Gentile, all nations. And how did Peter come to this realization? It came through Jesus Christ, of course, who is Lord of all.

Again we are told that in Jesus we see clearly for the first time the nature of God's heart and the divine plan for the universe. Peter is making the point that the revelation of God's universal love began at the Jordan River, when a divine anointing made clear that, in Jesus, the establishment of God's reign on earth has begun.

Jesus' works testify that he fits Isaiah's portrait of the suffering servant: Jesus brings sight to the blind and freedom to prisoners; and Jesus suffers for the sins of the people, taking on himself the burden that only divine love can bear.

Your voice should express an eagerness to explain all this when you proclaim Peter's words in this reading. You want to make it clear that when Jesus went down into the waters of the Jordan he began a journey that would end only when he returned to the Father in glory, having accomplished the salvation of the world.

GOSPEL Matthew's account of Jesus' baptism has the same objective that governs his entire gospel: to show that, in Jesus, the divine plan is being carefully worked out in every detail, and that every prediction concerning the Messiah is fulfilled in him.

John's reluctance tells us that he recognized Jesus as the chosen one (the servant described in the first reading). How did he know this? One can only speculate, but all speculation ends with Jesus' response: "God

GOSPEL   Matthew 3:13–17

A reading from the holy gospel according to Matthew

Jesus came from *Galilee* to *John* at the *Jordan*
    to be *baptized* by him.
John tried to *prevent* him, saying,
    "*I* need to be baptized by *you,*
    and yet you are coming to *me?*"

Jesus said to him in reply,
    "*Allow* it now, for thus it is *fitting* for us
    to fulfill all *righteousness.*"
Then he *allowed* him.

After Jesus was *baptized,*
    he came up from the *water* and *behold,*
    the *heavens* were *opened* for him,
    and he saw the Spirit of *God* descending like a *dove*
    and coming *upon* him.
And a *voice* came from the heavens, saying,
    "*This* is my beloved *Son,* with whom I am *well pleased.*"

The gospel is brief. Be sure you have the assembly's full attention before you begin.

There are three sections: (1) Jesus appears on the scene; (2) he dialogues with John; (3) Jesus is baptized, and the heavenly voice speaks.

Speak the heavenly voice's words as calm and firm rather than loud.

has commanded it, and we must obey." This is a deliberate assertion that this baptism is the moment when God will commission the Son to accomplish the work for which he was chosen, which is nothing less than the inauguration of God's reign on earth. And so it happens.

In Matthew, the voice that comes from heaven is meant to be heard by all. Matthew used the earlier gospel of Mark to compose his narrative and chose to change Mark's words from "*You* are my beloved Son" to "*This* is my beloved Son." The intention is to proclaim this divine epiphany as something for all to witness so that it not to be seen as a private revelation to Jesus alone.

Now that something of the significance of this event has been emphasized, we need to note the brevity of the text that describes it—a brevity that is seen in Mark and Luke as well. Remember the principle that brevity demands a slower, more deliberate pace. Remember, too, that the story is familiar to the assembly. How can you get your hearers to listen carefully to something they have heard over and over again? The answer is that you, the reader, must hear the story with fresh ears, gleaning from it all the significance it contains and proclaiming it with such vividness and strength that you draw the assembly into it.

One final caveat is in order. Be careful when you proclaim the words of the heavenly voice; don't deepen your voice to make it "sound like God." This kind of thing is never done in liturgical proclamation. Sometimes a gentle delivery of strong words makes them stronger!

2ND SUNDAY IN ORDINARY TIME

Lectionary #64

READING I   Isaiah 49:3, 5–6

A reading from the book of the prophet Isaiah

The LORD said to me: *You* are my *servant*,
   Israel, through whom I show my *glory*.
Now the LORD has *spoken*
   who *formed* me as his *servant* from the *womb*,
   that *Jacob* may be brought *back* to him
   and *Israel gathered* to him;
   and I am made *glorious* in the sight of the LORD,
   and my *God* is now my *strength*!

It is too *little*, the LORD says, for you to be my *servant*,
   to *raise up* the tribes of *Jacob*,
   and *restore* the *survivors* of *Israel*;
I will make you a *light* to the *nations*,
   that my *salvation* may reach to the *ends* of the *earth*.

This poem is packed with meaning that is not immediately obvious. A careful proclamation will cement the ideas in the minds of the members of the assembly so they will hear them echoed in the second reading and gospel.

Proclaim the last sentence with great breadth: slowly, emphatically, solidly.

READING I Today we begin the "green season." The liturgical color during Ordinary Time is green—symbolizing hope—and hope characterizes this longest season of the year. We celebrate only a few Sundays in Ordinary Time before Lent, but the season continues after the Easter season (usually in June) and carries us through to Advent (around December 1) and a new liturgical year. The season is not called "ordinary" because there's nothing special about it. Over the course of its Sundays, we see Jesus' ministry slowly reveal the nature of his mission and of the reign of God. There's nothing ordinary about that! It is, perhaps, more properly called "Ordinal Time" since it gets its name from the fact that the Sundays are numbered with ordinal numbers (second, third, fourth, and so on).

Notice that the seasons of the liturgical year are not separated by dramatic breaks. In fact, the entire year is one seamless garment—one season leading up to the next and flowing naturally from the one that preceded it. For example, the first reading today is the second of Isaiah's suffering servant songs. Last Sunday, on the feast of the Lord's baptism, we read the first of the songs. And in the gospel we hear John the Baptist elaborate on the significance of the event that inaugurated Jesus' public ministry. Next Sunday we will hear Jesus call the first of his disciples.

Notice that this reading is God's call to the servant to be a "light to the nations." Notice, too, that it speaks of God's will that salvation extend to the ends of the earth. In this ancient poem we see several of the themes Jesus will proclaim throughout his public ministry—the most dramatic of which is the universality of his mission.

READING II   1 Corinthians 1:1–3

A reading from the beginning of the first letter of Saint Paul to the Corinthians

Paul, called to be an *apostle* of Christ *Jesus* by the will of *God,*
    and *Sosthenes* our *brother,*
    to the church of *God* that is in *Corinth,*
    to you who have been *sanctified* in Christ Jesus,
    called to be *holy,*
    with all those *everywhere* who call upon the *name* of our *Lord*
    Jesus *Christ, their* Lord and *ours.*

Grace to you and *peace* from God our *Father*
    and the Lord Jesus *Christ.*

Don't let the punctuation guide you here. Go slowly and let each unit of meaning emerge clearly and distinctly. Sosthenes = SOS-thuh-neez

Read the final sentence broadly. It's a blessing.

READING II For the next month, the second reading will be taken from First Corinthians. Notice the formulaic nature its beginning: The reading doesn't continue past the introduction of the writer and the greeting. A standard opener for Paul, it includes a great deal of Christian conviction and belief. It reminds the Corinthians that they are a consecrated people, called to be holy. And, most important today, it goes on to point out that all who call on the name of the Lord Jesus, wherever they may be (beyond Corinth), are the people Paul addresses. Here

again is the statement about the universality of the Good News we heard in Isaiah.

The Corinthians needed to be reminded of their solidarity with all Christians. The same is true for us. We, too, need to be reminded that we belong to a worldwide communion of Christians, all of whom call upon the name of the Lord Jesus and have been consecrated and called to be holy. A deeper awareness of our oneness with all who bear the name Christian will hasten the coming of the reign of Christ on earth. Try to communicate something of this truth in your proclamation.

GOSPEL Ordinarily we will hear the gospel of Matthew proclaimed this year. (Year A is the year of the gospel of Matthew in the three-year cycle of the Sunday lectionary.) But John is read today instead to prolong our reflection on Epiphany's theme, the inauguration of Jesus' public ministry at his baptism. John's story of the baptism is considerably different from what we find in the other three gospels. That's because his purpose is to refute the view held by some that John the Baptist was superior to Jesus. In order to correct such a notion, the gospel writer does not

GOSPEL   John 1:29–34

A reading from the holy gospel according to John

John the *Baptist* saw *Jesus* coming toward him and said,
   "*Behold*, the Lamb of *God*, who takes away the *sin*
      of the *world*.
He is the one of whom I said,
   'A man is coming *after* me who ranks *ahead* of me
      because he *existed* before me.'
I did not *know* him,
   but the *reason* why I came *baptizing* with *water*
      was that he might be made *known* to Israel."

John testified *further*, saying,
   "I saw the *Spirit* come down like a *dove* from *heaven*
      and *remain* upon him.
I did not *know* him,
   but the one who *sent* me to baptize with *water* told me,
      'On whomever you see the *Spirit* come down and remain,
      he is the one who will baptize with the Holy *Spirit*.'
Now I have *seen* and *testified* that he is the Son of *God*."

give an account of the particulars of Jesus' baptism. Rather, he has John the Baptist give testimony to the meaning of the event. Notice that almost the entire reading is composed of the Baptist's words. And John the Baptist clearly says that the revelation of Jesus as the Lamb of God was the sole purpose of John's mission. Indeed, he picks up the evangelist's theme at the beginning of the gospel: "Jesus existed before me— before anyone—from all eternity!"

Having established the true Christian view of the relationship between the John the Baptist and Jesus, the gospel writer

concentrates on demonstrating that Jesus is indeed the servant of God described in the servant songs of Isaiah. It was revealed to John the Baptist that the one on whom the spirit of God descended would be the chosen one who would baptize the world with the Holy Spirit. The gospel writer's purpose, then, is to have John the Baptist himself show us that God's plan to save the world will be worked out through the chosen servant, Jesus. The Spirit that is upon him will stay with him throughout his ministry and demonstrate that he is the Lamb of God who takes away the sin of the world.

This reading is unusual in that you are not proclaiming the event of Jesus' baptism but relating its meaning through the words of John the Baptist. It would be inappropriate to assume the character of John the Baptist, of course, because these are not your words but his. However, your listeners need to hear all the conviction and strength of John's explanation of who Jesus is. Your overall purpose is to encourage the members of the assembly to say in their hearts what John the Baptist says out loud through you: "Now I see for myself: This truly is God's chosen servant."

3RD SUNDAY IN ORDINARY TIME

Lectionary #67

READING I   Isaiah 8:23 — 9:3

A reading from the book of the prophet Isaiah

First the Lord *degraded* the land of *Zebulun*
    and the land of *Naphtali;*
    but in the *end* he has *glorified* the *seaward* road,
    the land *west* of the *Jordan,*
    the District of the *Gentiles.*

Anguish has taken *wing, dispelled* is *darkness:*
    for there is no *gloom* where but *now* there was *distress.*

The people who walked in *darkness*
    have seen a great *light;*
    upon those who dwelt in the land of *gloom* a *light* has shone.
You have brought them abundant *joy*
    and great *rejoicing,*
    as they rejoice before you as at the *harvest,*
    as people make *merry* when dividing *spoils.*

For the *yoke* that *burdened* them,
    the *pole* on their *shoulder,*
    and the *rod* of their *taskmaster*
    you have *smashed,* as on the day of *Midian.*

The first part of this reading prepares for the second.
Zebulun = ZEB-yoo-luhn
Naphtali = NAF-tuh-lee

Here's the good news! Let it ring out.

Make the most of the poetic imagery.

Midian = MID-ee-uhn

READING I **The second half of this reading was proclaimed at Christmas Midnight Mass. Today in the gospel we hear Matthew assert that Isaiah's words are fulfilled in the ministry of Jesus. The use of this reading demonstrates how the liturgical year links all the times and seasons. Though Christmas is long over in the department stores, its meaning continues throughout the year: Jesus came to be the light of the world and to proclaim that the reign of God is at hand!**

To understand the imagery of the first half of the reading, you need to know that Zebulun and Naphtali were the first of Israel's twelve tribes to be conquered by the Assyrians because their lands were farthest north (closest to Assyria). For this reason the north was traditionally associated with darkness. The mention of Zebulun and Naphtali, then, provides Isaiah with a dramatic contrast to the great light of liberation that has now dawned over the people under their new king.

With the coming of Christ, a new age dawned over the world. And Christ brings

more than a new age; he ushers in the *final* age, for in the mystery of the incarnation heaven and earth are reconciled, the redemption of humankind is accomplished, death has been conquered and the reign of justice and peace has been established. Now all we need to do is to make these realities visible by following in the footsteps of Jesus. Theologians speak of this apparent contradiction as the "already but not yet" view of the reign of God. In other words, the life, death, resurrection and ascension of Christ

READING II 1 Corinthians 1:10–13, 17

A reading from the first letter of Saint Paul to the Corinthians

Paul is pleading earnestly here.

I *urge* you, brothers and sisters, in the name of our Lord
    Jesus *Christ*,
    that all of you *agree* in what you say,
    and that there be no *divisions* among you,
    but that you be *united* in the same *mind*
        and in the same *purpose*.

For it has been *reported* to me about you, my brothers and sisters,
    by *Chloe's* people, that there are *rivalries* among you.

Chloe = KLOH-ee

I mean that each of you is saying,
    "*I* belong to *Paul*," or "*I* belong to *Apollos*,"
    or "*I* belong to *Cephas*," or "*I* belong to *Christ*."

Be careful not to use a mocking tone here.
Just tell it straight.
Cephas = SEE-fuhs

The rhetorical questions are still pleading,
not scolding.

Is Christ *divided*?
Was *Paul* crucified for you?
Or were you *baptized* in the name of *Paul*?

For Christ did not send me to *baptize* but to preach the *gospel*,
    and not with the wisdom of *human* eloquence,
    so that the *cross* of Christ might not be *emptied*
        of its *meaning*.

---

accomplished our salvation and established God's reign. But this reign is as yet only partially realized—and our experience of the "not yet" is real indeed. Nevertheless, our faith gives us the insight to understand the "already" and the courage and strength to live good lives so that slowly but steadily the "already" replaces the "not yet."

READING II Paul is dealing with a real situation here. The people of Corinth had forgotten their fundamental

unity in Christ and had split into factions—some following the preaching of Apollos, some that of Paul, and others throwing their allegiance to Cephas (Peter). Paul is horrified. There is only one source of unity, Christ, who cannot be divided.

In a way, the same thing happens today, only in reverse. How many times have you heard someone say that they stopped going to church because this or that priest or nun scandalized them or treated them badly? Where did that person get the idea that an individual Christian's bad behavior makes

the church a bad choice? Have leaders in the church taught us to trust in them more than in Christ—as though we were incapable of knowing Christ except through religious authority? Such questions arise whenever our faith is misplaced.

The devotional life of members of the church can create division, too. Some swear by this saint or that devotion or this religious practice and are critical of those whose choices are different. It is, in fact, very easy to put our allegiance in the person or practice we can see rather than in Christ. And we make this mistake when we choose to live

GOSPEL Matthew 4:12–23

A reading from the holy gospel according to Matthew

There are five sections to this gospel. The first begins here.

Capernaum = kuh-PER-nay-*m
Zebulun = ZEB-yoo-luhn
Naphtali = NAF-tuh-lee

Section two begins with the quotation.

When *Jesus* heard that *John* had been *arrested,*
    he withdrew to *Galilee.*
He left *Nazareth* and went to live in *Capernaum* by the *sea,*
    in the region of *Zebulun* and *Naphtali,*
    that what had been said through Isaiah the *prophet*
    might be *fulfilled:*
    "Land of *Zebulun* and land of *Naphtali,*
    the way to the *sea,* beyond the *Jordan,*
    Galilee of the *Gentiles,*
    the people who sit in *darkness* have seen a great *light,*
    on those dwelling in a land overshadowed by *death*
    light has arisen."

Section three includes Jesus' announcement of the arrival of the kingdom of heaven.
Section four begins with Jesus' call of the first disciples.

From that time *on,* Jesus began to *preach* and say,
    "*Repent,* for the kingdom of *heaven* is at *hand.*"

As he was walking by the Sea of *Galilee,* he saw two *brothers,*
    Simon who is called *Peter,* and his brother *Andrew,*
    casting a *net* into the *sea;* they were *fishermen.*

by sight rather than faith. It's a temptation we all live with. But Paul's words today—during the celebration of the octave of prayer for Christian unity—wrench us away from such delusions and bring us back to the only foundation solid enough and large enough to hold all of us and our differences: the rock of Christ, in whom we became forever one in baptism.

GOSPEL Although a shorter version of the gospel is provided, the passage is not lengthy, and you would

do well to proclaim the whole text. Why? Because the longer form draws a striking connection between the "Christmas" text of the first reading from Isaiah (see the commentary on the first reading) and the earliest events of Jesus' ministry. The fullest meaning of the Christmas feast we celebrated almost exactly one month ago is proclaimed here: With the coming of Jesus, the light of the world, the darkness of sin and death has vanished. The reign of God is at hand!

Notice that Matthew makes the point that Jesus fulfills the prophecy of Isaiah by beginning his ministry in Gentile territory (Capernaum, near the lands of Zebulun and Naphtali mentioned by Isaiah). Matthew is always intent upon showing in Jesus the fulfillment of the Hebrew scriptures, and in this case he is also demonstrating that Jesus' ministry extends beyond Judea into the whole world. We cannot hear too often that the Good News is for everyone of every time and place.

Zebedee = ZEB-uh-dee

He said to them,
    "Come after *me*, and I will make you fishers of *men*."
At *once* they *left* their nets and *followed* him.
He walked along from there and saw two *other* brothers,
    James, the son of *Zebedee*, and his brother *John*.
They were in a *boat*, with their *father* Zebedee,
        mending their *nets*.
He *called* them, and *immediately* they *left* their boat
        and their father
        and *followed* him.

Section five describes the signs of God's reign manifested in Jesus' ministry.

He went around *all* of *Galilee*,
    teaching in their *synagogues*, proclaiming the *gospel*
        of the *kingdom*,
    and curing *every* *disease* and *illness* among the people.

[Shorter: Matthew 4:12–17]

In the second half of the gospel passage Jesus calls the first of the Twelve who represent for Matthew the restored twelve tribes of Israel. Two things strike us about this text. First, it is immediately clear that Jesus began his ministry by calling together a group of fellow disciples. Following Jesus means joining a group of fellow disciples. Nothing is less suited to Christianity than the notion that one can be a Christian in isolation from others. It simply can't be done.

This is true even of hermits. Even when living in solitude, if they are true to their vocation, they are more intimately united to their fellow believers in Christ than those of us who rub shoulders. Saint Benedict says of hermits that they become so only after "living in a monastery for a long time" with "the help and guidance of many."

The second thing that stands out here is the immediacy of the response to Jesus' invitation. Matthew says Simon and Andrew "at once" abandoned their nets, and James and John "immediately" left their boat and their father and followed him. What about

Simon's wife? What about Zebedee, James and John's father? What about their responsibilities to family and profession? The author of Matthew wants to make the point that one's response to Jesus must be immediate and wholehearted. We mustn't take the text as literally as some have—with disastrous results for their dependants—nor should we miss Matthew's point that following Christ requires an unhesitating response of the whole heart and mind, body and soul.

4TH SUNDAY IN ORDINARY TIME

Lectionary #70

READING I   Zephaniah 2:3; 3:12–13

Zephaniah = zef-uh-NĪ-uh

As is so often the case with prophecy, the form is poetry. There must be a higher degree of exaltation and solemnity in your voice than you would normally use for prose.

The second section of the reading begins here and contrasts with what precedes it.

The word "couch" in this sense is rare, and the translation is disputed. You might consider something like "Then they will pasture and lie down, and no one shall make them afraid."

A reading from the book of the prophet Zephaniah

Seek the LORD, all you *humble* of the earth,
    who have observed his *law*;
seek *justice*, seek *humility*;
    perhaps you may be *sheltered*
    on the day of the LORD's *anger*.

But I will leave as a *remnant* in your midst
    a people *humble* and *lowly*,
who shall take *refuge* in the name of the LORD:
    the remnant of *Israel*.
They shall do no *wrong*
    and speak no *lies*;
nor shall there be found in their mouths
    a *deceitful* tongue;
they shall *pasture* and couch their *flocks*
    with none to *disturb* them.

READING I   The day of the Lord's wrath and judgment is a common theme in Zephaniah. It foretells the fate that befalls a society that neither prizes justice nor seeks humility nor observes God's law. Although Zephaniah certainly qualifies as a prophet of doom—and we can all do with a grim reminder occasionally—there is a clear expression of hope in this lovely text. The "faithful remnant" is a concept found elsewhere in the scriptures. It refers to those who remain true to their faith in spite of terrible hardship, poor leadership and bad examples

all around them. How does this remnant remain faithful in the face of such horrors?

Humility seems to be the answer. This is not a fawning "ah, shucks" kind of timidity but an honest appraisal of one's worth. The word itself is derived from the Latin *humus,* meaning "earth." The concept of healthy humility pervades all the readings today. Zephaniah's contribution to the theme is clear enough: The humble take refuge in God; they do no wrong; they tell the truth; they are not deceitful. In a cynical society these are the "nice guys who finish last."

But that's okay. The humble know, without smugness, that the last shall be first.

In your proclamation, try to communicate something of the joy that comes from Zephaniah's brand of humility.

READING II   It is sometimes hard for us to realize just how revolutionary Christianity is. The weak are singled out; the lowest in the world's view are the apple of God's eye. It's not wrong to be highborn, world-wise, temporally powerful, looked up to or privileged—unless it fools

READING II   1 Corinthians 1:26–31

A reading from the first letter of Saint Paul to the Corinthians

Consider your own *calling,* brothers and sisters.
Not *many* of you were *wise* by *human* standards,
    not many were *powerful,*
    not many were of noble *birth.*
Rather, God chose the *foolish* of the world to *shame* the *wise,*
    and God chose the *weak* of the world to *shame* the *strong,*
    and God chose the *lowly* and *despised* of the world,
    those who count for *nothing,*
    to *reduce* to nothing those who are *something,*
    so that no *human being* might boast before *God.*

It is due to *him* that you are in Christ *Jesus,*
    who *became* for us *wisdom* from God,
    as well as *righteousness, sanctification,* and *redemption,*
    so that, as it is written,
    "Whoever *boasts,* should boast in the *Lord.*"

This reading has three sections. The first states facts that are negative at first glance.

The second section shows how apparently negative conditions are made positive by God.

The third section explains the consequences of God's action.

---

us into thinking we're worth more than other human beings. In fact, few of us occupy such lofty positions, and Paul says we should be glad of it. God's preference for the lowly is good news for most of us, and it truly does turn the world's values upside down.

Where is the evidence that we truly believe in this revolution? Church leaders often claim for themselves, and attempt to exert, a power over "the flock" they don't actually have. Those in exalted ecclesiastical positions often presume special privileges. On the whole, we're apparently not

willing to sacrifice much to feed the world's hungry. What we call "organized religion" often seems uninterested in—even unaware of—the kind of people Jesus loved most.

Am I painting too bleak a picture? Perhaps, but it should be clear that Paul's words to the Corinthians need a good proclamation and a good hearing today! We all need to learn how to boast in the Lord a little more and in ourselves a little less.

GOSPEL   With this gospel text we begin reading from one of our most precious possessions: the "sermon on the mount." Because Matthew is intent on showing Jesus to be the new Moses, he places Jesus teaching on a mountain. Matthew's original audience would not have failed to see the connection with Moses on Mount Sinai receiving the ten commandments for Israel. The church of Christ is the new Israel. In addition, although we may be more accustomed to teachers who stand, figures of authority in ancient times sat when

GOSPEL   Matthew 5:1–12a

A reading from the holy gospel according to Matthew

The first sentence sets the scene.

When Jesus saw the *crowds,* he went up the *mountain,*
    and after he had sat *down,* his disciples *came* to him.
He began to *teach* them, saying:
"Blessed are the poor in *spirit,*
    for *theirs* is the kingdom of *heaven.*
Blessed are they who *mourn,*
    for they will be *comforted.*

Pronounce the word "blessed" with two syllables, accent on the first: BLES-*d. Each beatitude must stand out on its own. Employ a wide range of vocal variety.

"Blessed are the *meek,*
    for they will *inherit* the *land.*
Blessed are they who *hunger* and *thirst* for *righteousness,*
    for they will be *satisfied.*

Give an extra pause here. We shift from personal attributes to cases that involve others.

"Blessed are the *merciful,*
    for they will be *shown* mercy.
Blessed are the clean of *heart,*
    for they will *see* God.

"Blessed are the *peacemakers,*
    for they will be called *children* of God.
Blessed are they who are *persecuted*
    for the sake of *righteousness,*
    for theirs is the kingdom of *heaven.*

These last two beatitudes are longer than the rest. Don't rush them.

"Blessed are you when they *insult* you and *persecute* you
    and utter every kind of *evil* against you falsely because of *me.*
Rejoice and be *glad,*
    for your *reward* will be *great* in *heaven.*"

The passage has an upbeat ending.

they taught. Thus Matthew highlights Jesus' authority as a teacher.

The list of those who are "blessed" is one of our greatest treasures. Known as the beatitudes, the list brings together in one memorable series formulas much of what Jesus taught by word and example. We must realize two things about the beatitudes. First, there is nothing here that cannot be found in the Hebrew scriptures, which Jesus knew well and quoted often. We often make the mistake of seeing the Old Testament as a mere prelude to the New. Nothing could

be further from Jesus' view, as he makes clear himself: "I have not come to abolish the law, but to bring it to perfection."

Second, the beatitudes are a portrait of Jesus himself: poor, lowly, merciful, single-hearted, peaceful, persecuted, sorrowful, hungry and thirsty for holiness. And if they are a portrait of Jesus, they are thus also a portrait of God. Though it may seem odd to attribute some of the beatitudes to God, clearly they appear in the life of Jesus, who is for us the fullest revelation of God. By living the divine dispositions of the beatitudes, we pattern our lives on the divine life itself.

Any list is challenging for a reader, who should want to avoid making it sound like a list! How can one make each of the beatitudes stand out clearly? Certainly the proclamation must be careful and a bit slower than usual. One cannot rush from one beatitude to the next and expect them to sink in. On the other hand, they should not be read as though each one stands alone. The secret to effective proclamation is always vocal variety: modulation of the voice, varied placement of emphasis, wide range of pitch and volume.

5TH SUNDAY IN ORDINARY TIME

Lectionary #73

READING I   Isaiah 58:7–10

A reading from the book of the prophet Isaiah

Thus says the LORD:
Share your *bread* with the *hungry*,
    shelter the *oppressed* and the *homeless*;
clothe the *naked* when you see them,
    and do not turn your *back* on your *own*.

Then your *light* shall break *forth* like the *dawn*,
    and your *wound* shall quickly be *healed*;
your *vindication* shall go before you,
    and the glory of the LORD shall be your rear *guard*.
Then you shall *call*, and the LORD will *answer*;
    you shall cry for *help*, and he will say: Here I *am*!

If you *remove* from your midst oppression,
        false *accusation* and malicious *speech*;
if you bestow your *bread* on the *hungry*
    and *satisfy* the *afflicted*;
then *light* shall rise for you in the *darkness*,
    and the *gloom* shall become for *you* like *midday*.

Any reading that begins with "Thus says the Lord" deserves special treatment. Be sure those important words ring out. Pause slightly before and after them.

Pay attention to the "If . . . then" structure of the text. It will guide you to an effective intonation.

"Here I am" is tricky. Be sure it isn't so light as to be comical. The best approach is to read straight through the line, without pausing or changing your tone of voice before "Here I am!"

READING I The prophets speak for God. Indeed, in its origin the word "prophet" means "to be a mouthpiece for." In common parlance we often reduce prophecy to foretelling the future. In the Hebrew tradition, the prophets just as frequently comment on or interpret the meaning of the past. And, as Isaiah does today, prophets often tell us how God wishes us to behave in the present.

The phrase "Thus says the Lord" always signals a solemn pronouncement from the mind of God as the prophet understands it.

It deserves a careful proclamation and an attentive hearing. Notice that this reading is constructed with the "If . . . then" pattern: "If you do these good things, then you will see good things." And the controlling image is light, which also appears in Jesus' words in the gospel. We are still not far from Christmas and Epiphany, when we celebrated the coming of the light of the world, which shattered the darkness of sin and death. And yet we are on the threshold of Lent. Ash Wednesday is three days away.

This reading looks both forward and backward: forward to the good works of a penitential season, backward to the glory that motivates our joyful penance.

Notice how practical our response to God's saving love must be. If you want to see light in the darkness, if you want to have your wounds healed and your prayers answered, then feed the hungry, shelter the homeless, clothe the naked and identify with the suffering of your fellow human beings. Let your proclamation encourage the members of the assembly to take up these good works.

Take this proclamation slowly and deliberately. Paul's thoughts here are splashed down rather than carefully structured, but they become perfectly clear if given enough space.

READING II   1 Corinthians 2:1–5

A reading from the first letter of Saint Paul to the Corinthians

When I *came* to you, brothers and sisters,
    proclaiming the *mystery* of *God*,
    I did not come with *sublimity* of words or of *wisdom*.
For I resolved to know *nothing* while I was with you
    except Jesus *Christ*, and him *crucified*.

I came to you in *weakness* and *fear* and much *trembling*,
    and my *message* and my *proclamation*
    were not with persuasive words of *wisdom*,
    but with a demonstration of *Spirit* and *power*,
    so that your *faith* might rest not on *human wisdom*
    but on the *power* of God.

READING II One of the problems Paul is addressing here is what seems to be a constant threat to our Christian faith. Because the Good News often appears too good to be true, minds that are uncomfortable with its dramatic simplicity feel obliged to devise more complex ways of expressing it. If the mystery can be captured in philosophical, even scientific, formulas, then we feel we have a firmer grip on it. Unfortunately, the end result is to eviscerate the mystery by reducing it to logic or something that seems like logic. The Corinthians were caught up in something like this, competing among themselves to squeeze eternal truths of faith into the limited confines of reason. They seemed to admire the sermon built on elaborate argument rather than on the stark simplicity and paradox of the cross.

Paul's solution to this perennial tendency is to place before our eyes the image of Christ crucified, an image he describes elsewhere as a stumbling block to some and foolishness to others. In purely human terms there is no way such an image can mean triumph over sin and death. Indeed, it looks like a terrible tragedy, an embarrassing failure. Only faith can see beyond such appearances: faith in the resurrection, faith in the fidelity of God, belief in the promises made to us by the one who was crucified.

Paul had learned earlier in Athens that any attempt to put the Christian mystery into philosophical restraints was doomed to failure. Thus in Corinth he limited himself to what he knew would eventually result in faith built not on human wisdom but on the power of God.

GOSPEL Matthew 5:13–16

A reading from the holy gospel according to Matthew

Jesus said to his *disciples*:
"*You* are the *salt* of the *earth*.
But if salt loses its *taste*, with what can it be *seasoned*?
It is no longer good for *anything*
    but to be thrown *out* and trampled *underfoot*.

"*You* are the *light* of the *world*.
A city set on a *mountain* cannot be *hidden*.
Nor do they light a *lamp* and then put it under a bushel *basket*;
    it is set on a *lampstand*,
    where it gives light to all in the *house*.
Just *so*, *your* light must shine before *others*,
    that they may *see* your good deeds
    and *glorify* your heavenly *Father*."

We hear "Jesus said to his disciples" many, many times. See if you can make the expression fresh.

Let the two images of salt and light ring out strongly, as though these metaphors are new to you.

There is a touch of ridiculousness here: Who would light a lamp and then cover it up?

Here is our purpose for being "light." Emphasize it.

GOSPEL The sermon on the mount continues. (See the gospel commentary from last Sunday.) In this passage Jesus gives us two of the most useful metaphors we have to guide our lives as Christians. Being the salt of the earth means that without us the world would be insipid and flat. It would lack the flavor it is supposed to have now that Christ has established his dominion on earth—the dominion that, as he told us, is within and among us.

We are the light of the world. It is our awesome privilege to brighten the world by acts of goodness so that those who see us doing good will give praise not to us but to our heavenly Father. As light, Christians enable people to see *God* at work and give *God* praise. Like the sun itself, which shines on the just and the unjust, we Christians show no partiality but let our light shine everywhere. We can say with the great philosopher Plato, "Nothing human is foreign to us."

The difference between a mirror and a lamp is a helpful illustration here. A mirror held up to reality adds nothing to it but reflects only what is before it. A lamp held up to reality adds something. It sheds light, casting shadows aside and illuminating the world around it, revealing its detail, adding variation in its color and brightening it with warmth. We are clearly meant to be lamps, not mirrors.

Remember when you proclaim this wonderful text that Jesus is describing what is, not what should be. There is a certainty in his words that should encourage us to be who and what we are. We are salt and light, for better or for worse. We have no choice in the matter, except to decide to be quality salt and brighter light.

ASH WEDNESDAY

Lectionary #219

READING I   Joel 2:12–18

A reading from the book of the prophet Joel

Even *now*, says the Lord,
    return to me with your whole *heart*,
      with *fasting*, and *weeping*, and *mourning*;
Rend your *hearts*, not your *garments*,
    and return to the *Lord*, your *God*.

For *gracious* and *merciful* is he,
    slow to anger, *rich* in kindness,
    and *relenting* in punishment.
Perhaps he will *again* relent
    and leave behind him a *blessing*,
Offerings and *libations*
    for the Lord, your *God*.

Blow the *trumpet* in *Zion*!
    proclaim a *fast*,
    call an *assembly*;
Gather the people,
    notify the congregation;
Assemble the *elders*,
    gather the *children*
    and the *infants* at the *breast*;
Let the *bridegroom quit* his room,
    and the bride her *chamber*.

Begin with an exalted tone. This is poetry, recognizable as such from the first words of the passage. And the feeling is upbeat because the Lord is forgiving, merciful and gracious.

This is a new section; pause before it. Then about ten short directives follow. Don't rush through them. Let each image sink in.

READING I   Though we may not look forward to Lent's abstinence and severity, we know it is important to acknowledge our sinfulness, the sober truth of our mortality, and the need to take stock of our lives. We come to church for ashes and prepare ourselves for an honest appraisal.

The members of the assembly are in a receptive mood, expecting a message that will help them live up to their lenten resolutions. You, the reader, have a wonderful opportunity to fulfill their expectations.

Notice first of all that the first reading is poetry. The prophet is calling the people to conversion, and he does so in exalted and beautiful language. When you proclaim these words with exaltation and communicate their beauty, you ennoble your listeners and their good intentions. You create the effect Joel intended.

The opening words "Even now . . ." imply "Even with things as bad as they are . . ." Joel is describing a bad situation; it is clear that the people's only recourse is to God. We know, of course, that our only reliable recourse is to God, but Lent reminds

us that we need to concentrate on that fundamental truth once again. Lent is a time for getting back to basics. It is a time for examining and reevaluating our priorities.

The trumpet call is a summons to come together and rally ourselves for action. Notice that the call is to the community as a whole. We are not entering the lenten season to engage in a lonely struggle all by ourselves. The entire church is called to this challenge. This makes our efforts not only

Between the *porch* and the *altar*
>   let the *priests*, the *ministers* of the Lord, *weep*,
And say, "*Spare*, O Lord, your *people*,
>   and make not your *heritage* a *reproach*,
>   with the nations *ruling* over them!
Why should they say among the *peoples*,
>   'Where is their *God*?'"

Then the Lord was stirred to *concern* for his land
and took *pity* on his people.

Pause again here, then read the last sentence with a sense of peaceful resolution.

| READING II | 2 Corinthians 5:20—6:2 |

A reading from the second letter of Paul to the Corinthians

We are *ambassadors* for *Christ*,
God as it were *appealing* through *us*.
We *implore* you, in Christ's name:
be *reconciled* to God!
For *our* sakes God made him who did not *know* sin to *be* sin,
so that in *him* we might become the very *holiness* of *God*.

As your fellow *workers*
we *beg* you not to receive the *grace* of God in *vain*.
For he says,
"In an *acceptable* time I have *heard* you;
on a day of *salvation* I have *helped* you."
Now is the acceptable time!
Now is the day of *salvation*!

This is a brief reading with two sections, and the prose is dense with meaning. The assembly will need time to absorb it.

The second section begins here. Renew the plea.

There is a sense of urgency in "Now! Now!"

---

easier but more gratifying. Because of our human tendency to get wrapped up in ourselves, especially when it comes to awareness of sin, the communal aspect of Lent reminds us that we are one in the body of Christ. Each one's sins affect all the rest, and the good works of each member reflect on the entire church.

| READING II | Notice first of all in this reading the plentiful plural pronouns: we, us, our, you, your. The use of these words creates an immediacy that can

make the reading more forceful, easier to listen to, more applicable to each hearer. It also creates a feeling of community, bringing us together. Make the most of it in your proclamation.

The first reading called us together and directed us to examine our lives as individuals and as a community. The second reading turns us outward as a community, reminding us that we, like Paul, are ambassadors for Christ in the world. A dimension of Lent involves an assessment of ourselves as a

church. How well are we doing as ambassadors for Christ? Is the church more attractive to outsiders this year than it was last year? What kind of image does the church present? Is it welcoming and inclusive? We hope so, but we know there is room for improvement in each of us as individual ambassadors and in the church as a whole.

Every time is an acceptable time; every day is a day of salvation. But we need to set aside special times and days to call ourselves back to the simplicity of our belief and mission. Paul begs us not to receive the

Be aware from the beginning that you are reading a carefully structured text (see the commentary). The first couple of lines state the principle. Three examples follow, stated with an easy-to-remember formula.

This is the first example. Experiment with emphasis on "you" to imply contrast with the hypocrites.

GOSPEL   Matthew 6:1–6, 16–18

A reading from the holy gospel according to Matthew

Jesus said to his *disciples*:
"Be on *guard* against performing religious *acts*
　　for people to *see*.
Otherwise expect no *recompense* from your heavenly *Father*.

When you give *alms*, for example,
do not blow a *horn* before you in synagogues and streets
　　like *hypocrites* looking for *applause*.
You can be sure of *this* much, they are *already* repaid.
In giving alms
you are not to let your *left* hand
　　know what your *right* hand is *doing*.
Keep your deeds of mercy *secret*,
and your *Father* who *sees* in secret will *repay* you.

grace of God in vain. By this statement he reminds us of what the Good News is, namely, that we have received the grace of God. Think of the implications of receiving that grace: divine acceptance, infinite love, total forgiveness, the assurance of eternal life. All of them are given for one reason only: God loves us. How terrible to think we could receive such wonders in vain!

GOSPEL   To understand Jesus' words here it is absolutely essential that we understand one thing clearly:

The good works we do, the sacrifices we make, the alms we give are simply a matter of justice. It is difficult for me to write a check for a needy cause without feeling like I have done something special. In one sense I have, of course, because I've recognized a need. But I must keep reminding myself that what I have given away always belonged to the needy person who received it. The extra prayers I say are simply what is appropriate. The fasting I do, the abstinence, is simply

deciding not to eat or drink something that really belongs to anyone who needs it more than I do.

Looking at our good lenten works this way shows how ridiculous it is to blow our horn, to brag about our piety or be an exhibitionist in our self-denial. We give things up because someone needs them more than we do. Rather than brag about our generosity, we might be embarrassed that we were keeping for ourselves what belonged to someone else. This is the kind revolutionary Christianity we get when we take Jesus at

The second example begins here: "Whenever you are praying . . ."

"When you are *praying*,
do not behave like the *hypocrites*
who love to stand and pray in *synagogues*
or on *street* corners in order to be *noticed*.
I give you my *word*, they are *already* repaid.
Whenever *you* pray, go to your *room*,
close your *door*, and pray to your Father in *private*.
Then your Father,
who sees what no *man* sees, will *repay* you.

The third example begins here: "When you fast . . ."

"When you *fast*,
you are not to look *glum* as the *hypocrites* do.
They *change* the appearance of their faces
so that others may *see* they are fasting.
I assure you, they are *already* repaid.
When *you* fast,
see to it that you *groom* your hair and *wash* your face.
In that way no one can *see* you are fasting
but your *Father* who is *hidden*;
and your Father who *sees* what is *hidden* will *repay* you."

his word. How long will it take us to realize that as long as there is one hungry person in the world, we're not doing our job?

With all this in mind, you will be able to proclaim this reading in a bright tone of voice. Your purpose is to strengthen the members of the assembly in their lenten resolutions by reminding them of the noblest way of carrying them out. The reading is not about hypocrites; it's about us.

There are three sections to the passage, each composed of three parts: "When you give alms . . . When you are praying . . . When you fast." Then, for each good work, Jesus admonishes us to avoid hypocrisy and to do our fasting, prayer and almsgiving secretly. This kind of formulaic teaching is common in scripture. It is probably a reflection of the oral tradition that existed long before these words were written down. The threefold pattern and the repeated phrases make the instruction easier to memorize.

Your proclamation can communicate something of this structure. The pattern should be discernible and even predictable. In this way, your listeners should be able to see how the reading builds upon itself so that the lesson becomes clearer and clearer. Allow the familiarity of the text to assist you. Enable the assembly to welcome these words of Jesus both in their familiarity and their challenge.

1ST SUNDAY OF LENT

Lectionary #22

READING I   Genesis 2:7–9; 3:1–7

A reading from the book of Genesis

The LORD *God formed* man out of the clay of the *ground*
    and blew into his *nostrils* the breath of *life*,
    and so man became a living *being*.
Then the LORD God planted a *garden* in *Eden*, in the *east*,
    and *placed* there the man whom he had *formed*.
Out of the *ground* the LORD God made various *trees* grow
    that were delightful to *look* at and good for *food*,
    with the tree of *life* in the *middle* of the garden
    and the tree of the knowledge of *good* and *evil*.

Now the *serpent* was the most *cunning* of all the animals
    that the LORD God had made.
The serpent asked the *woman*,
    "Did God really tell you *not* to eat
    from any of the trees in the *garden*?"
The woman *answered* the serpent:
    "We *may* eat of the fruit of the trees in the garden;
    it is only about the fruit of the tree
    in the *middle* of the garden that God said,
    'You shall *not* eat it or even *touch* it, lest you *die*.'"
But the serpent said to the woman:
    "You certainly will *not* die!
No, God knows well that the moment you *eat* of it
    your *eyes* will be *opened* and you will be like *gods*

The text reads better if you insert the article "the" before the word "man."

There is a new section here and a break in the narrative. Pause and begin with a fresh new tone.
Notice that the story has been edited. You will have to emphasize the first use of the word "woman" since her creation by God has been edited out.

READING I At the beginning of Lent we hear the story of the creation of human beings (or at least the creation of the first man; the story of the creation of the first woman is surprisingly omitted) and of how sin came into the world. It is one of the most familiar stories in human experience, common to both Jew and Christian, the subject of a wide range of literature from scholarly commentary to stage comedy. The characters of Adam, Eve and the serpent have appeared in every form of human expression, from Michelangelo's paintings to television commercials. The lure of the story is obvious.

Notice first of all that the reading is indeed a story—a piece of literature complete with situation, characters, plot, conflict and resolution. It is dynamic, moving from one element to the next and developing its overall point along the way. A beautiful scene is painted, characters are introduced into it, conflict arises, and we are left at the end with a different picture. The image of nakedness is compelling. Metaphorically,

we feel naked when our sins and failings are brought to light. Like Adam and Eve, we want to cover ourselves so that no one will see us as we really are. Here is an aspect of sinfulness we often miss in this story. Human nature has difficulty being honest about its failings, great determination in promoting its successes, and a spirit of self-sufficiency that makes reliance even on God difficult. The Genesis story is simple yet inexhaustible in its meaning, relevant to every age.

Storytelling is an ancient art. Stories connect us with our past, help explain our

A new section begins here as well.

who know what is *good* and what is *evil."*
The woman saw that the tree was *good* for food,
    pleasing to the *eyes*, and desirable for gaining *wisdom*.
So she *took* some of its fruit and *ate* it;
    and she also gave some to her *husband*, who was with her,
    and *he* ate it.

Then the eyes of *both* of them were *opened*,
    and they *realized* that they were *naked*;
    so they sewed *fig* leaves together
    and made *loincloths* for themselves.

The sadness of "lost innocence" is present in this passage.

READING II   Romans 5:12–19

A reading from the letter of Saint Paul to the Romans

Prepare this difficult reading with special care. Get the comparisons and contrasts exactly right. Don't take the shorter form; we need all of the text to understand it.

You can eliminate the word "men" here: "death came to all."

Brothers and sisters:
Through *one man sin* entered the world,
    and through sin, *death*,
    and thus death came to *all* men, inasmuch as all *sinned*—
    for up to the time of the *law*, sin was in the world,
    though sin is not *accounted* when there is no *law*.

But *death* reigned from *Adam* to *Moses*,
    even over those who did *not* sin
    after the pattern of the trespass of *Adam*,
    who is the *type* of the one who was to *come*.

There is a big transition here, but the *gift* is in no way, shape or form like the *offense*!

But the *gift* is not *like* the *transgression*.
For if by the *transgression* of the one, the many *died*,
    how much *more* did the *grace* of God
    and the gracious *gift* of the one man Jesus *Christ*

present and guide us into the future. Your task as proclaimer is to bring this familiar story to life in a way that will enable the members of the assembly to hear it again as if for the first time. Tell this ancient story with all the dignity it deserves, enlivening it with a wide range of vocal variety to make it fresh, but above all communicating its noble significance.

READING II Here is a classic piece of Pauline argumentation. It gives us Paul's view of how Christ, the second Adam, conquered the sin introduced

into the world by the first Adam (see the first reading). It is not an easy piece to read. Picture Paul thinking aloud and dictating to a scribe who is furiously trying to catch the words and thoughts Paul is tossing off in a rapid-fire delivery. Such a picture is not far off from what probably happened, and it will certainly impress you with the degree of care it takes to do justice to Paul's thought.

The argument is this: Sin (spiritual death) entered the world through Adam; forgiveness of sin (new life) enters the world with the arrival of Jesus Christ. But it's not

an even trade-off. Paul is at pains to impress us with how lopsided things are. Compared to the gift of life brought to us in Christ, Adam's sin is puny. In fact, there's no comparison. The sin we all share with Adam, and the death that resulted from it, has been annihilated by the overwhelming, abounding, overflowing grace and justification resulting from the sacrificial death of Christ.

The disproportion between Adam's sin and our redemption in Christ has always been a favorite theme in the church's tradition. One of the most dramatic statements of the theme appears in the Exsultet, that great

overflow for the *many.*
And the *gift* is not like the *result* of the one who *sinned.*
For after one *sin* there was the judgment
    that brought *condemnation;*
    but the *gift,* after *many* transgressions, brought *acquittal.*

For if, by the *transgression* of the one,
    death came to *reign* through that one,
    how much *more* will those who receive the abundance of *grace*
    and of the gift of *justification*
    come to reign in *life* through the one Jesus *Christ.*

In *conclusion,* just as through one *transgression*
    condemnation came upon all,
    so, through one *righteous* act,
    acquittal and *life* came to all.
For just as through the *disobedience* of the one man
    the many were made *sinners,*
    so, through the *obedience* of the one,
    the many will be made *righteous.*

[Shorter: Romans 5:12, 17–19]

Pause before this summary of Paul's argument. (appears in left margin beside the "In conclusion" stanza)

GOSPEL Matthew 4:1–11

A reading from the holy gospel according to Matthew

At that time *Jesus* was led by the *Spirit* into the *desert*
    to be *tempted* by the *devil.*
He *fasted* for forty *days* and forty *nights,*
    and *afterwards* he was *hungry.*
The *tempter* approached and said to him,

Tell the story as though the assembly has never heard it before. (left margin)

proclamation of the resurrection we hear at the Easter Vigil. It says, "How boundless your merciful love! To ransom a slave you gave away your Son! O happy fault! O necessary sin of Adam, which gained for us so great a Redeemer!"

You will have to study this reading quite carefully and read it aloud several times until the appropriate emphasis brings out the multitude of contrasts. Nearly every sentence contains not one but several comparisons or contrasts, all pointing out that the disobedience of Adam is overcome,

overpowered, obliterated and outweighed by the obedience of Christ.

GOSPEL The story of the temptation of Jesus in the desert is always proclaimed on the First Sunday of Lent. This year, Year A, we hear Matthew's account; Mark's is proclaimed in Year B (Mark 1:12–15) and Luke's in Year C (Luke 4:1–13). You might consider reading all three accounts so you can gain a sense of what is particularly important in Matthew's account.

The most immediate connection in the minds of your hearers might be the parallel between the 40 days of Lent and the 40 days Jesus spent in the desert. And, of course, that is certainly why this text is chosen for the beginning of this penitential season.

But there is much more to this story than meets the eye. Notice first of all that it is indeed a story, like the first reading from Genesis, a piece of literature complete with situation, characters, plot, conflict and resolution. It is dynamic, moving from one element to the next and revealing important truths along the way. A dramatic scene is

"If you are the Son of *God*,
command that these *stones* become loaves of *bread*."

He said in *reply*,
"It is *written*:
'One does not *live* on bread *alone*,
but on every *word* that comes forth
from the mouth of *God*.'"

Then the devil took him to the holy *city*,
and made him stand on the parapet of the *temple*,
and said to him, "If you are the Son of *God*,
throw yourself *down*.
For it is *written*:
'He will command his *angels* concerning you
and with their hands they will *support* you,
lest you dash your *foot* against a *stone*.'"
Jesus *answered* him,
"*Again* it is written,
'You shall not put the Lord, your *God*, to the *test*.'"

Then the devil took him up to a very high *mountain*,
and showed him all the *kingdoms* of the world
in their *magnificence*,
and he said to him, "All these I shall *give* to you,
if you will *prostrate* yourself and *worship* me."
At *this*, Jesus said to him,
"Get *away*, Satan!
It is *written*:
'The Lord, your *God*, shall you *worship*
and him *alone* shall you *serve*.'"

Then the devil *left* him and, *behold*,
angels came and *ministered* to him.

Do not rush into Jesus' replies. Prepare for them with a brief pause. Pause after them, too, because they bring each of the three sections to a close.

This is a new section. There should be a feeling of "And then . . ."
parapet = PAYR-uh-pit

This is another new section. There should again be a feeling of "And then . . ."

This is a beautiful final sentence. Only Matthew tells us of the ministering angels.

painted, Jesus and Satan are the players, conflict arises in the classic pattern of three, and the resolution brings the story to a peaceful end. Your awareness of this structure and these elements will contribute much to an effective proclamation.

As we have seen before, Matthew is intent on portraying Jesus as the new Moses. Moses led the people of Israel out of exile and into the desert, where they sojourned for 40 years—years filled with conflict and testing. But eventually they reached the promised land. The 40 days of Jesus' desert

experience are a parallel, as are his temptations. The first temptation (to turn stones into bread) reminds us of the manna in the desert and the eucharistic bread. The second temptation reminds us of the many times the Israelites put God to the test: "Is the Lord in our midst or not?" And the third temptation, most dramatic of all, reminds us of Israel's fall into idolatry when the people made the golden calf.

Jesus shows us that we live not on bread alone but on God's word. And Jesus himself is the Word who says "I am the true bread, come down from heaven." He also

teaches us that we need never question God's care for us, much less create situations that test it. Finally, we see Jesus assert the sovereignty of God, the sole object of our worship.

Matthew's account of the temptation is a rich and complex catechism that teaches us who Jesus is and what his mission will be. A careful proclamation, and your awareness of the layers of meaning, will do much to allow this familiar gospel text to have a new impact on your assembly, who knows it so well.

2ND SUNDAY OF LENT

Lectionary #25

READING I   Genesis 12:1–4a

A reading from the book of Genesis

The LORD said to *Abram*:
"Go *forth* from the land of your *kinsfolk*
    and from your *father's* house to a land that I will *show* you.

"I will make of you a *great nation*,
    and I will *bless* you;
I will make your name *great*,
    so that you will be a *blessing*.
I will *bless* those who *bless* you
    and *curse* those who *curse* you.
All the communities of the *earth*
    shall find *blessing* in *you*."

Abram *went* as the LORD *directed* him.

Abram = AY-br*m

The man's name is Abram. Be careful not to say Abraham. The name change comes later in Abram's life.

The blessing is a solemn pronouncement from the mouth of God. Pause before it, let each of the seven blessings be heard distinctly and separately, and pause slightly at the end.

Abram's obedience is the point here.

READING I **Blessed Pope John XXIII is remembered fondly for the many gestures of love and peace he made toward people of other faiths. One of the most memorable was directed to Jews when he reminded his fellow Catholics, "Spiritually, we are all Semites." In Eucharistic Prayer I we mention Abraham under the revered title "our father in faith." Today's brief first reading explains why Abraham is father to Jews, Christians and Muslims. All the families of the earth find blessing in Abraham.**

In all three years of the Sunday lectionary on the Second Sunday of Lent, the first reading is about Abraham. Notice that today he is still called Abram. God changes Abram's name to Abraham much later (when he is 99 years old) and tells him, as his new name implies, that he is to be the father of a host of nations. In Abraham we have a perfect model of obedience and trust in God.

Though the reading is brief, it contains one of the most beautiful blessings God ever pronounced. Notice that it is really seven blessings in one; in scripture the number seven generally signifies perfection. These

brief lines should be proclaimed with profound respect and a sense of wonder.

READING II **Several thoughts in this brief reading are appropriate for Lent. First, we are told, as Paul told Timothy, that the gospel will bring us our share of hardships. Hardship is not part of the gospel since the Good News is that God loves and saves us, but suffering is a consequence of living out the gospel in a world that finds it too good to be true. Second, the hardship we endure and the good we do are not payment**

READING II   2 Timothy 1:8b–10

A reading from the second letter of Saint Paul to Timothy

Beloved:
Bear your share of *hardship* for the gospel
    with the *strength* that comes from *God*.

He *saved* us and called us to a *holy* life,
    not according to our *works*
    but according to his own *design*
    and the *grace* bestowed on us in Christ *Jesus*
        before time *began*,
    but *now* made *manifest*
    through the *appearance* of our savior Christ Jesus,
    who *destroyed death* and brought *life* and *immortality*
    to light through the *gospel*.

Be sure the members of the assembly are silent and attentive before you begin.

There are seven units of thought in this section. Be sure you recognize them so you can proclaim this complex structure clearly.

GOSPEL   Matthew 17:1–9

A reading from the holy gospel according to Matthew

Jesus took *Peter*, *James*, and *John* his *brother*,
    and led them up a high *mountain* by *themselves*.
And he was *transfigured* before them;
    his *face* shone like the *sun*
    and his *clothes* became white as *light*.
And *behold*, Moses and *Elijah* appeared to them,
    conversing with him.

There is a brief introduction before the wonders begin. Start slowly.

The images are vivid. Make it your aim to paint this scene clearly for the assembly.

for grace, which by definition is a free gift of God and cannot be earned. Third, our efforts to do good (and our special efforts during Lent) are our spontaneous response to the revelation that God saves us totally out of love. Fourth, Christ Jesus holds out grace to us because he is God's eternal Word, sharing God's nature, and it is the nature of God to love freely and without limit. We didn't know this fully until Christ Jesus revealed it in the way he lived, in the message he spoke, in the death he died and in the resurrection and ascension.

Until we understand what Paul is saying here, a kind of bargain-counter theology will plague the practice of our faith. We will continue to wonder if we're "in" good enough with God and think maybe we ought to do more to curry favor. We will doubt the limitless nature of God's forgiveness and feel that we need to do something more to earn it. But the day will come when we will see God face to face and realize how mixed our motives were and how simple they could have been. Looking into the face of pure love, we will understand finally that the only

appropriate response is a grateful heart that does good things with total sincerity.

GOSPEL On the Second Sunday of Lent we always hear the story of the transfiguration. It is a beautiful, mysterious, strange and awesome story. It is a glimpse into another world, and it makes us wonder what it would have been like to be part of that privileged party of three.

Then *Peter* said to Jesus in *reply*,
  "*Lord*, it is *good* that we are here.
If you *wish*, I will make three *tents* here,
  one for *you*, one for *Moses*, and one for *Elijah*."

While he was still *speaking*, *behold*,
  a bright *cloud* cast a *shadow* over them,
  then from the cloud came a *voice* that said,
  "This is my beloved *Son*, with whom I am well *pleased*;
  listen to him."

When the disciples *heard* this, they fell *prostrate*
  and were very much *afraid*.
But *Jesus* came and *touched* them, saying,
  "*Rise*, and do *not* be afraid."
And when the disciples raised their *eyes*,
  they saw no one *else* but *Jesus alone*.

As they were coming *down* from the mountain,
  Jesus *charged* them,
  "Do not tell the *vision* to *anyone*
  until the Son of *Man* has been *raised* from the *dead*."

The mystery deepens when we hear the echo of the voice at Jesus' baptism. It is further confirmation of his origin and mission.

Pause here slightly, then renew the energy for a dramatic ending.

The point of the transfiguration is that the chosen three—Peter, James and John—behold Jesus' real nature as Messiah and, as he described himself, "the fulfillment of the law and the prophets." These are the same three disciples who go with Jesus to the garden of Gethsemane right before his arrest and see him in the throes of agony. At the transfiguration they glimpse who Jesus truly is, and the law (Moses) and the prophets (Elijah) take their proper place in relation to the one who brings them to their full meaning and significance.

Remembering that Matthew always portrays Jesus as the new Moses, we can understand that the transfiguration event is a further confirmation of Jesus' role as the ultimate deliverer and the one who will lead us to the final promised land. Peter's response is appropriate. He calls Jesus "Lord," and proposes a new festival of Tabernacles ("tents" or "booths"). Peter has seen who Jesus really is.

The bright cloud is Matthew's way of showing the divine presence, and the voice is meant to remind us of the initial commission given to Christ at his baptism. The mandate to keep silent about this strange vision until after the resurrection is to ensure that the scandal of the cross will not be diminished. Jesus, who is God's eternal Word and will rise from the dead, must nevertheless die a human death in order to conquer it once and for all.

Clearly, this special message must be proclaimed with great solemnity, awe and even a hint of mystery.

Lectionary #28

READING I Exodus 17:3–7

A reading from the book of Exodus

In those days, in their thirst for *water*,
    the people *grumbled* against Moses,
    saying, "Why did you ever make us leave *Egypt*?
Was it just to have us *die* here of *thirst*
    with our *children* and our *livestock*?"
So *Moses* cried out to the LORD,
    "What shall I *do* with this people?
A little *more* and they will *stone* me!"

The LORD *answered* Moses,
    "Go over there in front of the *people*,
    along with some of the *elders* of Israel,
    holding in your *hand*, as you go,
    the *staff* with which you struck the *river*.
I will be standing there in *front* of you on the *rock* in *Horeb*.
Strike the rock, and the *water* will flow from it
    for the people to *drink*."
This Moses *did*, in the presence of the *elders* of Israel.

The place was called *Massah* and *Meribah*,
    because the Israelites *quarreled* there
    and *tested* the LORD, saying,
    "Is the LORD in our *midst* or *not*?"

There are several voices here: the people, Moses, God, the narrator. Though appropriate vocal variety is important, do not adopt character voices. Liturgical proclamation is different from dramatic interpretation.

Pause slightly before the Lord's response to Moses.

Horeb = HOHR-eb

Pause before the final comment at the end of the narrative.
Massah = MAH-sah
Meribah = MAYR-ih-bah

The final question is abrupt. This is a rare kind of ending, but an effective one. Do not soften it, and do not rush on to "The word of the Lord." Let the question hang there a moment.

READING I Today's readings are saturated with water imagery, especially this first reading and the gospel. Water is one of our most basic needs; life as we know it is impossible without water. How natural, then, that water initiates us into Christian life. It is through the water of baptism that we became who we are: members of the body of Christ and heirs of the reign of God.

It may be difficult for us today to appreciate the image of water, perhaps because for many of us water is taken for granted. It was not so with the Israelites during their sojourn in the desert, as indeed it is not for many people today, for whom water is a precious commodity. If we lived in one of the more arid parts of the world, like Palestine, we might be able to appreciate the readings today at a more elemental level.

In this first reading we witness a serious confrontation between Moses and the unruly people he is leading through the

desert. They are panicky with thirst; Moses is frightened for his life. The real problem, of course, is that the people doubt that God will be with them in their need. Thus they ask a question that echoes in the heart of every believer who has undergone severe temptation or suffering: "Is the Lord with us or not?"

The words Massah and Meribah mean "quarrel" and "testing," as the text makes clear. You can indicate this by reading them with parallel emphasis. And don't shy away

READING II   Romans 5:1–2, 5–8

A reading from the letter of Saint Paul to the Romans

Brothers and sisters:
Since we have been *justified* by *faith*,
    we have *peace* with *God* through our Lord Jesus *Christ*,
    through whom we have gained *access* by faith
    to this *grace* in which we *stand*,
    and we boast in *hope* of the glory of *God*.

And *hope* does not *disappoint*,
    because the *love* of God has been *poured* out into our hearts
    through the Holy *Spirit* who has been *given* to us.
For *Christ*, while we were still *helpless*,
    died at the appointed time for the *ungodly*.
Indeed, only with *difficulty* does one die for a *just* person,
    though perhaps for a *good* person one *might* even
        find courage to *die*.
But *God proves* his love for us
    in that while we were still *sinners* Christ *died* for us.

There is a hint of disbelief in the goodness of this news, as if to say, "Can you believe it?"

The text is dense, though the thought will be clear if you proclaim it with great care and understanding.

Christ died for us "while we were still sinners"! Give due emphasis to this good news.

from the chilling question that ends the reading. It's a fact of life that we doubt and question, especially during difficult times. This reading acknowledges our weakness and then demonstrates that the Lord does appear among us. Doubting is not a sin; it is part of the struggle inherent in a life of faith. We have a lot in common with the grumbling Israelites—our ancestors in faith—and we need not be ashamed of it.

READING II Christianity is not about what we are supposed to do. It is about what has already been done for us by a loving God. As obvious as this, it is difficult to live out in the practice of our faith. We have been justified by faith; we have been reconciled with God; we have been granted access to grace. Notice how all this is in the past tense. It has happened. It's a given. "Have you been saved?" we are sometimes asked. Yes, we have. Have we accepted the salvation granted us out of

pure love? Do we believe God loves us infinitely and without reserve? Well, there's the challenge. But the more we come to believe it, the more spontaneous and joyous our response to love will be. Good works are done not in the hope of earning God's favor—we already have that. Rather, good works express our gratitude.

To demonstrate his point, Paul illustrates the difference between human and divine love. Yes, on rare occasions we hear

GOSPEL   John 4:5–42

A reading from the holy gospel according to John

Begin slowly and quietly (but audibly!) to
set the scene.
Samaria = suh-MAYR-ee-uh
Sychar = SĪ-kahr

Jesus came to a town of *Samaria* called *Sychar*,
    near the plot of land that *Jacob* had given to his son *Joseph*.
Jacob's *well* was there.
Jesus, *tired* from his *journey*, sat down there at the *well*.
It was about *noon*.

A *woman* of *Samaria* came to draw *water*.
Jesus *said* to her,
    "Give me a drink."
His *disciples* had gone into the *town* to buy *food*.

Be careful with "Give me a drink."
It should not sound hard or demanding.
Perhaps there can be a note of pleading or
even the hint of a question or request.

The woman is neither shy nor rude but
honest and straightforward.

The Samaritan woman said to him,
    "How can *you*, a *Jew*, ask *me*, a *Samaritan* woman,
        for a *drink*?"
—For *Jews* use *nothing* in common with *Samaritans*.—
Jesus answered and said to her,
    "If you knew the *gift* of God
    and *who* is saying to you, 'Give me a drink,'
    you would have asked *him*
    and he would have given *you living* water."

The following exchanges should not be too
solemn. There is every indication here that
a kind of gentle banter is going on. On
the other hand, a frivolous or joking tone
would be completely out of place.

The woman said to him,
    "Sir, you do not even have a *bucket* and the cistern is *deep*;
    where then can you *get* this living water?
Are you greater than our father *Jacob*,
    who *gave* us this cistern and drank from it *himself*
    with his *children* and his *flocks*?"

---

of one person giving up life itself out of love for another. Parents may sacrifice their own lives to save an endangered child, and they do so out of love for the child.

God's love for us in Christ is something like that, only greater. Christ died for us whether we deserved it or not. He died for us regardless of whether we care or not. He died for us whether or not we even hear about it until we meet him in glory! Perhaps

most amazing is that in dying for us, he made us deserving. But he chose to leave us free to believe this good news or not. That, too, is a sign of his love and respect.

GOSPEL   The readings for the Third, Fourth and Fifth Sundays of Lent this year (Year A) are so filled with basic images of our faith—water, light, death to life—that they may be read on those Sundays in Years B and C as well, in place of the readings proper to Years B and C. It is particularly fitting to exercise that option if there

are catechumens in the assembly who are being prepared for reception into the church at the Easter Vigil. Next Sunday we hear about light in the story of the man born blind. On the Fifth Sunday of Lent we hear about life beyond death in the story of Lazarus, whom Jesus brought back from the dead.

Today we see the Israelites thirsting for water in the desert. Today we hear Paul tell us that the love of God has been "poured out" into our hearts. And today we hear the

The point is that Jesus is greater than Jacob. Great leaders were often noted for the good wells they dug to provide for their people. Jesus surpasses them all.

Jesus answered and said to her,
  "Everyone who drinks *this* water will be thirsty *again*;
  but whoever drinks the water *I* shall give will *never* thirst;
  the water *I* shall give will become in him
  a *spring* of water welling up to eternal *life*."

The woman said to him,
  "Sir, *give* me this water, so that *I* may not be thirsty
  or have to keep coming here to *draw* water."

Jesus seems to set a trap here, but there is no hint of condemnation. It's more like a setup so he can reveal who he really is.

Jesus said to her,
  "*Go* call your *husband* and come *back*."
The woman answered and said to him,
  "I do not *have* a husband."
Jesus answered her,
  "You are *right* in saying, 'I do not have a husband.'
For you have had *five* husbands,
  and the one you have *now* is *not* your husband.
What you have said is *true*."

The woman said to him,
  "Sir, I can see that you are a *prophet*.
Our *ancestors* worshiped on this *mountain*;
  but *you* people say that the place to worship is in *Jerusalem*."
Jesus said to her,
  "*Believe* me, woman, the hour is coming
  when you will worship the Father
  neither on this mountain *nor* in Jerusalem.

There is no need for this challenge to sound condemnatory. It is a statement of fact, and the woman is clearly not offended by it. She already knows she is speaking with a prophet.

"*You* people worship what you do not *understand*;
  we worship what we *understand*,
  because *salvation* is from the *Jews*.

story of the "woman at the well," a gospel story so popular and well known it has acquired this special title.

Taking the shorter form of this gospel weakens its impact, so avoid that if at all possible. If you are concerned about the celebration taking too long, consider other legitimate ways to abbreviate the liturgy. If you are worried that the assembly will find such a long reading boring, use your most accomplished deacon or priest to proclaim this text. Better yet, employ three readers and proclaim the gospel as we do the passion

narratives on Palm Sunday and Good Friday. A narrator could read the narrative portions, along with the words of the disciples and the Samaritans. Another reader could proclaim the words of Jesus, and a third could proclaim the words of the woman. Such an approach will not only avert boredom, it will also bring a new life to the story. It goes without saying, I hope, that the three readers should spend considerable time and effort preparing!

Begin your study of this gospel by reminding yourself that, in the words of the gospel writer, "Jews have nothing to do with Samaritans." Then notice as you approach the end of the story that the Samaritans come to Jesus and beg him to stay with them awhile. While these startling expressions of reconciliation between groups known for their mutual hatred are not the central point of John's account, they color it from start to finish. You might recall as well that Jesus is breaking another taboo by speaking with a woman in public, and a Samaritan woman at that. It's not a bad thing to keep in mind the

But the hour is *coming*, and is now *here*,
> when *true* worshipers will worship the Father
>> in *Spirit* and *truth*;
> and indeed the Father seeks such people to worship him.
God is Spirit, and those who worship him
> must worship in Spirit and truth."

The woman said to him,
> "I know that the *Messiah* is coming, the one called the *Christ*;
> when he *comes*, he will tell us *everything*."
Jesus said to her,
> "*I* am he, the one *speaking* with you."

At that moment his *disciples* returned,
> and were *amazed* that he was talking with a *woman*,
> but still no one said, "What are you *looking* for?"
> or "Why are you *talking* with her?"
The woman *left* her water jar
> and went into the *town* and said to the people,
> "Come see a man who told me *everything* I have *done*.
Could he possibly be the *Christ*?"
They went out of the town and *came* to him.
Meanwhile, the disciples *urged* him, "Rabbi, *eat*."
But he said to them,
> "*I* have food to eat of which you do not *know*."
So the disciples said to one another,
> "Could someone have *brought* him something to eat?"

Jesus said to them,
> "*My* food is to do the will of the one who *sent* me
> and to finish *his* work.
Do you not say, 'In four months the *harvest* will be here'?
I tell you, look *up* and *see* the fields *ripe* for the harvest.

This is a thunderclap of truth. We can only imagine the woman's reaction. It is clearly an allusion to God's "I AM" in Exodus and would have been recognized by John's readers. Let it be followed by a significant pause.

John mentions the fact that "the woman left her water jar" for a reason; give it some emphasis.

The entrance of the disciples provides another opportunity for teaching.

reconciling power of Jesus' presence as we hear him, tired from his journey, ask for a drink of water and then reveal himself as the Messiah. Only one other time do we hear Jesus speak of his thirst—when he was lifted up on the cross and drew all the world to himself.

Though the story centers on water and its many associations, there are many other instances that urge us to look for the deeper meaning in the several topics raised in this encounter between Jesus and the Samaritan woman. The woman speaks of water, and Jesus turns the conversation to living water. The woman refers to Jacob, giver of the well, the source of the water, and Jesus makes it clear that indeed he is greater than Jacob. Jesus has a different kind of water to offer. The woman brings up the disagreement about where one should worship God, and Jesus explains that God is Spirit and can be worshiped anywhere by one with a truthful heart.

Even the disciples provide Jesus with an opportunity to speak of deeper matters. They urge him to eat something. He speaks of bringing the Father's work to completion as the food that sustains him. Finally, Jesus speaks of the gratuitous gift of God, Jesus himself. There is no need to sow, for the harvest is provided. God has done the work, and

The *reaper* is already receiving *payment*
    and gathering crops for eternal *life,*
    so that the *sower* and *reaper* can *rejoice* together.
For *here* the saying is verified that '*One* sows and *another* reaps.'
I sent you to *reap* what you have not *worked* for;
    others have done the *work,*
    and *you* are sharing the *fruits* of their work."

Many of the *Samaritans* of that town began to *believe* in him
    because of the word of the *woman* who testified,
    "He told me *everything* I have *done."*
When the Samaritans *came* to him,
    they invited him to *stay* with them;
    and he *stayed* there two *days.*
Many *more* began to believe in him because of his *word,*
    and they said to the *woman,*
    "We no longer believe because of *your* word;
    for we have heard for *ourselves,*
    and we know that this is *truly* the savior of the *world."*

[Shorter: John 4:5–15, 19b–26, 39a, 40–42]

Here is the ultimate payoff. The woman spreads the Good News, the Samaritans come to hear Jesus, and then they move from hearsay belief to personal faith. John has made the striking point that Jesus' mission is universal. This really is the Savior of the whole world!

we reap the grain without labor. God has become one with us: "Sower and reaper may rejoice together."

A sensitive proclamation should concentrate on revealing as much of the richness here as possible. The vivid imagery, the rich dialogue, the underlying issues of race and gender, the questions of the disciples and the conversion of the Samaritans make this gospel story one of the most formative, educational, and inspiring of the New Testament.

4TH SUNDAY OF LENT

Lectionary #31

READING I   1 Samuel 16:1b, 6–7, 10–13a

A reading from the first book of Samuel

The LORD said to *Samuel*:
   "Fill your *horn* with *oil*, and be on your *way*.
I am sending you to *Jesse* of *Bethlehem*,
   for I have chosen my *king* from among his *sons*."

As Jesse and his sons came to the *sacrifice*,
   Samuel looked at *Eliab* and thought,
   "Surely the LORD's *anointed* is here *before* him."
But the LORD said to *Samuel*:
   "Do not judge from his *appearance* or from his lofty *stature*,
   because I have *rejected* him.
Not as *man* sees does *God* see,
   because *man* sees the *appearance*
   but the LORD looks into the *heart*."

In the same way Jesse presented *seven sons* before Samuel,
   but Samuel said to Jesse,
   "The LORD has not chosen *any one* of these."
Then Samuel asked Jesse,
   "Are these *all* the sons you *have*?"
Jesse replied,
   "There is still the *youngest*, who is tending the *sheep*."
Samuel said to Jesse,
   "*Send* for him;
   we will not begin the sacrificial *banquet* until he *arrives* here."

Some verses have been omitted here, so there is no context for the words "to the sacrifice."
Eliab = ee-LĪ-uhb

The predictability is intentional here. The literary form used to tell this story is formulaic.

Again, the "sacrificial banquet" appears with no context.

READING I   Not as we see does God see! While we see only the outer appearance, God sees into the heart. All of today's readings are about light and darkness, blindness and sight, seeing without really seeing and the inability to see one's own blindness. We are reminded of the old truth, "There are none so blind as those who will not see."

The point of this reading is that God's ways and choices are different from our own, and God's choices are not to be questioned even when they seem unlikely. The presumption is that God sees the ultimate outcome of any choice, while we do not. This lesson is taught in the formulaic procession of Jesse's seven sons before the prophet Samuel, each one being rejected by the Lord despite Samuel's inclination to choose the eldest, the next eldest and so on.

Not surprisingly, considering the literary formula being followed here, it is David, Jesse's youngest son, that the Lord chooses, the one who seemed so unlikely a choice that his father had not even thought to present him. David comes on the scene and makes a good impression: young, handsome, ruddy. These are the kind of features that might draw us to choose David as a leader—and the very kind of external appearance by which God does not judge. Is there a contradiction here? Is God choosing by outward appearance? The point is that God sees into David's heart and knows he will be a good king, aside from his youth, physical appearance and the fact that Jesse never thought he had a chance.

Jesse *sent* and had the young man *brought* to them.
He was *ruddy*, a youth *handsome* to behold
    and making a *splendid* appearance.
The LORD said,
    "*There*—anoint *him*, for *this* is the one!"

Then Samuel, with the horn of *oil* in hand,
    anointed David in the presence of his *brothers*;
    and from *that* day *on*, the *spirit* of the LORD
        rushed upon David.

The last sentence, stating the proof of the validity of God's choice, deserves special emphasis.

READING II   Ephesians 5:8–14

A reading from the letter of Saint Paul to the Ephesians

Brothers and sisters:
You were once *darkness*,
    but *now* you are *light* in the *Lord*.
Live as children of *light*,
    for *light* produces every kind of *goodness*
    and *righteousness* and *truth*.

Try to learn what is *pleasing* to the Lord.
Take no part in the *fruitless* works of *darkness*;
    rather *expose* them, for it is shameful even to *mention*
    the things *done* by them in *secret*;
        but everything exposed by the *light* becomes *visible*,
        for everything that becomes visible *is* light.
Therefore, it says:
    "*Awake*, O sleeper,
    and *arise* from the *dead*,
    and *Christ* will give you *light*."

This is not a particularly easy text, for Paul's images tumble over one another. Nevertheless, the metaphor is clear: Those who are "light" do good deeds; those who are "darkness" do shameful deeds. Be what you are: light!

The final lines are a fragment from an ancient baptismal hymn. Read them boldly as the summons they clearly are.

God's choice is confirmed immediately as the spirit of the Lord rushes upon David. All the messianic promises associated with David's lineage (which culminate in Jesus) are thereby given credibility. Had the choice been left to human vision and perception, the outcome might have been very different. Not as we see does God see.

READING II Father Hugh Tasch, a monk of Conception Abbey, has penned some of the loveliest lyrics ever inspired by sacred scripture. This passage from Ephesians prompted him 40 years ago to write:

> Once you were darkness, Pharaoh's
>   prison band.
> Now you are sunlight, dwelling
>   in the Land.
> Walk then in sunlight, high
>   upon the shore.
> Rise from the waters, dying now
>   no more.

The strength of Paul's imagery here is the bluntness of his metaphors. He doesn't say we were *in* darkness; he says we *were* darkness itself. He does not say we are *in* the sunlight (of Christ); he says we *are* sunlight itself. This is how Paul shows us the dramatic change that takes place at baptism. As we prepare for Easter and the renewal of our baptismal vows, it is good to be reminded of the difference between what we used to be and what we are now.

The text is particularly important for those preparing for baptism. So closely is

GOSPEL   John 9:1–41

A reading from the holy gospel according to John

As Jesus passed by he saw a man *blind* from *birth*.
His *disciples* asked him,
    "Rabbi, who *sinned*, this *man* or his *parents*,
    that he was born *blind*?"

Jesus answered,
    "Neither *he nor* his parents sinned;
    it is so that the works of *God* might be made *visible*
        through him.
We have to *do* the works of the one who sent me while it is *day*.
Night is coming when *no one* can work.
While I am in the *world*, I am the *light* of the world."
When he had said this, he *spat* on the *ground*
    and made *clay* with the saliva,
    and *smeared* the clay on his *eyes*, and said to him,
    "Go *wash* in the Pool of *Siloam*"—which means *Sent*.
So he *went* and *washed*, and came back able to *see*.

His *neighbors* and those who had seen him *earlier*
        as a *beggar* said,
    "Isn't *this* the one who used to *sit* and *beg*?"
Some said, "It *is*,"
    but others said, "*No*, he just *looks* like him."
He said, "I *am*."
So they said to him, "How were your eyes *opened*?"
He replied,
    "The man called *Jesus* made *clay* and *anointed* my eyes
    and told me, 'Go to *Siloam* and *wash*.'
So I *went* there and *washed* and was able to *see*."

The opening line, "As Jesus passed by," is distracting. Passed by what? Pause after these words to make their meaning clearer.

"Blind from birth" is an important phrase. There is no other instance in the gospels of a person afflicted from birth. This is different from restoring sight; it is giving sight!

There are clear divisions in this story. Precede each one with a pause and begin in a fresh tone.

The dialogue is tight here. Take it slowly and deliberately.

---

light associated with baptism that the early church referred to the newly baptized as "those who have been illumined." This theme of light continues and is brought to fullness in the gospel narrative. Jesus proclaims publicly, "I am the light of the world," which is all the more reason to proclaim this brief passage carefully and clearly. It prepares us to hear Jesus' words with greater understanding.

GOSPEL The readings for the Third, Fourth and Fifth Sundays of Lent this year (Year A) are so filled with basic images of our faith—water, light, death to life—that they may be read on those Sundays in Years B and C as well, in place of the readings proper to Years B and C. It is particularly fitting to exercise that option if there are catechumens in the assembly who are being prepared for reception into the church at the Easter Vigil. Last Sunday we dealt with the image of water.

Moses struck the rock to provide water for the thirsty Israelites; Jesus revealed himself to the woman at the well as the Messiah who provides living water "leaping up to eternal life." Today we hear about light in the story of the man born blind. On the Fifth Sunday of Lent we will hear about life beyond death in the story of Lazarus, whom Jesus brought back from the dead.

And they said to him, "Where *is* he?"
He said, "I don't *know.*"

They brought the one who was once blind to the *Pharisees.*
Now Jesus had made *clay* and opened his eyes on a *sabbath.*
So then the *Pharisees also* asked him how he was able to see.
He said to them,
    "He put *clay* on my eyes, and I *washed,* and now I can *see.*"
So some of the Pharisees said,
    "This man is *not* from *God,*
    because he does not keep the *sabbath.*"
But *others* said,
    "How can a *sinful* man do such *signs?*"
And there was a *division* among them.

So they said to the blind man *again,*
    "What do you have to *say* about him,
    since he opened your eyes?"
He said, "He is a *prophet.*"

Now the Jews did not *believe*
    that he had been *blind* and gained his *sight*
    until they summoned the *parents* of the one
        who had gained his sight.
They asked *them,*
    "Is this your *son,* who you say was born *blind?*
How does he now *see?*"
His parents answered and said,
    "We *know* that this is our *son* and that he was *born blind.*
We do *not* know how he *sees* now,
    nor do we know *who* opened his eyes.
Ask *him,* he is of age;
    he can speak for *himself.*"

Here's the problem for the Pharisees: Jesus healed on the Sabbath, which was forbidden except when death threatened.

Replace "Jews" with "Jewish leaders (or authorities)." After all, everyone in the story is a Jew. There is more than a hint of bias against Jews in John. We need not perpetuate the anti-Semitism it has sometimes produced.

If this gospel narrative seems to you like a long reading, think of it instead as a short story! It has all the elements of that literary genre: situation, conflict, resolution, and so on. It is, literally and figuratively, about not seeing the light, being afraid to see the light, seeing the light, and refusing to see the light because we are convinced we already do!

This is another gospel passage that lends itself to effective proclamation with multiple readers. With careful preparation, three or four readers could proclaim this

story in the assembly in a new and refreshing way. One reader could take the words of Jesus, another those of the man born blind, and another those of the neighbors, the disciples, the parents of the blind man and the Pharisees. Needless to say, the passage must be proclaimed extremely well, which means that such a proclamation would require a great deal of preparation and rehearsal.

The man born blind could not see the light until Jesus, the light of the world, covered his eyes with mud, sent him to the pool to wash and restored his sight. A treasure chest of lenten, baptismal and messianic images tumble out before us in the story. Even the mudpack Jesus uses as a salve reminds us of the dust we are made of and to which we shall return. The pool of Siloam (meaning "one who is sent") reminds us of both the waters of baptism and Christ himself, who has been sent from God and who sends us

"His parents said this because they were afraid of the Jewish authorities, who had already agreed . . . ," and so on.

His parents said this because they were *afraid*
    of the Jews, for the Jews had already *agreed*
      that if anyone *acknowledged* him as the *Christ*,
    he would be *expelled* from the *synagogue*.
For *this* reason his parents said,
    "*He* is of age; question *him*."

Here again the dialogue is tight. Take it slowly.

So a *second* time they called the man who had been blind
    and said to him, "Give *God* the praise!
We know that *this* man is a *sinner*."
He replied,
    "If he is a *sinner*, I do not *know*.
One thing I *do* know is that I was *blind* and now I *see*."
So they said to him,
    "What did he *do* to you?
    How did he open your eyes?"
He answered them,
    "I told you *already* and you did not *listen*.
Why do you want to hear it *again*?
Do *you* want to become his disciples, *too*?"
They *ridiculed* him and said,
    "*You* are *that* man's disciple;
    we are disciples of *Moses*!
We *know* that God spoke to *Moses*,
    but we do not know where *this* one is *from*."

The man answered and said to them,
    "This is what is so *amazing*,
    that you do not know where he is *from*,
      yet he opened my *eyes*.
We *know* that God does not listen to *sinners*,
    but if one is *devout* and does his *will*, he *listens* to him.

forth through our baptismal commission to be light in the world's darkness.

But there are several kinds of blindness depicted here. Some characters even remain blind at the end of the story, choosing not to see because they are convinced their vision is not impaired. The Pharisees are downright annoying in their reluctance to believe the simple story of this simple man. He tells the story of his cure over and over to no avail: "I was blind. I did what this Jesus told me to do. Now I see. It's as simple as that." The Pharisees refuse to believe it, and the bystanders refuse to believe the man was blind in the first place.

The parents of the blind man are blinded by fear, and our hearts go out to them. They are afraid to acknowledge what Jesus did, afraid to get involved because the Pharisees can cause them real trouble. Here we have an example of an age-old evil: unjust and self-serving authorities who oppress people and, with threats of reprisal, keep them afraid to speak the truth. Whether such evil is blatant or subtle, it is still very much with us today. We are struck in this story by the degree of resistance to something wonderful. How many find the Good News too good to be true or even a threat to their own position?

Perhaps the most exciting development in the story is that the beggar, blind from birth, became an ambassador for Jesus, insisting that Jesus must be from God or he could not have performed such wonders. For this brave act of apostleship the blind man is excommunicated. But Jesus seeks him out and takes his belief one step further into ultimate sight: faith in the Son of God.

It is *unheard* of that anyone ever opened the eyes
    of a person *born* blind.
If this man were not from *God*,
    he would not be able to do *anything*."
They answered and said to him,
    "You were born *totally* in *sin*,
    and are *you* trying to teach *us*?"
Then they *threw* him *out*.

Don't miss the compassion here. Jesus seeks out the excommunicated man!

When Jesus *heard* that they had thrown him out,
    he *found* him and said, "Do you *believe* in the Son of *Man*?"
He answered and said,
    "Who *is* he, sir, that I *may* believe in him?"
Jesus said to him,
    "You have *seen* him,
    the one *speaking* with you is *he*."
He said,
    "I *do* believe, Lord," and he *worshiped* him.

Then Jesus said,
    "I *came* into this world for *judgment*,
    so that those who do *not* see *might* see,
    and those who *do* see might become *blind*."
Some of the *Pharisees* who were with him *heard* this
    and said to him, "Surely *we* are not also blind, *are* we?"
Jesus said to them,
    "If you *were* blind, you would have no *sin*;
    but *now* you are saying, 'We *see*,' so your sin *remains*."

The real tragedy is that the religious leaders had the obligation to point out the Messiah when at last he came. Now here he is, and yet they do not see him.

[Shorter: John 9:1, 6–9, 13–17, 34–38]

The story ends on a sad note. Perhaps the old expression "There are none so blind as those who will not see" is wrong. There are apparently some who are even more blind than willful blindness can make them. They are the ones who are convinced, even in their blindness, that they see clearly. However, one often gets the feeling that people in this last group protest too much. They know better, but panic in the face of what the truth might mean renders them helpless.

The consequences of becoming children of the light are quite profound. "Now you are sunlight, dwelling in the Land." That "Land" is the promised land into which Christ leads us through baptism. It is a land filled with new meaning and new brightness for those with eyes to see it. But it is a land whose promise is not yet fully realized. In the meantime, there is danger of compromise that could snuff out the light, keep it hidden, or force it behind a cloud of fear. We are desperately in need of Christ the Light but are often desperately fearful of the consequences of being illumined.

5TH SUNDAY OF LENT

Lectionary #34

READING I   Ezekiel 37:12–14

A reading from the book of the prophet Ezekiel

Thus says the Lord GOD:
O my *people*, I will *open* your *graves*
   and have you *rise* from them,
   and bring you *back* to the land of *Israel*.
Then you shall *know* that *I* am the LORD,
   when I open your *graves* and have you *rise* from them,
   O my *people*!

I will put my *spirit* in you that you may *live*,
   and I will *settle* you upon your *land*;
   thus you shall *know* that *I* am the LORD.
I have *promised*, and I will *do* it, says the LORD.

Any text that begins with "Thus says the Lord God" is a solemn proclamation. Such words are meant to catch our attention so that we will listen with special care. Speak the words with great conviction.

The repetition of "O my people" is meant to reassure us. Don't be reluctant to give the phrase the force and feeling it is clearly meant to convey.

Consider eliminating the final "says the Lord." This will make the dialogue formula "The word of the Lord" and the assembly's response much stronger.

READING I The first reading is brief but packed with good news. It must be proclaimed slowly, deliberately and with great care. Every line contains a promise that we rejoice to hear. The words are strangely beautiful, too. "Bring you back to the land of Israel" is loaded with meaning and nuance. "Open your graves" is slightly horrifying, but we know it is a promise of life beyond death. When God says, "I will put my spirit in you," we know God is promising something both tremendous and beyond our understanding.

All of these wonderful occurrences will convince us once and for all that God is truly the Lord of life and death. And to comfort us further, God promises to *keep* these awesome promises. The same theme of death and resurrection appears in all of today's readings. And there is a progression in the quality of our belief in the good things God wills for us.

The words you are reading come from a unique context, different from our own. Ezekiel is in the famous "valley of dry bones," looking forward to a day when Israel's exile will be ended and their suffering vindicated.

Being restored to the land that is their birthright would be very much like being raised from the dead for the people of Israel. Anything approaching our modern belief about the resurrection of the body came much later in Jewish thought. Nevertheless, the loving care God exhibits for the chosen people is seen as extending beyond destruction and death. In the end (whatever that end may be), the love of God (and the startling reality that God's spirit lives in us) will enable us to triumph.

Begin quite slowly; give yourself and the assembly time and space to relish the contrast between being "in the flesh" and being "in the spirit."

READING II   Romans 8:8–11

A reading from the letter of Saint Paul to the Romans

Brothers and sisters:
Those who are in the *flesh cannot* please *God*.
But *you* are *not* in the flesh;
    on the *contrary*, *you* are in the *spirit*,
    if only the *Spirit* of God *dwells* in you.
Whoever does *not* have the Spirit of Christ
        does not *belong* to him.

But if Christ *is* in you,
    although the *body* is *dead* because of *sin*,
    the *spirit* is *alive* because of *righteousness*.

If the *Spirit* of the one who raised *Jesus* from the dead
        dwells in you,
    the one who raised Christ from the dead
    will give life to *your* mortal bodies *also*,
    through his *Spirit* dwelling in you.

The last sentence is long and begins with a long conditional "if." Take a deep breath and proceed with care so that you can tie it all together.

GOSPEL   John 11:1–45

A reading from the holy gospel according to John

Now a man was *ill*, *Lazarus* from *Bethany*,
    the village of *Mary* and her sister *Martha*.
Mary was the one who had *anointed* the Lord with perfumed *oil*
        and dried his *feet* with her *hair*;
    it was her *brother* Lazarus who was ill.

READING II Easter is two weeks away. The catechumens who hear today's readings will be given a preview of the great truth of Easter resurrection. In this second reading and in the gospel we are inundated with words about death and life, flesh and spirit, grave and resurrection. Paul is at pains to explain to us that the Spirit of God dwelling in us is our guarantee that life does not end; it merely changes.

The evidence for the truth of our belief, Paul says, is the resurrection of Jesus. Most challenging for the reader here is a deft handling of the paradox that Paul presents. Our bodies are dead to sin because our spirits are alive in God. And our mortal bodies, which carry in them many signs of death (illness, pain, sin), are nonetheless enlivened by the spirit we received at baptism. Unfortunately, this text has led many to believe and preach that we must despise the body because it is mortal.

Nothing could be further from Paul's meaning. The physical body is, after all, the only instrument we have for doing the good works of the Spirit that lives in us. It is possible to love and respect the body without being a slave to it. There is a great deal of difference between being "in the flesh" and being flesh. We don't have much choice on this side of heaven with regard to being flesh. But we certainly can choose not to be "in the flesh" rather than "in the spirit," that is, guided by the spirit and not by the flesh.

The evidence that we have the Spirit of God in us is found in the way we lead our lives even now: not putting our trust in fallible and corruptible flesh, for the flesh is subject to weakness and sin. No, we lead lives of holiness because we are "in the Spirit" and the Spirit is in us, a power that both enlivens and surpasses our mortal nature.

"The one you love is ill" is a striking way of naming a dear friend; the name isn't necessary.

John begins to insert his teaching about Jesus into the story of the event. Lazarus' illness will be an opportunity for the glory of God to shine and the conversion of many.

When Jesus waits two more days to go to Lazarus, he makes it clear that he is confident of his mastery over death. The more obstacles placed in his way, the more dramatic his victory will be.

This is an elusive passage, but it surely indicates that the disciples would understand why Jesus has to go back to Judea if they could see more clearly what his ultimate mission is to be. It has the feeling of a proverb: "Let us do it now, for now is the right time."

The "sleep versus death" discussion is simply John's way of emphasizing that Lazarus is really dead and that Jesus will do far more than wake him from slumber.

So the sisters sent *word* to Jesus saying,
 "*Master*, the one you *love* is *ill*."
When Jesus *heard* this he said,
 "*This* illness is *not* to end in *death*,
 but is for the glory of *God*,
 that the *Son* of God may be *glorified* through it."

Now Jesus *loved* Martha and her sister and Lazarus.
So when he heard that he was *ill*,
 he *remained* for two *days* in the place where he *was*.
Then *after* this he said to his *disciples*,
 "Let us go back to *Judea*."
The disciples said to him,
 "*Rabbi*, the Jews were just trying to *stone* you,
 and you want to go *back* there?"
Jesus answered,
 "Are there not twelve *hours* in a *day*?
If one walks during the *day*, he does not *stumble*,
 because he sees the *light* of this world.
But if one walks at *night*, he *stumbles*,
 because the light is not *in* him."

He said this, and then told them,
 "Our friend *Lazarus* is *asleep*,
 but I am going to *awaken* him."
So the disciples said to him,
 "*Master*, if he is *asleep*, he will be *saved*."
But Jesus was talking about his *death*,
 while *they* thought that he meant ordinary *sleep*.
So then Jesus said to them *clearly*,
 "*Lazarus* has *died*.
And I am *glad* for you that I was not *there*,
 that you may *believe*.

GOSPEL The readings for the Third, Fourth and Fifth Sundays of Lent this year (Year A) are so filled with basic images of our faith—water, light, death to life—that they may be read on those Sundays in Years B and C as well, in place of the readings proper to Years B and C. It is particularly fitting to exercise that option if there are catechumens in the assembly who are being prepared for reception into the church at the Easter Vigil. Two Sundays ago we dealt with the image of water. Moses struck the rock to provide water for the thirsty Israelites; Jesus revealed himself to

the woman at the well as the Messiah who provides living water "leaping up to eternal life." Last Sunday we heard about what it means to be children of the light and about Jesus as the light of the world in the story of the man born blind. Today we hear about life beyond death in the story of the raising of Lazarus.

If today's gospel narrative seems to you like a long reading, think of it instead as a short story. Like the gospel stories we have heard for the last two Sundays, the story of Lazarus has all the elements of the literary genre we call short story: situation, conflict,

characters, point of view and resolution. It is, literally and figuratively, about death, victory over death and the promise of resurrection for all of us in Jesus, who proclaims, "I myself am the resurrection and the life."

Although it is not especially lengthy, this is another gospel narrative that lends itself to effective proclamation with multiple readers. With careful preparation, three readers could proclaim this story in the assembly in a new and refreshing way. One reader could take the words of Jesus, another those of the disciples and Mary and

Didymus = DID-ih-muhs

Let us *go* to him."
So *Thomas*, called Didymus, said to his fellow disciples,
    "Let us *also* go to *die* with him."

When Jesus *arrived*, he found that Lazarus
    had already been in the *tomb* for four *days*.
Now *Bethany* was *near* Jerusalem, only about two miles *away*.
And many of the *Jews* had come to Martha and Mary
    to *comfort* them about their brother.
When Martha heard that *Jesus* was coming,
    she went to *meet* him;
    but *Mary* sat at *home*.
Martha said to Jesus,
    "Lord, if you had *been* here,
    my brother would not have *died*.
But even *now* I know that whatever *you* ask of God,
    God will *give* you."
Jesus said to her,
    "Your *brother* will *rise*."

Martha said to him,
    "I *know* he will rise,
    in the *resurrection* on the last *day*."
Jesus told her,
    "*I* am the resurrection *and* the *life*;
    whoever believes in *me*, even if he *dies*, will *live*,
    and everyone who lives and believes in *me* will *never* die.
Do you *believe* this?"
She said to him, "*Yes*, Lord.
I have come to believe that you are the *Christ*, the Son of *God*,
    the one who is *coming* into the *world*."

Here is the heart of John's account. Notice that it falls precisely in the center of the narrative. These words must be proclaimed with special (and memorable) conviction.

Martha, and a third the words of the narration. Needless to say, the passage must be proclaimed extremely well, and so such a proclamation would require a great deal of preparation and rehearsal.

John's strange and wonderful story about the raising of Lazarus is filled with strong emotions, dramatic scenes and profound teaching about the person of Jesus. The combination of narrative with discussion is explained by the fact that John has taken a preexisting account of Lazarus being brought back to life and has overlaid it with his own special brand of teaching.

The Lazarus story appears in John's gospel shortly before Jesus is captured, tried and crucified. It is the event that most directly results in his condemnation by those who were seeking to kill him. In the other gospels, it is another event that turns the officials against Jesus: the cleansing of the temple. The effect of John's arrangement is striking, since Jesus proclaims immediately before his death and resurrection the words that form the heart of today's story: "I

am the resurrection and the life." All the elements of the story point toward these words and put them in bold relief.

We learn first that Lazarus is a special friend, so we might think that Jesus would hasten to his side in his sickness. But his delay gives the author of the story the opportunity to point out that time is irrelevant. The degree of Lazarus' illness is also irrelevant. Jesus is the master of life and death. The entire event, as Jesus says, is an opportunity for the Son of Man (Jesus himself) to be glorified.

When she had said this,
  she went and called her sister Mary *secretly*, saying,
  "The *teacher* is here and is *asking* for you."
As soon as she *heard* this,
  she rose *quickly* and *went* to him.
For Jesus had not yet come into the *village*,
  but was still where Martha had *met* him.
So when the Jews who were *with* her in the house *comforting* her
  saw Mary get up quickly and go *out*,
  they *followed* her,
  presuming that she was going to the *tomb* to *weep* there.

When Mary came to where *Jesus* was and *saw* him,
  she fell at his *feet* and said to him,
  "Lord, if *you* had been here,
  my *brother* would not have *died*."
When Jesus saw her *weeping* and the Jews who had come
    with her weeping,
  he became *perturbed* and deeply *troubled*, and said,
  "Where have you *laid* him?"
They said to him, "Sir, come and *see*."
And *Jesus* wept.
So the Jews said, "See how he *loved* him."
But some of them said,
  "Could not the one who opened the eyes of the *blind* man
  have done something so that *this* man would not have *died*?"

So *Jesus*, perturbed *again*, came to the *tomb*.
It was a *cave*, and a *stone* lay across it.
Jesus said, "Take away the *stone*."
Martha, the dead man's *sister*, said to him,
  "Lord, by *now* there will be a *stench*;
  he has been *dead* for *four days*."

Emotions run high in this section. Even Jesus is "perturbed and deeply troubled." In the shortest verse in the Bible (John 11:35), the Lord of Life is in tears. In both the Latin Vulgate and the King James Version of the Bible, two words are used: *"Jesus flevit"; "Jesus wept."* The very brevity of the verse makes it strong. Pause briefly here.

The drama of the scene reaches its climax. Nothing could make the reality of death more vivid than the "stench." In a masterful literary and theological stroke, John juxtaposes the horror of bodily corruption with the glory of victory over it. The final command, "Lazarus, come out," is preceded by a prayer by which Jesus reminds us of his relationship with the Author of life.

When the disciples protest Jesus' decision to go back to Judea (where he is in trouble with the authorities), the author has the opportunity to show that this too is irrelevant. What does the master of life and death have to fear from such dangers?

The strange poetic response of Jesus to the apostles' protest is difficult to understand. It certainly means that Jesus sees the outcome of the situation more clearly than his followers do. And he also seems to be saying, "Open your eyes and see what I have been trying to teach you: You have been enlightened by belief in me; you have

nothing to fear from anyone. If you still feel unequal to the risk and challenge of being my follower, believe more strongly and the light within you will increase."

But the proverbial feeling of the saying indicates something more like, "Strike while the iron is hot," or "For everything there is an appointed time." In other words, Jesus is saying there is a time for doing what must be done, and there is a time for delaying what must be done until a more propitious time arrives. The daylight hours are a good time for walking; when night comes, it's best to postpone the walk until

you can see the road. It's possible that this proverb or saying has been inserted into John's Lazarus story because it seems apropos of the disciples hesitancy to take the risk of returning to Judea. It could be as simple as "It's now or never!"

Thomas the Twin responds either with real courage or impulsive enthusiasm— or perhaps with an "Oh, what the heck!" resignation. Whatever the motive behind his energetic response, it is obviously a decision to accept the consequences of being a disciple.

Jesus said to her,
"Did I not *tell* you that if you *believe*
you will see the glory of *God*?"

So they took away the *stone*.
And Jesus raised his *eyes* and said,
"*Father*, I *thank* you for *hearing* me.
I know that you *always* hear me;
but because of the *crowd* here I have said this,
that they may *believe* that you *sent* me."

And when he had said this,
he *cried out* in a loud *voice*,
"*Lazarus*, come *out*!"
The dead man came *out*,
tied hand and foot with *burial* bands,
and his *face* was wrapped in a *cloth*.
So Jesus said to them,
"*Untie* him and let him *go*."

The purpose of the entire event is fulfilled. Those who witnessed it put their faith in Jesus.

Now *many* of the Jews who had come to *Mary*
and *seen* what he had done began to *believe* in him.

[Shorter: John 11:3–7, 17, 20–27, 33b–45]

The discussion about the difference between sleep and death is John's way of impressing upon us even further that Jesus is actually going to raise the dead, not merely revive the seriously ill. And the fact that Lazarus has been dead for four days impresses the witnesses of the miracle even more. Custom and law required burial within 24 hours since modern-day means of preserving a corpse were not available. The central point is further stressed: Nothing can hinder the master of life and death.

It is also John's intent in this story to prefigure the imminent suffering of Jesus himself. The personal grief and emotional stress that Jesus expresses at the loss of his friend is a prediction of his own passion and death. But that suffering and death, too, will be overcome when God raises Jesus from the dead.

Finally, John points out to us in the last sentence of this reading that all the signs had their intended effect: "This caused many of the Jews . . . to put their faith in him." In your proclamation of John's account of this wonderful occurrence, realize that it is packed with instruction for the assembly. Some of that instruction is direct: "I am the resurrection and the life. Believe in me and you will rise from the dead." Some of the instruction is indirect: Jesus' emotional involvement here is unusually dramatic. If the Lord Jesus seems far away from our experience at times, here is a poignant glimpse into the tenderness of his vulnerable humanity. There may be no more vivid illustration of the fact that Jesus "shared completely in our weakness." The historical facts are important, but they are primarily the framework to support the fundamental doctrine of Christ's mastery over sin and its ultimate consequence: death.

PALM SUNDAY OF THE LORD'S PASSION

Lectionary #37

GOSPEL AT THE PROCESSION   Matthew 21:1–11

A reading from the holy gospel according to Matthew

When *Jesus* and the *disciples* drew near *Jerusalem*
    and came to *Bethphage* on the Mount of *Olives*,
    Jesus sent two disciples, *saying* to them,
    "Go into the *village* opposite you,
    and *immediately* you will find an *ass* tethered,
    and a *colt* with her.
Untie them and bring them *here* to me.
And if anyone should *say* anything to you, reply,
    'The *master* has need of them.'
Then he will send them at *once*."

This *happened* so that what had been spoken through the *prophet*
    might be *fulfilled*:
    "Say to daughter *Zion*,
    '*Behold*, your *king* comes to you,
    meek and riding on an *ass*,
    and on a *colt*, the *foal* of a beast of *burden*.'"

The disciples *went* and did as Jesus had *ordered* them.
They brought the *ass* and the *colt* and laid their *cloaks* over them,
    and he *sat* upon them.
The very large *crowd* spread their *cloaks* on the *road*,
    while *others* cut *branches* from the *trees*
    and *strewed* them on the *road*.
The crowds *preceding* him and those *following*

These quiet preparations for Jesus' entry into Jerusalem all have the single purpose that Matthew makes explicit and you should emphasize: to fulfill what was said by the prophet.
Bethphage = BETH-fayj

Be sure this sounds like a quotation.

We are about to remember this procession with one of our own. Make the details clear.

PROCESSION GOSPEL We begin the holiest week of the year with a triumphant shout of praise to Jesus, the Son of David. But we do so with mixed feelings, for we already know that the second proclamation from the gospel today will recount Jesus' suffering and death. The twofold nature of this special day is reflected in the two names by which it is called: Palm Sunday and Passion Sunday.

The liturgy begins with a procession patterned after Jesus' triumphal entry into Jerusalem. The penitential rite is omitted and, after a greeting and brief instruction,

Matthew's gospel account of the joyous procession is proclaimed, and the assembly commemorates and celebrates it in a tangible way. Matthew's purpose is to demonstrate that the prophet from Nazareth is actually the promised Messiah. But this Messiah differs greatly from the expected one. This is no conquering hero entering the city astride the foal of a pack animal, and yet he is acclaimed "blessed." Matthew rolls the images of royalty, humility, divinity and humanity into one, creating a dramatic scene fraught with theological complexity.

Our shouts of acclamation will become cries of horror when we see that this Messiah will rule from a cross, an instrument of death. Only next week, after the celebration of the resurrection, will we understand the paradoxical scene Matthew places before us. Knowing as we do what is to come before we witness Jesus' triumph over death, our shouts of acclamation are ritualized and subdued. The red vestments worn for the procession signify royalty, but red is also the color of blood.

As always, the reader does not imitate the cries of the crowd but narrates them. Liturgical proclamation is not a reenactment but a solemn retelling of what happened.

kept *crying out* and saying:
"*Hosanna* to the Son of *David*;
blessed is he who *comes* in the name of the *Lord*;
hosanna in the *highest*."

And when he entered *Jerusalem*
the whole *city* was *shaken* and asked, "Who *is* this?"
And the crowds *replied*,
"This is *Jesus* the *prophet*, from Nazareth in *Galilee*."

Lectionary #38

READING I   Isaiah 50:4–7

A reading from the book of the prophet Isaiah

You are announcing the proclaimer's creed! Your tongue has been trained most effectively by your faith experience.

The Lord GOD has given me
    a well-*trained* tongue,
that I might *know* how to speak to the *weary*
    a *word* that will *rouse* them.
Morning after *morning*
    he opens my *ear* that I may *hear*;
and I have not *rebelled*,
    have not turned *back*.

Every day, every moment, is an opportunity to "hear" more clearly so that you may proclaim more clearly.

I gave my *back* to those who *beat* me,
    my *cheeks* to those who plucked my *beard*;
my *face* I did not *shield*
    from *buffets* and *spitting*.

The poetry of the suffering servant songs demands an exalted delivery. The meaning is deeper than the actual words.

The Lord GOD is my *help*,
    therefore I am not *disgraced*;
I have set my face like *flint*,
    knowing that I shall *not* be put to *shame*.

READING I | Who is speaking in this brief first-person narrative from Isaiah's poetic depiction of the suffering servant? The one who is persecuted for doing the Lord's work? As Christians we see Jesus in the role of the servant, especially today when we hear the record of his suffering at the hands of his persecutors. But the voice also belongs to the God of heaven and earth, now revealed to be a God of compassion, intimately involved with creation.

It is also the voice of those who have spoken on God's behalf throughout history: Jeremiah, the prophet who was called to live out the suffering of God's people; Israel, God's chosen people who have suffered so much because of that honor; and, indeed, the men and women of every time and place who have shared the pain of the suffering poor and carried the burden of straying sinners.

You speak for all these as you proclaim this text. The members of the assembly should find themselves speaking these words and so experience a renewal of their oneness with and responsibility for a pain-ridden world. There are perhaps no stronger words in scripture than these for describing those faithful servants who are able to "set their faces like flint" toward the difficulties they must encounter to be true to a God of righteousness in a world marred by injustice.

READING II | The second chapter of Paul's letter to the Philippians contains one of the most moving and beautiful sketches of Christ's mission and person. Your purpose here is to move your hearers to imitate their noble model: to be selfless, humble, obedient and confident of ultimate victory through the name that has been bestowed on them, "Christian."

READING II   Philippians 2:6–11

A reading from the letter of Saint Paul to the Philippians

Christ *Jesus*, though he was in the form of *God*,
    did not regard *equality* with God
    something to be *grasped*.
Rather, he *emptied* himself,
    taking the form of a *slave*,
    coming in *human* likeness;
    and found *human* in appearance,
    he *humbled* himself,
    becoming *obedient* to the point of *death*,
    even death on a *cross*.

Because of this, *God* greatly *exalted* him
    and *bestowed* on him the *name*
    which is above *every* name,
    that at the name of *Jesus*
    every *knee* should *bend*,
    of those in *heaven* and on *earth* and *under* the earth,
    and every tongue *confess* that
    Jesus *Christ* is *Lord*,
    to the glory of *God* the *Father*.

There are clearly two sections with two sets of contrasting images: (1) emptied, slave, human, humbled, obedient, death; and (2) exalted, name above every name, bent knees, confessing tongues, the glory of God. Make the contrasts clear.

A new section begins here. Pause slightly before beginning it.

The final section builds through to the end. The exalted cry "Jesus Christ is Lord!" should be proclaimed with more solemnity than volume.

Most striking of all is that the model placed before us is God, who is just as much God in suffering as in glory. Suffering is not merely something endured for a time because it leads to glory. Rather, suffering and glory are the natural mix that defines God and us as disciples.

When we proclaim that "Jesus Christ is Lord to the glory of God the Father," we are accepting the apparent contradiction of Christian life. Since Jesus is the perfect model of perfect acceptance of the paradox, "every knee must bend" to acknowledge and imitate that perfection.

Here is the Easter mystery in a nutshell. And it surely is a mystery! How well can any of us live up to Paul's challenge to make Christ's attitude our own? Why do our hearts rise to its challenge and sink in the face of it at the same moment? Have we come face to face with the reason why this observation has been made so often: "We don't know whether Christianity will work or not because it's never been tried"? As you read this amazing passage, try to assist your listeners in asking themselves such questions.

PASSION   It is rare these days that the accounts of the passion on Palm Sunday and Good Friday are proclaimed by one reader. Everyone seems to sense the efficacy of employing several readers (at least three), not only because the text is long, but because it seems to demand a kind of ritual dramatization to bring it fully to life. This is not to say, however, that a full-scale reenactment or even a "dramatic interpretation" of the passion is to be preferred over a proclamation. The liturgical context does not lend itself to anything approaching theatrical presentation. The liturgy is ritualized

Throughout the passion narrative, it is important to emphasize the deeper meaning rather than the literal facts. For example, whenever Matthew notes that an event took place to fulfill the scriptures, the assembly should be able sense the reappearance of this central theme.

We begin with the scandal of betrayal. The word "traitor" is from the Latin *tradere*, meaning "to hand over." The phrase is used twice in the opening paragraph, and a pun is involved. Jesus is "handed over" so that he can "hand over" his life for the salvation of the world. Human betrayal is transformed into divine fidelity.

The Passover meal is the context in which Jesus explains his passing over from death to life. Only when that passing over is fully accomplished will we share the cup with Jesus in eternity.

There is no melodrama in the dialogue of betrayal as presented by Matthew. Keep the delivery calm. Otherwise the inevitability of all things happening in accord with prophecy is compromised.

PASSION   Matthew 26:14—27:66

The Passion of our Lord Jesus Christ according to Matthew

(1) One of the *Twelve*, who was called Judas *Iscariot*,
   went to the chief *priests* and said,
   "What are you willing to *give* me
   if I hand him *over* to you?"
They *paid* him thirty pieces of *silver*,
   and from that time *on* he looked for an *opportunity*
      to hand him *over*.

(2) On the *first* day of the Feast of Unleavened *Bread*,
   the *disciples* approached Jesus and said,
   "Where do you want us to *prepare*
   for you to eat the *Passover*?"
He said,
   "Go into the *city* to a certain *man* and *tell* him,
   'The *teacher* says, "My appointed *time* draws *near*;
   in *your* house I shall celebrate the *Passover*
      with my *disciples*."'"
The disciples then *did* as Jesus had *ordered*,
   and prepared the *Passover*.

(3) When it was *evening*,
   he reclined at *table* with the Twelve.
And while they were *eating*, he said,
   "*Amen*, I *say* to you, *one* of you will *betray* me."
Deeply *distressed* at this,
   they began to *say* to him one after *another*,
   "*Surely* it is not *I*, Lord?"
He said in *reply*,
   "He who has dipped his hand into the *dish* with me

behavior and requires the kind of restraint and dignity that respects the solemnity and weight of its content and purpose. The liturgy never reenacts its subject matter. It memorializes and commemorates what it celebrates, but the liturgy does not try to re-create what has been done once and for all. Those who take creative approaches to the proclamation of the passion narratives must keep in mind that they are presenting precisely that, a narrative, not a script.

Perhaps the form of proclamation most true to liturgical tradition is the singing or chanting of the passion by three cantors—one taking the voice of the evangelist, one the voice of all speakers except Jesus and one the voice of Jesus. The solemnization of the passion achieved through this kind of presentation is unforgettable and quite moving, and never sentimental. In an age awash in cinematic realism, the kind of heightened solemnity demanded by the liturgy may seem less immediate and more formal. Nevertheless, it must be maintained if we are to avoid trivializing its subject matter.

In recent years the members of the assembly have been provided copies of the passion text and have read aloud the words of the crowds. While this practice may seem to accomplish a higher degree of participation, it also requires that the assembly follow along with the proclaimers (to be ready for their "part") and so cannot fully attend as *hearers*, which is their proper form of participation during the proclamation of God's word at every liturgy. The benefits of this practice should not be presumed but carefully evaluated in the light of fundamental liturgical and pastoral principles.

is the one who will *betray* me.
The Son of Man indeed *goes*, as it is *written* of him,
but *woe* to that man *by* whom the Son of Man is *betrayed*.
It would be *better* for that man if he had never been *born*."
Then *Judas*, his *betrayer*, said in reply,
"Surely it is not *I*, Rabbi?"
He *answered*, "You have *said* so."

(4) While they were *eating*,
Jesus took *bread*, said the *blessing*,
broke it, and giving it to his *disciples* said,
"*Take* and *eat*; this is my *body*."
Then he took a *cup*, gave *thanks*, and gave *it* to them, saying,
"*Drink* from it, *all* of you,
for this is my *blood* of the *covenant*,
which will be *shed* on behalf of *many*
for the forgiveness of *sins*.
I *tell* you, from now *on* I shall not *drink* this fruit of the vine
until the day when I drink it with you *new*
in the kingdom of my *Father*."
Then, after singing a *hymn*,
they went out to the Mount of *Olives*.

(5) *Then* Jesus said to them,
"This *night all* of you will have your *faith* in me *shaken*,
for it is *written*:
'I will strike the *shepherd*,
and the *sheep* of the flock will be *dispersed*';
but after I have been raised *up*,
I shall go *before* you to *Galilee*."
Peter said to him in *reply*,
"Though *all* may have their faith in you shaken,
mine will *never* be."

Jesus quotes scripture to indicate his foreknowledge of the inevitable. Matthew is writing (and we are reading) after the fact.

Whatever practice is observed in your community, it should try to meet the challenge of a long proclamation (potentially tedious if not done well) and avoid the excesses of a presentation so elaborate or literal that the assembly is preoccupied with the manner of proclamation at the expense of the message.

The story of Christ's passion and death is told in a more or less straightforward narrative by all four evangelists. Over the three-year lectionary cycle we read Matthew, Mark and Luke on Passion Sunday. John's account is read every year on Good Friday.

It is important to realize that each of the four writers had more in mind than a literal telling of the events. Each had a particular point of view and a particular purpose. Thus, the accounts differ from one another. For this reason it is important to choose a mode of proclamation that serves the faith-building insight offered rather than the events related.

Matthew's guiding purpose in the way he recounts the passion narrative, as it is throughout his gospel, is to demonstrate in every detail that what happens to Jesus fulfills the scriptures. Thus it is important in the delivery of the Matthean account to

emphasize the implied and explicit indications that the scriptures are being fulfilled. Though much of this must be done in the homily, the proclaimers who understand Matthew's purpose can help the narrative achieve it.

(1) The conflict begins with a betrayal. The event immediately preceding this one, the story of the woman who anointed Jesus' head with costly perfume, an anointing described by Jesus himself as a preparation for his burial, puts the horror of Judas' scheme in bold relief. Matthew has thus

Jesus said to *him*,
  "*Amen*, I *say* to you,
    this very *night* before the *cock* crows,
    you will *deny* me three *times*."
Peter said to *him*,
  "Even though I should have to *die* with you,
    I will not *deny* you."
And *all* the disciples spoke *likewise*.

Then Jesus came with them to a place called *Gethsemane*,
    and he said to his disciples,
    "Sit *here* while I go over *there* and *pray*."
He took along *Peter* and the two sons of *Zebedee*,
    and began to feel *sorrow* and *distress*.

Then he said to them,
  "My soul is *sorrowful* even to *death*.
Remain here and keep *watch* with me."
He *advanced* a little and fell *prostrate* in *prayer*, saying,
  "My *Father*, if it is *possible*,
    let this cup *pass* from me;
    yet, not as *I* will, but as *you* will."
When he returned to his *disciples* he found them *asleep*.
He said to *Peter*,
  "So you could not keep *watch* with me for one *hour*?
Watch and *pray* that *you* may not undergo the test.
The *spirit* is *willing*, but the *flesh* is *weak*."
Withdrawing a *second* time, he prayed *again*,
  "My *Father*, if it is not *possible* that this cup *pass*
    without my *drinking* it, your *will* be *done*!"
Then he returned once *more* and found them *asleep*,
    for they could not keep their *eyes* open.

Gethsemane = geth-SEM-uh-nee

Jesus takes with him the same three disciples who witnessed his transfiguration. As they had glimpsed his glory, so now they will see his wrenching struggle. Like ourselves, they were very attentive to the glory but find it difficult to attend to the suffering.

moved us from a scene of consummate love to an act of complete selfishness.

It would be a mistake to read Judas' betrayal too literally. Matthew is intent on showing us that Judas is simply another agent in the fulfillment of scripture, which clearly foretold that an act of betrayal would lead to the death of the suffering servant. William F. Barclay, in his *Daily Study Bible Commentary on Matthew,* makes the fascinating observation that Judas may never have meant for Jesus to die. He may have intended only to force Jesus into action, to put him in a situation in which his divine

power would be necessary to avert the tragedy of his death. Such a view certainly makes Judas a more complex human being, more than a greedy coward. Even so, Judas' refusal to accept the messianic plan as Jesus intended it has tragic consequences. We may not like the idea of a dying Savior as much as a heroic risen Christ. We may prefer to see representations of the cross rather than the crucifix, but our preferences will never change the fact that our risen Lord chose to show his love for us in bloody self-sacrifice.

(2) In this paragraph Matthew shows us that Jesus is fully aware of all that is about to happen to him and that he controls it from start to finish. Throughout his passion, Jesus is a willing participant, not a passive victim.

(3) The Passover begins at sundown, and the events that take place on this night are dark indeed. Again, Jesus refers to scripture and the prediction that his betrayal would take place in the context of a meal. The significance of the context here is greater when we realize that the shared meal in ancient Near Eastern culture was a

He *left* them and withdrew *again* and prayed a *third* time,
    saying the same thing *again*.
Then he *returned* to his disciples and said to them,
    "Are you still *sleeping* and taking your *rest?*
Behold, the hour is at *hand*
    when the Son of *Man* is to be handed over to *sinners*.
Get *up*, let us *go*.
Look, my betrayer is at *hand*."

(6) While he was still *speaking*,
    Judas, one of the Twelve, arrived,
        accompanied by a large *crowd*, with *swords* and *clubs*,
        who had come from the chief *priests* and the *elders*
            of the people.
His betrayer had arranged a *sign* with them, saying,
    "The man I shall *kiss* is the one; *arrest* him."
Immediately he went over to Jesus and said,
    "*Hail*, Rabbi!" and he *kissed* him.
Jesus *answered* him,
    "*Friend*, do what you have *come* for."
Then stepping forward they laid *hands* on Jesus and *arrested* him.

And *behold*, one of those who *accompanied* Jesus
    put his hand to his *sword*, drew it,
    and struck the high priest's *servant*, cutting off his *ear*.
Then Jesus *said* to him,
    "Put your *sword* back into its *sheath*,
    for all who *take* the sword will *perish* by the sword.
Do you think that I cannot call upon my *Father*
    and he will not provide me at this *moment*
    with more than twelve *legions* of *angels?*
But then how would the *Scriptures* be *fulfilled*
    which say that it *must* come to *pass* in this *way?*"

Here again is the expression "handed over." We realize the bitter irony that the Father has "handed over" the Son, not in betrayal as Judas will, but in fulfillment of the scripture.

sign of special unity and friendship. Being betrayed by one who shared a dish with you was the ultimate treachery.

Matthew's version of the identification of the betrayer is simple. Judas' question is answered in a straightforward manner: "Yes, you are the one." Was this exchange made in secret so the others did not hear it?

(4) This brief description of the Last Supper explains the divine motive: to forgive sins and to establish the reign of God upon earth. This is accomplished in the context of a covenant, a new relationship between God and creation, a "new and everlasting

covenant," as we hear at every Mass. Unlike the old covenant, this new one shows us the face of God in utter clarity for the first time. Jesus is the face of God. In his self-sacrificing love, we catch a dramatic and convincing glimpse of how God loves us. Even centuries later, and until time disappears into eternity, we will try to comprehend a love of such intensity. We may even find it impossible to believe. But there it is, and it is the foundation of our faith. At the end of this meal that has sanctified every meal since, Jesus and the apostles sang the psalm that concluded every Passover meal.

Its refrain, "God's mercy endures forever," takes on an entirely new meaning.

(5) The prediction of Peter's denial (despite his protest) and the inability of the disciples to stay awake at Gethsemane provide Matthew with effective emphasis on the fulfillment of the prophet Isaiah's "suffering servant songs" in the person of Jesus. The point is that *all* will abandon Jesus, even those whose love seems strongest. Notice that the mood of the text is calm: There is no recrimination of the Twelve even as their denial is predicted and protested. Jesus even assures them that they will see him

Again, it all has to happen as the prophets foretold. Be sure this relentless theme is emphasized.

Caiaphas = KAY-uh-fuhs

At that hour Jesus said to the *crowds,*
   "Have you come out as against a *robber,*
   with *swords* and *clubs* to seize me?
Day after *day* I sat *teaching* in the *temple* area,
   yet you did not *arrest* me.
But *all* this has come to *pass*
   that the writings of the *prophets* may be *fulfilled.*"
Then all the disciples *left* him and *fled.*

(7) Those who had *arrested* Jesus led him *away*
   to *Caiaphas* the *high* priest,
   where the *scribes* and the *elders* were assembled.

Peter was *following* him at a *distance*
   as far as the high priest's *courtyard,*
   and going *inside* he sat down with the *servants*
      to see the *outcome.*
The chief *priests* and the entire *Sanhedrin*
   kept trying to obtain false *testimony* against Jesus
   in order to put him to *death,*
   but they found *none,*
   though many false *witnesses* came forward.

Finally two came forward who stated,
   "This man said, 'I can *destroy* the temple of *God*
   and within three days *rebuild* it.'"
The *high* priest *rose* and *addressed* him,
   "Have you no *answer?*
What are these men *testifying* against you?"
But Jesus was *silent.*
Then the high priest said to him,
   "I *order* you to tell us under *oath* before the living *God*
   whether you are the *Christ,* the *Son* of God."

again and that all will be well. The dominion he came to establish will put past, present and future in right relationship with God. Furthermore, the struggle within Jesus to accept his gruesome fate, and to do so completely abandoned by his friends, emphasizes the nobility and totality of his obedience, the virtue *par excellence* of God's suffering servant.

(6) Although Judas' kiss has become a horrifying symbol of hypocrisy and betrayal, we should not think of Judas either as a brute or as a faceless instrument of God's pre-ordained plan. That is far too simplistic. It

removes Judas from human experience and makes him an arbitrary hammer in the hand of a vengeful God. It is much more likely that Judas was terribly misled by his erroneous expectations of Jesus and took matters into his own hands, hoping he could force Jesus to emerge as the warring Messiah that Judas wanted him to be. Judas shows us a side of being human that is complex, elusive and terrifying. His tragic story deserves awed and humble contemplation.

The disciple who strikes the high priest's servant allows Matthew to make a meaningful point. By mutilating the ear of

the high priest's servant, the attacker has symbolically rendered the high priest himself unfit for office according to ancient Jewish law. Matthew is saying in effect that the old law is passing away and a new order is being established. Finally, Matthew puts into Jesus' own mouth the words that explain the evangelist's governing theme: "How would the scriptures be fulfilled if things did not proceed in this way?"; and "All has happened to fulfill the writings of the prophets."

(7) Clearly, Jesus is innocent—a point that Matthew must make in the strongest

Because Jesus describes himself with a messianic text, he clearly refers to himself as Messiah. This is blasphemy to those who do not believe it.

Jesus said to him in reply,
  "You have *said* so.
But I *tell* you:
  From now *on* you will *see* 'the Son of Man
  seated at the right hand of the *Power*'
  and 'coming on the clouds of *heaven*.'"
Then the *high* priest tore his *robes* and said,
  "He has *blasphemed*!
What further *need* have we of *witnesses*?
You have now *heard* the blasphemy;
  what is your *opinion*?"
They said in reply,
  "He deserves to *die*!"
Then they *spat* in his *face* and *struck* him,
  while some *slapped* him, saying,
  "*Prophesy* for us, Christ: who is it that *struck* you?"

Galilean = gal-ih-LEE-uhn

(8) Now *Peter* was sitting *outside* in the *courtyard*.
One of the *maids* came over to him and said,
  "You *too* were with *Jesus* the *Galilean*."
But he *denied* it in front of *everyone*, saying,
  "I do not know what you are *talking* about!"
As he went out to the *gate*, *another* girl saw him
  and said to those who were there,
  "*This* man was with *Jesus* the *Nazarene*."
Again he denied it with an *oath*,
  "I do not *know* the man!"
A little later the *bystanders* came over and said to Peter,
  "*Surely* you too are one of them;
  even your *speech* gives you away."
At that he began to *curse* and to *swear*,
  "I do *not know* the man."
And *immediately* a *cock* crowed.

possible way. He not only says that the chief priests were looking for *false* testimony, but he goes on to say that none could be found, despite the many false witnesses who came forward. If you think about it for a moment, how difficult is it to find *false* testimony? Those who wanted to put Jesus to death were motivated by jealousy and hatred, not a concern for the truth. Yet, even with the most ignoble motives and unlimited scope for perjury, they could find no case against Jesus.

Jesus was found guilty of blasphemy not because he claimed to be God but because he quoted Daniel 7:13, a clear reference to the Messiah that he attributes to himself. But, again, he does not fulfill the expectations of those who awaited a conquering hero. Matthew teaches us a crucial lesson here: The challenge for every believer and for the church is to let Jesus be the Messiah he came to be. This may be the most difficult lesson of all. Throughout history and in every Christian life we see the struggle to accept Jesus on his own terms. Any Christian community that feels justified in excluding, judging, condemning or attacking any of God's creatures fails to accept Jesus as the Messiah he is and is guilty of the same horrific mistake made by those who here rend their garments as they cry, "Death to this imposter!"

The physical abuse that accompanies the authorities' hysteria shows how base human prejudice can be. All semblance of courtroom justice has disappeared; every trace of a fair trial or a presumption of innocence is gone. The mockery of Jesus' claim to be Messiah shows us how low hatred brings those consumed by it. The truth has become irrelevant, as it always does when we act out of willful ignorance or fear.

Then Peter remembered the *word* that Jesus had *spoken*:
"Before the *cock* crows you will *deny* me *three times*."
He went out and began to *weep bitterly*.

When it was *morning*,
all the chief *priests* and the *elders* of the people
took *counsel* against Jesus to put him to *death*.
They *bound* him, led him *away*,
and handed him over to *Pilate*, the *governor*.

(9) Then *Judas*, his *betrayer*, seeing that Jesus had been *condemned*,
deeply *regretted* what he had done.
He *returned* the thirty pieces of *silver*
to the chief priests and elders, saying,
"I have *sinned* in betraying *innocent* blood."
They said,
"What is that to *us*?
Look to it *yourself*."
Flinging the money into the *temple*,
he *departed* and went off and *hanged* himself.
The chief priests *gathered up* the money, but said,
"It is not *lawful* to deposit this in the *temple* treasury,
for it is the price of *blood*."
After *consultation*, they used it to buy the *potter's* field
as a *burial* place for *foreigners*.
That is why that field even *today* is called the Field of *Blood*.
Then was *fulfilled* what had been said through *Jeremiah*
the prophet,
"And they took the thirty pieces of *silver*,
the *value* of a man with a *price* on his head,
a price set by some of the *Israelites*,

Again, the theme of being "handed over" appears. Jesus is "handed over" to Pilate, then the one who "handed him over" repents.

(8) Jewish law measures infidelity, disloyalty or treason by degrees, and here we see Peter commit these sins in their gravest form. The denial is threefold; it is total, uncompromising, relentless and without mitigation. And, of course, we see Jesus' prediction of Peter's betrayal fulfilled (even as Peter proclaimed his loyalty). The bitterness of Peter's repentance emphasizes both the depth of his infidelity and the sincerity of his sorrow.

(9) In Judas' betrayal and death, the prophecy of Jeremiah is fulfilled. The "blood money" involved is used to pay for a burial place for an outcast or criminal. Again, Matthew's point here is that every detail of the passion narrative is foreshadowed in the ancient scriptures, the prophets and the oral tradition. In Jesus, the long history of God's dealings with the chosen people has come full circle when, in the person of the suffering servant, Israel's sins are taken away and placed upon the shoulders of their creator. We will never fully fathom the terror or the splendor of this mystery.

(10) In the dialogue between Jesus and Pilate, Matthew emphasizes the authenticity of Jesus' identity, his innocence and the injustice of his condemnation. In answer to Pilate's question, Jesus gives a response that forces the responsibility for his death back on those who perpetrate it. The name "Barabbas" literally means "son of the father" (*bar* corresponds to "son," *abbas* to father). Jesus is also "Son of the Father,"

and they paid it out for the *potter's* field
just as the *Lord* had *commanded* me."

(10) Now *Jesus* stood before the *governor*, who *questioned* him,
"Are you the *king* of the *Jews*?"
Jesus said, "You *say* so."
And when he was accused by the chief *priests* and *elders*,
he made no *answer*.
Then *Pilate* said to him,
"Do you not *hear* how many things they are *testifying*
against you?"
But he did not *answer* him one *word*,
so that the *governor* was greatly *amazed*.

Now on the occasion of the *feast*
the governor was accustomed to *release* to the crowd
one *prisoner* whom they *wished*.
And at *that* time they had a *notorious* prisoner called *Barabbas*.
So when they had *assembled*, Pilate said to them,
"Which *one* do you want me to *release* to you,
Barabbas, or Jesus called *Christ*?"
For he *knew* that it was out of *envy*
that they had handed him *over*.

While he was still seated on the *bench*,
his *wife* sent him a *message*,
"Have nothing to *do* with that righteous *man*.
I suffered *much* in a *dream* today because of him."

The chief priests and the elders *persuaded* the crowds
to ask for *Barabbas* but to *destroy* Jesus.
The governor said to them in reply,
"*Which* of the two do you want me to *release* to you?"
They answered, "*Barabbas*!"

Jesus' refusal to answer Pilate shows us that he has chosen not to defend himself and so is in charge of his own destiny. He is not proven guilty but chooses his own fate. How else could the scriptures be fulfilled?

Barabbas = buh-RAB-uhs

of course, and the point is that the people choose the wrong "son of the father" for release. The dream of Pilate's wife and her remark that Jesus is a "holy" man serve to emphasize further Jesus' innocence.

The figure of Pilate has fascinated commentators through the ages. He is clearly not presented as a villain or a ruthless tyrant. His awkward position, caught as he is in a political struggle as well as a theological one, reveals him to be a master of compromise. While there's no virtue in his posture, there seems to be no venom either. It is important for the gospel writers to show that

Jesus' own people are responsible for his death. As the prologue to John's gospel states, "He came to what was his own, but his own people did not accept him."

On the other hand, Pilate's refusal to take responsibility teaches us a great deal about how to be a Christian. Though he literally washes his hands of Jesus' death, he cannot escape the charge of refusing to protect an innocent person from unjust condemnation. Is such a crime any less heinous? Is it less sinful to walk away from injustice

than to perpetrate it? Can we claim to be disciples of Jesus and "wash our hands" of situations in which people are treated with indignity? The consequences of Pilate's refusal to get involved are shocking. Our own failure to act when we might have made a difference perpetuates Pilate's.

(11) The soldiers mock Jesus as yet another pathetically doomed revolutionary from the ranks of a conquered race. Rome occupied the land, enslaved the people and treated upstarts with great cruelty. Mockery is a customary response when a group thinks itself superior to all others. It continues

Pilate said to them,
  "Then what shall I do with *Jesus* called *Christ*?"
They all said,
  "Let *him* be *crucified*!"
But he said,
  "*Why*? What *evil* has he done?"
They only shouted the *louder*,
  "Let him be *crucified*!"

When Pilate *saw* that he was not *succeeding* at *all*,
  but that a *riot* was breaking out *instead*,
  he took *water* and washed his *hands* in the sight of the *crowd*,
  saying, "I am *innocent* of this man's *blood*.
Look to it *yourselves*."
And the *whole people* said in reply,
  "His blood be upon *us* and upon our *children*."
Then he released *Barabbas* to them,
  but after he had Jesus *scourged*,
  he handed him *over* to be *crucified*.

(11) Then the *soldiers* of the governor took Jesus
    inside the praetorium
  and gathered the whole *cohort* around him.
They stripped off his *clothes*
  and threw a scarlet *military* cloak about him.
Weaving a *crown* out of *thorns*, they placed it on his *head*,
  and a *reed* in his right *hand*.
And *kneeling* before him, they *mocked* him, saying,
  "*Hail*, King of the *Jews*!"
They *spat* upon him and took the *reed*
  and kept *striking* him on the *head*.
And when they had *mocked* him,
  they *stripped* him of the cloak,

Like the details in preparation for the Passover meal, the details here are all part of Matthew's demonstration of Jesus' passion as the fulfillment of scripture.

today wherever prejudice and bigotry appear. By bearing the insults of the Roman soldiers and the false charges of the Jewish authorities, Jesus shows us for all time the consequences of social injustice. As long as there is one person who is denied the dignity bestowed by a loving creator, the world will be unfit for the reign of God.

Notice the different motives for rejecting Jesus here. The Roman soldiers and Pilate regard him as a nuisance and reject him without regard for his innocence or guilt. But the Jewish authorities regard him

as a threat to their own influence over the people because he claims to be the Messiah, although he fulfills none of their expectations of the Messiah. Thus Jesus becomes a political pawn for both Roman imperial authority and Jewish leader, through which Pilate placates the Jewish leaders and the Jewish leaders raise their status in the eyes of the people. No matter how people are used as a means to a political end, the results are always tragic.

(12) Simon of Cyrene is pressed into service out of necessity. Jesus has endured so much at this point that he is simply too

weak to carry the cross. But this coming Friday we will hear John's account of the passion, and the gospel's author makes the point that Jesus carried the cross by himself. Such apparent inconsistencies teach us to read the word of God not as pure history but as a collection of many points of view. John's passion narrative makes it clear throughout that Jesus is divinity in human form, reigning from the cross. It would not suit John's argument to portray Jesus as in need of assistance. Matthew's point of view is different, as is Mark's, whose

dressed him in his *own* clothes,
and led him *off* to *crucify* him.

Cyrenian = sī-REE-nee-uhn

(12) As they were going out, they met a *Cyrenian* named *Simon*;
    this man they pressed into *service*
    to carry his *cross*.

Golgotha = GOL-guh-thuh

And when they came to a place called *Golgotha*
    —which means Place of the *Skull*—
    they gave Jesus *wine* to drink mixed with *gall*.
But when he had *tasted it*, he *refused* to drink.

(13) After they had *crucified* him,
    they divided his *garments* by casting *lots*;
    then they sat down and kept *watch* over him there.

And they placed over his *head* the written *charge* against him:
    This is *Jesus*, the King of the *Jews*.
Two *revolutionaries* were crucified *with* him,
    one on his *right* and the other on his *left*.

Those passing by *reviled* him, shaking their *heads* and saying,
    "*You* who would destroy the *temple* and *rebuild* it
        in three days,
    save *yourself*, if you are the Son of *God*,
    and come *down* from the cross!"

Likewise the chief *priests* with the *scribes* and *elders*
        mocked him and said,
    "He saved *others*; he cannot save *himself*.
So he is the *king* of Israel!
Let him come *down* from the cross *now*,
    and we will *believe* in him.
He trusted in *God*;
    let him *deliver* him now if he *wants* him.

narrative goes so far as to identify Simon as the father of Alexander and Rufus; Luke gives us the detail that Simon carried the cross and followed behind Jesus.

The drink of wine offered to Jesus was drugged with gall, a potion meant to deaden somewhat the pain of crucifixion. This was a common practice and an act of mercy on the part of more humane witnesses. Matthew makes the point that Jesus refused to drink it because he is resolved not to mitigate the suffering he chooses to endure for our sakes.

(13) Psalm 22 threads its way through the narrative from here on. It is the psalm most associated with Jesus' suffering and contains the desolate cry Jesus will utter toward the end, "My God, my God, why have you forsaken me?" It tells the story of God's chosen one being humiliated and persecuted for the sins of the people, and includes references to lots being cast for his clothing and the taunt that he relied on God, who has now apparently abandoned him. The gospel writers show the fulfillment of all these references in Jesus, who is therefore clearly demonstrated to be God's chosen one.

(14) The darkness, the torn temple curtain, the earthquake and appearance of the dead are all signs that heighten the cosmic dimensions of Jesus' death. Matthew's purpose here, as always, is to show that the world is changed forever. The old order of things has passed away, and a new world has been born. The torn curtain is an especially rich sign: The curtain that separated the Holy of Holies in the temple from all but the high priest is rent from top to bottom. The Holy of Holies was the earthly dwelling of the spirit of God. Jesus' appearance on

For he said, '*I* am the Son of *God.*'"
The *revolutionaries* who were *crucified* with him
    also kept abusing him in the *same way.*

(14) From noon *onward*, *darkness* came over the whole *land*
    until *three* in the *afternoon.*
And about three o'clock Jesus *cried out* in a loud *voice*,
    "*Eli, Eli, lema sabachthani*?"
    which means, "My *God*, my *God*, *why* have you *forsaken* me?"
Some of the *bystanders* who heard it said,
    "This one is calling for *Elijah.*"
Immediately one of them ran to get a *sponge*;
    he soaked it in *wine*, and putting it on a *reed*,
    gave it to him to *drink.*
But the *rest* said,
    "*Wait*, let us see if Elijah comes to *save* him."
But Jesus cried out *again* in a loud voice,
    and gave up his *spirit.*

[Here all kneel and pause for a short time.]

And *behold*, the veil of the *sanctuary*
    was *torn in two* from *top* to *bottom.*
The *earth* quaked, *rocks* were split, *tombs* were opened,
    and the bodies of many *saints* who had fallen *asleep*
        were *raised.*
And coming forth from their *tombs* after his *resurrection*,
    they entered the holy *city* and appeared to *many.*

The *centurion* and the men with him who were
        keeping *watch* over Jesus
    feared *greatly* when they saw the earthquake
    and all that was happening, and they said,
    "*Truly*, this *was* the Son of God!"

Eli, Eli, lema sabachthani = ay-LEE, ay-LEE, luh-MAH sah-bahk-TAH-nee
Though there are many references to Psalm 22 in the passion narrative, this one is an explicit quotation—from the original language and translated by Matthew. The reader must pronounce the foreign words with absolute clarity and conviction. Any uncertainty or stumbling here will severely compromise the proclamation.

The catastrophes recall earlier predictions of signs of the end of time. They are dramatic evidence that Jesus' death has brought about the beginning of the end of the old order and has inaugurated the new.

centurion = sen-TOOR-ee-uhn

---

earth overcomes the separation between God and humanity. In Jesus we see God's face revealed—not in its divine glory, of course, but in its nature as loving, compassionate, life-giving and victorious over death.

It is interesting that none of Jesus' own people give voice to a recognition of what all these dramatic signs mean, but the pagan centurion and his men, upon seeing all that was happening, are terror-stricken and say, "This was the Son of God!" Is Matthew making the point that those who should have recognized Jesus do not, but

those whose minds are less filled with pre-conceptions do? If so, what a powerful lesson for us! Over and over again we are reminded that Jesus cannot be locked into a formula or in any way limited. Christians will never have the comfort of a faith that is fully delineated in a catechism or totally captured in dogmatic formulas. Every Christian and every Christian church can profit from Matthew's reminder that, at the foot of the cross, it was the pagan who saw clearly what the religious zealots did not.

(15) The presence of the women at the foot of the cross is an embodiment of steadfast love at its most durable, able to withstand all adversity and the most wrenching tragedy. Their presence makes the absence of the Twelve all the more shocking, demonstrating again the futility of human expectations. We might expect the Twelve (or at least the Eleven) to be stalwart, but we are shown a very different group of devotees. It is an image we should carry forward into our daily experience of Christian devotion and our evaluation of it.

Magdalene = MAG-duh-luhn

Zebedee = ZEB-uh-dee

Arimathea = ayr-ih-muh-THEE-uh

(15) There were many *women* there, looking on from a *distance*,
    who had *followed* Jesus from *Galilee, ministering* to him.
Among them were Mary *Magdalene* and Mary
        the mother of *James* and Joseph,
    and the mother of the sons of *Zebedee*.

When it was *evening*,
    there came a *rich* man from *Arimathea* named *Joseph*,
    who was himself a *disciple* of Jesus.
He went to *Pilate* and asked for the *body* of Jesus;
    then Pilate ordered it to be handed *over*.
Taking the body, Joseph wrapped it in clean *linen*
    and laid it in his new *tomb* that he had hewn in the *rock*.
Then he rolled a huge *stone* across the *entrance* to the tomb
        and *departed*.
But Mary *Magdalene* and the *other* Mary
    remained sitting there, facing the *tomb*.

The many details regarding the security of the tomb heighten the miracle of the resurrection. Matthew may be trying to forestall claims that the disciples stole Jesus' lifeless body away, or he may be contesting rumors still in circulation at the time the gospel was being written.

(16) The next *day*, the one following the day of *preparation*,
    the chief priests and the Pharisees
    gathered before *Pilate* and said,
    "Sir, we remember that this *impostor* while still *alive* said,
    'After *three days* I will be *raised up*.'
Give *orders*, then, that the grave be *secured* until the third day,
    lest his *disciples* come and *steal* him and say to the people,
    'He has been *raised* from the *dead*.'
This *last* imposture would be worse than the *first*."
Pilate said to them,
    "The guard is *yours*;
    go, secure it as best you *can*."
So they went and *secured* the tomb
    by fixing a *seal* to the *stone* and setting the *guard*.

[Shorter: Matthew 27:11–54]

A silent and eerie picture ends the narrative. The huge stone is in place covering the tomb where Jesus lies, the women are in attendance, and a guard has been assigned to watch. The sense of anticipation is palpable. A quiet ending and an extended moment of absolute silence should prolong the feeling.

The passion of Jesus is framed by acts of pure love offered by women. A woman anoints Jesus' feet with precious perfume at Bethany—an act recognized by Jesus as a prophecy of his death—and a woman appears again at the tomb when the prophecy has come to pass.

(16) In this final paragraph, Matthew takes care to forestall any notion that Jesus did not rise from the dead but was instead stolen from his tomb by his disciples. No doubt such theories were still in circulation as Matthew crafted his account of these

events, and he is at pains to refute them. Indeed, Matthew's concern about denials of the resurrection can serve as a guide to understanding his entire approach to Jesus' suffering and death. Like the accounts of the other evangelists, Matthew's account has a purpose and is more like a homily than a mere historical record. Events are told in such as way as to emphasize a particular point of view, which in Matthew's case is to show that Jesus' life, death and resurrection are all in fulfillment of the ancient scriptures. Matthew would have us see in Jesus the fulfillment the ancient prophecies and

promises, so that we could then proclaim with the centurion—in the *present* tense— "Clearly, this *is* the Son of God!"

HOLY THURSDAY: EVENING MASS OF THE LORD'S SUPPER

Lectionary #39

READING I Exodus 12:1–8, 11–14

A reading from the book of Exodus

The LORD said to *Moses* and *Aaron* in the land of *Egypt*,
"*This* month shall stand at the *head* of your *calendar*;
   you shall reckon it the *first* month of the *year*.
Tell the whole *community* of Israel:
   On the *tenth* of this month every one of your *families*
      must procure for itself a *lamb*, one *apiece* for each *household*.
If a family is too *small* for a whole *lamb*,
   it shall join the nearest *household* in procuring one
   and shall *share* in the lamb
   in proportion to the number of *persons* who *partake* of it.

"The lamb must be a *year-old male* and without *blemish*.
You may take it from either the *sheep* or the *goats*.
You shall *keep* it until the *fourteenth* day of this month,
   and *then*, with the whole *assembly* of Israel *present*,
   it shall be *slaughtered* during the evening *twilight*.
They shall take some of its *blood*
   and apply it to the two *doorposts* and the *lintel*
   of every house in which they *partake* of the lamb.
That same *night* they shall *eat* its roasted *flesh*
   with unleavened *bread* and bitter *herbs*.

A solemn proclamation from the Lord God begins this evening's liturgy of the word and the great Paschal Triduum. The solemnity of solemnities has begun. From the original celebration of Passover, when the Lord liberated Israel from captivity, we progress over the next three days to the fulfillment of Passover, when the risen Christ liberates us from sin and death. Let the weight of this reading shine through your proclamation.

READING I The holiest days of the liturgical year begin with this evening's celebration of the eucharist. And the three days we call the Triduum (Holy Thursday evening through Easter Sunday evening) are not three celebrations but one: the Passover of the Lord. Notice that all three readings this evening describe a communal gathering around a supper table. The image of a banquet leads us from Holy Thursday to the wedding banquet of the risen Lamb in heaven, the eternal Easter. For Christians, the experience of the shared meal is always sacred.

The first reading is a detailed description of the ritual Passover seder meal commemorating Israel's escape from slavery in Egypt. Notice that it is a family meal. So important is the family dimension of the seder that smaller families who cannot afford or consume a whole lamb are to join with their neighbors for the feast. What began in an earlier age as a simple sacrifice takes on the important dimension of participation, signified by eating the sacrificial offering in a communal setting. It is not too great a leap from the Passover seder to the eucharistic meal that is the summit and source of our life.

The intricate details of the reading are not as important as the significance of the overall event. It is obviously a form of the meal that Jesus shared with his disciples on the night before he died and should allow us to experience a gratifying link with our ancient past.

The details of how the Passover meal is eaten reveal the urgency of the situation. The pilgrim people have to be ready for travel. Having one's "loins girt" means being dressed for physical labor. We are not passive observers; we participate in these marvelous deeds.

"*This* is how you are to *eat* it:
  with your *loins* girt, *sandals* on your *feet* and your *staff*
    in hand,
  you shall eat like those who are in *flight*.
It is the *Passover* of the LORD.

"For on this *same* night I will go through *Egypt*,
  striking *down* every *firstborn* of the land, both *man* and *beast*,
  and executing *judgment* on all the *gods* of Egypt—*I*, the LORD!

"But the *blood* will mark the houses where *you* are.
Seeing the blood, I will *pass over* you;
  thus, when I strike the land of *Egypt*,
  no destructive blow will come upon *you*.

"*This* day shall be a memorial *feast* for you,
  which all your *generations* shall *celebrate*
  with *pilgrimage* to the LORD, as a perpetual *institution*."

READING II   1 Corinthians 11:23–26

A reading from the first letter of Saint Paul to the Corinthians

Brothers and sisters:
I received from the *Lord* what I also handed on to *you*,
  that the Lord *Jesus*, on the night he was *handed over*,
  took *bread*, and, after he had given *thanks*,
  broke it and said, "This is my *body* that is for *you*.
Do this in *remembrance* of me."

In the same way also the *cup*, after supper, saying,
  "This *cup* is the *new* covenant in my *blood*.

Some of the most important pieces of our history and tradition are expressed in brief statements. This reading is one of them, and so it must be proclaimed with great deliberation.

In proclaiming this text, strive to create an atmosphere of solemn significance. Ceremonies that are made holy by time and devout practice almost compel our attention as we prepare to carry out the Lord's command to celebrate the eucharistic meal as a perpetual memorial of his sacrificial love for us.

READING II Here we have the eucharistic tradition in Paul's words. How rich is this word "tradition," from the Latin *tradere.* It means "to hand on" or "to

hand over"; Paul uses it in both senses here. Paul hands on to us the tradition of what Jesus did at the Last Supper. Jesus used the ancient ceremony that was "handed on" through his Jewish tradition, and he did all this on the night that he was "handed over" by Judas. A good lector ought to be aware of how the reading turns on the meaning and intricate use of "tradition."

Paul's emphasis is not on what Jesus did, but on what the assembled community of the church does when it gathers in his

memory. Difficulties among the Corinthians Paul addressed had led to rival factions and the exclusion of the poor from the eucharistic meal in that place. Paul is reminding the church at Corinth that the purpose of this holy meal is to proclaim the Lord's death until the end of time, a duty that must never exclude others or be confused with gatherings of lesser significance.

In this brief reading you use Paul's words to remind the members of your assembly what they are about to do in the Holy Thursday celebration. You remind them of its solemnity and its meaning. Whenever we

Do this, as often as you *drink* it, in *remembrance* of me."
For as often as you eat this *bread* and drink the *cup*,
    you proclaim the *death* of the Lord until he *comes*.

Emphasize this final sentence. Consider its meaning so that your proclamation will impress its significance upon the assembly.

GOSPEL   John 13:1–15

A reading from the holy gospel according to John

Before the feast of *Passover*, Jesus *knew* that his *hour* had *come*
    to pass from *this* world to the *Father*.
He *loved* his own in the world and he loved them to the *end*.

The *devil* had already induced *Judas*, son of Simon the *Iscariot*,
        to hand him *over*.
So, during *supper*,
    fully *aware* that the Father had put everything into his *power*
    and that he had *come* from God and was *returning* to God,
    he *rose* from supper and took off his outer *garments*.
He took a *towel* and tied it around his *waist*.
Then he poured *water* into a *basin*
    and began to *wash* the disciples' *feet*
    and *dry* them with the *towel* around his *waist*.

He came to Simon *Peter*, who said to him,
    "*Master*, are you going to wash my *feet*?"
Jesus *answered* and said to him,
    "What I am *doing*, you do not *understand* now,
    but you *will* understand *later*."
Peter said to him, "You will *never* wash *my* feet."
Jesus answered him,
    "Unless I *wash* you, you will have no *inheritance* with me."

On the feast of Passover, the Lord Jesus passes over from death to life. Let the assembly hear John's play on the word.

There is another play on words here: Judas hands Jesus over to betrayal, and Jesus hands over his life so that he can hand everything back to the Father, who handed everything over to him. Iscariot = is-KAYR-ee-uht

Let the dialogue be a narrative, not a reenactment.

gather for the eucharist we proclaim the Lord's death until he comes again in glory.

GOSPEL It may strike us as strange that our celebration of Holy Thursday does not include a gospel account of Jesus' words "Take and eat; take and drink." Matthew, Mark and Luke all record these words. But today we read from the gospel of John, which does not record the "words of institution," although the events described here clearly occur within the context of the Passover seder.

John's account of the Last Supper, however, gives us something just as precious as Jesus' words. The evangelist records the dramatic and moving scene of Jesus washing the feet of his disciples. In doing so, John gives us profound insight into the meaning and consequence of the eucharist. We can put it quite plainly: Our celebration of the eucharist requires that we wash one another's feet, serve one another, revere Christ present in one another. It means that we become great only by serving all the

rest. To refuse to serve is to refuse salvation. In the second reading, Paul gave us the words of Christ's sacrificial love. In John's gospel we hear the words that tell us what it means to accept that love.

The washing of the feet is made all the more striking by the presence of Judas, the betrayer. He is not excluded from the washing, even though Jesus refers to him as unclean. And since the washing of feet symbolizes the ultimate act of service, it reveals an even deeper level of the meaning of the eucharist: No one—not even a traitor—is undeserving of our loving service.

Simon Peter said to him,
  "*Master*, then not only my *feet*, but my *hands*
    and *head* as *well*."
Jesus said to him,
  "Whoever has *bathed* has no *need*
    except to have his *feet* washed,
  for he is clean all *over*;
  so *you* are clean, but not *all*."
For he knew who would *betray* him;
  for *this* reason, he said, "Not *all* of you are clean."

So when he had washed their *feet*
  and put his *garments* back on and reclined at *table* again,
  he said to them, "Do you *realize* what I have *done* for you?
You call me '*teacher*' and '*master*,' and rightly *so*, for indeed I *am*.
If *I*, therefore, the *master* and *teacher*, have washed *your* feet,
  you ought to wash one *another's* feet.
I have given you a *model* to follow,
  so that as *I* have done for *you*, you should *also* do.

The secret of effective proclamation here is to get the right emphasis on the pronouns. Practice diligently so that Jesus' definition of authentic ministry makes an impression on your hearers.

Peter's refusal to allow Jesus to wash his feet indicates two things: Peter still does not fully understand the kind of Messiah Jesus is, nor does he understand the full implication of the meal he is sharing with Jesus. And how could he? That understanding will come fully only with the resurrection. Note well, though, that Peter understands enough to know that he wants to be part of Jesus' mission and plan. He may not understand it fully, but he trusts Jesus enough to submit his doubts and questions to the will of his master. How beautifully Peter shows us our own faith experience: We do not fully understand either, but faith in the person of Jesus enables us to follow his example and submit to his teaching.

GOOD FRIDAY: CELEBRATION OF THE LORD'S PASSION

Lectionary #40

READING I   Isaiah 52:13—53:12

A reading from the book of the prophet Isaiah

The reading begins on a bright note, despite the grotesque images that follow.

See, my *servant* shall *prosper*,
   he shall be raised *high* and greatly *exalted*.
Even as many were *amazed* at him—
   so *marred* was his *look* beyond human *semblance*
   and his *appearance* beyond that of the sons of *man*—
so shall he *startle* many *nations*,
   because of him *kings* shall stand *speechless*;
for those who have not been *told* shall *see*,
   those who have not *heard* shall *ponder* it.

Rhetorical questions are powerful. They help the assembly "tune in" again. Make the most of them.

Who would *believe* what we have *heard*?
   To *whom* has the arm of the LORD been revealed?
He grew up like a *sapling* before him,
   like a *shoot* from the parched *earth*;
there was in him no *stately* bearing to make us *look* at him,
   nor *appearance* that would *attract* us to him.
He was *spurned* and *avoided* by people,
   a man of *suffering*, accustomed to *infirmity*,
one of those from whom people *hide* their *faces*,
   spurned, and we held him in no *esteem*.

At this point we move from simple narrative to an examination of the meaning underlying it. You are explaining the suffering servant's mission.

Yet it was our *infirmities* that he bore,
   our sufferings that he *endured*,
while we thought of him as *stricken*,
   as one *smitten by* God and *afflicted*.

READING I | This is the fourth and most significant of the four "suffering servant songs" from the book of Isaiah. The liturgy applies the text and the term "suffering servant" to Jesus and his redemptive mission. Originally, of course, the application of the term was to the whole people of Israel. The servant is really God's servants, and the language of poetry has collected the people of God into one figure. Even the most basic awareness of the history (both ancient and modern) of the Jewish people enables us to hear the suffering servant songs with heartrending poignancy.

It is not certain whether Jesus actually applied this text to himself, but it has been applied to him in the liturgy since the earliest Christian writers began to interpret his life, mission, passion and death. He is seen as the culmination of the suffering servant theme, fulfilling the Isaian prophecy in every detail. No other scriptural text is more suitable for the Good Friday liturgy.

One implicit idea must be communicated in the proclamation: Obedience is the suffering servant's greatest virtue and the ultimate reason why the servant triumphs and wins salvation. It is obedience to God that ennobles the servant's agony and wins the allegiance and contrition of all who witness the servant's pain. The second reading today makes this point clearly: Even though Jesus was God's own Son, he became obedient because of what he suffered. The idea that the servant became obedient unto death already makes the servant a heroic figure. The idea that the servant's death gives life to others makes the servant even more than a hero: The servant becomes a personification of God's creative and redemptive love, which is precisely who Jesus is, of course.

But he was *pierced* for *our* offenses,
    crushed for *our* sins;
upon him was the *chastisement* that makes us *whole*,
    by his *stripes* we were *healed*.

We had all gone *astray* like *sheep*,
    each following his *own* way;
but the LORD laid upon *him*
    the guilt of us *all*.

Though he was harshly *treated*, he *submitted*
    and opened not his *mouth*;
like a *lamb* led to the *slaughter*
    or a *sheep* before the *shearers*,
    he was *silent* and opened not his *mouth*.

Oppressed and *condemned*, he was taken *away*,
    and who would have thought any *more* of his *destiny*?
When he was *cut off* from the land of the *living*,
    and *smitten* for the sin of his *people*,
a *grave* was assigned him among the *wicked*
    and a *burial* place with *evildoers*,
though he had done no *wrong*
    nor spoken any *falsehood*.
But the LORD was pleased
    to *crush* him in *infirmity*.

If he gives his *life* as an *offering* for *sin*,
    he shall see his *descendants* in a *long* life,
    and the will of the LORD shall be *accomplished* through him.

Because of his *affliction*
    he shall see the *light*
    in *fullness* of days;

Patience and quiet endurance are not the same as submissiveness. This should sound strong, not pitiful or weak.

There must be a significant pause here. Let the horror of it sink in.

Begin anew with a fresh tone of voice, for this is the good news.

This is a lengthy reading, or, more properly, a lengthy poem. The rich images build throughout the passage until we are caught up in a morass of mixed emotions. We are filled with admiration for the servant's humility and meekness. We are suffused with guilt and gratitude for the servant's willingness to suffer so that we could be freed from sin and justified in the sight of God. We are reminded of countless thousands of martyrs who have suffered for their beliefs, been persecuted for their skin color, race, creed, sex, sexual orientation or social status. And, sadly, we are reminded that such persecution continues even in our own day, which makes the text as appropriate today as it was when it was written. The suffering and death of those whom the world persecutes is precious in God's sight and will be vindicated.

Jesus, the suffering servant, can suffer no more, having triumphed over death. But his kingdom on earth has not yet come to perfection, and he is still put to death in the suffering members of his mystical body. That tells us two things. First, our suffering has meaning and significance; we are not merely victims of cruel fate. Second, we know that the ultimate victory is ours, won for us by a loving redeemer. Nothing can separate us from the love of Christ.

A worthy proclamation of this moving text requires exceptional skill, careful preparation and a heart full of compassion.

READING II The author of the letter to the Hebrews is writing to comfort Jewish Christians who have been alienated from the Jewish tradition because of their faith in Jesus. This part of the letter assures them that Jesus is the perfect high priest, whose perfect and unique sacrifice

through his *suffering*, my servant shall justify *many*,
   and their *guilt* he shall *bear*.

Therefore I will give him his *portion* among the *great*,
   and he shall divide the *spoils* with the *mighty*,
because he *surrendered* himself to *death*
   and was counted among the *wicked*;
and he shall *take away* the sins of *many*,
   and win *pardon* for their *offenses*.

Utter confidence should fill these final lines. Allow for a significant pause before saying "The word of the Lord."

READING II   Hebrews 4:14–16; 5:7–9

A reading from the letter to the Hebrews

Brothers and sisters:
Since we have a great *high* priest who has passed
   through the *heavens*,
   Jesus, the Son of *God*,
   let us hold *fast* to our *confession*.
For we do *not* have a high priest
   who is unable to *sympathize* with our *weaknesses*,
   but one who has *similarly* been tested in every *way*,
   yet without *sin*.
So let us *confidently* approach the throne of *grace*
   to receive *mercy* and to find *grace* for timely *help*.

In the days when Christ was in the *flesh*,
   he offered *prayers* and *supplications* with loud *cries* and *tears*
   to the one who was able to *save* him from *death*,
   and he was *heard* because of his *reverence*.

There is more than a hint of pleading here: "Don't be afraid; approach God with bold confidence!"

Now you explain how Jesus accomplished what he did. It is a model for us.

---

has brought all others to fulfillment. There is no further need for sacrificial victims to take away our sins and justify us in the sight of God. Jesus has done that once and for all. The eucharist we celebrate continues Christ's sacrifice, a perfect sacrifice offered by a high priest who identifies completely with our weakness.

The effect of hearing this text on Good Friday is that we understand more clearly the way Jesus functions as the source of eternal salvation. Jesus is both divine and human, and is therefore the perfect mediator. He shares our humanity and shares with us his

divinity. As God and human, Jesus has made us one with himself in reconciling love.

Jesus knows our temptations—he underwent them. He knows our suffering— he taught us obedience by enduring them. This is why we can approach the throne of grace with utter confidence. We know we will be heard and understood by the one who has experienced all that we have. This is the great good news: God is revealed to us in Jesus, whom we know intimately. There is no longer any need to appease God. Our sacrificial offerings express our loving gratitude.

Oddly, we have a hard time believing that the Good News is that simple or that wonderful. And yet it is. We have a great high priest who has passed through the heavens: Jesus, the Son of God, who has shown us that God is love.

PASSION   It is very rare these days that the accounts of the passion on Palm Sunday and Good Friday are proclaimed by one reader. Everyone seems to sense the efficacy of employing several readers (at least three), not only because the text is long but because the narrative seems

Son though he *was*, he learned *obedience* from what he *suffered*;
and when he was made *perfect*,
he became the *source* of eternal *salvation* for all who
obey him.

PASSION   John 18:1—19:42

The Passion of our Lord Jesus Christ according to John

(1) *Jesus* went out with his *disciples* across the Kidron *valley*
to where there was a *garden*,
into which he and his disciples *entered*.
Judas his *betrayer also* knew the place,
because Jesus had *often* met there with his *disciples*.
So *Judas* got a band of *soldiers* and *guards*
from the chief *priests* and the *Pharisees*
and *went* there with *lanterns*, *torches*, and *weapons*.

Jesus, knowing *everything* that was going to *happen* to him,
went out and said to them, "Whom are you *looking* for?"
They answered him, "*Jesus* the *Nazarene*."
He said to them, "*I AM*."
Judas his *betrayer* was *also* with them.
When he said to them, "*I AM*,"
they turned *away* and fell to the *ground*.
So he *again* asked them,
"Whom are you *looking* for?"
They said, "*Jesus* the *Nazarene*."
Jesus answered,
"I *told* you that *I AM*.

Kidron = KID-ruhn
John's narrative moves from place to place, progressing inexorably from the garden to Golgotha. In each location there is an important revelation, a dynamic interplay of characters, a revelation and a kind of resolution. Then the action moves on. Many commentators have made mention of the dramatic action in John's narrative. The various stages of this action must be set off by clear transitions (pauses, tones of voice, a different proclaimer, and so on).
Nazarene = naz-uh-REEN

to demand such a proclamation to bring it to life. This is not to say, however, that a full-scale reenactment or a dramatic interpretation of the passion is to be preferred over a proclamation. The liturgy does not lend itself to anything approaching theatrical presentation, which can be quite effective on stage (if superbly done). No, the liturgy is ritual behavior and requires the kind of restraint and dignity that respects the solemnity and weight of its content and purpose. The liturgy never reenacts its subject matter. It memorializes, commemorates and recalls the paschal mystery. It does not re-create what has

already been accomplished once and for all. Those who take creative approaches to the proclamation of the passion narratives must keep in mind that they are presenting precisely that, a narrative, not a script. In an age awash in cinematic realism, the kind of heightened solemnity demanded by the liturgy may seem less immediate and more formal. Nevertheless, it must be maintained if we are to avoid trivializing its subject matter.

Perhaps the form of proclamation most true to liturgical tradition is the singing or chanting of the passion by three cantors,

one taking the voice of the gospel writer, one the voice of all speakers except Jesus, and one the voice of Jesus. The solemnization of the passion achieved with this kind of proclamation can be quite moving.

In recent years the members of the assembly have been provided copies of the text of the passion to allow them to read aloud the words of the crowds. While this practice may seem to accomplish a higher degree of participation, it also requires the members of the assembly to follow along with the proclaimers (to be ready for their "part"), which prevents them from fully

So if you are looking for *me*, let *these* men go."
This was to *fulfill* what he had said,
  "I have not lost *any* of those you *gave* me."

Malchus = MAL-kuhs

(2) Then Simon *Peter*, who had a *sword*, drew it,
  struck the *high* priest's *slave*, and cut off his right *ear*.
The slave's *name* was *Malchus*.
Jesus said to Peter,
  "Put your *sword* into its *scabbard*.
Shall I not drink the *cup* that the Father *gave* me?"

So the band of *soldiers*, the *tribune*, and the Jewish *guards*
    seized Jesus,
  bound him, and brought him to *Annas* first.

The action moves to the residence of
Annas, then on to a meeting with the high
priest, Caiaphas.
Annas = AN-uhs
Caiaphas = KAY-uh-fuhs

He was the father-in-law of *Caiaphas*,
  who was *high* priest that year.
It was *Caiaphas* who had *counseled* the Jews
    that it was *better* that *one* man should die
      rather than the *people*.

(3) Simon Peter and *another* disciple *followed* Jesus.
Now the *other* disciple was *known* to the high priest,
  and he entered the *courtyard* of the high priest with *Jesus*.
But *Peter* stood at the gate *outside*.
So the *other* disciple, the acquaintance of the *high* priest,
  went out and spoke to the *gatekeeper* and brought Peter *in*.
Then the *maid* who was the gatekeeper said to Peter,
  "You are not one of this man's *disciples*, are you?"
He said, "I am *not*."
Now the *slaves* and the *guards* were standing
    around a charcoal *fire*
  that they had made, because it was *cold*,
  and were *warming* themselves.
Peter was *also* standing there keeping warm.

**Notice that the denials of Peter are
separated by the interrogation of Jesus
by the high priest. Peter is in the shadows
listening to Jesus testify to his public
teaching. The irony is compelling.**

---

attending to the proclamation. The benefits of this practice should not be presumed but carefully evaluated in the light of fundamental liturgical and pastoral principles.

Whatever practice is observed in your community, it should try to meet the challenge of a long proclamation (potentially tedious if not done well) and avoid the excesses of a presentation so elaborate or literal that the assembly is preoccupied with the manner of proclamation at the expense of the message.

The story of Christ's passion and death is told in more or less straightforward narrative by all four evangelists. Over the course of the three years of the Sunday lectionary, we read Matthew, Mark and Luke on Passion Sunday. John's account is read every year on Good Friday. It is important to realize that each of the four writers had more in mind than a literal account of the events. Each had a particular point of view and purpose, and so the accounts differ from each other. For this reason, it is important to choose a mode of proclamation that serves

the faith-building insight offered rather than the events related.

Last Sunday we heard Matthew's passion narrative, which emphasizes that Jesus fulfills all the prophecies about the Messiah who would deliver God's people from exile and restore them to God's favor forever. For Matthew, Jesus is the suffering servant foretold in Isaiah, the new Moses who delivers God's law in perfect form, the great and mighty king whom the prophets proclaimed as liberator of the chosen people.

John's passion narrative portrays Jesus in a different light. As always in John, Jesus

There is a danger here of making Jesus sound defensive. He makes no defense; he simply tells the truth, quietly, strongly, gently.

(4) The *high* priest *questioned* Jesus
  about his *disciples* and about his *doctrine*.
Jesus *answered* him,
  "I have spoken *publicly* to the world.
I have always taught in a *synagogue*
  or in the *temple* area where all the Jews *gather*,
  and in *secret* I have said *nothing*. Why ask *me*?
Ask those who *heard* me what I said to them.
They *know* what I said."

When he had said this,
  one of the temple *guards* standing there *struck* Jesus and said,
  "Is this the way you answer the *high* priest?"
Jesus answered him,
  "If I have spoken *wrongly*, *testify* to the wrong;
  but if I have spoken *rightly*, why do you *strike* me?"
Then *Annas* sent him *bound* to *Caiaphas* the *high* priest.

Now Simon Peter was *standing* there keeping *warm*.
And they *said* to him,
  "You are not one of his *disciples*, are you?"
He *denied* it and said,
  "I am *not*."
One of the *slaves* of the high priest,
  a *relative* of the one whose *ear* Peter had cut off, said,
  "Didn't I see you in the *garden* with him?"
Again Peter denied it.
And *immediately* the *cock* crowed.

Now the action moves to the praetorium and thus into the world of the Gentiles. Here John reveals the prediction and fulfillment of the kind of death Jesus will die.

(5) Then they brought Jesus from *Caiaphas* to the *praetorium*.
It was *morning*.
And they *themselves* did not *enter* the praetorium,
  in order not to be *defiled* so that they could eat the *Passover*.

---

is the eternal Word, the divine creator of the universe, who appeared in the flesh to redeem us in love. John clearly plays down the physical sufferings of Jesus in order to emphasize his divine nature, origin and purpose. The entire gospel of John is preoccupied with Jesus as king and priest, which sets it apart from the other three gospels.

You will notice as you read John's account that Jesus is much more in control of the situation than in the other three passion narratives, even (and perhaps especially) when he would seem by human estimation to be most vulnerable. Within the

first few sentences of John's passion narrative we are reminded that *Jesus is aware of all that will happen to him.* There are no surprises, and, indeed, Jesus directly or indirectly guides the course of events from his arrest to his crucifixion. Let this awareness guide you as you proclaim the text.

To some, Jesus seems less accessible, more distant, in John than in Matthew, Mark or Luke. And yet it is John who reveals more directly than the others that Jesus is the Father's love made flesh, a love that is noble and ennobling, exalted but intimate, eternal but expressed with deep human emotion.

(1) It is remarkable that such an impressive contingent appears to arrest Jesus. There is a cohort of soldiers as well as temple police, armed with weapons and carrying lanterns and torches. Why is such an army necessary to apprehend an itinerant preacher who has no history of violence and no band of fighters to protect him? At least one answer is that John intends to show that no force, however great, can prevail against the Son of God. The inequity of the situation is almost ridiculous but for the larger point being made. One word from Jesus and the assembled forces retreat and

So *Pilate* came out to them and said,
    "What *charge* do you bring against this man?"
They answered and said to him,
    "If he were not a *criminal*,
    we would not have handed him *over* to you."
At *this*, Pilate said to them,
    "Take him *yourselves*, and judge him according to *your* law."
The Jews answered him,
    "We do not have the *right* to execute anyone, "
    in order that the *word* of Jesus might be *fulfilled*
    that he said indicating the kind of *death* he would die.

So *Pilate* went back into the *praetorium*
    and *summoned* Jesus and said to him,
    "Are *you* the King of the *Jews*?"
Jesus *answered*,
    "Do you say this on your *own*
    or have others *told* you about me?"
Pilate answered,
    "*I* am not a Jew, am I?
Your own *nation* and the chief *priests* handed you over to me.
What have you *done*?"
Jesus answered,
    "*My* kingdom does not belong to *this* world.
If my kingdom *did* belong to this world,
    my *attendants* would be *fighting*
    to keep me from being handed *over* to the *Jews*.
But as it *is*, my kingdom is not *here*."
So Pilate said to him,
    "Then you *are* a king?"
Jesus answered,
    "You *say* I am a king.

The questioning of Jesus by Pilate must be handled with great care. Presume that Pilate is genuinely curious and that Jesus is sincerely trying to explain the sense in which he is, indeed, a king. If a blatant contest of wills is communicated, Pilate's later discomfort will not seem believable.

fall to the ground. The words Jesus speaks clearly echo the great "I AM" from Exodus, God's response to Moses' question "Who should I say has sent me?" The army that has come to arrest a troublemaker finds itself face to face with divinity. Their response testifies to Jesus' true identity.

Notice, too, that Jesus is in charge, as he will be throughout his trial. He has the first and the last words, indeed the only words, except for the responses to his questions. And the scene of his arrest ends with the order he gives: "Let these men go." The

order is obeyed, as it must be, to fulfill his own prophecy: "I have not lost any of those you gave me." In John's gospel the figure of Jesus is authoritative. He is not only the central figure, he is the one who directs all that happens to him. That calmly assertive authority must be communicated in the proclamation of John's passion narrative.

(2) Peter's impulsive move to protect Jesus gets a response that reminds us of another time when Peter acts without understanding. Earlier in the gospel, Peter reproaches Jesus after hearing him speak of his approaching suffering and death.

"Lord," he says, "do not say this; such a thing must not be." And Jesus responds, "Away from me! You are thinking in human terms rather than God's." Here, too, Jesus must remind Peter that God's plan is different from what anyone expected. And why is there no retaliation from the arresting cohort? Because Jesus, not the soldiers, is directing matters here.

Another point is being made here: By severing the ear of the high priest's servant, Peter has symbolically rendered the high priest himself unfit for office according to

For this I was *born* and for this I came into the *world*,
  to testify to the *truth*.
Everyone who belongs to the *truth listens* to my voice."
Pilate said to him, "What *is* truth?"

(6) When he had said this,
  he *again* went out to the *Jews* and said to them,
  "I find no *guilt* in him.
But you have a *custom* that I release one *prisoner*
    to you at *Passover*.
Do you want me to release to you the King of the *Jews*?"
They cried out again,
  "Not *this* one but *Barabbas*!"
Now *Barabbas* was a *revolutionary*.

(7) Then Pilate took Jesus and had him *scourged*.
And the *soldiers* wove a *crown* out of *thorns*
    and placed it on his *head*,
  and *clothed* him in a purple *cloak*,
  and they came to him and said,
  "*Hail*, King of the *Jews*!"
And they *struck* him repeatedly.

Once *more* Pilate went out and said to them,
  "*Look*, I am bringing him *out* to you,
  so that you may *know* that I find no *guilt* in him."
So Jesus came *out*,
  wearing the crown of *thorns* and the purple *cloak*.
And he said to them, "*Behold*, the man!"

When the chief *priests* and the *guards saw* him they cried out,
  "*Crucify* him, *crucify* him!"
Pilate said to them,
  "Take him *yourselves* and crucify him.

Pilate finds no reason to put Jesus to death. We must remember that, for it is a statement of his innocence. Pilate tries to placate the crowd by having Jesus scourged, but it is not enough.

Barabbas = buh-RAB-uhs

ancient Jewish law. The evangelist is saying in effect that the old law is passing away, and a new order is being established.

(3) It is a mistake to oversimplify Peter's denial as presented by John. He does deny the Lord, just as Jesus predicted he would. But John points out that Peter (in company with another disciple) followed Jesus closely when he was taken to trial. Later in the narrative we are reminded that Simon Peter is present throughout the questioning in the high priest's courtyard. Why is he there, so dangerously close? And why does he deny knowing Jesus when he is asked?

Is it fear for his own safety, or simple expediency so that he can continue to remain close to the proceedings? For that matter, what kind of courage did it take for Peter to raise his sword against the large arresting cohort? It is only when the cock crows that Peter disappears from the scene, presumably shaken by the fulfillment of Jesus' prediction, but also perhaps because he has finally seen clearly Jesus' resolve to carry out a divine plan that included the necessity of his death. Peter's denial can be seen as far more than simple infidelity to a promise or a cowardly betrayal of a friend. It is much

more likely that his struggle presents us with a model for our own struggle to come to accept a Messiah who brings salvation in a way different from what we expect or hope or even like. Peter's life after the resurrection shows us the empowerment that comes with that acceptance, regardless of past failures during the struggle that precedes it.

The way John interweaves Peter's denials with Jesus' bold defense of the truth during his trial is striking. As truth and falsehood are thus played out, each puts the other in bold relief. Truth appears to lose; Jesus is condemned to death. Falsehood

The questioning continues. Pilate comes across as a man genuinely seeking to do the right thing. The Jewish leaders seem blindly bent on killing Jesus at any cost. This passage reveals John's strong anti-Jewish sentiment. It cannot be concealed in the proclamation.

Gabbatha = GAB-uh-thuh

I find no *guilt* in him."
The Jews answered,
    "We have a *law*, and *according* to that law he ought to *die*,
    because he *made* himself the Son of *God*."

Now when Pilate heard *this* statement,
    he became even *more* afraid,
    and went back into the *praetorium* and said to Jesus,
    "Where are you *from*?"
Jesus did not *answer* him.

So Pilate said to him,
    "Do you not *speak* to me?
Do you not know that I have power to *release* you
    and I have power to *crucify* you?"
Jesus answered him,
    "You would have *no* power over me
    if it had not been *given* to you from *above*.
For *this* reason the one who handed me *over* to you
    has the *greater* sin."
Consequently, Pilate tried to *release* him; but the *Jews* cried out,
    "If you *release* him, you are not a Friend of *Caesar*.
Everyone who makes himself a *king* opposes *Caesar*."

When Pilate heard *these* words he brought Jesus out
    and *seated* him on the *judge's* bench
    in the place called *Stone Pavement*, in Hebrew, *Gabbatha*.
It was *preparation* day for *Passover*, and it was about *noon*.
And he said to the Jews,
    "*Behold*, your *king*!"
They cried out,
    "Take him *away*, take him *away*! *Crucify* him!"

appears to win; Peter escapes being identified with a criminal. The dramatic irony is palpable: We know even as we hear the account that appearances are not reality.

(4) Jesus' bold dialogue with the high priest Annas makes John's emphasis clear: The real authority here lies with the one charged with the crime, not with the one who brings the charge. Notice that the high priest is given no words at all. Only Jesus' words are recorded. Furthermore, Jesus questions and directs the questioner, indicating not only that his authority is from above but that the high priest is not even following proper procedure. According to Jewish law, the high priest should not be questioning the defendant or forcing him to incriminate himself; he should be questioning witnesses both for and against him. For this impudence Jesus is physically abused, a common enough response to someone who points out injustice. How often does it happen that those in high position regard themselves as being above the law? Annas wanted to get rid of this nuisance and was willing to do anything to do so. Jesus nevertheless has the last word, a resounding indictment of the whole process: "Why do you hit me for telling the truth?"

(5) In the exchange between Pilate and Jesus, John most clearly reveals the divine kingship of Jesus that is the writer's real interest. Jesus speaks at length of his dominion, which does not belong to this world, and boldly asserts his true purpose and mission. Later, Pilate is frightened when Jesus reminds him of the true source of all power. Pilate's discomfort reveals John's desire to show us the convincing power of Jesus' words.

Pilate again tries to resist but ultimately surrenders his will to that of the mob.

Pilate said to them,
  "Shall I crucify your *king*?"
The chief *priests* answered,
  "We have no king but *Caesar*."

Then he handed him *over* to them to be *crucified*.

Golgotha = GOL-guh-thuh

The action now moves toward Golgotha. Jesus carries his cross by himself. There is no one to help him in John's account because Jesus is in charge here and needs no help.

(8) So they *took* Jesus, and, carrying the cross *himself*,
  he went out to what is called the Place of the *Skull*,
  in Hebrew, *Golgotha*.
There they *crucified* him, and *with* him two *others*,
  one on either *side*, with Jesus in the *middle*.

Pilate *also* had an *inscription* written and put on the *cross*.
It read,
  "*Jesus* the *Nazarene*, the *King* of the *Jews*."
Now many of the Jews *read* this inscription,
  because the *place* where Jesus was crucified was near the *city*;
  and it was written in *Hebrew*, *Latin*, and *Greek*.

So the chief *priests* of the Jews said to Pilate,
  "Do not write 'The *King* of the *Jews*,'
  but that he *said*, 'I am the King of the Jews'."
Pilate answered,
  "What I have *written*, I have *written*."

There is a significant transition here. After Pilate's famous words, "What I have written, I have written," let there be a dramatic pause. The deed has been done.

The details that follow all prove that Jesus is the long-awaited Messiah-king.

When the soldiers had *crucified* Jesus,
  they took his *clothes* and *divided* them into four *shares*,
  a share for each *soldier*.
They also took his *tunic*, but the tunic was *seamless*,
  woven in one *piece* from the top down.
So they said to one another,
  "Let's not *tear* it, but cast *lots* for it to see whose it will *be*,"

Pilate was in a vulnerable position, caught between Rome and Palestine, and he responds to the situation as those who have sold themselves to the systems of power often do. He tries to wash his hands of the situation and avoid responsibility for what happens.

As we watch this scene unfold, the sense of irony increases with every exchange between these two rulers: one who rules heaven and earth but needs no trappings of royalty to prove it; and another who has all the outward signs of power but is unable even to help the innocent man before him.

Pilate is one of the saddest figures in history. He put himself in the terrible position of not being able to do the right thing even when he knows what to do.

(6) Barabbas means "son of the father" or "the father's son" (*bar* correspond to "son," *abbas* to "father"). In the other gospels we learn that the man's full name was Jesus Barabbas. So we have two figures here with the same name: Jesus, son of the father. And, from the point of view of the author, the crowd chooses the wrong one, although the people's choice allows the

true Son of the Father to complete his mission. Furthermore, Barabbas is described by John as an insurrectionist or revolutionary. And, of course, Jesus is also a revolutionary, but on an entirely different plane.

(7) The Roman soldiers at the crucifixion see Jesus as just another in a long line of puny revolutionaries from an inferior race. The fact that he has claimed to be a king makes him all the more ridiculous in their eyes. In our eyes, blessed with hindsight, Jesus becomes an even more tragic figure when we see him being abused by those who had no idea who he was.

Clopas = KLOH-puhs

hyssop = HIS-uhp

After Jesus utters his final words and gives up his spirit, all kneel for a short time. Allow a significant period of silence (no less than 15 seconds, and 30 would be better). When all rise, wait until all noise ceases before continuing.

The calm that follows the storm characterizes the closing paragraphs. Let them move slowly, confidently, to the simple conclusion of the story. After the proclamation, all should be seated and, with no rush, the homily begins. It is a somber moment.

in order that the passage of *Scripture* might be *fulfilled*
   that says:
"They divided my *garments* among them,
and for my *vesture* they cast *lots.*"
This is what the soldiers did.

Standing by the *cross* of Jesus were his *mother*
   and his mother's sister, *Mary* the wife of *Clopas,*
   and Mary of *Magdala.*

When Jesus saw his *mother* and the *disciple* there whom he *loved*
   he said to his mother, "*Woman,* behold, your *son.*"
Then he said to the *disciple,*
   "Behold, your *mother.*"
And from that *hour* the disciple took her into his *home.*

After *this, aware* that everything was now *finished,*
   in order that the *Scripture* might be *fulfilled,*
   Jesus said, "I *thirst.*"
There was a *vessel* filled with common *wine.*
So they put a *sponge* soaked in wine on a sprig of *hyssop*
   and put it up to his *mouth.*
When Jesus had *taken* the wine, he said,
   "It is finished."
And bowing his *head,* he handed over the *spirit.*

[Here all kneel and pause for a short time.]

Now since it was *preparation* day,
   in order that the *bodies* might not remain
   on the cross on the *sabbath,*
   for the sabbath day of *that* week was a *solemn* one,
   the Jews *asked* Pilate that their *legs* be broken
   and that they be taken *down.*

The food for thoughtful meditation here is plentiful. John presents a drama so fraught with irony, contradiction and paradox that we cannot exhaust the richness of its implication and application. It is the experience of faith painted in brutal strokes. Believing in what we cannot see, we see the person in whom we believe being ridiculed. The divine creator of heaven and earth wills to subject himself to earthly power in order to redeem the earth and reunite it with heaven.

Three kings appear in this passage: the King of the Jews, rejected by those whose name he bears; a "king of shreds and patches," ridiculed and mocked by those he came to save in love; and the king of the universe, recognized only by a faithful remnant that will proclaim his sovereignty throughout the world. When the mob cries, "We have no king but Caesar," they utter the most grotesque blasphemy. But in that same breath they prepare the way for their own redemption by unknowingly becoming participants in God's plan to save the world.

(8) There is no Simon of Cyrene in John's gospel to help Jesus carry the cross. The sovereignty of Jesus is thus asserted again in John's account of the passion. In many other details of the narrative, John carries out his purpose. The seamless garment for which the soldiers cast lots, the thirst quenched by sour wine and the fact that Jesus' legs are not broken all provide John the opportunity to show the scriptures being fulfilled in Jesus. John, the eyewitness, is gathering testimony in defense of this Messiah-king, for whom the world had waited so long but whom it failed recognize when he appeared.

Notice, too, that there are no jeering crowds at the foot of the cross. Instead Jesus' mother and the writer himself along

So the *soldiers* came and broke the legs of the *first*
    and then of the *other one* who was crucified with Jesus.
But when they came to *Jesus* and saw that he was already *dead*,
    they did not break *his* legs,
        but *one* soldier thrust his *lance* into his side,
        and *immediately blood* and *water* flowed out.

An *eyewitness* has *testified*, and his testimony is *true*;
    he *knows* that he is speaking the *truth*,
        so that you *also* may come to *believe*.

For this *happened* so that the *Scripture* passage might be *fulfilled*:
    "Not a *bone* of it will be *broken*."
And *again another* passage says:
    "They will *look* upon him whom they have *pierced*."

Arimathea = ayr-ih-muh-THEE-uh

After *this*, Joseph of *Arimathea*,
    secretly a *disciple* of Jesus for fear of the *Jews*,
    asked *Pilate* if he could remove the *body* of Jesus.
And Pilate *permitted* it.
So he came and *took* his body.

aloes = AL-ohz

Nicodemus, the one who had first come to him at *night*,
    also came bringing a mixture of *myrrh* and *aloes*
    weighing about one hundred *pounds*.
They took the *body* of Jesus
    and *bound* it with *burial* cloths along with the *spices*,
    according to the Jewish *burial* custom.
Now in the *place* where he had been *crucified* there was a *garden*,
    and in the garden a new *tomb*, in which no one
        had yet been *buried*.
So they laid Jesus *there* because of the Jewish *preparation* day;
    for the tomb was *close by*.

with a few others stand by his side. Jesus is not totally abandoned, as he is in the other gospel accounts. And although he is subjected to the most horrible indignities, Jesus' dignity is palpable throughout. Those who mock Jesus in John's passion narrative sink lower with every attempt to raise themselves above the object of their hatred.

As we look at Jesus in John's passion narrative, we see a much more voluble and assertive victim than we saw in Matthew's account last Sunday. Jesus responds differently to his situation in John. He is treated differently, too. The inscription on the cross ("Jesus the Nazarene, the King of the Jews") appears in three languages, an indication that this king's reign is universal. Even the demand to change the inscription cannot get it altered, for Jesus *is* king of the Hebrews, as well as king of the Romans and the Greeks. He is king of the entire universe. When Pilate utters those unforgettable words, "What I have written, I have written," he becomes an unwitting ambassador for Christ the King.

In John, Jesus *reigns* from his cross. In a final decree he sends out the proclamation "It is finished." His spirit is not taken from him; he commends it and the world into the hands of the Father. Even after his death, the signs of his reign continue. The enormous quantity and richness of the materials Nicodemus provides for Jesus' burial are more appropriate for a king than a crucified criminal. Our proclamation of John's view of the suffering and dying Jesus must always strive to assert the royal dignity he retains at every moment.

EASTER VIGIL

Lectionary #41

READING I Genesis 1:1—2:2

A reading from the book of Genesis

In the *beginning*, when God created the *heavens* and the *earth*,
    the earth was a formless *wasteland*, and *darkness*
        covered the *abyss*,
    while a mighty *wind* swept over the *waters*.

Then God said,
    "Let there be *light*," and there *was* light.
God saw how *good* the light was.
God then *separated* the light from the *darkness*.
God called the light "*day*" and the darkness he called "*night*."
Thus *evening* came, and morning *followed*—the *first* day.

Then God said,
    "Let there be a *dome* in the middle of the *waters*,
    to separate *one* body of water from the *other*."
And so it *happened*:
    God *made* the dome,
    and it separated the water *above* the dome
        from the water *below* it.
God called the dome "the *sky*."
Evening came, and morning *followed*—the *second* day.

Then God said,
    "Let the *water* under the *sky* be gathered into a single *basin*,
    so that the dry *land* may appear."

The Vigil began in darkness and silence, as does this reading. Do not begin until absolute stillness settles over the assembly. Then let your proclamation of Genesis start quietly, for you need to build through to the end.

Do not rush from one section to the next. Refresh your tone of voice with each "Then God said."

Each "Let . . ." must be authoritative. God creates the world with a word!

READING I Genesis, the "book of beginnings," was the source of our first reading on the First Sunday of Lent. Now, as the celebration of the paschal mystery reaches its highest point, we read from it again to include all of creation in the great work Jesus is about to accomplish on our behalf.

There is one controlling idea that runs throughout this wonderful story of creation: God the Almighty is the source of all life, the cause and the ultimate goal of every living thing, and the one who sustains everything in existence. But to put it that way renders this awesome truth colorless and dull. The author of this creation account knows by instinct that great truths must be told in memorable ways. And what is more memorable than the first chapter of Genesis?

The reading before you is immense, profound, laden with centuries of tradition and countless generations of use. Because

And so it *happened*:
   the water *under* the sky was gathered into its *basin*,
   and the dry *land* appeared.
God called the dry land "the *earth*,"
   and the basin of the *water* he called "the *sea*."
God saw how *good* it was.
Then God said,
   "Let the earth bring forth *vegetation*:
   every kind of *plant* that bears *seed*
   and every kind of *fruit* tree on earth
   that bears *fruit* with its *seed* in it."
And so it *happened*:
   the earth brought forth every *kind* of plant that bears seed
   and every *kind* of fruit tree on earth
   that bears fruit with its *seed* in it.
God saw how *good* it was.
Evening came, and morning *followed*—the *third* day.

Then God said:
   "Let there be *lights* in the dome of the *sky*,
   to separate *day* from *night*.
Let them mark the fixed *times*, the *days* and the *years*,
   and serve as *luminaries* in the dome of the *sky*,
   to shed *light* upon the earth."
And so it *happened*:
   God made the two great *lights*,
   the *greater* one to govern the *day*,
   and the *lesser* one to govern the *night*;
   and he made the *stars*.
God set them in the dome of the sky,
   to shed *light* upon the earth,
   to govern the *day* and the *night*,
   and to separate the *light* from the *darkness*.

Remember that you are continuing to build. A significant jump should be detected as you proclaim the creation of the lights of heaven.

it is so familiar, however, there is some risk that its words will be "tuned out" if you, the proclaimer, exert less than your finest skill. Strive for a mode of proclamation that reveres the text, loves the message and makes it fresh. This does not mean that you exaggerate in any way; rather, it means you prepare and proclaim carefully and sensitively, so that the way you read the text asserts its importance. It is a ringing proclamation of cosmic significance and deserves all the nobility and sincerity you can muster.

You cannot help but notice the refrain-like repetition of several phrases. There is a repetitive kind of rhythm that is part of the author's intention. For one thing, before we had the ease of printed text, the refrains would make the passage easier to memorize. But there is another reason for these refrains: They produce an almost hypnotic effect, giving the story more of the feeling of a long-revered fable, even a formula. It marches through the seven days with gratifying predictability, relying precisely on the

"Let the water *teem* . . ." Let the power of the words do their job. Something of the prodigality of nature is asserted here. The water isn't just filled with abundant life, it *teems* with it.

God saw how *good* it was.
Evening came, and morning *followed*—the *fourth* day.

Then God said,
  "Let the water *teem* with an abundance of living *creatures*,
  and on the *earth* let *birds* fly beneath the dome of the sky."
And so it *happened*:
  God created the great *sea* monsters
  and all *kinds* of swimming creatures with which
    the water *teems*,
  and all *kinds* of winged *birds*.
God saw how *good* it was, and God *blessed* them, saying,
  "Be *fertile*, *multiply*, and *fill* the water of the seas;
  and let the *birds* multiply on the *earth*."
Evening came, and morning *followed*—the *fifth* day.

Then God said,
  "Let the earth bring forth all *kinds* of living *creatures*:
  cattle, *creeping* things, and wild *animals* of all *kinds*."
And so it *happened*:
  God made all *kinds* of wild animals, all *kinds* of cattle,
  and all kinds of *creeping* things of the earth.
God saw how *good* it was.

Then God said:
  "Let us make *man* in our *image*, after our *likeness*.
Let them have *dominion* over the *fish* of the sea,
  the *birds* of the air, and the *cattle*,
  and over *all* the wild animals
  and all the *creatures* that crawl on the *ground*."
God *created* man in his *image*;
  in the image of *God* he created him;
  male and *female* he created them.

familiarity that makes for enjoyable listening. Each time you proclaim the refrains "God saw how good it was," or "And so it happened," you assert the sovereignty of God's creative love. Don't rush these refrains in the fear that the assembly will be bored by them. Relish each occurrence, realizing that the power of the refrains lies precisely in the assembly's awareness that they come with soothing regularity.

Let your proclamation be guided by your own awareness that one simple truth underlies this account of creation: All that is comes from the heart of a loving God, and all of it is good! "Rejoice, O earth, in shining splendor, radiant in the brightness of your King."

God *blessed* them, saying:
  "Be *fertile* and *multiply*;
  fill the earth and *subdue* it.
Have *dominion* over the fish of the *sea*, the birds of the *air*,
  and all the living things that move on the *earth*."

God *also* said:
  "*See*, I give you every seed-bearing *plant* all over the *earth*
  and every *tree* that has seed-bearing *fruit* on it to be your *food*;
  and to all the *animals* of the land, all the birds of the *air*,
  and all the living creatures that crawl on the *ground*,
  I give all the green *plants* for *food*."
And so it *happened*.

God looked at *everything* he had made, and he found it
    very *good*.
Evening came, and morning *followed*—the *sixth* day.

Thus the *heavens* and the *earth* and all their *array*
    were *completed*.
Since on the *seventh* day God was *finished*
  with the work he had been doing,
  he *rested* on the seventh day from all the work
    he had *undertaken*.

[Shorter: Genesis 1:1, 26–31a]

After the sixth day, begin to reduce the intensity and close on the same quiet note with which you began. A significant pause must precede "The word of the Lord" (which is never thrown away as an afterthought).

READING II Genesis 22:1–18

A reading from the book of Genesis

God put *Abraham* to the *test*.
He *called* to him, "*Abraham*!"
"Here I *am*," he replied.

The purpose (to test Abraham) is stated abruptly in the opening words. Follow them with a pause. Then be careful with "Here I am." Try emphasizing "am" rather than "here" to avoid a childish sound.

READING II For the Christian, the story of Abraham and Isaac has long been a compelling symbol or prefiguring of the sacrifice of God's Son for the redemption of the world. Abraham is perfectly obedient; Isaac is perfectly innocent.

Isaac even bears the wood for his sacrifice upon his own shoulders. In Eucharistic Prayer I, we proclaim Abraham to be "our father in faith," and so he is, because of the beautiful blessing and promise he receives at the end of the reading.

Our first response to this story may be horror at God's demand of such a sacrifice.

But we need to remind ourselves of the purpose of the story and what the writer wants us to take from it. This is always the case with scripture: The message is always more than the mere historical details. By the time the Abraham and Isaac story was written, human sacrifice was no longer practiced

**Moriah = moh-RĪ-uh
holocaust = HOL-uh-kawst**

Note the immediacy of Abraham's response to this horrific command. This is not because he is heartless but because he has total faith in God's goodness.

Then God said:
    "Take your son *Isaac*, your only *one*, whom you *love*,
    and go to the land of *Moriah*.
There you shall offer him *up* as a *holocaust*
    on a *height* that I will point *out* to you."

Early the next *morning* Abraham saddled his *donkey*,
    took with him his son *Isaac* and two of his *servants* as *well*,
    and with the *wood* that he had cut for the *holocaust*,
    set *out* for the place of which God had *told* him.

On the *third* day Abraham got *sight* of the place from *afar*.
Then he said to his *servants*:
    "Both of you stay *here* with the donkey,
    while the *boy* and I go on over *yonder*.
We will *worship* and then come *back* to you."
Thereupon Abraham took the *wood* for the holocaust
    and laid it on his son Isaac's *shoulders*,
    while he *himself* carried the *fire* and the *knife*.

Abraham's trust ("God will provide") is also a prediction of the outcome of the story.

As the two walked on together, Isaac *spoke*
        to his father Abraham:
    "*Father*!" Isaac said.
"*Yes*, son," he replied.
Isaac continued, "Here are the *fire* and the *wood*,
    but where is the *sheep* for the holocaust?"
"*Son*," Abraham answered,
    "God *himself* will provide the *sheep* for the holocaust."
Then the two continued going forward.

When they came to the place of which God had *told* him,
    Abraham built an *altar* there and arranged the *wood* on it.
Next he tied *up* his son *Isaac*,
    and put him on *top* of the wood on the *altar*.

among the Israelites. That's part of the point of the story. As a way of proclaiming God's sovereignty, the firstborn of every creature belonged to God. And each firstborn human child was "redeemed" by the substitute of an animal sacrifice.

The focus throughout the reading is Abraham's willingness to relinquish what he loves most to God's sovereignty. It is the ultimate test for all believers to arrive at the kind of faith that relinquishes control and affirms God to be in charge of life as a provident guardian. Indeed, this is the meaning

of the name that Abraham bestows on the site where the sacrifice took place. The translation of "Yahweh-yireh" is complex, but it means God will see that the covenant and promise will be kept. As God provided the ram for sacrifice in place of Isaac, so God will see to the redemption of the people of the covenant.

Let the messenger's voice be strong and calm, not urgent.

Then he reached out and took the knife to *slaughter* his son.
But the LORD's *messenger* called to him from heaven,
  "*Abraham, Abraham!*"
"Here I *am*," he answered.
"Do not lay your *hand* on the boy," said the messenger.
"Do not do the least *thing* to him.
I *know* now how *devoted* you are to God,
  since you did not *withhold* from me your own beloved *son*."
As Abraham looked about,
  he spied a *ram* caught by its *horns* in the *thicket*.
So he went and took the ram
  and offered *it* up as a holocaust in place of his *son*.
Abraham *named* the site *Yahweh-yireh*;
  hence people now say, "On the *mountain* the LORD will *see*."

Because of this outcome, the firstborn that belongs to God is redeemed by the substitution of an animal sacrifice. We cannot help but think here of the Lamb of God, sacrificed to redeem us.
Yahweh-yireh = Yah-way-YEER-ay

This is the great blessing explaining why we call Abraham "our father in faith." Note that all the nations of the earth, not just Abraham's people, shall be blessed.

Again the LORD's messenger called to Abraham from heaven
    and said:
  "I swear by *myself*, declares the LORD,
  that because you acted as you *did*
  in not withholding from me your beloved *son*,
  I will *bless* you *abundantly*
  and make your *descendants* as countless
  as the stars of the *sky* and the sands of the *seashore*;
  your descendants shall take *possession*
  of the gates of their *enemies*,
  and in your *descendants* all the *nations* of the earth
    shall find *blessing*—
  all *this* because you *obeyed* my *command*."

[Shorter: Genesis 22:1–2, 9a, 10–13, 15–18]

The reward for Abraham's obedience and service is the beautiful blessing that concludes the passage. It should be read with breadth and conviction. The assembly will instinctively draw the parallels between Abraham and Isaac, and God the Father and Jesus. A revered foreshadowing of Jesus' sacrifice in obedience to his Father's will

takes on special meaning for us as we celebrate the paschal mystery on this holiest of nights.

"Father, how wonderful your care for us! How boundless your merciful love! To ransom a slave you gave away your Son."

READING III The story of the crossing of the Red Sea—surely one of the most beloved in Jewish and Christian traditions—recounts a central event in salvation history. It is the classic image of a people being delivered from captivity. As the Israelites pass through the waters and

We see a people cowering in fright, afraid to move forward until their leader instructs them in no uncertain terms to put their trust in God. Then the feeling of resolve and courage begins to build as God manifests divine power on their behalf.

The important words are "I am the Lord." Both sides must learn this lesson, just as we learn it sometimes when we make the mistake of siding with Pharaoh!

These are strong images! Let your proclamation match them.

READING III   Exodus 14:15—15:1

A reading from the book of Exodus

The LORD said to *Moses*, "Why are you crying *out* to me?
Tell the *Israelites* to go *forward*.
And *you*, lift up your *staff* and, with hand *outstretched*
     over the *sea*,
   split the sea in *two*,
   that the Israelites may pass *through* it on dry *land*.
But I will make the *Egyptians* so *obstinate*
   that they will go in *after* them.
Then I will receive *glory* through *Pharaoh* and all his *army*,
   his *chariots* and *charioteers*.
The Egyptians shall *know* that *I am the* LORD,
   when I receive *glory* through *Pharaoh*
   and his *chariots* and *charioteers*."

The *angel* of God, who had been *leading* Israel's camp,
   now *moved* and went around *behind* them.
The column of *cloud* also, leaving the *front*,
   took up its place *behind* them,
   so that it came *between* the camp of the *Egyptians*
   and that of *Israel*.
But the cloud *now* became *dark*, and thus the night *passed*
   without the rival camps coming any closer *together*
     all night *long*.

Then *Moses* stretched out his *hand* over the *sea*,
   and the LORD *swept* the sea
   with a strong east *wind* throughout the *night*
   and so turned it into dry *land*.

arrive safely on the other shore, leaving their pursuers behind, so we pass through the waters of baptism and are admitted into the fellowship of the Body of Christ, leaving sin and death behind.

The imagery of these parallel events has been beautifully captured in a brief song by Father Hugh Tasch, OSB, of Conception Abbey, Conception, Missouri:

> Once you were darkness, Pharaoh's
>   prison band.
> Now you are sunlight dwelling
>   in the Land.
> Walk, then, in sunlight, high
>   upon the shore.
> Rise from the waters, dying now
>   no more.

So important is the Red Sea crossing in our Christian tradition that this reading is obligatory tonight even if others are omitted for pastoral reasons. In your community there may be catechumens awaiting baptism at this very moment. Let your proclamation be for them in a special way. Let it echo what we heard in the Exsultet at the beginning of this holy night: "This is the night

This is a vivid story, like an action movie.
We must sense the energy here but not
lose ourselves in the details. God's solid
and uncontestable power is the point.

When the *water* was thus *divided*,
   the *Israelites* marched into the *midst* of the sea on dry *land*,
   with the water like a *wall* to their *right* and to their *left*.

The *Egyptians* followed in *pursuit*;
   all Pharaoh's *horses* and *chariots* and *charioteers*
     went *after* them
   right into the *midst* of the *sea*.
In the *night* watch just before *dawn*
   the LORD cast through the column of the fiery *cloud*
   upon the Egyptian *force* a *glance* that threw it into a *panic*;
   and he so *clogged* their *chariot* wheels
   that they could hardly *drive*.
With *that* the Egyptians sounded the *retreat* before Israel,
   because the LORD was fighting for them *against* the Egyptians.

Then the LORD told Moses, "Stretch out your *hand* over the *sea*,
   that the *water* may flow *back* upon the Egyptians,
   upon their *chariots* and their *charioteers*."
So Moses stretched out his hand over the sea,
   and at *dawn* the sea flowed *back* to its normal *depth*.
The *Egyptians* were fleeing *head on* toward the *sea*,
   when the LORD *hurled* them into its *midst*.
As the water flowed *back*,
   it *covered* the *chariots* and the *charioteers*
     of Pharaoh's whole *army*
   which had *followed* the Israelites into the *sea*.
Not a single *one* of them *escaped*.

But the *Israelites* had marched on dry *land*
   through the *midst* of the sea,
   with the water like a *wall* to their *right* and to their *left*.
Thus the LORD *saved* Israel on that day
   from the *power* of the *Egyptians*.

The conclusion should not be anti-
climactic. Keep the energy level up.

when first you saved our ancestors: you freed the people of Israel from their slavery and led them dry-shod through the sea."

READING IV After hearing of the exercise of divine power on behalf of the chosen people, we now hear a gentle proclamation of God's love for them. It would be difficult to find a more moving expression of devotion than this one. It is a poem of intimacy between God and the holy city, Jerusalem. It refers first to Jerusalem's people, the race God has chosen, but is ultimately addressed to all humankind.

In this love song we see evidence of a stormy relationship, which should not surprise us. Any relationship that strives for genuine union between two independent hearts will have its turbulent times. But in this reading, as in our experience, the difficulties encountered in honest love serve only to make that love stronger.

The theme of Israel's exile is clear in the image of the abandoned wife. The promise of deliverance and prosperity is just as clear in the *shalom* or "peace" of the next generation. The marital bond is often employed in

When Israel *saw* the Egyptians lying *dead* on the *seashore*
   and *beheld* the great *power* that the LORD
   had *shown* against the Egyptians,
   they *feared* the LORD and *believed* in him
     and in his servant *Moses.*

Then Moses and the Israelites sang this *song* to the LORD:
   I will sing to the LORD, for he is gloriously triumphant;
   horse and chariot he has cast into the sea.

READING IV   Isaiah 54:5–14

A reading from the book of the prophet Isaiah

The One who has become your *husband* is your *Maker*;
   his *name* is the LORD of *hosts*;
your *redeemer* is the *Holy* One of *Israel*,
   called *God* of all the *earth.*
The LORD calls you *back*,
   like a *wife* forsaken and grieved in spirit,
   a *wife* married in *youth* and then cast *off*,
   says your God.

For a brief *moment* I *abandoned* you,
   but with great *tenderness* I will take you *back.*
In an outburst of *wrath*, for a *moment*
   I hid my *face* from you;
but with enduring *love* I take *pity* on you,
   says the LORD, your *redeemer.*

How can the all-powerful God of hosts also be a loving spouse? Let the exhilarating paradox exert its power!

The prophet gives God a human voice, speaking in the frailty of human language. Thus the desire for intimacy prevails over struggle and infidelity.

scripture as the only one intimate enough to describe God's love for Israel.

The same bond describes the love between Christ and the church. Christ is the bridegroom who has rescued his beloved from every danger and given his life for her happiness. Conjugal bliss is an appropriate image as we celebrate this holiest of nights.

As we heard in the Exsultet: "O night truly blessed, when heaven is wedded to earth and we are reconciled with God."

READING V   Scripture scholars believe that the author of this passage of poetry lived and struggled in a poor community. It's not surprising, then, that we find here images of a sumptuous banquet and the encouraging message that

the riches promised come at no cost from the hand of a loving provider. The prophet appeals to his audience in images his hearers can understand.

Beyond the local circumstances that gave birth to Isaiah's poetry, this reading shows us the kind of sustenance that comes

This is for *me* like the days of *Noah*,
    when I *swore* that the *waters* of Noah
    should never *again deluge* the earth;
so I have sworn not to be *angry* with you,
    or to *rebuke* you.
Though the *mountains* leave their *place*
    and the *hills* be *shaken,*
my *love* shall *never* leave you
    nor my covenant of *peace* be *shaken,*
    says the LORD, who has *mercy* on you.

O *afflicted* one, *storm*-battered and *unconsoled,*
    I lay your *pavements* in *carnelians,*
    and your *foundations* in *sapphires;*
I will make your *battlements* of *rubies,*
    your *gates* of *carbuncles,*
    and all your *walls* of precious *stones.*

All your children shall be *taught* by the LORD,
    and *great* shall be the *peace* of your children.
In *justice* shall you be *established,*
    far from the fear of *oppression,*
    where *destruction* cannot come *near* you.

The combination of strength and tenderness here is moving.

carnelians = kahr-NEEL-yuhnz

carbuncles = KAHR-bung-k∗lz

The repetition of the word "children" means you must emphasize other words in the sentence. See the emphasis markings.

Utter confidence and peace bring the reading to a close.

READING V   Isaiah 55:1–11

A reading from the book of the prophet Isaiah

Thus says the LORD:
All you who are *thirsty,*
    come to the *water!*
You who have no *money,*

Another message of consolation is solemnly presented here. Let your proclamation concentrate on the strength of the message, avoiding a softness that would be inappropriate.

from trust in a God who is a provident Father. Isaiah's prophecy predicts a future time of peace and prosperity. Again we are presented with a vision of the end times (heaven), and we are encouraged to see the signs that indicate the imminent arrival of those times: the mercy and redemptive love of God, symbolized here in the image of a banquet.

The great challenge to faith, of course, is to see the signs of God's perfect love in an imperfect world. It takes genuine, profound and ongoing conversion. It means acknowledging deep down that God's ways are different from our own and then aligning our ways with those of the divine: mercy over vengeance, persons over things, love over security. In fervent prayer for such insight, we do not change God's will; we change ourselves.

Finally, we are reminded here that God's word is irrevocable and will accomplish the purpose for which you proclaim it.

"Bread" is a symbolic term here, signifying the nourishment of wisdom. Recall Jesus' words: "My food and drink is to do the will of God who sent me."

come, receive *grain* and *eat;*
come, without *paying* and without *cost,*
   drink *wine* and *milk!*
Why spend your *money* for what is not *bread,*
   your *wages* for what fails to *satisfy?*
Heed me, and you shall eat *well,*
   you shall *delight* in rich *fare.*
Come to me *heedfully,*
   listen, that you may have *life.*
I will *renew* with you the *everlasting* covenant,
   the *benefits* assured to *David.*

As I made him a *witness* to the *peoples,*
   a *leader* and commander of *nations,*
so shall *you* summon a nation you knew *not,*
   and nations that *knew* you *not* shall *run* to you,
because of the LORD, your *God,*
   the *Holy* One of *Israel,* who has *glorified* you.

"So shall you summon . . ." This is a tongue-twister. Either take it slowly or alter it to something manageable, such as, "Thus you will call out to a nation . . ."

Seek the LORD while he may be *found,*
   call him while he is *near.*
Let the *scoundrel forsake* his way,
   and the *wicked* man his *thoughts;*
let him turn to the LORD for *mercy;*
   to our *God,* who is generous in *forgiving.*

Make this inclusive by using plural forms: "Let scoundrels forsake their ways, and the wicked their thoughts; let them turn . . ."

For *my* thoughts are not *your* thoughts,
   nor are *your* ways *my* ways, says the LORD.
As high as the *heavens* are above the *earth,*
   so high are *my* ways above *your* ways
   and *my* thoughts above *your* thoughts.

The paschal mystery we are celebrating is our best evidence that God's word has been accomplished: "This is the night when Jesus Christ broke the chains of death and rose triumphant from the grave."

READING VI | The sixth and seventh readings of the Vigil remind us that without the intervention of God's love we would still be slaves to sin and death. The governing image is Israel's exile and unfaithfulness. As Israel was rescued from exile and restored to God's favor, so it is with us this night. "This is the night when first you saved our ancestors: you freed the people of Israel from their slavery and led them dry-shod through the sea."

The poetry of Baruch is a call to awareness. The cosmic imagery creates a sense of the immensity and universality of God's

This is a powerful image of how God's word does its work. For you who proclaim it, know that you are enabling the word to achieve its purpose, despite your weakness or strength. Take courage.

For just as from the *heavens*
    the *rain* and *snow* come down
and do not *return* there
    till they have *watered* the earth,
    making it *fertile* and *fruitful*,
giving *seed* to the one who *sows*
    and *bread* to the one who *eats*,
so shall my *word* be
    that goes forth from my *mouth*;
my word shall not return to me *void*,
    but shall do my *will*,
    achieving the *end* for which I *sent* it.

In the paschal mystery we celebrate tonight, we see that God's word has indeed achieved its purpose in the resurrection of Jesus Christ.

READING VI   Baruch 3:9–15, 32 — 4:4

A reading from the book of the prophet Baruch

Baruch = buh-**ROOK**

Anytime you encounter the words "Hear, O Israel," you have come upon a solemn pronouncement. The most fundamental of Jewish prayers, the Shema, begins with these words: "Hear, O Israel, the Lord our God is One!"

Hear, O Israel, the *commandments* of *life*:
    listen, and know *prudence*!
How *is* it, Israel,
    that you are in the land of your *foes*,
    grown *old* in a *foreign* land,
defiled with the *dead*,
    accounted with those destined for the *netherworld*?
You have *forsaken* the fountain of *wisdom*!
Had you walked in the way of *God*,
    you would have dwelt in enduring *peace*.

These are harsh words, but we need to hear how much we need God's loving redemption.

---

domain. Above all, it is a call to seek wisdom, that most insightful of virtues that enables us to see how different our ways are from God's and to reorient ourselves to God's way of dealing with the world. Wisdom is a gift from God and a manifestation of God. It is withheld from none, not reserved to the intelligent or denied to the

simple. It enables us to see God revealed in every aspect of creation, from the four-footed beasts to the stars in heaven. To find wisdom we must resist our tendency to shortsightedness and raise our eyes to the universe.

In his historical context the prophet is calling out to Israel, dispersed as its people are throughout the pagan world. If they are concerned that they cannot serve God well in the midst of foreigners, they must be

reminded that their exile is the result of failing to serve God well in their homeland. The prophet's indictment may seem harsh, but he is more eager to point out that wisdom is available wherever we are because God has revealed the word by which we can guide our behavior and our devotion. It is discernible in nature but even more so in the hearts of the just, who have loved the

The rhetorical questions center on God as creator and sustainer of all that is. Wisdom begins when we realize, as we heard in the last reading, that God's ways are different from our own.

Learn where *prudence* is,
 where *strength*, where *understanding*;
that you may know *also*
 where are length of *days*, and *life*,
 where light of the *eyes*, and *peace*.
Who has found the place of *wisdom*,
 who has entered into her *treasuries*?

The One who knows *all* things knows *her*;
 he has *probed* her by his *knowledge*—
the One who *established* the earth for all *time*,
 and *filled* it with four-footed *beasts*;
 he who *dismisses* the light, and it *departs*,
 calls it, and it *obeys* him *trembling*;
before whom the *stars* at their posts
 shine and *rejoice*;
when he *calls* them, they answer, "Here we *are!*"
 shining with *joy* for their Maker.

Such is our *God*;
 no *other* is to be *compared* to him:
he has traced out the whole *way* of *understanding*,
 and has given her to *Jacob*, his *servant*,
 to *Israel*, his beloved *son*.

Since then she has *appeared* on *earth*,
 and *moved* among *people*.
She is the *book* of the precepts of *God*,
 the *law* that endures *forever*;
all who *cling* to her will *live*,
 but those will *die* who *forsake* her.

Turn, O Jacob, and *receive* her:
 walk by her *light* toward *splendor*.

Wisdom appeared on earth in the love God has for us. If we can learn and believe that we are loved, we will become truly wise.

law and whose lives make the goodness of God visible.

In a dramatic way, Baruch is discouraging us from seeking tidy answers to specific questions. Serving God well means seeing the world in a certain way and behaving accordingly. There is no rule book or catechism that can instill such vision or guarantee that we have aligned our ways with God's. Only wisdom can do that. But

Baruch tells us not to be discouraged. Even when we merely search for wisdom we already serve God well.

READING VII Israel's exile and return to the land of their ancestors is central to their faith, which is why so much of the Hebrew scriptures dwell on the subject. The prophet Ezekiel is a colorful writer. His images range from the harshest

condemnations (as we find in this reading) to the most tender expressions of God's redeeming power. When the facts of the case are harsh, Ezekiel pulls no punches.

Bad as it is, however, Israel's infidelity is no worse than human infidelity at any age. What is most distressing is that the chosen people have profaned the name of the God who chose them. It is no different with us.

Give not your *glory* to *another*,
  your *privileges* to an *alien* race.
Blessed are we, O Israel;
  for what pleases *God* is *known* to us!

READING VII   Ezekiel 36:16–17a, 18–28

Ezekiel = ee-ZEE-kee-uhl

A reading from the book of the prophet Ezekiel

The word of the LORD came to me, saying:
  Son of *man*, when the house of *Israel* lived in their *land*,
  they *defiled* it by their *conduct* and *deeds*.
Therefore I poured out my *fury* upon them
  because of the *blood* that they poured out on the *ground*,
  and because they *defiled* it with *idols*.
I *scattered* them among the *nations*,
  dispersing them over *foreign* lands;
  according to their *conduct* and *deeds* I *judged* them.

But when they came among the *nations wherever* they came,
  they served to *profane* my holy *name*,
  because it was said of them: "*These* are the people of the LORD,
  yet they had to leave their *land*."

So I have *relented* because of my holy *name*
  which the house of *Israel profaned*
  among the *nations* where they *came*.
Therefore say to the house of Israel: *Thus* says the Lord GOD:
  Not for *your* sakes do I act, house of *Israel*,
  but for the sake of my holy *name*,
  which you *profaned* among the nations to which you *came*.

These are tough words to proclaim and to hear. But our sins do bring evil upon the earth, and we need to be reminded of the consequences of our actions. The amazing thing is that God can bring good even out of evil. God will love Israel back into favor.

Chosen as we are by a merciful and loving God, our refusal to be merciful and loving is all the more terrible.
  But again God relents, as we have come to expect, since mercy always triumphs over justice where God is concerned. Although our homecoming is said to be for the sake of the holiness of God's great name among the foreign nations—and not because God pities us—we are nevertheless to be reestablished as the people of the covenant.

Ezekiel's point is that neither our good deeds nor our bad ones nor our repentance *earn* the love of God. That love is gratuitous, always a gift freely given by God, for it is God's nature. God *makes* us holy in spite of ourselves. Again, as we heard in the Exsultet: "This is the night when Christians everywhere, washed clean of sin and freed from all defilement, are restored to grace and grow together in holiness."
  On this night of all nights, we need to be reminded that the sacrificial love demonstrated in Christ's death and resurrection is

a totally free act of love. We can accept it with grateful hearts, or we can reject it with stony ones; there is no way we can *earn* it. We can, however, heed the voice of the prophet and respond to love with the new hearts of flesh God has given us. "What good would life have been to us, had Christ not come as our Redeemer?"

EPISTLE   Finally we come to the reading that ties all the others together in the Christian tradition. It adds

I will prove the *holiness* of my great name,
 profaned among the *nations*,
 in whose *midst* you have *profaned* it.
Thus the nations shall *know* that *I* am the LORD,
 says the Lord GOD,
 when in their sight I *prove* my holiness through *you.*

For I will take you *away* from among the *nations*,
 gather you from all the foreign *lands*,
 and bring you *back* to your *own* land.

I will sprinkle clean *water* upon you
 to *cleanse* you from all your *impurities*,
 and from all your *idols* I will *cleanse* you.

I will give you a *new* heart and place a new *spirit* within you,
 taking from your bodies your *stony* hearts
 and giving you *natural* hearts.
I will put my *spirit* within you and make you *live* by my *statutes*,
 careful to observe my *decrees*.
You shall *live* in the land I gave your *fathers*;
 you shall be *my* people, and I will be your *God.*

The image of hearts of flesh versus hearts of stone is powerful. A heart of stone may be hard for many reasons: sinfulness, sorrow, resentment, suffering. Appeal to the stony hearts without scolding.

Pay attention to the words "my people" and "your God." Lovers always have the sense of possessing each other. How wonderful to be claimed as God's own!

them all up and shows us that the resurrection of Christ is the culmination of God's intervention in the world since its creation. It begins with a powerful rhetorical question: "It's not possible, is it," Paul asks, "that you don't understand the consequences of your baptism?" The question must be proclaimed so that the members of the assembly will spontaneously cry out in their hearts: "We do understand! Our old selves have died with Christ; our new selves have risen with him."

Thus begins a masterful comparison between baptism and death, and between Jesus' bodily resurrection and our spiritual resurrection. But it's more complex than that. Paul's argument is not tidy, nor was it meant to be. He draws together images of life, death, baptism, resurrection and sin in order to emerge with the clear conviction that baptism has transformed us, just as the resurrection has transformed Jesus.

We know by experience that in many ways we appear to be the same as we were before baptism. But the spiritual insight we must capture here is that, appearances notwithstanding, we are totally changed by baptism.

Baptism is union with Christ in his death and resurrection. It is a death to our old selves and a new life in Christ. Sin no longer has any power over us because Christ's death put an end to death, which is the ultimate consequence of sin. Obviously, a dead

A reading from the letter of Saint Paul to the Romans

Brothers and sisters:
Are you *unaware* that we who were *baptized* into Christ *Jesus*
  were *baptized* into his *death?*
We were indeed *buried* with him through baptism into *death,*
  so that, just as Christ was *raised* from the dead
  by the glory of the *Father,*
  we *too* might live in *newness* of *life.*

For if we have grown into *union* with him
  through a *death* like his,
  we shall also be *united* with him in the *resurrection.*
We know that our *old* self was *crucified* with him,
  so that our *sinful* body might be done *away* with,
  that we might no longer be in *slavery* to sin.
For a *dead* person has been *absolved* from sin.
If, then, we have *died* with Christ,
  we believe that we shall *also live* with him.

We know that *Christ, raised* from the dead, dies no *more;*
  death no longer has *power* over him.
As to his *death,* he died to sin *once* and for *all;*
  as to his *life,* he lives for *God.*
Consequently, you *too* must think of *yourselves*
  as being *dead* to sin
  and *living* for *God* in Christ *Jesus.*

The opening rhetorical question is always effective. Make the most of it.

This is a difficult text. It follows its own logic (as Paul so often does) not in syllogistic form but by unfolding the basic premise that we have died and risen with Christ. Here are the implications of that fact. Proceed slowly and let Paul's meditation unfold.

The last sentence is the practical consequence of all that precedes it. It tells us how to behave because of what we believe.

person cannot sin. The dead are outside the power of sin. This is true of us as well because our union with Christ's death has killed that part of us that was subject to sin.

The bottom line, and the great good news, is that we are also united with Christ in his resurrection. The age-old promise of victory over death and sin has come to fruition in the paschal mystery we have gathered to celebrate this very night. "The power of this holy night dispels all evil, washes guilt away, restores lost innocence, brings mourners joy; it casts out hatred, brings us peace and humbles earthly pride."

GOSPEL None of the gospel writers gives us specific information about what happened at the resurrection, what went on inside the tomb between the moment of Jesus' burial and his glorious appearance outside the tomb. There were no witnesses, of course, and Jesus did not volunteer any information about the matter in his discussions with the disciples after the resurrection.

The fact that we have no information in this regard demonstrates that resurrection is totally beyond our comprehension or ability to describe it. We have evidence that it happened, but we have no idea how it happened. We are forced back to the only conclusion available: The totally transcendent God intervened in nature and history and raised Jesus from the dead in a wonderful way that we can cannot understand

GOSPEL Matthew 28:1–10

A reading from the holy gospel according to Matthew

Do not neglect the beauty of the phrase "as the first day of the week was dawning." The proclamation of the resurrection is the dawning of a new day, a new week, a new era!

The angel sat on the stone for a reason. The seated position is reserved for the most solemn of proclamations.

After the *sabbath*, as the *first* day of the week was *dawning*,
  Mary *Magdalene* and the *other* Mary came to see the *tomb*.
And *behold*, there was a great *earthquake*;
  for an angel of the *Lord* descended from heaven,
  approached, rolled *back* the stone, and *sat* upon it.
His *appearance* was like *lightning*
  and his *clothing* was white as *snow*.
The *guards* were *shaken* with *fear* of him
  and became like *dead* men.

Then the *angel* said to the women in *reply*,
  "Do not be *afraid*!
I *know* that you are seeking *Jesus* the *crucified*.
He is not *here*, for he has been *raised* just as he *said*.
Come and see the place where he *lay*.
Then go *quickly* and tell his *disciples*,
  'He has been *raised* from the *dead*,
  and he is going *before* you to *Galilee*;
  there you will *see* him.'
  Behold, I have *told* you."

As the women hurry away, the dramatic scene seems to be closing. But the reading continues, "And behold . . . "!

Then they went away *quickly* from the tomb,
  fearful yet *overjoyed*,
  and ran to *announce* this to his *disciples*.

And *behold*, Jesus *met* them on their way and *greeted* them.
They *approached*, embraced his *feet*, and did him *homage*.
Then Jesus said to them, "Do not be *afraid*.
Go tell my brothers to go to *Galilee*,
  and *there* they will *see* me."

Pronounce the final words of Jesus with utter calm and quiet strength. Christ has truly risen and his disciples will see him. The struggle is over, the triumph won.

but can only accept in stunned faith. And this is precisely the state of mind in which the gospel writers, especially Matthew, want us to be.

Matthew's narrative here is a solemn announcement of the accomplished fact accompanied by several manifestations of divine power: earthquake, angel, lightning, dazzling garments. They are Matthew's way of asserting that God alone is responsible for this wonder. Knowledge cannot comprehend it; our emotions cannot contain it; the evidence will not let us deny it. But the wisdom of faith can embrace it with unparalleled joy!

Just when we think we've seen all that our overwhelmed senses can bear, we hurry away from the tomb to obey the angel's bidding and find ourselves face to face with the Master himself, whose coming was foretold to us, whose teaching delighted us, whose tender touch healed us. We witnessed his betrayal and death, we attended his burial, and yet now we hear his voice again. And the first words he utters encompass all he has done for us: "Peace! Do not be afraid."

"Most blessed of all nights, chosen by God to see Christ rising from the dead! Of this night scripture says: 'The night will be as clear as day: it will become my light, my joy!' "

EASTER SUNDAY

Lectionary #42

READING I   Acts 10:34a, 37–43

A reading from the Acts of the Apostles

Peter proceeded to speak and said:
"You *know* what has happened all over *Judea*,
      beginning in *Galilee* after the *baptism*
      that *John* preached,
      how God anointed *Jesus* of *Nazareth*
      with the Holy *Spirit* and *power*.
He went about doing *good*
      and *healing* all those *oppressed* by the *devil*,
      for *God* was with him.

"*We* are *witnesses* of all that he *did*
      both in the country of the *Jews* and in *Jerusalem*.
They put him to *death* by hanging him on a *tree*.
This man God *raised* on the *third day* and granted
            that he be *visible*,
      not to *all* the people, but to *us*,
      the witnesses *chosen* by God in *advance*,
      who *ate* and *drank* with him after he rose from the *dead*.

"He *commissioned* us to *preach* to the people
      and *testify* that *he* is the one appointed by *God*
      as *judge* of the *living* and the *dead*.
To *him* all the *prophets* bear *witness*,
      that *everyone* who *believes* in him
      will receive *forgiveness* of *sins* through his *name*."

This reading is packed with information. It must be taken slowly, meditatively and in a natural conversational tone. You are not Peter, but you are telling the story in his words.

Notice the "we" and "us," which give your proclamation immediacy and a kind of intimacy with the assembly.

The dramatic simplicity of the final sentence deserves special emphasis. The most important word, perhaps, is "everyone."

READING I Today is the solemnity of solemnities, the greatest feast on the liturgical calendar. The paschal celebration peaked during last night's Vigil, and now we bask in the glory of the resurrected Lord for the 50-day season of Easter, which culminates in the celebration of the coming of the Holy Spirit on Pentecost. During the rest of the liturgical year, the first reading is taken from the Old Testament. But during Easter the first reading comes from the Acts of the Apostles, the wonderful account of the early Christian community's struggles and triumphs.

We begin today with Peter's summary of the life, work, death and resurrection of Jesus. It is a reminder that Jesus is Lord and lives in our midst. The recurrent theme here is that Peter and the others who received their commission from the risen Lord were eyewitnesses of his glory. Of particular note is that they proclaim Christ to be the judge of the living and the dead. The concern about the "last days" and the end of time reminds us that the risen Christ is now with God the Father, having completed the work for which he was sent. The words of the creed take on a startling immediacy today: "He

will come again in glory to judge the living and the dead."

Now we hear Peter teaching what Jesus said so often about himself during his earthly ministry: All the prophets have testified to the coming of the Messiah, and their expectations have been fulfilled in Jesus. Furthermore, although our sins brought Jesus to the cross, his suffering and death have healed us. What is the appropriate response to this good news? All that we have to do is believe in Christ crucified and risen.

Notice the elevating effect of this text. Encourage those in the assembly to raise their sights.

The contrast between being hidden and being revealed must be emphasized.

READING II   Colossians 3:1–4

A reading from the letter of Saint Paul to the Colossians

Brothers and sisters:
If then you were *raised* with *Christ*, seek what is *above*,
    where Christ is *seated* at the right hand of *God*.
Think of what is *above*, not of what is on *earth*.
For you have *died*, and your life is *hidden* with Christ in *God*.
When Christ your *life* appears,
    then you *too* will appear with him in *glory*.

Or:

One image (yeast) controls this reading. Be sure you understand it (see the commentary) and enable the assembly to understand it. The shorter the reading, the more careful and deliberate the proclamation must be!

READING II   1 Corinthians 5:6b–8

A reading from the first letter of Saint Paul to the Corinthians

Brothers and sisters:
Do you not know that a little *yeast* leavens all the *dough*?
Clear *out* the *old* yeast,
    so that you may become a *fresh* batch of dough,
        inasmuch as you are *unleavened*.
For our paschal *lamb*, *Christ*, has been *sacrificed*.
Therefore, let us *celebrate* the feast,
    not with the *old* yeast, the yeast of *malice* and *wickedness*,
    but with the *unleavened* bread of *sincerity* and *truth*.

There is a choice of second readings today. Speak with the liturgy coordinator or the homilist to find out which reading will be used.

READING II COLOSSIANS. Notice how brief some readings, such as this one, are. As complicated as it may sometimes seem, the Good News of Jesus Christ can be summarized in a few words. It is the simplest of messages: Christ has died, Christ is risen, Christ will come again.

Sometimes we need to remind ourselves how beautifully simple our faith can be.

Paul's words make it clear that we are living an entirely new life as a result of our baptism, which we renew at today's Mass. When Paul says that our life is hidden now with Christ, he means there is more to come and that the work of salvation is not complete until the end of time. Scholars speak of "partially realized eschatology," a formidable phrase meaning that the reign of God is established on earth but has not yet reached perfection. Another way of putting it is "already, but not yet!" Christ's reign is already victorious, but it is not yet fully visible to us. It will no longer be hidden when Christ returns in glory. When he appears, we will also appear as we really are—completely transformed through the waters of baptism.

Living in faith is a matter of realizing who we really are in spite of who we sometimes seem to be. It is a matter of living out our true identity in Christ rather than the false identity of sinfulness. By faith we know that we are "already" raised up to eternal life with Christ. By setting our hearts

GOSPEL   John 20:1–9

A reading from the holy gospel according to John

On the first day of the *week*,
    Mary of *Magdala* came to the *tomb* early in the *morning*,
    while it was still *dark*,
    and saw the *stone* removed from the *tomb*.
So she *ran* and went to Simon *Peter*
    and to the *other* disciple whom Jesus *loved*, and *told* them,
    "They have taken the *Lord* from the *tomb*,
    and we don't know where they *put* him."

So *Peter* and the *other* disciple went out and *came* to the tomb.
They both *ran*, but the *other* disciple ran *faster* than Peter
    and arrived at the tomb *first*;
    he bent down and saw the *burial* cloths there, but did
        not go in.

When Simon Peter arrived *after* him,
    he went *into* the tomb and saw the *burial* cloths there,
    and the cloth that had covered his *head*,
    not with the *burial* cloths but *rolled up* in a separate *place*.
Then the *other* disciple *also* went in,
    the one who had arrived at the tomb *first*,
    and he *saw* and *believed*.
For they did not yet *understand* the *Scripture*
    that he *had* to *rise* from the *dead*.

It is early Sunday morning; it is not the Sabbath, the seventh day, the day of rest, but the first day of a new week. The Christian observance of Sunday rather than the Jewish Sabbath begins here.

Mary presumes the body has been stolen, but the disciples see evidence to the contrary (see the commentary).

These details can be proclaimed in a tone of voice that offers them as evidence of the resurrection. That is their purpose. Experiment.

---

on this higher realm we can lessen the evidence that it has "not yet" appeared!

1 CORINTHIANS. Paul's words here were prompted by the presence in the Corinthian community of a person of evil influence. Paul is reminding the community that one bad apple can spoil the whole barrel. But he uses an image common in his day: yeast, which leavens all the dough. With its fermentation process, yeast is an effective simile for evil. It works its effect subtly but with obvious results.

When Paul refers to Christ as "our paschal lamb," unleavened bread immediately comes to mind. Unleavened bread (made without yeast) is still eaten at Jewish Passover meals, along with the Passover lamb, in memory of God's command to Israel to be ready for a speedy escape from Egypt. There was no time to wait for the dough to rise.

For all of us, in the context of the Easter celebration, the image reminds us of the need to restore our baptismal innocence. The overall effect of the reading is to make a good case for the need to purify ourselves of

wickedness, restore our baptismal innocence and lead renewed lives of simple sincerity and truthfulness.

The gospel from the Easter Vigil may be read at any Mass on Easter Sunday, at any time of the day. Luke 24:13–35 may be used at an afternoon or evening Mass.

GOSPEL   Last night at the Vigil we heard Matthew's account of the resurrection, or rather his description of events that followed the resurrection. The

Lectionary #46

AFTERNOON GOSPEL Luke 24:13–35

A reading from the holy gospel according to Luke

That very *day*, the *first* day of the week,
  two of Jesus' *disciples* were going
  to a *village* seven miles from *Jerusalem* called *Emmaus*,
  and they were *conversing* about all the things
    that had *occurred*.
And it *happened* that while they were *conversing* and *debating*,
  Jesus *himself* drew near and *walked* with them,
  but their *eyes* were prevented from *recognizing* him.

He asked them,
  "What are you *discussing* as you walk along?"
They *stopped*, looking *downcast*.
One of them, named *Cleopas*, said to him in *reply*,
  "Are you the *only* visitor to *Jerusalem*
  who does not *know* of the things
  that have taken *place* there in these days?"

And he replied to them, "What *sort* of things?"
They said to him,
  "The things that happened to *Jesus* the *Nazarene*,
  who was a *prophet* mighty in *deed* and *word*
  before *God* and all the *people*,
  how our chief *priests* and *rulers* both handed him *over*
  to a sentence of *death* and *crucified* him.
But we were *hoping* that he would be the one to *redeem* Israel;
  and besides all *this*,
  it is now the third *day* since this took *place*.

Here again we have a compromised beginning: "That very day . . ." prompts the question "What very day?" Omit it and begin, "On the first day of the week . . ."

Emmaus = eh-MAY-uhs

Proclaim this wonderful story with all the dignity and feeling you can. It deserves to be "heard again for the first time."

Cleopas = KLEE-oh-puhs

Note the dramatic effect Jesus' question has. They are incredulous.

There is much dialogue here with very little intervening text. Be sure it's clear when the speaker changes.

gospel writers offer evidence of Jesus' resurrection, not proof of a scientific kind. Such proof was not available to them, nor is it to us. The overall purpose in the way John describes the scene is to testify to the disciples' response of faith when they saw the empty tomb. No further proof was necessary for him. The same is true of us. No amount of physical evidence can force us into believing. Faith is always a gift from God that we are free to accept or refuse.

John's account contains some unique features. For example, the race between John and Peter has John arriving at the tomb first. The meaning of this detail is more than an observation that John is the younger and swifter of the two. It is a statement about John's special position as "the disciple whom Jesus loved." The same point is made when John enters the empty tomb and makes his act of faith: "He saw and believed." This is the powerful testimony of an eyewitness who has the clarity of vision unique to those who love deeply and are likewise loved.

The almost tedious description of the burial cloth and the head cloth folded up neatly by itself offers evidence that the body of Jesus had not been stolen, as was feared by the authorities and presumed here by Mary. The scene is orderly rather than chaotic; the disorder one would expect to be left by grave robbers is absent. It corrects Mary's presumption and refutes any similar claim.

The passage includes an almost contradictory parenthetical remark by the writer. Immediately following John's profession of faith ("he saw and believed"), we are reminded that the disciples did not yet understand that Jesus had to rise from the

The disciples seem to move back and forth between high hopes and bitter disappointment.

Some *women* from our group, however, have *astounded* us:
 they were at the *tomb* early in the *morning*
 and did not find his *body*;
 they came *back* and reported
 that they had *indeed* seen a vision of *angels*
 who announced that he was *alive*.

"Then some of those *with* us went to the tomb
 and found things *just* as the women had *described*,
 but *him* they did *not* see."

Let there be no hint of rebuke in Jesus' words here. Clearly the disciples take no offense.

And he said to them, "Oh, how *foolish* you are!
How slow of *heart* to *believe* all that the *prophets* spoke!
Was it not *necessary* that the Christ should *suffer* these things
 and enter into his *glory*?"

The word is opened.

Then beginning with *Moses* and all the *prophets*,
 he *interpreted* to them what *referred* to him
 in all the *Scriptures*.
As they approached the *village* to which they were *going*,
 he gave the *impression* that he was going on *farther*.
But they *urged* him, "*Stay* with us,
 for it is nearly *evening* and the day is almost *over*."
So he went in to *stay* with them.

The bread is broken.

And it *happened* that, while he was *with* them at *table*,
 he took *bread*, said the *blessing*,
 broke it, and *gave* it to them.

The disciples recognize the Lord.

With that their *eyes* were *opened* and they *recognized* him,
 but he *vanished* from their *sight*.

---

dead. Notice that what they did not understand was the *scripture* testifying to the resurrection. This they will understand only when the risen Lord appears to them, opens their minds to the scripture's meaning and then ascends to resume his place in glory at the Father's side.

The process implied here reflects our own religious experience during the 50 days of Easter. We also have our understanding stretched and fleshed out by the risen Lord's teaching before he ascends to the Father and sends the Holy Spirit to teach all of us the truth.

AFTERNOON GOSPEL Whenever you have the opportunity to proclaim a gospel narrative from Luke, consider yourself empowered in a special way. Well proclaimed, Luke can stir faith to new heights. He tells his stories with such warmth and immediacy that many of the events in Jesus' life are remembered in Luke's version above that of the other gospel writers. This is one of his most memorable and poignant narratives. Before the reform of the lectionary mandated by the Second Vatican Council, the day on which this

gospel was read was called "Emmaus Day." (By the way, it is pronounced "eh-MAY-us," "not EE-mouse"!)

The story of the disciples on the road to Emmaus is filled with the kind of vivid detail and human emotion that make the story both moving and unforgettable. The scene is tranquil, even sad, as the disciples make their way along the seven-mile journey, discussing the tragic result of their hope that Jesus would be the Messiah to set Israel free. But they are also marveling at news of a resurrection brought to them by some of their group.

Then they said to each other,
    "Were not our hearts *burning* within us
    while he *spoke* to us on the *way* and opened the *Scriptures*
        to us?"

So they set out at *once* and returned to *Jerusalem*
    where they found gathered together
    the *eleven* and those *with* them who were saying,
    "The Lord has *truly* been *raised* and has appeared to *Simon*!"

Then the *two* recounted
    what had taken place on the *way*
    and how he was made *known* to them in the *breaking* of *bread*.

We do not know precisely why they do not recognize Jesus when he joins them on their trek, but, as is customary for this gospel, the author is probably saving the recognition until the trio breaks bread together. Luke could also be saying that none of us can recognize Jesus unless we look with the eyes of faith and listen with the heart. In any event, the disciples are stopped in their tracks by Jesus' feigned ignorance of the events they are discussing. "What things?" he asks, setting the scene for the gratifying and gentle revelation.

We may be startled by what sounds like a rebuke on the lips of Jesus: "Oh, how foolish you are!" But there is no need for this to sound reproachful. After all, Jesus has strung them along to prepare for this moment. When you read his words, imagine him reaching out to place his hand on the arm of his companions and shaking his head in mock scorn. There is no dignity lost in such an image, and the words take on the sound of an encouraging teacher nudging a young student toward deeper insight.

Finally, notice what leads up to the disciples' recognition of Jesus and the meaning of his explanation. It is not until after the scriptures have been opened and the bread broken that they see him for who he is. In what other context do we gather to open the scriptures and break bread together? Luke has provided us with the essentials of a Christian eucharistic liturgy, as he so often does in the gospel. When word and action are joined, the eyes of the disciples are opened, and they recognize Jesus. And they respond to this recognition in the only way a Christian can: They rush out to share the Good News.

2ND SUNDAY OF EASTER

Lectionary #43

READING I   Acts 2:42–47

A reading from the Acts of the Apostles

They *devoted* themselves
    to the *teaching* of the *apostles* and to the *communal* life,
    to the breaking of *bread* and to the *prayers*.

Awe came upon *everyone*,
    and many *wonders* and *signs* were done through the *apostles*.

All who *believed* were *together* and had all things in *common*;
    they would sell their *property* and *possessions*
    and *divide* them among *all* according to each one's *need*.
Every *day* they *devoted* themselves
    to *meeting* together in the *temple* area
    and to breaking *bread* in their *homes*.
They ate their meals with *exultation* and sincerity of *heart*,
    praising *God* and enjoying *favor* with all the *people*.
And every day the Lord *added* to their number
      those who were being *saved*.

The first sentence lists four activities of the early church. Give each one its proper emphasis.

This is an early statement of social justice in practice, an idealized snapshot of fervent faith. Let your proclamation inspire the assembly to emulate such goodness.

The effect of genuine Christian community is that others are eager to join.

READING I — **Throughout the season of Easter the first reading is taken from the Acts of the Apostles, that wonderful account of the early Christian community's struggles and triumphs. It provides us with a view of how the risen Christ guided the newly formed church. This brief passage is one of our greatest treasures, giving us the earliest picture of the church at work and prayer.**

In fact these verses describe the ideal church or Christian community of any time or place—a group of Christians who love to be together and who look out for one another's well being. Despite the size and complexity of the modern diocese and parish, this description of community should be our goal.

In these faith-filled days of Easter, this reading can serve as an impetus toward genuine renewal, and it deserves the most sensitive and sincere proclamation you can bring to it. It should not surprise you that an effective reading of this passage could bring many in the assembly to a new realization of what "Christian community" means. Remember that as a proclaimer your ministry moves the members of the assembly toward greater zeal in living the Christian ideal in their lives.

The greatest evidence that the Christian community is living up to its name is that it wins the approval of those outside it and encourages them to become members themselves. May it be said of us as it was said of the early believers, "Behold these Christians! How they love one another!"

READING II — **After the traditional greeting, the first letter of Peter begins with a baptismal hymn, followed by the author's consoling message that our new**

READING II   1 Peter 1:3–9

A reading from the first letter of Saint Peter

Blessed be the *God* and *Father* of our Lord Jesus *Christ,*
    who in his great *mercy* gave us a *new birth* to a *living hope*
    through the *resurrection* of Jesus Christ from the *dead,*
    to an *inheritance* that is *imperishable, undefiled,*
        and *unfading,*
    kept in *heaven* for you
    who by the power of *God* are *safeguarded* through *faith,*
    to a *salvation* that is ready to be *revealed* in the final *time.*

In this you *rejoice,* although now for a *little* while
    you may have to *suffer* through various *trials,*
    so that the *genuineness* of your faith,
    more precious than *gold* that is *perishable* even though
        tested by *fire,*
    may prove to be for *praise, glory,* and *honor*
    at the *revelation* of Jesus Christ.

Although you have not *seen* him you *love* him;
    even though you do not *see* him now yet *believe* in him,
    you *rejoice* with an indescribable and glorious *joy,*
    as you attain the *goal* of your faith, the *salvation* of your *souls.*

The first section is a hymn of acclamation. Begin with great dignity and solemnity.

Don't get lost in the disjointed assertions here. Give each one its due.

The change of tone here is obvious. But again, let the meaning of each sense unit be your guide.

Notice that you are testifying to the belief of the members of your assembly. They should feel confident when they hear this.

birth in baptism unites us forever with the resurrected Lord. It is a relationship sustained by God, a relationship that enables us not only to endure the trials of life but to triumph over death itself. Notice, too, that the message is oriented toward the "end time," when Jesus Christ will appear in glory. Resurrection and eternal life are the meaning of Easter and our final destination.

Begin by recognizing the two parts of the reading: a hymn, which is followed by the author's interpretation of its meaning. The hymn is an acclamation and employs a poetic structure that cannot be read in the

same way as the prose that follows it. Even the prose continues in an exalted tone and must be read with regard to each clause rather than to complete sentences. Indeed, the entire reading is only a few sentences, so the content must be proclaimed with little regard to punctuation. Although this is not uncommon in scripture, it can cause you to move much too rapidly through the text. Analyze each sense unit so that you can proclaim it clearly.

After the hymn, a significant pause and a more quiet approach will provide effective contrast between the two sections. This

does not mean less volume but less exaltation and more intensity, since Peter now turns to the realities of trial and distress. Although our life of grace has begun, it will not come to fullness until Christ returns in glory. In the meantime, distress is an opportunity for our faith to mature and make us ready for the glorious day of Christ's return. Moreover, we can grow in faith with complete confidence that we are sustained in it through God's own power. There is no greater security than that.

The final paragraph is filled with peace, flowing from the knowledge that we can

GOSPEL   John 20:19–31

A reading from the holy gospel according to John

On the *evening* of that first day of the week,
    when the *doors* were *locked*, where the disciples were,
    for fear of the *Jews*,
    Jesus came and stood in their *midst*
    and said to them, "*Peace* be with you."
When he had *said* this, he showed them his *hands* and his *side*.
The disciples *rejoiced* when they saw the Lord.

Jesus said to them *again*, "*Peace* be with you.
As the Father has sent *me*, so I send *you*."

And when he had said this, he *breathed* on them
        and said to them,
    "Receive the Holy *Spirit*.
Whose sins you *forgive* are *forgiven* them,
    and whose sins you *retain* are *retained*."

Thomas, called *Didymus*, one of the *Twelve*,
    was not *with* them when Jesus came.
So the *other* disciples said to him, "We have seen the *Lord*."
But he said to them,
    "Unless I see the mark of the *nails* in his *hands*
    and put my *finger* into the *nailmarks*
    and put my *hand* into his *side*, I will *not* believe."

Now a week *later* his disciples were *again* inside
    and Thomas was *with* them.
Jesus came, although the *doors* were *locked*,
    and stood in their *midst* and said, "*Peace* be with you."

By all accounts the tone of John's gospel is often anti-Jewish. You may wish to replace the word "Jews" here with "authorities."

Be absolutely sure to emphasis the word "Peace" and not the preposition "with" in both instances of the greeting.

The Holy Spirit is the breath of God. The word "breathed" is important. Likewise, emphasize the words "forgive" and "forgiven," not "sins."

Pause here and refresh your conversational tone.
Didymus = DID-ih-muhs

Thomas is not refusing faith, he is struggling toward it.

---

believe even though we have not seen, which is what faith is after all. We will hear this theme developed again in today's gospel.

GOSPEL This gospel narrative is a two-part story, one within the other, and concludes with the gospel writer's comment on its meaning, as we find so often in John. It is the first appearance of Jesus to his disciples after the resurrection and follows directly on last Sunday's gospel of the tender dialogue between Jesus and Mary Magdalene.

The writer is making two points by being at pains to tell us that the disciples were cowering behind locked doors. First, the disciples had reason to fear the authorities because they had been associated with a revolutionary. Second, there are no locks capable of hindering the presence of Christ. Keep in mind always that the gospel writers have little interest in recording historical data. Every detail has a significance beyond the literal and obvious. We can lock ourselves away from God's influence in any way we choose, but none of those choices can exclude the divine presence.

There is a message of comfort here as well. Jesus is there to calm the disciples' fears and embolden and empower them for the work ahead. The bestowal of the Holy Spirit is crucially important for the growth of the church. And isn't it striking that the first power given the disciples was that of forgiving sins? Why not the power to heal, to preach, to resist temptation, to be fearless in the face of persecution and hardship? Forgiveness is the first gift, of course, because the only lasting freedom is from slavery to sin. That freedom enables us to exercise all the other powers. When Christ

There should be no sense of rebuke here. Be matter-of-fact. Both Thomas and those who have not seen are "blessed."

Again we have a change of tone. The gospel writer is commenting on the story and explaining the reason for telling it.

Then he said to *Thomas,* "Put your finger *here* and see my *hands,*
    and bring your *hand* and put it into my *side,*
    and do not be *un*believing, but *believe.*"
Thomas *answered* and said to him, "My *Lord* and my *God*!"

Jesus said to him, "Have you come to believe
    because you have *seen* me?
Blessed are those who have *not* seen and have *believed.*"

Now, Jesus did many *other* signs in the presence of his disciples
    that are not *written* in this book.
But *these* are written that you may come to *believe*
    that Jesus is the *Christ,* the Son of *God,*
    and that *through* this belief you may have *life* in his *name.*

empowers us to forgive each other's sins, he empowers us in every other way. It is a purely spiritual and sacramental power, a power greater than any temporal power as far as human beings are concerned.

Now we launch into the story within the story. Thomas is often made to sound like a bullish and stubborn unbeliever when his refusal to believe is overemphasized. But Thomas does not say he will never believe; he says that he needs a good reason to believe. He is called "doubting Thomas," not "denying Thomas." Read Thomas' words with an emphasis on "believe," implying,

"Of course, I want to believe, but I can't without some evidence."

When Jesus appears a week later, Thomas gets the evidence he needs and provides Jesus with the perfect opportunity to teach us what faith is. There is no sense of rebuke in Jesus' reply to Thomas' affirmation of faith. Rather, the reply is for all succeeding generations of Christians (like the assembly before you), who are challenged to believe without seeing. Here is an echo of Peter's words in the second reading today: "You've never seen him, but you believe in him."

Why are we expected to believe without seeing? Belief is stronger than knowledge. Belief draws us beyond ourselves; mere knowledge is limited to facts. Belief motivates us to increase our belief; knowledge can bring us to a standstill. We do need help to believe, just as Thomas did, and that is why John tells us this story. The final paragraph makes his purpose clear: You will need help believing in Jesus, so these signs have been recorded by eyewitnesses to help you. Your faith through hearing will bring you new life as a Christian, one who bears the name of your redeemer.

3RD SUNDAY OF EASTER

Lectionary #46

READING I   Acts 2:14, 22–33

A reading from the Acts of the Apostles

Then *Peter* stood up with the *Eleven*,
  raised his *voice*, and *proclaimed*:
"You who are *Jews*, indeed *all* of you staying in Jerusalem.
Let this be *known* to you, and *listen* to my *words*.
You who are *Israelites*, *hear* these words.
Jesus the *Nazarene* was a man *commended* to you by *God*
  with mighty *deeds*, *wonders*, and *signs*,
  which God *worked* through him in your *midst*,
    as you yourselves *know*.
This *man*, delivered up by the set *plan* and *foreknowledge*
    of God,
  you *killed*, using *lawless* men to *crucify* him.

"But *God* raised him *up*, *releasing* him from the throes of death,
  because it was *impossible* for him to be *held* by it.
For *David* says of him:
  'I saw the Lord *ever* before me,
  with *him* at my right hand I shall *not* be *disturbed*.
  Therefore my *heart* has been *glad* and my tongue has *exulted*;
  my flesh, *too*, will dwell in *hope*,
  because you will not *abandon* my soul to the *netherworld*,
  nor will you suffer your *holy* one to see *corruption*.
  You have made *known* to me the paths of *life*;
  you will fill me with *joy* in your *presence*.'

To avoid perpetuating the sin of anti-Semitism, you may wish to say: "People of Judea and all who live in Jerusalem."

Peter is addressing us in these words as much as his original audience.

The quotation from Psalm 16 is part of a poem. Alter your tone accordingly.

READING I   Our new edition of the lectionary is not without its weaknesses. Here is one of them. The old edition began this reading with "On the day of Pentecost Peter stood up . . ." Why the new edition begins with the words "Then Peter stood up . . ." is a mystery. It is a distraction that immediately makes us ask "When?" I suggest you begin as the older edition did or delete the word "Then."

In the design of the lectionary, the first reading is from Acts of the Apostles throughout the season of Easter, which allows us to see the work of the risen Christ in the church right up until the fiftieth and final day of the Easter season, Pentecost.

The strength and courage with which Peter delivers the discourse is already a sign that the risen Christ is at work. Here we have one of the earliest sermons on the meaning and consequences of Christ's death and resurrection. The fact that Peter charges his listeners with partial responsibility for Christ's death makes the message all the more striking, even disturbing.

Notice immediately, however, Peter's assertion that everything happened according to the purpose and plan of God. Peter's purpose is not to condemn those who put Jesus to death. They could never have done this on their own, or even with the help of outsiders, had it not been part of the divine plan for salvation. The point is that Jesus is victorious over death because he was perfectly obedient to the Father to the bitter end.

"My brothers, one can *confidently* say to you
about the patriarch *David* that he *died* and was *buried*,
and his *tomb* is in our midst to this *day*.
But since he was a *prophet* and knew that God had sworn
an *oath* to him
that he would set one of his *descendants* upon his *throne*,
he *foresaw* and *spoke* of the resurrection of the *Christ*,
that neither was he *abandoned* to the *netherworld*
nor did his *flesh* see *corruption*.

The final lines are filled with confidence and joy.

"God *raised* this Jesus;
of this we are all *witnesses*.
Exalted at the right hand of God,
he received the promise of the Holy *Spirit* from the Father
and poured him *forth*, as you *see* and *hear*."

READING II 1 Peter 1:17–21

A reading from the first letter of Saint Peter

Beloved:
If you invoke as *Father* him who judges *impartially*
according to each one's *works*,
conduct yourselves with *reverence* during the time
of your *sojourning*,
realizing that you were *ransomed* from your futile conduct,
handed on by your *ancestors*,
not with *perishable* things like *silver* or *gold*
but with the precious *blood* of *Christ*
as of a *spotless* unblemished *lamb*.

This is a formal and exalted text, and is complex in structure. Be sure each element is given its proper emphasis.

There was no way death could keep Jesus in its grasp, Peter says, because he had conquered it on the cross, delivering us from the spiritual death of separation from God. And, according to Peter's interpretation of David's words (in Psalm 16, which is the responsorial psalm following the reading), the scriptures that foretold God's special care for the chosen one were fulfilled in Christ. Here is further evidence that death had no possibility of holding Jesus in the grave. If it couldn't hold Jesus, it can't hold us either.

READING II We hear from Peter twice today, first in Acts, then in First Peter. In the second reading we continue the text from last Sunday, and we will continue reading First Peter for five more weeks. You may wish to consult the other commentaries to get a better sense of the entire letter.

Today's passage could be called a sermon on hope. Peter uses words that compare our present condition to that of the Israelites in exile. Through our baptism and the redemptive death and resurrection of Jesus, heaven is our home, and until we get there we wander in a kind of exile not unlike the one suffered by the chosen people. But such a sad state of affairs does not mean we can live unguarded lives, nor should it let us surrender to sorrow. The writer encourages us to live in hope of the glory that is to come, a glimpse of which we have seen in the paschal mystery.

The writer applies another ancient image from Israel's history to Jesus: the

Again, many thoughts are expressed in this tight little treatise. Allow each one to stand out.

He was *known* before the foundation of the *world*
    but *revealed* in the *final* time for *you*,
    who *through* him believe in *God*
    who *raised* him from the *dead* and gave him *glory*,
    so that your *faith* and *hope* are in *God*.

GOSPEL   Luke 24:13–35

A reading from the holy gospel according to Luke

Here again we have a compromised beginning: "That very day . . ." prompts the question "What very day?" Omit it and begin, "On the first day of the week . . ." Emmaus = eh-MAY-uhs

Proclaim this wonderful story with all the dignity and feeling you can. It deserves to be "heard again for the first time."

Note the dramatic effect Jesus' question has. They are incredulous.
Cleopas = KLEE-oh-puhs

That very *day*, the *first* day of the week,
    two of Jesus' *disciples* were going
    to a *village* seven miles from *Jerusalem* called *Emmaus*,
    and they were *conversing* about all the things
        that had *occurred*.
And it *happened* that while they were *conversing* and *debating*,
    Jesus *himself* drew near and *walked* with them,
    but their *eyes* were prevented from *recognizing* him.

He asked them,
    "What are you *discussing* as you walk along?"
They *stopped*, looking *downcast*.
One of them, named *Cleopas*, said to him in *reply*,
    "Are you the *only* visitor to *Jerusalem*
    who does not *know* of the things
    that have taken *place* there in these days?"

---

unblemished sacrificial lamb slain for our passover from death to life. Jesus' blood atoned for our sins, just as God had planned from the beginning of the world. The conclusion is clear: If God gave the Son (the Lamb of God) for our redemption, then our hope and trust are well placed. God's will and call are irrevocable. If God wills to save us, we will be saved! Let this confidence ring out in your proclamation.

GOSPEL Whenever you have the opportunity to proclaim a gospel narrative from Luke, consider yourself empowered in a special way. Well proclaimed, Luke can stir faith to new heights. He tells his stories with such warmth and immediacy that many of the events in Jesus' life are remembered in Luke's version above that of the other gospel writers. This is one

of his most memorable and poignant narratives. Before the reform of the lectionary mandated by the Second Vatican Council, the day on which this gospel was read was called "Emmaus Day." (By the way, it is pronounced "eh-MAY-us," not "EE-mouse"!)

    The story of the disciples on the road to Emmaus is filled with the kind of vivid detail and human emotion that make the story both moving and unforgettable. The scene is tranquil, even sad, as the disciples make their

There is much dialogue here with very little intervening text. Be sure it's clear when the speaker changes.

And he replied to them, "What *sort* of things?"
They said to him,
   "The things that happened to *Jesus* the *Nazarene*,
    who was a *prophet* mighty in *deed* and *word*
    before *God* and all the *people*,
    how our chief *priests* and *rulers* both handed him *over*
    to a sentence of *death* and *crucified* him.
But we were *hoping* that he would be the one to *redeem* Israel;
   and besides all *this*,
   it is now the third *day* since this took *place*.

The disciples seem to move back and forth between high hopes and bitter disappointment.

Some *women* from our group, however, have *astounded* us:
   they were at the *tomb* early in the *morning*
   and did not find his *body*;
   they came *back* and reported
   that they had *indeed* seen a vision of *angels*
   who announced that he was *alive*.

"Then some of those *with* us went to the tomb
   and found things *just* as the women had *described*,
   but *him* they did *not* see."

Let there be no hint of rebuke in Jesus' words here. Clearly the disciples take no offense.

And he said to them, "Oh, how *foolish* you are!
How slow of *heart* to *believe* all that the *prophets* spoke!
Was it not *necessary* that the Christ should *suffer* these things
   and enter into his *glory*?"

The word is opened.

Then beginning with *Moses* and all the *prophets*,
   he *interpreted* to them what *referred* to him
   in all the *Scriptures*.
As they approached the *village* to which they were *going*,
   he gave the *impression* that he was going on *farther*.
But they *urged* him, "*Stay* with us,
   for it is nearly *evening* and the day is almost *over*."
So he went in to *stay* with them.

way along their seven-mile journey, discussing the tragic result of their hope that Jesus would be the Messiah to set Israel free. But they are also marveling at news of a resurrection brought to them by some of their group.

    We do not know precisely why they do not recognize Jesus when he joins them on their trek, but, as is customary for this gospel, the author is probably saving the recognition until the trio breaks bread together. Luke could also be saying that none of us can recognize Jesus unless we look with the eyes of faith and listen with the heart. In any event, the disciples are stopped in their tracks by Jesus' feigned ignorance of the events they are discussing. "What things?" he asks, setting the scene for the gratifying and gentle revelation.

    We may be startled by what sounds like a rebuke on the lips of Jesus: "Oh, how foolish you are!" But there is no need for this to sound reproachful. After all, Jesus has strung them along to prepare for this moment. When you read his words, imagine him reaching out to place his hand on the arm of his companions and shaking his head in mock scorn. There is no dignity lost in such an image, and the words take on the

The bread is broken.

And it *happened* that, while he was *with* them at *table*,
   he took *bread*, said the *blessing*,
   broke it, and *gave* it to them.

The disciples recognize the Lord.

With that their *eyes* were *opened* and they *recognized* him,
   but he *vanished* from their *sight*.

Then they said to each other,
   "Were not our hearts *burning* within us
   while he *spoke* to us on the *way* and opened the *Scriptures*
      to us?"

So they set out at *once* and returned to *Jerusalem*
   where they found gathered together
   the *eleven* and those *with* them who were saying,
   "The Lord has *truly* been *raised* and has appeared to *Simon*!"

Then the *two* recounted
   what had taken place on the *way*
   and how he was made *known* to them in the *breaking* of *bread*.

sound of an encouraging teacher nudging a young student toward deeper insight.

Finally, notice what leads up to the disciples' recognition of Jesus and the meaning of his explanation. It is not until after the scriptures have been opened and the bread broken that they see him for who he is. In what other context do we gather to open the scriptures and break bread together? Luke has provided us with the essentials of a Christian eucharistic liturgy, as he so often does in the gospel. When word and action are joined, the eyes of the disciples are opened, and they recognize Jesus. And they respond to this recognition in the only way a Christian can: They rush out to share the Good News.

4TH SUNDAY OF EASTER

Lectionary #49

READING I   Acts 2:14a, 36–41

A reading from the Acts of the Apostles

Then *Peter* stood up with the *Eleven*,
    raised his *voice*, and *proclaimed*:
"Let the whole *house* of Israel *know* for *certain*
    that *God* has made both *Lord* and *Christ*,
    this *Jesus* whom you *crucified*."

Now when they *heard* this, they were cut to the *heart*,
    and they *asked* Peter and the other apostles,
    "What are we to *do*, my brothers?"
Peter said to them,
    "*Repent* and be *baptized*, every *one* of you,
    in the name of Jesus *Christ* for the forgiveness of your *sins*;
    and you will receive the *gift* of the Holy *Spirit*.
For the *promise* is made to *you* and to your *children*
    and to *all* those far *off*,
    whomever the Lord our God will *call*."

He testified with many *other* arguments,
        and was *exhorting* them,
    "*Save* yourselves from this *corrupt* generation."
Those who *accepted* his message were *baptized*,
    and about three *thousand* persons were *added* that day.

This is a bold announcement. Emphasize God's role in exalting Jesus as Messiah and Lord.

Here is a message for all time. The call to conversion is as true for the assembly before you as it was for the original hearers.

There is both challenge and consolation in this final section. Rejoice in the growth that the fledgling church experienced on this occasion.

READING I Peter demonstrates his new-found courage as he continues his Pentecost sermon. The point of this sermon is clear: Jesus of Nazareth is the long-awaited Messiah, despite all evidence to the contrary. Certainly he is not the kind of Messiah that Israel had expected, but Israel's Messiah he is. Peter is quite brave in pointing out to his hearers that they were responsible for Jesus' death. But apparently he was convincing for we see the profound effect his preaching had on his audience.

When the people ask what they can do in the face of such a charge, Peter answers their question in words that mean far more than they seem to at first glance. Of course we must change our selfish ways, but a great deal more is implied than changing our behavior. Christian conversion is more a matter of seeing things in a new way, seeing more clearly what Jesus has done for us. For Peter's audience it meant moving away from old expectations of a conquering hero and embracing the revelation of a self-giving God.

Once we open ourselves to the full realization of the immensity of God's love, reformation of life is spontaneous. And apparently those who heard Peter speak underwent such a conversion. They saw things in a new way and began to understand God's plan for salvation through Jesus. Thus, 3,000 were baptized that day, not so much in order to be saved as to give expression to their newfound conviction that God willed to save them. God takes the initiative; we respond to compelling love.

Every time you proclaim this good news, you invite the members of your assembly to move ever more closely toward genuine conversion, to see things in a completely new light and realize that God's saving love

READING II   1 Peter 2:20b–25

A reading from the first letter of Saint Peter

Beloved:
If you are *patient* when you *suffer* for doing what is *good,*
    this is a *grace* before *God.*
For to *this* you have been *called,*
    because Christ *also* suffered for *you,*
    leaving you an *example* that you should *follow* in his *footsteps.*
"He committed *no* sin, and no *deceit* was found in his *mouth.*"

When he was *insulted,* he returned *no* insult;
    when he *suffered,* he did not *threaten;*
    instead, he handed himself *over* to the one who judges *justly.*

He *himself* bore our *sins* in his *body* upon the *cross,*
    so that, *free* from sin, we might *live* for *righteousness.*
By his *wounds* you have been *healed.*

For you had gone *astray* like *sheep,*
    but you have now *returned* to the *shepherd* and *guardian*
        of your *souls.*

The image of the suffering servant is central to our belief about Jesus' role in our redemption. You may wish to consult the commentary on the first reading for Good Friday.

Think of the irony in the idea that Jesus' wounds healed our wounds. It sums up the significance of Jesus' sacrifice and, indeed, the meaning of Easter.

---

is an utterly free gift to which we respond with unmodified joy.

READING II This is the third of six consecutive Sundays on which the second reading is from the first letter of Peter. You may wish to consult earlier commentaries to get an overall view of the letter and its context.

No one escapes suffering in this life. We strive to relieve it, we do all we can to minimize it, and there may be times when we resent it bitterly. But it is a fact of life that cannot be denied. Peter is not saying here that there is virtue in needless suffering, nor that we can tolerate suffering inflicted on the defenseless. On the contrary, Jesus made it clear by the example of his ministry that suffering is to be relieved whenever possible. Peter message is that, given the fact of human suffering, we can find strength to endure it through the example of Jesus' own redemptive suffering.

In itself, suffering is an evil, the consequence of a fallen world. It will have no place in God's eternal reign. But in the meantime it can be for us an occasion of grace. The Christian sees suffering as an opportunity bring good out of evil, just as Jesus did. Isaiah the prophet summed it up in the well-known phrase "By his wounds we are healed."

Jesus is the sacrificial lamb led willingly to the slaughter. By enduring suffering and death he became the shepherd and guardian of our souls. In his nonviolent response to those who tortured him and put him to death, Jesus modeled total reliance on the God who judges with justice. Our suffering will not be meaningless for us when we identify with Jesus the suffering servant, by whose suffering our suffering is redeemed.

GOSPEL   John 10:1–10

A reading from the holy gospel according to John

Jesus said:
"*Amen, amen*, I *say* to you,
  whoever does not enter a *sheepfold* through the *gate*
  but climbs over *elsewhere* is a *thief* and a *robber*.
But whoever enters through the *gate* is the *shepherd* of the sheep.
The gatekeeper *opens* it for him, and the *sheep* hear his *voice*,
  as the shepherd calls his own sheep by *name*
    and leads them *out*.
When he has driven out all his *own*,
  he walks *ahead* of them, and the sheep *follow* him,
  because they *recognize* his *voice*.
But they will not follow a *stranger*;
  they will run *away* from him,
  because they do not recognize the *voice* of strangers."
Although Jesus used this figure of *speech*,
  the *Pharisees* did not *realize* what he was trying to *tell* them.

So Jesus said again, "*Amen, amen*, I *say* to you,
  I am the gate for the sheep.
All who came *before* me are *thieves* and *robbers*,
  but the sheep did not *listen* to them.
I am the gate.
Whoever enters through *me* will be *saved*,
  and will come *in* and go *out* and find *pasture*.
A *thief* comes only to *steal* and *slaughter* and *destroy*;
  I came so that they might have *life*
    and have it more *abundantly*."

Notice that Jesus begins his discourse with a formula. It predicts an important and solemn pronouncement. This is true whenever you encounter a passage beginning with such words as, "Amen, amen, I say to you," or "Truly, I assure you," or "Verily, verily, I say unto you."

There is no neat and logical arrangement of the images here. Jesus is both shepherd and gate, and the shepherd enters through the gate, opened by the keeper. But they are effective in the way they shift back and forth.

What his hearers do not grasp is that Jesus is claiming to be the Messiah. Any others who claim that role he must be false.

Another formula introduces an important point. Do not neglect it.

The gospel passage ends with a much-loved text. Proclaim it boldly.

GOSPEL | Today's responsorial psalm is the universally loved Psalm 23, with its response, "The Lord is my shepherd." In the second reading we hear Peter describe Jesus as the shepherd of souls. The image appears again in this gospel text, making it clear why today is sometimes referred to as Good Shepherd Sunday.

But there is another image in this reading: Jesus calls himself the gate by which the sheep enter. The two images come together in one narrative to help us understand more fully our relationship to Jesus. In addition, Jesus contrasts himself with bad shepherds, whom the sheep will not follow, and with the thief, who does not use the gate but breaks in by another way to harm the sheep.

We, the members of the church, are the sheep. Some have objected to this comparison on the grounds that sheep are stupid animals. But this objection misses the very clear point of the comparison, which centers on the shepherd, not on the flock. There are good shepherds, and there are bad shepherds. Jesus is the perfect model of the good shepherd who gives his life for his sheep.

This gospel reading is full of helpful images and parallels, most of which are easy to grasp. One central point should be stressed: The sheep follow the shepherd because they recognize his or her voice. This is literally true. A flock of sheep will only follow its own shepherd's voice. It is true from the standpoint of faith as well. When we know the true shepherd's voice through informed faith, we will not follow false shepherds or mistake the allure of self-centered fantasies for the voice of the true Messiah. Jesus is the model for all who are called to leadership; he is the gate by which we enter the fold of his faithful.

5TH SUNDAY OF EASTER

Lectionary #52

READING I   Acts 6:1–7

A reading from the Acts of the Apostles

As the *number* of *disciples* continued to *grow*,
    the *Hellenists* complained against the *Hebrews*
    because their *widows*
    were being *neglected* in the daily *distribution*.
So the *Twelve* called together the *community* of the disciples
        and said,
    "It is not *right* for us to *neglect* the word of *God*
        to serve at *table*.
Brothers, *select* from among you *seven reputable men*,
    filled with the *Spirit* and *wisdom*,
    whom we shall *appoint* to this task,
    whereas *we* shall devote ourselves to *prayer*
    and to the *ministry* of the *word*."

The proposal was *acceptable* to the whole *community*,
    so they chose *Stephen*, a man filled with *faith*
        and the Holy *Spirit*,
    also *Philip, Prochorus, Nicanor, Timon, Parmenas*,
    and *Nicholas* of *Antioch*, a *convert* to Judaism.
They *presented* these men to the *apostles*
    who *prayed* and laid *hands* on them.

Prejudice knows no time or place. The Twelve are dealing with a real scandal here, but they deal with it promptly and effectively.

Prochorus = PRAH-kuh-ruhs
Nicanor = nī-KAY-ner
Timon = TĪ-muhn
Parmenas = PAHR-muh-nuhs
Antioch = AN-tee-ahk

READING I   Here we are presented with an account of the inauguration of a new ministry in the church. It grew out of a genuine need, as all genuine ministry does. The leaders are concerned with both aspects of Christian community, spiritual and temporal. While not neglecting their primary task of preaching and prayer, they know that the material needs of the community have to be addressed, too. Their answer to the situation is to delegate and distribute tasks.

The history here has a practical lesson for us. Cultivating one's own spiritual life is not enough; public works of charity alone are not sufficient either. Faith finds its expression in good works, and good works in turn build faith. Those who feel they are Christian simply because they foster a private relationship with God have veered from their true calling.

Your challenge in proclaiming this text is to convey the importance of practical matters in the life of faith. Every parish has its pragmatic concerns, and the scriptures can teach us how to deal with them effectively.

In the story before us, the most urgent matter at hand is social justice and, perhaps, prejudice against some members of the community. The Twelve successfully arbitrate differences between Greeks and Jews—a remarkable achievement when we realize the long-term enmity between these two groups. Their approach to the situation gives us another instance of the power of Christian faith to be a force for reconciliation.

The final paragraph describes in a beautiful way the success of the early church in attracting new members into the

The final section is clearly a broader commentary on the growth of the church. Pause before it, and let it be the joyful conclusion it is.

The word of God continued to *spread*,
  and the *number* of the disciples in *Jerusalem* increased *greatly*;
  even a large group of *priests* were becoming *obedient*
    to the *faith*.

READING II   1 Peter 2:4–9

A reading from the first letter of Saint Peter

Beloved:

Notice that you are using direct address here ("you," "yourselves"), which is always effective. The assembly is immediately more attentive when they hear themselves being addressed directly.

Come to him, a *living* stone, *rejected* by human *beings*
  but *chosen* and *precious* in the sight of *God*,
  and, like *living* stones,
  let *yourselves* be built into a spiritual *house*
  to be a holy *priesthood* to offer spiritual *sacrifices*
  acceptable to God through Jesus *Christ*.

For it says in *Scripture*:

Learn how to proclaim quotations without relying on words to introduce them. This is done with a slight pause and an elevation of tone.

  "*Behold*, I am laying a *stone* in *Zion*,
  a *cornerstone*, *chosen* and *precious*,
  and whoever *believes* in it shall *not* be put to *shame*."
Therefore, its *value* is for you who have *faith*,
    but for those *without* faith:
  "The stone that the builders *rejected*
  has become the *cornerstone*,
  A stone that will make people *stumble*,
  and a *rock* that will make them *fall*."
They *stumble* by disobeying the *word*, as is their *destiny*.

---

fold. The priests referred to are religious leaders of the Jewish tradition who might be expected to resist Christianity more strongly than others.

This passage requires extra preparation. Consult the pronunciation keys provided in the margin for the correct pronunciation of the list of proper names. There must never be any hesitation by the proclaimer in such matters. Stumbling over unusual words guarantees that the assembly will be distracted from the message and drawn to the reader's struggle. It is difficult to emphasize this too much. Your credibility must not be

compromised by an impression that you did not do your homework. Both the assembly and the sacred texts deserve your best effort in the performance of your ministry.

READING II We have been reading from the first letter of Peter for the last three Sundays and will continue for two more. To get a feel for the context and overall thrust of Peter's message, you may wish to consult earlier and later commentaries.

The image of Christ as a "living stone" enables the author to demonstrate that Christ is a rock-solid foundation for those who believe in him and a rock wall of obstacles for those who find belief difficult. Any honest Christian will tell you that there are times when Jesus Christ seems to be both. If you can appreciate the struggle involved in your own faith journey, you will communicate it to your hearers to their benefit.

The most effective tone to adopt in proclaiming such a passage is one of sadness and empathy. Certainly we can't communicate superiority or disdain. Proclaim the text

The final paragraph is a trumpet blast. We are defined in four glorious phrases. Don't rush through them.

You are "a *chosen* race, a royal *priesthood*,
  a holy *nation*, a people of his *own*,
  so that you may announce the *praises*" of him
  who called you out of *darkness* into his wonderful *light*.

GOSPEL   John 14:1–12

A reading from the holy gospel according to John

Jesus said to his *disciples*:
  "Do not let your *hearts* be *troubled*.
You have faith in *God*; have faith also in *me*.
In my Father's *house* there are *many* dwelling places.
If there were *not*,
  would I have *told* you that I am going to prepare
    a *place* for you?
And if I *go* and prepare a *place* for you,
  I will come *back* again and take you to *myself*,
  so that where *I* am you *also* may be.
Where I am *going* you *know* the *way*."

Thomas said to him,
  "Master, we do *not* know where you are going;
  how can we know the *way*?"

Jesus said to him, "*I* am the way and the *truth* and the *life*.
No one comes to the *Father* except through *me*.
If you know *me*, then you will also know my *Father*.
From now on you *do* know him and have *seen* him."

The text begins with a message from Jesus but soon becomes a conversation. Conversation demands greater vocal variety, more deliberate delivery and careful pauses.

Thomas contradicts Jesus. "We do not know . . ." But it is a request for clarification rather than an outburst of frustration.

---

as it is: a difficult saying that we can never fully understand. At the same time we should rejoice in being a "chosen people." The final sentence here is filled with gratitude at being claimed as God's own, and one of the most striking developments in our history is the gradual realization that God's call to salvation is universal. Those who know the joy of being "chosen" also take on the happy task of increasing their number by inviting all the world to join them.

GOSPEL We are approaching the celebrations of Ascension and Pentecost. Today's gospel reading prepares us for what is to come. Jesus says that it is necessary for him to leave this world so that even greater works than his can be accomplished. How can this be? The answer he gives is that he will send the Holy Spirit, and in the power of that Spirit his work will pervade the entire world. History bears him out on this point, though much remains to be done.

The affectionate exchanges between Jesus and Thomas and Philip must be proclaimed with all the encouragement that is so clearly present in Jesus' words. There is no rebuke or even disappointment in his tone as he encourages Philip one more time to recognize him as the manifestation of the Father's love. More than that, he answers Philip's request with a question. "You still do not know me?" Jesus continues by repeating what he has said before: "The Father and

We are eternally grateful for Philip's question. It is our own, and the answer is clear: "If you want to know the Father, if you want to see the Father, look at me."

Philip said to him,
  "Master, *show* us the Father, and that will be *enough* for us."

Jesus said to him, "Have I been with you for so *long* a time
  and you still do not *know* me, Philip?
Whoever has seen *me* has seen the *Father*.
How can you say, '*Show* us the Father'?
Do you not *believe* that I am *in* the Father
  and the Father is in *me*?
The words that I *speak* to you I do not speak on my *own*.
The *Father* who *dwells* in me is doing his *works*.
Believe me that *I* am in the *Father* and the *Father* is in *me*,
  or *else*, believe because of the works *themselves*.
Amen, *amen*, I *say* to you,
  whoever *believes* in me will do the *works* that I do,
  and will do *greater* ones than these,
  because I am *going* to the *Father*."

Jesus gives us a choice: Believe he is in the Father, or look at the evidence of his works. It amounts to the same thing. Jesus' work is the work of the Father because the Father and Jesus are one.

I are one." Like Philip, we all tend to keep asking similar questions and wanting clearer explanations. But the simple (and awesome) message here is that whenever we want to know what God is like, we must look at Jesus—his life, ministry, words, death, resurrection and ascension. The Holy Spirit he sends enables us to have this kind of vision, if we will only open ourselves to it.

Nothing can take the sadness out of this encounter. Jesus is about to leave his friends, with whom he has been through so much. Here, too, there is consolation, even in the sadness. We all know the pain of separation from a loved one through death or other circumstances. In Jesus' consoling words we hear words of comfort for our pain and the reason for our hope. A time is coming when there will be no more pain of separation, only the joy of reunion in eternity.

In your proclamation of this moving passage, the members of the assembly will hear the sadness of separation. But emphasize Jesus' words of encouragement, which spur them forward with renewed faith and hope.

6TH SUNDAY OF EASTER

Lectionary #55

READING I   Acts 8:5–8, 14–17

A reading from the Acts of the Apostles

Notice here that you are telling a
straightforward narrative. There is no
interpretation of the meaning of the
events, and yet their significance must be
abundantly clear in your proclamation.
Samaria = suh-MAYR-ee-uh

Philip went down to the city of *Samaria*
    and proclaimed the *Christ* to them.
With one *accord*, the crowds paid *attention*
        to what was said by Philip
    when they *heard* it and saw the *signs* he was doing.
For unclean *spirits*, crying out in a loud *voice*,
    came out of many *possessed* people,
    and many *paralyzed* or *crippled* people were cured.
There was great *joy* in that city.

Now when the apostles in *Jerusalem*
    heard that *Samaria* had accepted the word of *God*,
    they sent them *Peter* and *John*,
    who went down and *prayed* for them,
    that they might receive the Holy *Spirit*,
    for it had not yet *fallen* upon *any* of them;
    they had only been *baptized* in the name of the Lord *Jesus*.
Then they laid *hands* on them
    and they *received* the Holy Spirit.

There is a danger of rushing this reading.
Be sure to pause at the natural halfway
point, and maintain a deliberate,
careful pace.

READING I The Acts of the Apostles is a compelling account of the early church, recording both successes and failures, good times and bad. Philip's departure for Samaria coincides with a great persecution of the church in Jerusalem. It should not surprise us that the church experienced persecution shortly after its founding. Any revolutionary movement, fueled with great fervor, is bound to attract the malicious attention of those who feel threatened by it.

Can this be the same Philip who last week begged Jesus for a glimpse of God to fortify his faith? It is, and his missionary efforts in Samaria—raising the place's joy to a fever pitch—demonstrate how much he took Jesus' reply to heart. So that this new community of believers can be clearly associated with the center of the new faith (Jerusalem), Peter and John are sent down as officials to bestow the Holy Spirit.

Though this reading is a straightforward telling of events, it is filled with dramatic images and enormous enthusiasm. In your proclamation, communicate the energetic commitment of the early missionaries and the joy of the new converts.

In places where the Ascension of the Lord is celebrated next Sunday, May 12, the second reading and the gospel of the Seventh Sunday of Easter (lectionary #59) may be read today. Check with the liturgy coordinator or homilist to find out which readings will be used today.

READING II We have been reading from the first letter of Peter for the last four Sundays and will continue to do so through next Sunday. You may wish to refer

There is a quiet strength, conviction, trust and peace in this text that is extraordinary. Let your proclamation reflect these qualities.

Here is a thumbnail sketch of the purpose of Christ's suffering, our model and consolation in our own suffering.

READING II   1 Peter 3:15–18

A reading from the first letter of Saint Peter

Beloved:
Sanctify Christ as *Lord* in your *hearts.*
Always be *ready* to give an *explanation*
    to anyone who *asks* you for a *reason* for your *hope,*
    but do it with *gentleness* and *reverence,*
    keeping your *conscience* clear,
    so that, when you are *maligned,*
    those who *defame* your good conduct in Christ
    may *themselves* be put to shame.
For it is better to suffer for doing *good,*
    if that be the will of *God,* than for doing *evil.*

For Christ *also* suffered for sins *once,*
    the *righteous* for the sake of the *unrighteous,*
    that he might *lead* you to *God.*
Put to *death* in the *flesh,*
    he was brought to *life* in the *Spirit.*

to earlier commentaries to get a sense of the letter's overall content and significance.

Today we hear the words of a man who has grown wise and confident in his faith. He is clearly a seasoned master of Christian living, and he has become so in the midst of much suffering and struggle. As you may have noticed, the author of First Peter returns frequently to the matter of suffering for one's faith. He makes it clear throughout that genuine faith cannot escape struggle.

When you consider how ridiculous Christian hope can sound to the cynical ear, it is not surprising that we should be called

on to account for our faith. We proclaim a crucified Master who told us that it is better to serve than to be served. We are willing to suffer for our good deeds because then we are closely identified with a suffering servant whose wounds have healed our own. No wonder we are called upon to explain ourselves! Indeed, if we are not so challenged, we need to wonder why.

How do we respond? We needn't worry about that, Peter says, as long as our consciences are clear and we respond with gentle reverence. So much for talk of "doing battle for the faith"—gentle reverence isn't

much of a battle cry. So much for "defending the faith"—faith, by definition, is an indefensible position. Not even death itself threatens our hope, so what is there to defend? We defend only our manner of life, which should defend itself by virtue of its good works.

GOSPEL | The important thing about this gospel passage is that it moves us away from the resurrected Jesus to show us the new manner of his presence in the world: the Spirit of truth. We

GOSPEL John 14:15–21

A reading from the holy gospel according to John

Jesus said to his *disciples*:
"If you *love* me, you will keep my *commandments*.
And I will ask the *Father*,
    and he will give you another *Advocate* to be with you *always*,
    the Spirit of *truth*, whom the *world* cannot *accept*,
    because it neither *sees* nor *knows* him.
But *you* know him, because he *remains* with you,
    and will be *in* you.

"I will not leave you *orphans*; I will *come* to you.
In a *little* while the *world* will no longer *see* me,
    but *you* will see me, because *I* live and *you* will live.
On that day you will *realize* that *I* am in my *Father*
    and *you* are in *me* and *I* in *you*.

"Whoever has my *commandments* and *observes* them
    is the one who *loves* me.
And whoever loves *me* will be *loved* by my *Father*,
    and *I* will love him and *reveal* myself to him."

Jesus is speaking throughout the entire passage. A tone of gentle encouragement and unshakeable love should characterize your proclamation.

Jesus speaks as a loving parent. This must be read slowly. It is complex: "I in my Father"; "you in me"; "I in you."

This is not easy to proclaim. There are many levels of emphasis necessary to bring out the full meaning and progression of thought.

---

are prompted more than ever to see life with spiritual rather than material vision. We are taught to walk by faith, not by sight.

The charm and attraction we have for the image of Jesus walking the earth in his resurrected body must be transformed by wisdom and insight that enable us to see in the coming of the Spirit an even more intimate union with Christ. It was not an easy adjustment for the apostles, nor is it for us.

But love makes it possible, and that is the point of Jesus' words to us today. The proof of our love is that we obey Jesus, and we can give true obedience because we

love, and are loved by, the one we obey. In other words, to continue what sounds like a circular argument, our obedience is grounded in love and in obeying we demonstrate our love for the one to whom we are obedient. Indeed, the command we observe is to love! How far this removes us from any view of Christianity as an ethical code! We submit to external codes of conduct because there are reprisals if we don't. We submit to the Lord's commandments because we love and trust the one who commands us to love.

How clear can your proclamation make this to the assembly? Can you communicate

the revolutionary concept of loving obedience that Jesus asks of us? Remember that Jesus himself recognized that "the world" cannot accept it because the world does not recognize him for who he is. Perhaps the best you can do as proclaimer is to help your hearers see Jesus a bit more clearly, to recognize him and to love him. The bottom line in Christianity is that our obedience, our faith, our love is centered on the person of Jesus, God's love made visible. Centered anywhere else, our obedience, faith and love will be burdensome.

ASCENSION OF THE LORD

Lectionary #58

READING I Acts 1:1–11

A reading from the beginning of the Acts of the Apostles

Theophilus = thee-OF-uh-luhs

There is a sweeping summary here of "all that Jesus did and taught." Communicate something of the vastness of the text.

In the *first* book, Theophilus,
   I dealt with all that Jesus *did* and *taught*
   until the day he was *taken up*,
   after giving *instructions* through the Holy *Spirit*
   to the *apostles* whom he had *chosen*.
He presented himself *alive* to them
   by many *proofs* after he had *suffered*,
   appearing to them during forty days
   and *speaking* about the *kingdom* of *God*.

The order to stay in Jerusalem until they had received the Holy Spirit is significant. The good news was to be proclaimed beginning in Jerusalem and then throughout the world. We are the "new Jerusalem" and the "new Israel."

While *meeting* with them,
   he *enjoined* them not to depart from *Jerusalem*,
   but to *wait* for "the *promise* of the Father
   about which you have heard me *speak*;
   for *John* baptized with *water*,
   but in a few *days you* will be baptized with the Holy *Spirit*."

When they had gathered together they *asked* him,
   "*Lord*, are you at this time going to restore
   the kingdom to *Israel*?"
He answered them, "It is not for you to *know* the *times*
      or *seasons*
   that the *Father* has established by his own *authority*.

If the Ascension of the Lord is celebrated next Sunday, May 12, today's readings are used in place of those for the Seventh Sunday of Easter.

READING I When the first reading is announced like this one, "A reading from the beginning of the Acts of the Apostles," the assembly takes special notice. In this case its members' special attention will be richly rewarded. Luke, the great storyteller, is the author here. The first book he refers to is, of course, his gospel

narrative. Theophilus (Greek for "one who loves God") may have been a specific person, but it is more likely that the writer is addressing all readers of good will.

Luke's point at the beginning of his second book is to show how God's plan to save the world continues in one great sweep from the time of Jesus' ministry and beyond. The good news of Jesus' victory will spread from Jerusalem to all of Judea, Samaria and the ends of the known world.

The question the apostles ask about the restoration of Israel has larger implications than we might think. There is the literal

aspect of the question, which Jesus does not answer, saying only that such knowledge is reserved to God. We know some early Christians saw the reconstitution of Israel in the community established by Christ—the "new Israel." Luke is surely hinting at this theme here.

In effect, Luke teaches us what a life of faith is. It is not a life of certainty; rather, it is a life of believing and acting on that belief. Jesus' physical disappearance from the historical scene allows his spiritual presence to completely permeate time and space.

Pause slightly at the end of Jesus' words.

But you will receive *power* when the Holy *Spirit* comes upon you,
  and you will be my *witnesses* in *Jerusalem*,
  throughout *Judea* and *Samaria*,
  and to the ends of the *earth*."

When he had *said* this, as they were looking *on*,
  he was *lifted up*, and a *cloud* took him from their *sight*.
While they were looking intently at the *sky* as he was *going*,
  suddenly two *men* dressed in white *garments*
    stood *beside* them.

**There is no rebuke in the angels' question.
It is a rhetorical remark to strengthen the
following statement about Jesus' return.**

They said, "Men of *Galilee*,
  why are you *standing there* looking at the *sky*?
This *Jesus* who has been taken *up* from you into *heaven*
  will *return* in the same *way* as you have seen him
    going into heaven."

READING II   Ephesians 1:17–23

A reading from the letter of Saint Paul to the Ephesians

Brothers and sisters:
May the *God* of our *Lord* Jesus *Christ*, the Father of *glory*,
  give you a Spirit of *wisdom* and *revelation*
  resulting in *knowledge* of him.

**Notice that the reading is a list of petitions
and assertions. Ignore the punctuation, and
read the sense units. Good vocal variety will
enable you to communicate the complicated
levels of subordination.
Except for words like "head," "body" and
"feet," all the nouns here are abstract.
This means that your proclamation must
be deliberate, varied and slow.**

May the eyes of your *hearts* be *enlightened*,
  that you may *know* what is the *hope* that belongs to his *call*,
  what are the riches of *glory*
  in his *inheritance* among the *holy* ones,
  and what is the surpassing *greatness* of his *power*
  for us who *believe*,

Remember the angels' question at the empty tomb: "Why do you look for the living among the dead?" The angels' question on the mount of the ascension brings the point home. "Why stand looking up at the skies? Jesus will return. Meanwhile, the business at hand is to tell the world all that he did and taught."

READING II This second reading celebrates Christ's role in the saving plan of God. It must be proclaimed with high energy and a joyful voice. The first paragraph is a greeting and a blessing, a prayer for all who hear it. We pray that we may be granted the kind of wisdom and inner vision that will enable us to walk by faith and not by sight. Now that we no longer experience Jesus' bodily presence, we must see him in the world in other ways.

The second paragraph gives us a glimpse of the risen Christ at the right hand of God. He through whom the heavens and the earth were created has now returned to heaven where he continues to intercede for us. Jesus and the Father are one.

The final paragraph portrays Christ as the ruler of the world, head of his body the church, which is now guided by the Holy Spirit. God has revealed the fullness of love among us, and we have received that fullness in the person of Christ.

Though this reading is not particularly easy (the thoughts tumble over one another), anything less than a powerful proclamation will not do it justice.

GOSPEL Today's first reading began with the announcement "A reading from the beginning of the Acts of the Apostles." The proclamation of the gospel

in accord with the *exercise* of his great *might*,
which he worked in *Christ*,
raising him from the *dead*
and *seating* him at his right *hand* in the *heavens*,
far above every *principality*, *authority*, *power*, and *dominion*,
and every *name* that is *named*
not only in *this* age but also in the one to *come*.

And he put *all* things beneath his *feet*
and gave him as *head* over all things to the *church*,
which is his *body*,
the *fullness* of the one who fills *all* things in every *way*.

Make something of the assertion that the church is Christ's body. We cannot hear this too often or too strongly.

GOSPEL   Matthew 28:16–20

A reading from the conclusion of the holy gospel according to Matthew

Do not neglect the interesting assertion that some of the apostles were still doubtful. Those doubts are dispelled when they see the resurrected Lord. We are helped in our own doubts by the testimony of these eyewitnesses.

The voice of the risen Christ must be filled with peace and strength, dignity and warmth.

Do not neglect "therefore."

The eleven *disciples* went to *Galilee*,
to the *mountain* to which Jesus had *ordered* them.
When they *saw* him, they *worshiped*, but they *doubted*.

Then Jesus *approached* and said to them,
"All *power* in *heaven* and on *earth* has been given to *me*.
Go, therefore, and make *disciples* of all *nations*,
baptizing them in the name of the *Father*,
and of the *Son*, and of the Holy *Spirit*,
teaching them to *observe* all that I have *commanded* you.

Pause before the final message of comfort. It is a much-loved saying of Jesus and deserves special emphasis.

"And *behold*, I am with you *always*, until the end of the *age*."

---

begins, "A reading from the conclusion of the holy gospel according to Matthew." On the feast of the Ascension, when we celebrate the completion of Jesus' earthly ministry and his return to glory, the readings give us a tidy summary of all that Jesus did and taught, and a commission to spread the word far and wide.

Matthew's final words to us present a dramatic scene indeed, and it is filled with significance far beyond the words he uses to describe it. First of all, the meeting takes place on a mountain. In Matthew (who always sees Jesus as the new Moses), many

important events take place on a mountaintop: the sermon on the mount, the transfiguration, the crucifixion and now the ascension. Moses received the ten commandments on Mount Sinai; Jesus proclaims the new law in the same conspicuous way, emphasizing its importance.

The resurrected Jesus reveals himself here in a new way. He is now revealed as the Christ, the ruler of the universe, with all authority in heaven and on earth. It is in that authority that he utters the great missionary challenge to the eleven who remained faithful. The word "therefore" in this passage is

crucially important. Jesus is saying, "Because I have full authority, I can send you forth with every assurance that your mission will be successful. And because I have full authority, my presence will never desert you."

No Christian can neglect this commission. If the universal call to evangelize fills us with dread or feelings of insecurity, we need to take to heart the final promise of Matthew's gospel, "I am with you always."

7TH SUNDAY OF EASTER

Lectionary #59

READING I   Acts 1:12–14

A reading from the Acts of the Apostles

After *Jesus* had been taken up to *heaven* the *apostles*
    returned to *Jerusalem*
    from the mount called *Olivet*, which is *near* Jerusalem,
    a sabbath day's journey *away*.

When they entered the *city*
    they went to the upper *room* where they were *staying*,
    Peter and *John* and *James* and *Andrew*,
    Philip and *Thomas*, *Bartholomew* and *Matthew*,
    James son of *Alphaeus*, Simon the *Zealot*,
    and *Judas* son of *James*.

All these *devoted* themselves with one accord to *prayer*,
    together with some *women*,
    and *Mary* the *mother* of Jesus, and his *brothers*.

Here we have a quiet scene, following immediately upon the drama of the ascension. It is quiet and straightforward but filled with anticipation.

**Read the names of the Eleven with expert clarity and confidence. Consult a pronunciation guide if necessary.
Alphaeus = AL-fee-uhs
Zealot = ZEL-uht**

READING II   1 Peter 4:13–16

A reading from the first letter of Saint Peter

Beloved:
Rejoice to the extent that you *share* in the *sufferings* of *Christ*,
    so that when his *glory* is revealed
    you may *also* rejoice *exultantly*.

It should startle the assembly that it is being counseled to rejoice over suffering. It is a startling concept by any standard.

> **If the Ascension of the Lord is celebrated today, see pages 162–64 for the appropriate readings.**

READING I **Three things happen in this brief reading: The apostles** return to Jerusalem after witnessing Jesus' ascension; they come together as a community; and they watch in prayer as they await the coming of the Holy Spirit (which we will celebrate next Sunday on Pentecost). In a way, it is the perfect picture of the church today. Though we have received the Holy Spirit, we are constantly on the watch for the Spirit's coming in new ways. God's spirit is dynamic, always appearing in our midst and in the individual believer, and never yet coming in total fullness.

Luke, the author of Acts, sees the resurrection, the ascension and the coming of the Spirit as three distinct events in time. He explicitly mentions that Jesus spent 40 days on earth after the resurrection. We should not take this too literally lest we miss the point that the number 40 is frequently used to indicate fullness or completion, even a kind of perfection. Jesus also spent 40 days in the desert during his temptation. Israel spent 40 years in exile. The number speaks more of the fullness of God's presence in these events than it does of historical time.

We, of course, live within the constraints of time, and we remember and celebrate the events in Christ's life accordingly. But as we make the round of the liturgical year, year after year, it is important to remember that salvation has come in all its fullness, even though we do not experience its completion yet. As we gather in prayer and watchful preparation for the feast of Pentecost next Sunday, we are fully aware

List the sins carefully and thoughtfully. There are many ways to be a thief or murderer.

If you are *insulted* for the name of *Christ*, *blessed* are you,
   for the Spirit of *glory* and of *God rests* upon you.

But let *no* one among you be made to suffer
   as a *murderer*, a *thief*, an *evildoer*, or as an *intriguer*.
But whoever is made to suffer as a *Christian*
    should not be *ashamed*
   but glorify *God* because of the *name*.

GOSPEL   John 17:1–11a

A reading from the holy gospel according to John

Jesus raised his eyes to *heaven* and said,
"*Father*, the *hour* has *come*.
Give *glory* to your son, so that your *son* may glorify *you*,
   just as you gave him *authority* over all *people*,
   so that your son may give eternal *life* to all you *gave* him.
Now *this* is eternal life,
   that they should *know* you, the only *true* God,
   and the one whom you *sent*, Jesus *Christ*.

"I *glorified* you on *earth*
   by accomplishing the *work* that you gave me to *do*.
Now glorify *me*, Father, *with* you,
   with the glory that I *had* with you before the world *began*.

"I revealed your *name* to those whom you *gave* me
    out of the world.
They belonged to *you*, and you gave them to *me*,
   and they have *kept* your *word*.

Though the text is completely abstract (containing no concrete images), a careful and loving proclamation will make it vivid.

This parenthetical remark has been added by the author. Make this obvious by altering your tone.

Here the subject of Jesus' prayer switches from his relationship with the Father to his relationship with his disciples and *their* relationship to the Father and to Jesus himself.

---

that the Spirit has indeed already come, making us a redeemed and Spirit-filled people.

READING II Today we conclude a series of six readings from the first letter of Peter. It has accompanied us throughout the Easter season. We may think it odd that Peter, in this "resurrection" letter, keeps returning to the idea of suffering. But Peter is a realist who feels compelled to assure us that suffering is a part of every life, just as it was a part of Jesus' life. But that is not his main point, of course. He points out that suffering is not meaningless

because it unites us more closely with Jesus in both his suffering and his glory.

There are two reasons for suffering: (1) We have sinned and feel the consequences of sin; and (2) we have done well (by being good Christians) and are persecuted because of it. We can avoid the first, though we still sin, and our sins affect others just as theirs affect us. The second reason for suffering is cause for rejoicing. This is not an easy lesson to learn, especially in prosperous cultures that have devised countless ways to stave off suffering. We recoil from suffering by natural instinct, and we do our best to

relieve it in others. Nevertheless, it comes to everyone in some form. When it comes as a result of living our faith boldly, we are truly one with Jesus. That is Peter's point.

We often call the Holy Spirit the Paraclete, which means "comforter." Our acceptance of that Spirit and the insight it brings enables us to look on suffering as a participation in the life, death and resurrection of Christ. That is surely cause for thanks and praise.

GOSPEL The gospel reading today is difficult and unusual, made

Now they *know* that everything you *gave* me is from *you*,
   because the words you gave to *me* I have given to *them*,
   and they *accepted* them and truly *understood*
     that I *came* from you,
   and they have *believed* that you *sent* me.

"I pray for *them*.
I do *not* pray for the *world* but for the ones you have *given* me,
   because they are *yours*, and everything of *mine* is yours
   and everything of *yours* is *mine*,
   and I have been *glorified* in them.
And *now* I will no longer be *in* the world,
   but *they* are in the world, while *I* am coming to *you*."

The pronouns must be carefully and subtly emphasized to make the meaning clear.

up entirely of the words of Jesus, which are abstract and mysterious. There are no concrete images to hold our imagination, and we have to put our best thinking skills to work to both proclaim it well and to listen to its message.

The passage is not a short story, sermon or parable. It is a prayer, Jesus' long prayer at the Last Supper on the night before he died. It is not a farewell prayer by any means, but it does recall and consecrate his earthly ministry. It is, in a way, a last will and testament wherein Jesus makes clear that he now entrusts to his disciples what

the Father had entrusted to him, namely the good news of salvation.

It is because his disciples have believed in him that Jesus can say he has been glorified. The point is that our belief in the work Jesus accomplished for us glorifies him and makes his work effective. Like the first disciples, we believe and so are distinct from the nonbelieving world, even though we still live in the world. For this reason Jesus prays for us.

Perhaps the most moving thing about the text is the intimate relationship it reveals between Jesus and the Father. It speaks of

the life they had together before Jesus came into the world, indeed before the world began (a favorite theme in John). It speaks of Jesus' joy in seeing that the disciples have come to believe that he and the Father are one and that all that Jesus gave them was given him by the Father. And it poignantly acknowledges that even the disciples Jesus has were given him by the Father. As a model of prayer, it has never been surpassed. Nevertheless, it is not easy to proclaim and must read with great care, deliberation and love.

PENTECOST VIGIL

Lectionary #62

READING I — Genesis 11:1–9

A reading from the book of Genesis

This is a simple story with a clear lesson. Tell it straightforwardly but with all the energy it contains.

Shinar = SHĪ-nahr

bitumen = bih-TOO-m*n

The whole *world* spoke the same *language*, using the
    same *words*.
While the people were *migrating* in the *east*,
    they came upon a *valley* in the land of *Shinar* and *settled* there.
They said to one another,
    "*Come*, let us mold *bricks* and *harden* them with *fire*."
They used bricks for *stone*, and bitumen for *mortar*.

Then they said, "*Come*, let us build ourselves a *city*
    and a *tower* with its *top* in the *sky*,
    and so make a *name* for ourselves;
    otherwise we shall be *scattered* all over the *earth*."

The LORD came down to *see* the city and the tower
    that the people had built.
Then the LORD said: "If now, while they are *one* people,
    all speaking the same *language*,
    they have started to do *this*,
    nothing will later *stop* them from doing
        whatever they *presume* to do.

God uses the royal plural: "Let us then go down . . ."

Let us then go *down* there and *confuse* their *language*,
    so that one will not *understand* what another *says*."

Thus the LORD *scattered* them from there all over the *earth*,
    and they stopped *building* the city.

There is a choice of first readings today. Speak with the liturgy coordinator or pastor to find out which reading will be used.

READING I | GENESIS. The story of the Tower of Babel is one of several options for the vigil celebration because tomorrow's first reading (Acts 2:1–11) alludes to it. While God punishes those who build the tower because of their pride by dividing their one language into many, the linguistic divisions among peoples are bridged by the unifying power of the Holy Spirit on Pentecost. The effect of juxtaposing these readings is twofold. First, it shows us that our understanding of God has grown and changed over the centuries, becoming clearest in the person of Jesus. Secondly, it emphasizes Luke's controlling theme about the universality of God's saving plan for the world. All the nations have become the chosen people.

In this delightful story from Genesis we see a traditional explanation for the many diverse tongues spoken by the peoples of the earth. In the story from Acts we see a traditional explanation for the rapid spread of the gospel. God's jealousy in the Genesis reading makes more sense when we realize that the people were defying God's command to settle in their respective homelands. Their disobedience brings punishment

Babel = BAB-*l (Notice the similarity to "babble.")

That is why it was called *Babel*,
    because *there* the LORD confused the *speech* of all the *world*.
It was from that place that he *scattered* them all over the *earth*.

Or:

Notice that this story has two parts. First, God reminds the people (through Moses) of their deliverance from Egypt and secures their promise of obedience. Then comes a display of divine power.

READING I   Exodus 19:3–8a, 16–20b

A reading from the book of Exodus

Moses went up the mountain to *God*.
Then the LORD *called* to him and said,
"*Thus* shall you say to the house of *Jacob*;
    tell the Israelites:
    You have *seen* for *yourselves* how I *treated* the *Egyptians*
    and how I *bore you up* on eagle *wings*
    and *brought* you here to *myself*.

"*Therefore*, if you hearken to my *voice* and keep my *covenant*,
    you shall be my *special possession*,
    dearer to me than all *other* people,
    though all the *earth* is mine.
You shall *be* to me a kingdom of *priests*, a *holy* nation.
That is what you must tell the *Israelites*."

So Moses *went* and *summoned* the *elders* of the people.
When he set before them
    all that the LORD had *ordered* him to tell them,
    the people all answered *together*,
    "Everything the LORD has *said*, we will *do*."

upon them; willful pride creates division among them, as it does to this day.

This is a classic fable, one of many in Genesis that make the point that God is the creator and cause of everything that is. Proclaim the story with all the skill you have as a storyteller. There is a timeless moral lesson here, perhaps all the more relevant in a world that continues to "shrink," as we become more and more aware of ourselves as a global village.

EXODUS. The second option for the first reading shows us the traditional signs of God's powerful intervention in Israel's history: smoke, cloud, fire and a thunderous roar. With the coming of the Holy Spirit, fire reveals God's presence, a brilliant image of the all-consuming nature of God's love and the fervor of those who are filled with it.

In this reading we encounter the awesome occasion when God gives the law to Israel through Moses. The chapter following this one in Genesis lists the ten commandments. The parallels between the giving of the law and the coming of the Spirit are easy to see, as are the differences between the two events.

In both events the people are brought into a covenant relationship with God, and

Read the signs of God's power as a narrative, not a reenactment.

On the morning of the *third* day
    there were peals of *thunder* and *lightning*,
    and a heavy *cloud* over the mountain,
    and a very loud *trumpet* blast,
    so that all the people in the camp *trembled*.
But *Moses* led the people *out* of the camp to meet *God*,
    and they *stationed* themselves at the *foot* of the mountain.
Mount *Sinai* was all wrapped in *smoke*,
    for the LORD came down upon it in *fire*.
The smoke *rose* from it as though from a *furnace*,
    and the whole *mountain* trembled *violently*.
The *trumpet* blast grew *louder* and *louder*,
        while Moses was *speaking*,
    and God *answering* him with *thunder*.

When the LORD came *down* to the top of Mount *Sinai*,
    he summoned *Moses* to the *top* of the mountain.

Or:

There is a dialogue between God and Moses; it is not a one-sided decree.

READING I   Ezekiel 37:1–14

Ezekiel = ee-ZEE-kee-uhl

This wonderful story is vivid and has always captured the imagination. You are speaking for Ezekiel in the first person ("I"), which makes the scene more immediate.

A reading from the book of the prophet Ezekiel

The hand of the LORD came upon me,
    and he led me *out* in the *spirit* of the LORD
    and set me in the center of the *plain*,
    which was now filled with *bones*.
He made me *walk* among the bones in every *direction*
    so that I *saw* how *many* they were on the surface of the plain.

both events are characterized by theophanies (dramatic signs of God's presence). In the first, God entrusts to Israel the fundamental law by which all succeeding generations will live. In the second, the presence of the Holy Spirit confers the power to preach the gospel on an assembly made up of peoples from many parts of the world.

Clearly we are beginning to understand that God's redemptive love is intended for all the nations of the earth. Empowered by the divine Spirit, we are able to spread the Good News of this new covenant—revealed to us in Jesus, God's love made visible.

EZEKIEL. The third option for today's first reading is the story of the valley of the dry bones, made justly famous by the wonderful African American spiritual that gave it a

place in popular culture: "Dem bones, dem bones, dem dry bones!" It is the story of a faithful and loving God restoring his beloved Israel to new life. Ezekiel foresees the revival of a destitute people, who reclaim their rightful place through the mercy of a God who is not hindered by death or the grave.

Take the changes in the dialogue slowly. God asks several rhetorical questions here. It's part of the narrative style.

prophesy = PROF-uh-sī

sinews = SIN-yooz

This reminds us of the "spirit of life" God blew into the nostrils of Adam.
prophesied = PROF-uh-sīd

How *dry* they were!
He asked me:
　　Son of man, can these bones come to *life*?
I answered, "Lord GOD, you *alone* know that."

Then he said to me:
　　Prophesy over these bones, and *say* to them:
　　Dry *bones*, hear the *word* of the LORD!
Thus says the Lord GOD to these bones:
　　See! I will bring *spirit* into you, that you may come to *life*.
I will put *sinews* upon you, make *flesh* grow over you,
　　cover you with *skin*, and put *spirit* in you
　　so that you may come to *life* and know that *I* am the LORD.

I, Ezekiel, prophesied as I had been *told*,
　　and even as I was *prophesying* I heard a *noise*;
　　it was a *rattling* as the bones came *together*, *bone* joining *bone*.
I saw the *sinews* and the *flesh* come upon them,
　　and the skin *cover* them, but there was no *spirit* in them.

Then the LORD said to me:
　　Prophesy to the *spirit*, *prophesy*, son of man,
　　and *say* to the spirit: Thus says the Lord GOD:
　　From the four winds *come*, O spirit,
　　and *breathe* into these *slain* that they may come to *life*.
I prophesied as he *told* me, and the spirit *came* into them;
　　they came *alive* and stood *upright*, a vast *army*.

Then he said to me:
　　Son of man, these *bones* are the whole house of *Israel*.
They have been saying,
　　"Our bones are *dried up*,
　　our *hope* is *lost*, and we are *cut off*."

The day of restoration comes in a new way on Pentecost. God's promise to place a new spirit within the people, giving them hearts of flesh to replace their stony ones, takes on a whole new meaning in the light of Pentecost fire.

Ezekiel foretold the fulfillment of God's promises at the end of time. The Pentecost event in Acts recounts the fulfillment of that promise and the inauguration of that end-time even now.

The familiarity of this wonderful story is part of its charm. Your proclamation should convey suspense, awe, wonder and power so that the assembly will hear the passage in a fresh way.

JOEL. In this fourth option for the first reading, we see the signs of God's power in smoke and fire as the spirit of God is poured out on all living flesh. No longer are the gifts of prophecy reserved for a chosen few. Instead, the whole people, from youngest to oldest and from least to greatest, will prophesy in the Lord's name.

The horrific images of blood, smoke, fire and darkness are necessary to impress us with the vastness of God's power and our total dependence on divine mercy. The Day of the Lord will be terrible only if we rebel against the goodness of God. Everyone who

The poignancy of God's solemn promise ("O my people, O my people") should be felt in your proclamation.

Therefore, *prophesy* and say to them: *Thus* says the Lord *GOD*:
O my *people*, I will open your *graves*
and have you *rise* from them,
and bring you *back* to the land of *Israel*.

Then you shall *know* that *I* am the LORD,
when I open your *graves* and have you *rise* from them,
O my *people*!
I will put my *spirit* in you that you may *live*,
and I will *settle* you upon your *land*;
thus you shall *know* that *I* am the LORD.
I have *promised*, and I will *do* it, says the LORD.

Or:

A reading from the book of the prophet Joel

Thus says the *Lord*:
I will pour out my *spirit* upon all *flesh*.
Your *sons* and *daughters* shall *prophesy*,
your *old* men shall dream *dreams*,
your *young* men shall see *visions*;
even upon the *servants* and the *handmaids*,
in those days, I will pour out my *spirit*.
And I will work *wonders* in the *heavens* and on the *earth*,
blood, *fire*, and columns of *smoke*;
the *sun* will be turned to *darkness*,
and the *moon* to *blood*,

Here we have a solemn proclamation from the mouth of God. This is exalted poetry.

prophesy = PROF-uh-sī

calls upon the name of the Lord will be rescued from it. They are the remnant that will remain.

The image of the faithful remnant is a favorite in Hebrew scriptures. It is a positive image rather than a negative one. It does not mean that only a few shall be saved; rather, it makes the point that, no matter how bad things seem, God never abandons the faithful.

It is difficult for us to appreciate fully the richness of God's spirit and how it transforms those upon whom it rests. It is the breath and life and substance of God, not merely a ghostly phantasm. The spirit of God is palpably real and enables those who receive it to see things as God sees them, to reorient their lives to right relationship with God, to live their full dignity as God's creatures and to proclaim God's goodness to the world around them. To receive a portion of God's spirit is to receive a portion of God's life.

This is what happens on Pentecost. All the world, people of every race and tongue, receive that spirit and speak of the marvels God has accomplished in a language that all can understand: the language of love, justice, respect and humility.

at the coming of the *day* of the LORD,
    the *great* and *terrible* day.

Then everyone shall be *rescued*
    who *calls* on the name of the LORD;
for on Mount *Zion* there shall be a *remnant*,
    as the LORD has said,
and in *Jerusalem survivors*
    whom the LORD shall *call*.

Notice that the narrative changes from first person ("I") to third person ("the Lord"), but it is still God speaking.

Despite the terrifying images, the reading ends with a comforting promise.

READING II   Romans 8:22–27

A reading from the letter of Saint Paul to the Romans

Brothers and sisters:
We *know* that all *creation* is *groaning* in *labor* pains
    even until *now*;
    and not only *that*, but we *ourselves*,
    who have the *firstfruits* of the Spirit,
    we *also* groan within ourselves
    as we wait for *adoption*, the redemption of our *bodies*.

For in *hope* we were *saved*.
Now *hope* that *sees* is *not* hope.
For who *hopes* for what one *sees*?
But if we hope for what we do *not* see, we wait with *endurance*.

In the same *way*, the Spirit *too* comes to the *aid* of our weakness;
    for we do not *know* how to pray as we *ought*,
    but the Spirit *himself* intercedes with inexpressible *groanings*.

The use of "we," "our" and "us" gives you an immediate rapport with the assembly. Make use of it.

Let the rhetorical question be a real question. Pause slightly after it.

Notice throughout that Paul presents a problematic condition followed by "But . . ." Let the contrast ring out.

READING II Though the thought here is clear and simple, its expression is complex. It is a vivid portrayal of our present spiritual condition. We rejoice in the assurance that faith gives us at the same moment we long for its promise to be complete. We long fervently for the peace that comes from union with God even as we struggle to maintain that relationship through prayer. We should take great comfort in hearing that the Spirit helps us in our weakness. Even wanting to pray is itself a prayer, for the Spirit is at prayer within our very desire. Perhaps we really begin to pray when we grow tired of "saying prayers" and let the Spirit take over.

This most striking thing about this text is the enormous dignity Paul accords hopeful believers. The Spirit, dwelling within us, gives our efforts, our suffering and our weakness the same nobility we see in the struggles of Jesus.

We should not regret that we must live in hope, subject to all the miseries of the flesh. How could it be otherwise? Is it possible to hope for something we already have? Indeed, we hope for what we cannot see and do not yet have. And we do so in patient endurance, the same patient endurance we see in Jesus at Gethsemane, before Pilate and on the cross. We keep that cross before us daily precisely because we know what lies beyond it. Life itself presents us with the cross; Spirit-filled hope draws us on toward the resurrection.

The final paragraph is complex in structure. Take it deliberately.

And the one who searches *hearts*
    knows what is the *intention* of the Spirit,
because he *intercedes* for the *holy* ones
according to God's *will.*

GOSPEL   John 7:37–39

A reading from the holy gospel according to John

This is a brief gospel text that makes up in power what it lacks in length.

On the *last* and *greatest* day of the feast,
    Jesus stood up and *exclaimed,*
    "Let anyone who *thirsts* come to *me* and *drink.*
As *Scripture* says:
    'Rivers of *living* water will flow from *within* him
        who *believes* in me.'"

Clearly the second half of the reading is John's commentary on Jesus' outcry. Make this clear in your proclamation.

He said this in reference to the *Spirit*
    that those who came to *believe* in him were to *receive.*
There *was,* of course, no Spirit *yet,*
    because *Jesus* had not yet been *glorified.*

GOSPEL   The festival the gospel passage refers to is the Jewish feast of Tabernacles, which included scripture readings and the ceremonial drawing of water to celebrate the great day of Israel's restoration, when "You will draw water joyfully from the springs of salvation" (Isaiah 12:3). We sang this song at the Easter Vigil.

Jesus announces that those who thirst for living water must find it in him. He is the spring of salvation Isaiah had foretold. The parenthetical commentary by John equates the "living water" with the outpouring of the Holy Spirit at Pentecost, following Jesus' resurrection and ascension. His point, written with the benefit of hindsight, is that the sacrificial death of Jesus made the Spirit's coming possible.

Notice that Jesus is not speaking of himself as being the source of living water but instead says that all those who drink of him shall have the spring of salvation flow from within them. Clearly, we are recipients of the water and the Spirit so that we can become sources of living water in the world. To drink from the fountain is to *become* a fountain.

PENTECOST

Lectionary #63

READING I   Acts 2:1–11

A reading from the Acts of the Apostles

This is quite a dramatic event, requiring your best effort to convey the awe and delight of those who witnessed it.

These natural phenomenon signify God's power. They are familiar to us from the Hebrew scriptures but always fascinating.

When the time for *Pentecost* was fulfilled,
    they were all in one place *together*.
And *suddenly* there came from the *sky*
    a *noise* like a strong driving *wind*,
    and it filled the entire *house* in which they were.
Then there appeared to them *tongues* as of *fire*,
    which *parted* and came to *rest* on each *one* of them.
And they were all *filled* with the Holy *Spirit*
    and began to speak in different *tongues*,
    as the Spirit *enabled* them to *proclaim*.

Now there were devout *Jews* from every nation under *heaven*
    staying in Jerusalem.
At this *sound*, they gathered in a large *crowd*,
    but they were *confused*
    because *each one* heard them speaking in his own *language*.
They were *astounded*, and in *amazement* they asked,
    "Are not all these people who are speaking *Galileans*?
Then how does each of us *hear* them in his *native language*?
We are *Parthians*, *Medes*, and *Elamites*,
    inhabitants of *Mesopotamia*, *Judea* and *Cappadocia*,

Master these proper names! They're quite a mouthful, but stumbling over them will compromise your credibility as a proclaimer.
Galileans = gal-ih-LEE-uhnz
Parthians = PAHR-thee-uhnz
Medes = meedz
Elamites = EE-luh-mīts
Mesopotamia = mes-uh-poh-TAY-mee-uh
Judea = joo-DEE-uh
Cappadocia = kap-uh-DOH-shuh

READING I **Remember the story of the tower of Babel from Genesis (Genesis 11:1–9; see the commentary for the vigil of Pentecost)? Today's reading from Acts reverses the situation. Whereas the people who built the tower out of pride had their one language divided into many, the people who experience the coming of the Spirit see their diverse languages made intelligible to all. The point is clear: The coming of the Holy Spirit binds together all the nations of the world.**

When did this marvelous event take place? According to Luke in this reading, it is on the Jewish feast of Pentecost, which commemorates the giving of the law on Mount Sinai, an event also accompanied by wind and fire. In today's gospel reading from John, the coming of the Holy Spirit occurs when the risen Lord first appears to his disciples. (We heard this same gospel passage on the Second Sunday of Easter.) Luke clearly wants to associate the new Pentecost with the old and show it to be the fulfillment of ancient prophecies. John places the event in the context of the commission to forgive sins.

The writers of the scriptures always have their reasons for situating events in certain contexts. The coming of the Spirit, in any case, cannot be limited to any particular moment in history. It is a constant and dynamic reality. Most important are the consequences of the Spirit's dynamism in the church. Never limited to place or time, it is poured out upon the whole world at every moment in every created thing. The earth is filled with the goodness of God. The faith-filled heart can perceive it everywhere.

Pontus = PON-tuhs
Phrygia = FRIJ-ee-uh
Pamphylia = pam-FIL-ee-uh
Libya = LIB-ee-uh
Cyrene = si-REE-nee
Cretans = KREE-tuhnz

Pontus and *Asia*, *Phrygia* and *Pamphylia*,
Egypt and the districts of *Libya* near *Cyrene*,
as well as travelers from *Rome*,
both *Jews* and *converts* to Judaism, *Cretans* and *Arabs*,
yet we hear them speaking in our own *tongues*
of the mighty acts of *God*."

READING II   1 Corinthians 12:3b–7, 12–13

A reading from the first letter of Saint Paul to the Corinthians

Brothers and sisters:
No one can say, "Jesus is *Lord*," except by the Holy *Spirit*.
There are different *kinds* of spiritual *gifts* but the same *Spirit*;
    there are different forms of *service* but the same *Lord*;
    there are different *workings* but the same *God*
    who produces *all* of them in *everyone*.
To each *individual* the manifestation of the Spirit
    is given for some *benefit*.

As a body is *one* though it has *many parts*,
    and all the *parts* of the body, though *many*, are *one* body,
    so also *Christ*.
For in one *Spirit* we were all *baptized* into one *body*,
    whether *Jews* or *Greeks*, *slaves* or *free* persons,
    and we were all given to *drink* of one *Spirit*.

The reading begins abruptly. Be sure the assembly is settled and quiet before you begin. The first sentence is crucial.

The rhetorical device at work here, repetition of "there are . . . but," is effective. Use vocal variety to make the most of it.

The great theme of Paul, unity in the one Spirit, dominates the second half of the reading.

READING II   The Corinthians had to constantly struggle with divisions in their community. This is the context in which Paul penned the reading assigned to today's feast. He encourages the community to unify itself under the one Lord Jesus Christ, who sent his Spirit as the bond of unity in the church.

It makes no sense for Christians to squabble over whose spiritual gifts are greater. All genuine gifts and charisms come from the one God, and the test of their authenticity is the degree to which they build up or divide the community in whose service they are to be exercised. Again, the gifts of the Spirit create unity in the church; divisiveness is a sure sign that the gift does not come from God.

The gift of speaking in tongues had led the Corinthians to rank themselves, which is always a mistake in Christian communities. Speaking in tongues is a gift. Those who do not receive it have no doubt received a different gift, perhaps less dramatic but no less important. There are many gifts, but they all come from the same Spirit.

GOSPEL   In this brief passage from John's gospel (which we heard on the Second Sunday of Easter), Jesus breathes the Holy Spirit upon the disciples and the Easter celebration comes full circle. With the gift of the Holy Spirit, Jesus' work on earth is complete. The Spirit empowers the disciples to continue the work of redemption in full awareness of the abiding presence of Christ through the power of the Spirit.

John's painstaking effort to make clear that the Jesus who appears to his disciples is really the same Jesus they knew before

GOSPEL John 20:19–23

A reading from the holy gospel according to John

On the *evening* of that *first* day of the *week*,
    when the doors were *locked*, where the *disciples* were,
    for fear of the *Jews*,
    Jesus came and stood in their *midst*
    and said to them, "*Peace* be with you."
When he had *said* this, he showed them his *hands* and his *side*.
The disciples *rejoiced* when they saw the Lord.

Jesus said to them *again*, "*Peace* be with you.
As the *Father* has sent *me*, so *I* send *you*."

And when he had said this, he *breathed* on them
        and said to them,
    "*Receive* the Holy *Spirit*.
Whose *sins* you forgive are *forgiven* them,
and whose sins you *retain* are *retained*."

This is a brief gospel, but it tells of a major event in the life of the church. Proclaim it with great care and breadth.

Emphasize "Peace" each time, not "with."

We are sent forth just as Jesus was. Our commission in the world is identical to his.

---

his death is fascinating. Though we may be more impressed by the risen Lord's ability to pass through closed doors, there is more at stake here than such feats. Jesus is not a ghost, as he himself says in more than one post-resurrection appearance. Jesus shows the disciples his hands and side, which still bear the marks of his wounds. We know this because the text that immediately follows relates the "doubting Thomas" story, in which the wounds play a prominent role. So who or what is this being that stands before the happy disciples? He is clearly not mortal, but he is still the teacher the disciples

knew and loved. The most important point John is making is that the risen Christ is *real,* however incomprehensible his new mode of existence might be. Not only is he real, he is *really present* despite any obstacle, whether it be a closed door or a closed heart.

The author describes disciples' recognition and subsequent joy with what may be the understatement of the ages: "The disciples rejoiced when they saw the Lord." Your proclamation of this line will have to go beyond the meaning of the literal words to capture the exultation hidden there.

Finally, we witness the giving of the Holy Spirit. The power to forgive sins or to hold them bound is clearly a commission to spread the gospel of Jesus and to bring all people to belief and baptism. Baptism is the great sign of forgiveness of sin and of incorporation into the fold of Christ. Jesus' mission is accomplished, but his work of redemption continues through those he now sends forth in the power of the Holy Spirit.

HOLY TRINITY

Lectionary #164

READING I   Exodus 34:4b–6, 8–9

A reading from the book of Exodus

This is a dramatic and solemn scene, in which God the all-transcendent is revealed as intimately present to the chosen people.

Early in the *morning Moses* went up Mount *Sinai*
    as the LORD had *commanded* him,
    taking along the two stone *tablets*.

Having come down in a *cloud*, the LORD stood with Moses there
    and proclaimed his *name*, "LORD."
Thus the LORD passed *before* him and cried *out*,
    "The *LORD*, the *LORD*, a *merciful* and *gracious* God,
    slow to anger and *rich* in *kindness* and *fidelity*."

"The Lord, the Lord, the Lord"—make the most of each use.

Moses at *once* bowed down to the *ground* in *worship*.
Then he said, "If I find *favor* with you, O Lord,
    do come along in our *company*.
This is indeed a *stiff-necked* people; yet *pardon* our wickedness
        and sins,
    and *receive* us as your *own*."

God emboldens Moses to ask this favor by revealing that the divine presence is approachable.

READING I   The concept of God as three persons (Father, Son and Holy Spirit) in one is impossible to grasp, and yet the trinitarian notion of God is absolutely central to most (although not all) Christian believers. On the solemnity of the Ascension we heard Jesus send his disciples into the world to baptize with a formula most of us learned when we were very young: "In the name of the Father, and of the Son and of the Holy Spirit." We can't fathom the depth and full meaning of this first thing we learned about our faith. We need to remind ourselves occasionally that standing in awe of the mystery will always be the most appropriate posture for us. It keeps us from getting sentimental about God.

To proclaim this first reading from Exodus on the feast of the Holy Trinity is an exercise in isogesis, that is, reading into the scriptures what its human author did not intend but what we believe in light of the revelation of God in Jesus. God's self-revelation as a trinity of persons came very gradually through the centuries. God has not changed, of course, but our limited understanding of God's nature has continually developed thanks to God's grace. The revelation came most fully, we Christians believe, in Jesus, in whose life and death we glimpse enough to know that God is all-good, all-loving and has shown us how to be creatures worthy of our Creator.

In this reading, God reveals the divine name to Moses three times. But that name is then expanded upon: God is merciful, gracious, loving, faithful, and so on. Moses' immediate impulse is to bow his head and worship. His awed reverence in response to tender affection teaches us a great deal about our relationship with God, as does the bold request Moses makes.

READING II   2 Corinthians 13:11–13

A reading from second letter of Saint Paul to the Corinthians

Brief readings like this can be over before
the assembly has begun to listen. Prepare
them to listen with a brief silence after
the announcement of the reading.

Paul encourages us to live the life of the
Trinity here: harmony, peace, love.

Make the final sentence expansive,
emphasizing the special quality assigned
to each person of the Trinity.

Brothers and sisters, *rejoice. Mend* your *ways,*
     encourage one another,
   agree with one another, live in *peace,*
   and the *God* of love and peace will be *with* you.
Greet one another with a holy *kiss.*
All the *holy* ones greet *you.*

The *grace* of the Lord Jesus *Christ*
   and the *love* of *God*
   and the *fellowship* of the Holy *Spirit* be with *all* of you.

READING II These last three verses of Paul's second letter to the community at Corinth have been chosen for today's feast because they conclude with a trinitarian formula. It is probably an expansion of the simpler greeting Paul used so often: "The grace of the Lord Jesus Christ be with you."

Notice the attributes ascribed to each person of the Trinity, and make the most of them in your proclamation. Grace (God's favor) comes through Jesus Christ. Love (God's nature) comes to us from the Father in the person of Jesus Christ. Fellowship (unity) is the unifying force of the Spirit that makes us one in community. Thus we emulate the life of the trinitarian God, who is a communion of three persons, completely one. There is no finer model for the Christian church.

GOSPEL Nicodemus went to speak with Jesus under cover of darkness. He had to because he was a leading Pharisee and could not risk open association with this strange but compelling teacher until he had tested his credentials. We can be forever grateful to Nicodemus for his courage in taking this risk. His encounter with Jesus has left us with words that have been quoted lovingly among Christians ever since.

John 3:16 is a thumbnail sketch of God's initiative on our behalf. When examined closely, this saying of Jesus can rid us of a number of misguided notions about our faith. First of all, God took the initiative in loving us. Once taken, that initiative is never withdrawn. This means that our entire life is a grateful response to God, a fact that should give us a clear idea of what prayer and good works are all about. The response to "I love you" is ordinarily not "What do you want me

John 3:16 is so familiar that your proclamation must be carefully studied to
make it fresh and new. Do not belabor it,
of course, but proclaim it with obvious
understanding and appreciation.

The second half is a commentary on the
implications of the preceding verse. It
implies "therefore . . ."

Believing is life; not believing is death,
whether physical or spiritual. The point
here is that believing is the only sensible
option. God does not condemn; condemnation can only be self-inflicted.

GOSPEL   John 3:16–18

A reading from the holy gospel according to John

God so *loved* the world that he *gave* his only *Son*,
 so that everyone who *believes* in him might not *perish*
 but might have eternal *life*.

For God did *not* send his Son into the world
 to *condemn* the world,
 but that the world might be *saved* through him.
Whoever *believes* in him will *not* be condemned,
 but whoever does *not* believe has *already* been condemned,
 because he has *not* believed in the *name* of the only
  Son of *God*.

to do about that?" It is "I love you, too," followed spontaneously by evidence that we
mean what we say.

 Second, God's initiative took the form
of a human being like ourselves so that we
could "see" God, in the person of Jesus, as
we had never seen God before. If we want
to know God, we must get to know Jesus. In
the morass of human affairs, conflict, codes
of behavior, ethical quagmires and the
alarming complexity of organized religion,
we must learn about Jesus and believe in
him as a person. When we believe in the
person of Jesus, we make good choices.

When we are merely aware of his words
and deeds, even if we admire them, we
reduce them to a code of behavior, and we
make poor choices. We are then guided by
our current selections from the code and
lose sight of the person, the person who did
not say, "I will show you the way," but, "I
am the way, the truth and the life."

 And third, the *only* response required of
us is to believe in the Son. We need only
believe that God who is love loves us infinitely, exactly as we are at every given
moment. We needn't worry about avoiding
sin, being punished or being good. Once we

believe we are loved as God indeed loves
us, we will quite naturally respond with
similar love.

 Believing this way takes a lifetime for
some, an instant for others. Time is irrelevant.
From the moment we begin to *want* to believe
in this way, we become truly Christian. It
really is that simple, despite our perceptions
to the contrary. And it is refreshing at least,
life-altering at best, to put aside those perceptions and take Jesus at his word.

BODY AND BLOOD OF CHRIST

Lectionary #167

READING I   Deuteronomy 8:2–3, 14b–16a

Deuteronomy = doo-ter-AH-nuh-mee

The key concept in this reading is remembrance. Moses must keep reminding the disheartened people to rely on their memory of God's fidelity in the past to carry them through the present.

There is a paradox here: God gives food to remind us that we need more than food to live! Jesus quotes this passage during his temptation in the desert.

saraph = SAYR-uhf

A reading from the book of Deuteronomy

Moses said to the *people*:
"*Remember* how for forty *years* now the LORD, your *God*,
    has directed *all* your journeying in the *desert*,
    so as to *test* you by *affliction*
    and find out whether or not it was your *intention*
    to *keep* his *commandments*.

He therefore let you be *afflicted* with *hunger*,
    and then *fed* you with *manna*,
    a food *unknown* to you and your *fathers*,
    in order to *show* you that not by bread *alone* does one live,
    but by every *word* that comes forth
        from the mouth of the LORD.

"Do not *forget* the LORD, your God,
    who brought you out of the land of *Egypt*,
    that place of *slavery*;
    who *guided* you through the vast and terrible *desert*
    with its saraph *serpents* and *scorpions*,
    its *parched* and waterless *ground*;
    who brought forth *water* for you from the flinty *rock*
    and *fed* you in the desert with *manna*,
    a food *unknown* to your *fathers*."

READING I We celebrate this feast because of historical developments that led to the perception of the eucharistic bread and wine as objects for adoration as well as food for Christian living. The church clearly asserts that it is both, and today's celebration should remind us of the central place the eucharist has in our faith. It is the source and summit of all we profess as believers. When we eat Christ's body and drink Christ's blood we are united with God and one another in a bond that exceeds anything we can experience or understand on a merely human level. Believing in that oneness with God and neighbor will alter the way we think and live.

The first reading was chosen for this celebration because it helps develop the theological connection between manna and the eucharistic bread, a connection Jesus himself makes in today's gospel. But beyond that, Moses here reminds the discouraged Israelites that God's fidelity is beyond question. "Take heart," he says, "and remember how God saved us in the desert by sending manna from heaven and water from the rock. God did not abandon us then and will not abandon us now."

God's everlasting faithfulness is the point of this reading and of this feast. In the body and blood of Christ we have a perpetual pledge of God's provident love. Celebrating the eucharist creates the people of God, bringing all the proofs of God's love throughout history right into the present moment.

O sacred banquet,
in which Christ is received,
the memorial of his passion
    is celebrated,
and a pledge of future glory is given
    to us!

This is a brief reading. Be sure the assembly ready to listen before you begin. There are rhetorical questions here. Proclaim them to elicit a silent response in your listeners' hearts.

Finally, in response to their "Yes, we know that!" you remind them of the consequences of what they know.

READING II 1 Corinthians 10:16–17

A reading from the first letter of Saint Paul to the Corinthians

Brothers and sisters:
The cup of *blessing* that we bless,
  is it not a *participation* in the blood of *Christ*?
The *bread* that we *break*,
  is it not a participation in the *body* of Christ?

Because the loaf of *bread* is *one*,
  we, though *many*, are one *body*,
  for we all *partake* of the one *loaf*.

For most of this reading you are quoting Jesus directly. Your awareness of that will enhance your proclamation.

GOSPEL John 6:51–58

A reading from the holy gospel according to John

Jesus said to the Jewish *crowds*:
  "*I* am the living *bread* that came down from *heaven*;
  whoever *eats* this bread will live *forever*;
  and the bread that *I* will give
  is my *flesh* for the life of the *world*."

The *Jews quarreled* among themselves, saying,
  "How can this man give us his *flesh* to eat?"

Jesus said to them,
  "*Amen, amen*, I say to you,
  unless you *eat* the *flesh* of the Son of Man and *drink* his *blood*,
  you do not have *life* within you.

Jesus goes on at some length to develop his point. Like those who first heard him, we must move from the literal to the deeper meaning.

READING II Two rhetorical questions comprise this brief text, and a statement of the effect of celebrating the eucharist sums it up. Rhetorical questions are a dramatic way of saying that the answer should be obvious. The answer Paul expects in the hearts of his hearers is, "Of course! How could it be otherwise?" Try to elicit the same kind of response by the way you proclaim these questions.

In Paul's summary statement we see the horizontal dimension of the eucharist. By partaking of the body and blood of Christ we

are joined to him and to one another in a unity of love that makes selfishness and individualism unthinkable. To eat and drink this sacrament while denying the full dignity of any living creature is to bring condemnation upon ourselves. Eucharistic unity dispels prejudice, exclusivity, pride, disdain, arrogance, false humility or any other expression of separation among people. Is not loving service of one another the natural expression of such unity? Of course! How could it be otherwise?

GOSPEL The final two sentences make it clear why this text was chosen for today's feast. Jesus reminds his audience that the bread that came down from heaven (manna, in the first reading) was God's way of sustaining the chosen people. Likewise, but in a much more dramatic and lasting way, Jesus has come down from heaven for the same purpose—not to give us food for the journey but to *be* our food for the journey.

It was only after his death and resurrection, of course, that the full implication of Jesus' words about being the bread of life

The manna came from God; Jesus came from God. The difference is that Jesus nourishes us not for the day but forever.

"Whoever *eats* my flesh and *drinks* my blood
  has *eternal* life,
  and I will *raise* him on the last *day*.
For my *flesh* is true *food*,
  and my *blood* is true *drink*.
Whoever eats my *flesh* and drinks my *blood*
  remains in me and I in *him*.

"Just as the living Father *sent* me
  and I have *life* because of the Father,
  so also the one who *feeds* on me
  will have *life* because of me.
This is the bread that came down from *heaven*.
Unlike your *ancestors* who *ate* and still *died*,
  whoever eats *this* bread will live *forever*."

was understood. It is through hindsight that the evangelist John (and the contemporary reader) knows what Jesus is saying about eating his flesh and drinking his blood. It is no surprise that he would be questioned about such an unusual and even (to his audience) repulsive assertion. "How can this man give us his flesh to eat?" is a perfectly natural response. Only the supernatural response (faith) can accept him at his word.

We would do well to remind ourselves that Jesus gives us *himself* in the eucharist, not divided or in part, but his very *self:* his life, his being, his force, his soul and divinity. It is best not to concentrate on our worthiness to receive him (who could ever be worthy?) but rather to dwell on how desperately we *need* to receive him to sustain ourselves.

10TH SUNDAY IN ORDINARY TIME

Lectionary #88

READING I   Hosea 6:3–6

A reading from the book of the prophet Hosea

Proclaim the reading as poetry through your cadence and pace. Make the most of the images: dawn, day, rain, cloud, dew.

In their *affliction*, people will say:
"Let us *know*, let us *strive* to *know* the *Lord*;
    as certain as the *dawn* is his *coming*,
    and his *judgment* shines forth like the light of *day*!
He will *come* to us like the *rain*,
    like *spring* rain that waters the *earth*."

There are two rhetorical questions. God should not sound peevish here! Make the questions bright and strong.
Ephraim = EE-fray-im

What can I *do* with you, *Ephraim*?
    What can I do with *you*, *Judah*?
Your piety is like a morning *cloud*,
    like the *dew* that early passes *away*.
For this reason I *smote* them through the *prophets*,
    I *slew* them by the words of my *mouth*;

The final thought will be heard again in the words of Jesus in today's gospel. Make it stand out.

for it is *love* that I desire, *not* sacrifice,
    and *knowledge* of God rather than *holocausts*.

READING I The Sundays in Ordinary Time number 33 or 34. They begin after the Christmas season, are interrupted by Lent and Easter, and resume after Pentecost. There is no "First Sunday in Ordinary Time," because that Sunday is always the feast of the Baptism of the Lord. The two solemnities we just celebrated (Holy Trinity and Body and Blood of Christ) also replace Sundays in Ordinary Time. After Pentecost, the Sundays in Ordinary Time resume wherever they must so that the Thirty-fourth Sunday in Ordinary Time (Christ the King) falls the week before the First Sunday of Advent. This explains why we left Ordinary Time on the Fifth Sunday in Ordinary Time and resume it on the Tenth Sunday in Ordinary Time.

By the way, Ordinary Time is a misleading term. Maybe we should call it "Ordinal Time," because that's what it is: the times of the year when we designate the Sundays with ordinal numbers (the *Tenth* Sunday in Ordinary Time, the *Eleventh* Sunday in Ordinary Time, and so forth).

The first reading provides us with a good theme as we launch again into the "green" season of Ordinary Time: Let us strive to know the Lord! This is the time of year when, undistracted by the drama of special feasts, we can settle into some serious listening and get to know the Lord more deeply.

The Hosea text is poetry, not prose, discernible immediately because of its parallelism, in which each line is restated or echoed in the line that follows it. This is a favorite device of Hebrew poetry, and the proclaimer must take it into account. Getting a feel for the parallelism will enable you to proclaim the text with much greater sensitivity and clarity.

READING II   Romans 4:18–25

A reading from the letter of Saint Paul to the Romans

Brothers and sisters:
Abraham believed, *hoping* against *hope*,
    that he would become "the *father* of many *nations*,"
    according to what was said, "Thus shall your *descendants* be."
He did not *weaken* in faith when he considered his own *body*
    as already *dead*—for he was almost a *hundred* years *old*—
    and the dead *womb* of *Sarah*.
He did not *doubt* God's promise in *unbelief*;
    rather, he was *strengthened* by *faith* and gave *glory* to God
    and was fully *convinced* that what he had *promised*
    he was also able to *do*.

That is why it was *credited* to him as *righteousness*.
But it was not for him *alone* that it was written
    that it was *credited* to him;
    it was also for *us*, to whom it *will be* credited,
    who *believe* in the one who raised Jesus our *Lord* from the *dead*,
    who was *handed over* for our *transgressions*
    and was *raised* for our *justification*.

The reading presents Abraham as a real human being whose faith was constant despite reasons for not believing. It's a practical example for us.

The negative makes the point stronger.

Here's the point of the story: Because he kept faith, Abraham found righteousness with God.

READING II │ The second reading will be taken from Paul's letter to the Romans for 14 Sundays in a semi-continuous fashion. You may want to look ahead at other commentaries to get an overall feel for the letter.

Abraham is called "our father in faith." It was with Abraham that God established the covenant with the chosen people, the covenant that continues still, brought to perfection in Jesus Christ. Despite the apparent hurdle of old age, Abraham had faith in God's promise that he would become the father of many nations. And indeed he has,

beginning with Isaac, who then became the father of Jacob. Sarah his wife was old, too, and when she heard that her "dead" womb would be fertile, she laughed—not the best response to a divine promise, although certainly understandable! Sarah's untimely snickers did not go unrecorded: The name Isaac means "laughter."

Paul recounts this ancient story to show us something of the nature of faith. Like Abraham, most of us see our faith as a kind of "hoping against hope" at times. But faith is still faith, even when it flickers. The

important thing is to trust in God's ways, so different from our own, and go on believing.

GOSPEL │ According to the gospel that bears his name, Matthew was the fifth disciple called by Jesus. The first four were fishermen: Peter, Andrew, James and John. This fifth is a tax collector. Despite the less-than-charitable feelings we might have for the IRS, there is no sin in being a tax collector. Matthew's job was detestable to his own people because he collected taxes placed on them by the

"As Jesus passed on from there . . ."
From where? Consider using, "As Jesus
walked along . . . ," or the earlier
translation, "As Jesus moved about . . ."
Matthew's immediate response should
be obvious by the way you proclaim
the words.

Prepare for Jesus' response with a slight
pause after the Pharisees' question.

Make the quotation sound like a quotation.

GOSPEL Matthew 9:9–13

A reading from the holy gospel according to Matthew

As Jesus passed on from there,
  he saw a man named *Matthew* sitting at the *customs* post.
He said to him, "*Follow* me."
And he got up and *followed* him.
While he was at *table* in his *house*,
  many *tax* collectors and *sinners* came
  and *sat* with Jesus and his *disciples*.
The Pharisees *saw* this and said to his *disciples*,
  "*Why* does your teacher *eat* with *tax* collectors and *sinners*?"

He *heard* this and said,
  "Those who are *well* do not *need* a physician, but the *sick* do.
Go and learn the *meaning* of the words,
  'I desire *mercy*, not *sacrifice*.'
I did not come to call the *righteous* but *sinners*."

despised Romans, who occupied their land. The people not only resented him but considered him a traitor of sorts.

But he was obviously not a bad man. Not only does he respond immediately to the Lord's call, but many tax collectors and sinners join him and Jesus at table. He may have influenced them to follow him in following the Lord. Clearly, the point is that disciples of Jesus do not have to present credentials of worthiness. Jesus likes the company of sinners. And why not? These are the people he came to save. All men and

women are sinners, especially those who think they are not.

Jesus quotes a saying from the Hebrew scriptures that organized religion will always have difficulty observing. Mercy is greater than sacrifice. Mercy is greater than justice. Mercy is the hallmark of the Christian. And mercy like God's does not have to be earned or deserved. The more institutionalized our religion gets, the more difficulty it has being merciful. It tends to cultivate its own concerns and look inward, which can make the outsider (the "sinner") feel less than welcome, unworthy of belonging. More than

once I have failed utterly in convincing those who feel unworthy of coming to church that they are the most welcome of all. They see too much evidence to the contrary.

The words of Jesus are often difficult to take to heart. They sound too idealistic, too out of touch with our daily grind. If they were words isolated from deeds, we might justify our feeling that what Jesus asks exceeds our capabilities. But Jesus' words are always put into action, as they are in this gospel story, which encourages us to be doers of the word and not hearers only.

11TH SUNDAY IN ORDINARY TIME

Lectionary #91

READING I   Exodus 19:2–6a

A reading from the book of Exodus

Sinai = SĪ-nī

In those days, the *Israelites* came to the desert of *Sinai*
    and pitched *camp*.
While Israel was *encamped* here in front of the *mountain*,
    Moses went *up* the mountain to *God*.
Then the LORD *called* to him and said,
    "Thus shall you say to the house of *Jacob*;
    tell the Israelites:
    You have seen for *yourselves* how I treated the *Egyptians*
    and how I bore *you* up on *eagle* wings
    and *brought* you here to *myself*.
Therefore, if you *hearken* to my *voice* and *keep* my *covenant*,
    you shall be my special *possession*,
    dearer to me than all other *people*,
    though all the *earth* is mine.
You shall be to me a kingdom of *priests*, a *holy* nation."

Moses is the prophet who speaks for God. Let God's directive to him ring out.

There is poignant intimacy in the expression "brought you here to myself." A covenant involves two parties. This is how we respond to God's goodness.

"A kingdom of priests"—all are privileged to serve in God's presence.

READING I   The first reading is always from the Hebrew scriptures (except during the Easter season when we read from the Acts of the Apostles) and is chosen more or less to complement the gospel. Sometimes, either because of a particular feast or happy coincidence, the message of the second reading also echoes the themes of the other two, as it does today. The problem with such an approach is that we might begin to think that the Hebrew scriptures have little value except as "fulfilled" or "interpreted" by the Christian scriptures.

Nothing could be further from the truth. The Hebrew scriptures stand on their own as a record of God's developing relationship with the Jewish people, and, through them, us as well. We believe God's plan to save all creation came to perfect completion in Jesus, but that in no way lessens the importance of God's constant and continuing relationship with the Jewish people.

In this passage from Exodus, we see what we might call "God's initiative" to us. We can see that initiative continuing in the gospel and the second reading. We sometimes get so preoccupied with our duties as believers, our obligations as members of the church, that we forget that God moved toward us first. The whole notion of "seeking God" needs to be tempered with the acknowledgement that God sought us first.

It was the Lord God who chose Moses to lead the Israelites through the desert. God had seen the misery and suffering of enslaved Israel and took the initiative to lead them to freedom. Once Moses overcame his reluctance to be God's mouthpiece (which is what "prophet" means), it became clear to him that this God of theirs was energetically promoting their welfare.

READING II   Romans 5:6–11

A reading from the letter of Saint Paul to the Romans

Brothers and sisters:
Christ, while we were still *helpless*,
    yet *died* at the appointed *time* for the *ungodly*.
Indeed, only with *difficulty* does one *die* for a *just* person,
    though *perhaps* for a *good* person
    one *might* even find courage to *die*.
But God *proves* his *love* for us
    in that while we were still *sinners* Christ died for us.
How much *more* then, since we are now *justified* by his *blood*,
    will we be *saved* through him from the *wrath*.

Indeed, if, while we were *enemies*,
    we were *reconciled* to God through the *death* of his *Son*,
    how much *more*, once *reconciled*,
    will we be *saved* by his *life*.
Not only *that*,
    but we also *boast* of God through our *Lord* Jesus *Christ*,
    through whom we have now *received* reconciliation.

Why does God take the initiative? God is love and, by its very nature, love moves out toward others. "Goodness diffuses itself," the Greek philosophers tell us. Those who see the God of the Hebrew scriptures primarily as a harsh and angry judge don't know the scriptures very well.

READING II Not only did God take the initiative in loving us (see the first reading), but that same initiative is at work in the sacrificial death of Jesus. God proves in an incontestable way that we are loved far beyond any considerations of worthiness. We cannot remind ourselves too often that being a Christian means first and foremost that we are on the receiving end of God's goodness.

The mind-blowing marvel of our faith is that we have been redeemed in total love by a God whose love is completely benevolent. Christianity is not about what we must do to be saved; Christianity is about what has been done to save us.

In this exquisitely crafted passage, Paul clearly takes delight in drawing out for us the consequences of God's love. How can we be concerned about "wrath," which does not represent God's anger so much as the tragedy of being unfit at the final judgment? If God saved us in the midst of our sins, how can we doubt our salvation now that we are redeemed?

Finally, our hope is so sure and our joy is so great that we make God our boast every day of our lives. There is no presumption in Paul's ecstatic certainty of salvation. There is, rather, an enviable faith-filled confidence, one that he urges us to share.

GOSPEL   Matthew 9:36—10:8

A reading from the holy gospel according to Matthew

The narrative begins with an important phrase preceding the subject. Be sure it's not lost. Wait until the assembly is settled and ready to listen.

At the *sight* of the *crowds*, Jesus' *heart* was moved
    with *pity* for them
because they were *troubled* and *abandoned*,
    like *sheep* without a *shepherd*.
Then he said to his *disciples*,
    "The *harvest* is *abundant* but the *laborers* are *few*;
    so ask the *master* of the harvest
    to send out *laborers* for his harvest."

We can wonder what kind of authority included such marvels. Don't rush through it.

Then he *summoned* his twelve disciples
    and gave them *authority* over unclean *spirits*
    to drive them *out* and to cure every *disease* and every *illness*.
The *names* of the twelve *apostles* are *these*:
    first, *Simon* called *Peter*, and his brother *Andrew*;
    James, the son of *Zebedee*, and his brother *John*;
    Philip and *Bartholomew*, *Thomas* and *Matthew*
        the *tax* collector;
    James, the son of *Alphaeus*, and *Thaddeus*;
    Simon from *Cana*, and Judas *Iscariot* who *betrayed* him.

Master the less-familiar names. Your credibility as proclaimer must not be compromised by a few proper names!
Zebedee = ZEB-uh-dee
Alphaeus = AL-fee-uhs

Jesus sent *out* these twelve after *instructing* them *thus*,
    "Do not go into *pagan* territory or enter a *Samaritan* town.
Go *rather* to the *lost* sheep of the house of *Israel*.
As you go, make this *proclamation*:
    'The *kingdom* of *heaven* is at *hand*.'
Cure the *sick*, raise the *dead*, cleanse *lepers*, drive out *demons*.
Without *cost* you have *received*; without *cost* you are to *give*."

The second to the last sentence is a list. Don't rush through it. Each item must ring out.

GOSPEL   The movement of God's love toward the world (the "initiative" God took) we saw in the first two readings is seen again in the compassion Jesus feels for the crowds in the gospel story. It is the same God and the same compassion we heard about in the first reading. We can also see it in the selection of the Twelve, who are to take a message of hope and consolation to all the people of Israel. Not only are the Twelve to proclaim that the reign of God is at hand, they are also to drive away evil and cure the sick, raise the dead and cleanse the leper. Their ministry is to be

like God's: freely given without expectation of return.

Though it may trouble us to hear Jesus exclude some people and places from his mission—Gentiles, pagan territory and Samaritan towns—we must remember that we are witnessing the very beginning of the proclamation of Good News. We need to remind ourselves that salvation comes from the Jews, as Jesus himself says. Their special claim as the chosen people is in no way diminished. It is right that they should be the first to hear that "the kingdom of God is at hand!"

We must also remember that it was only gradually that God's plan of universal salvation came to be acknowledged. Indeed, the presumption was that the "house of Israel" was the object of Jesus' mission. The gradual revelation that the gospel was to be preached to all the world came as a shock to those who first heard it. We can imagine stunned disciples asking incredulously: "Even to the Gentiles?" And Jesus response is, of course, "Yes, even to the Gentiles, indeed even to the ends of the earth."

12TH SUNDAY IN ORDINARY TIME

Lectionary #94

READING I — Jeremiah 20:10–13

A reading from the book of the prophet Jeremiah

Jeremiah said:
"I hear the *whisperings* of *many*:
　'*Terror* on every *side*!
　Denounce! let us *denounce* him!'
All those who were my *friends*
　are on the *watch* for any *misstep* of mine.
'Perhaps he will be *trapped*; then we can *prevail*,
　and take our *vengeance* on him.'

"But the LORD is with me, like a mighty *champion*:
　my persecutors will *stumble*, they will *not* triumph.
In their *failure* they will be put to utter *shame*,
　to *lasting, unforgettable confusion.*

"O LORD of *hosts*, you who test the *just*,
　who probe *mind* and *heart*,
let me witness the *vengeance* you take on them,
　for to *you* I have entrusted my *cause.*

"*Sing* to the LORD,
　praise the LORD,
for he has *rescued* the life of the *poor*
　from the *power* of the *wicked*!"

Clearly this is a poetic text. The enemies are larger than life. The confidence is of epic proportions. It must be proclaimed nobly and grandly.

Halfway through, the tone changes: "*But* [pause] the Lord is with me . . ."

The final lines change from prayer to exultation.

READING I Jeremiah and Jesus have always been identified with each other because of their sufferings at the hands of their enemies. But more than that, Jesus echoes both Jeremiah's pain and his confidence in the face of such trials. Clearly, this reading has been chosen to complement the encouraging words Jesus speaks to the newly commissioned Twelve in today's gospel.

Notice how the text moves from a lament to a song of grateful confidence. It could be a model prayer for us when we find ourselves in difficult times. There is nothing stoic about Jeremiah's outcry. He states the case exactly as he feels it, and he pulls no punches in his description of the enemies who are arrayed against him. There is always a bit of denial in stoicism, a certain resignation. The stoic's approach to tribulation seems incomplete, never moving beyond gritted teeth. The approach of Jeremiah and Jesus seems healthier. They certainly grit their teeth, but beyond that there is the open-mouthed shout of confidence in their strength to endure, which comes from trust in God.

We've all known people whose sufferings made them bitter and angry, and none of us is above such a response. Some suffer to such a dramatic degree that we wonder how they endure it, much less see beyond it. On the other hand, we've all known others who suffer greatly and yet do not succumb to bitter resignation. Something enables them to continue to love life, to care for those around them and to maintain a joyful hope. Jeremiah's words can move us away from resentment and closer to confident assurance that God is our mighty champion, the dread warrior who joins us in battle and guarantees victory.

READING II Romans 5:12–15

A reading from the letter of Saint Paul to the Romans

The text is complicated. Take it slowly, even analytically.

Brothers and sisters:
Through *one* man *sin* entered the *world*,
    and through *sin*, *death*,
    and thus *death* came to *all* men, inasmuch as all *sinned*—
    for up to the time of the *law*, sin was *in* the world,
    though sin is not *accounted* when there is no *law*.

The syntax gets convoluted here. Let careful emphasis and vocal variation make it clear.

But *death* reigned from *Adam* to *Moses*,
    even over those who did not *sin*
    after the *pattern* of the trespass of *Adam*,
    who is the *type* of the one who was to *come*.

Here's the point: "*But* [pause] the gift . . . !"

But the *gift* is not *like* the *transgression*.
For if by the *transgression* of the one the many *died*,
    how much *more* did the grace of *God*
    and the gracious *gift* of the *one* man Jesus *Christ*
    overflow for the *many*.

READING II This justly famous passage from Paul's letter to the Romans demonstrates how mercy triumphs over justice, grace over sin, Christ's death over death itself. The masterful image of Christ as the second Adam is rich and complex. Paul uses the image both for comparison and contrast. The text is something of a jumble of likes and dislikes, and is not particularly easy to proclaim. It requires a great deal of vocal variety and degrees of emphasis to make it work.

The reading says that sin (spiritual death) entered the world through Adam; forgiveness of sin (spiritual life) enters the world through Christ. When we were laboring under the effect of Adam's sin, Christ freed us through forgiveness. This, however, sounds like mere tit for tat. Paul is eager to point out how much greater Christ's redemptive act is in its effects than Adam's sinful act was. Going far beyond parity, grace came in superabundance to obliterate the abundance of sin: "Where sin did once abound, grace now abounds much more."

Though we make a great deal of sin, it is a paltry thing in the face of Christ's victory. Though we labor under the effects of sinfulness, our struggle now is nothing compared to the glory to come. Christ's power to forgive sin, which he shared with his church, renders sin completely powerless. We can make this comparison in many ways, but the bottom line is that God's loving mercy goes far beyond the forgiveness we need. It makes one wonder why so many Christians are so obsessed with sin. We'd be a much more effective church if we were obsessed with grace!

GOSPEL Matthew continues Jesus' instruction to the Twelve as

GOSPEL   Matthew 10:26–33

A reading from the holy gospel according to Matthew

Jesus said to the *Twelve*:
"Fear *no* one.
Nothing is *concealed* that will not be *revealed*,
    nor *secret* that will not be *known*.
What I say to you in the *darkness*, speak in the *light*;
    what you hear *whispered*, proclaim on the *housetops*.

"And do not be *afraid* of those who kill the *body*
        but cannot kill the *soul*;
    rather, be afraid of the one who can destroy
        both soul and body in *Gehenna*.
Are not two *sparrows* sold for a small *coin*?
Yet not *one* of them falls to the *ground*
        without your Father's *knowledge*.
Even all the hairs of your *head* are counted.
So do not be *afraid*; you are worth *more* than *many* sparrows.

"Everyone who *acknowledges* me before *others*
    I will acknowledge before my heavenly *Father*.
But whoever *denies* me before others,
    I will deny before my heavenly *Father*."

Throughout this passage you are using direct address (Jesus to the Twelve), which always makes the text more immediate for the assembly.

A tone of utter certainty about these matters is most appropriate.

Gehenna = geh-HEN-nah

This is a rhetorical question. Let it provoke the obvious response in your listeners.

The choice for us is shockingly simple: Either acknowledge Christ or deny him!

he commissions them to preach the Good News. He warns them that their mission will inevitably bring them suffering. The first reading (Jeremiah) introduced the idea that suffering is part and parcel of life for those who proclaim the gospel.

The first section of the text, about darkness and light, is not immediately clear to us unless we catch its eschatological thrust; it's partly a description of how things will be at the end of time. The day will come when the reign of God will be fully established and obvious to all the world. But it also refers to the effect of the preaching of the

Twelve. What is not yet known (darkness) is to be proclaimed boldly by them in the light of day. What they hear from Jesus now in private, they are to proclaim from the housetops to all the world. The dominion that Jesus established is a dynamic reality. It is not waiting quietly to be revealed. It is being revealed in every good word and deed at every moment. At the end of time, when Christ returns in glory, what is being revealed now will become even clearer.

The second part of the reading is a comforting reminder of how much the Father loves us and how that love is greater than

any threat or danger. But it concludes with a challenging lesson in what commitment means. It means acknowledging God to others during the best and the worst of times. It means that the way we live with each other must acknowledge God's goodness and provident care. Anything less is a denial of Christ that will receive Christ's denial in return. More than a threat, this hard saying is simply an explanation of how to live in the only way that really works. Proclaim it for the obvious truth it is.

13TH SUNDAY IN ORDINARY TIME

Lectionary #97

READING I   2 Kings 4:8–11, 14–16a

A reading from the second book of Kings

This is a lovely little story. Capture the assembly's attention with the formulaic first words: "One day . . ."
Elisha = ee-LĪ-shuh
Shunem = SH<u>OO</u>-nem

One day *Elisha* came to *Shunem*,
    where there was a woman of *influence*, who urged him
        to *dine* with her.
Afterward, *whenever* he passed by, he used to *stop* there to *dine*.
So she said to her *husband*, "I know that *Elisha* is
    a *holy* man of *God*.
Since he visits us *often*, let us arrange a little *room* on the *roof*
    and *furnish* it for him with a bed, table, chair, and lamp,
    so that when he *comes* to us he can *stay* there."
Sometime *later* Elisha *arrived* and *stayed* in the room *overnight*.

The woman welcomes the prophet and will receive the prophet's reward. (See the gospel for today.)

Gehazi = geh-HAY-zī

Later Elisha asked, "Can something be *done* for her?"
His servant *Gehazi* answered, "*Yes!*
    She has no *son*, and her *husband* is getting *on* in years."
Elisha said, "*Call* her."
When the woman had been *called* and stood at the *door*,
    Elisha *promised*, "This time *next* year
    you will be fondling a baby *son*."

There is tenderness in the way the prophet makes the promise. He doesn't say simply that she will have a son but that she will hold a son lovingly in her arms.

READING I Here is a warm and touching story of hospitality and gratitude. Both the woman's generosity and the prophet's kindness in return are examples of graciousness. Let your proclamation communicate as much of these qualities as possible. The compilers of the lectionary obviously chose this text because it exemplifies what Jesus says in today's gospel reading: Whoever welcomes a prophet is rewarded accordingly.

The larger meaning will not escape the attentive reader or hearer. The prophet's role is to speak for God. Whether the message is one of warning or comfort (or both, which is most often the case), the prophet must proclaim it courageously. At the same time, those who speak for God cannot do so with authenticity unless they speak with compassion, remembering that all have sinned and that conversion is an ongoing and dynamic process.

There are many ways to speak for God. Some are dramatic, as in Elisha's promise to the woman that she would bear a child.

Some seem negligible in the eyes of the world but are never so in the eyes of God, as Jesus reminds us in the gospel for today.

READING II Paul once again uses somewhat tortured logic—by our standards—to share an important theological insight. It will take a dynamic and sensitive proclamation to communicate the various levels of contrast and comparison he relies on to get his point across. Careful preparation, vocal variety and a deliberate delivery will help you succeed.

READING II   Romans 6:3–4, 8–11

A reading from the letter of Saint Paul to the Romans

Brothers and sisters:
Are you *unaware* that we who were *baptized* into Christ *Jesus*
    were baptized into his *death*?
We were indeed *buried* with him through baptism into *death*,
    so that, just as Christ was *raised* from the dead
    by the *glory* of the *Father*,
    we *too* might live in newness of *life*.

If, then, we have *died* with Christ,
    we believe that we shall also *live* with him.
We know that *Christ*, *raised* from the dead, dies no *more*;
    death no longer has *power* over him.
As to his *death*, he died to sin *once* and for *all*;
    as to his *life*, he lives for *God*.
Consequently, you *too* must think of yourselves as *dead* to *sin*
    and *living* for *God* in Christ *Jesus*.

Read the commentary carefully. This reading is packed with meaning but is not particularly easy to proclaim.

Use varying degrees of emphasis to make the contrasts and comparisons clear.

The last sentence implies something like "Therefore, it should be obvious that . . ." It is very upbeat!

The initial rhetorical question prompts the answer, "Of course we are aware of that!" Thus begins his masterful comparison between baptism and death, between Jesus' resurrection and our own. But it's a bit more complex than that. Paul's arguments are never tidy, nor did he mean them to be. He immerses his thought in images of life, death, baptism, resurrection and sin in order to emerge with the clear conviction that baptism has changed us into completely new beings.

Our experience tells us that in many ways we seem to be the same after baptism as we were before. The spiritual insight Paul wants us to get, however, is that, appearances notwithstanding, we are totally changed after baptism. Because we have been "buried" with Christ in baptism, we have also "risen" with Christ to a whole new way of living. Sin no longer has any power over us because Christ's death was death to sin, once for all.

Consider those who have died. They are outside the power of sin. We are dead to sin and alive in Christ. That part of us that was alive to sin (within its power) has died. Forgiveness is our assurance of union with Christ, and forgiveness is abundantly available for the asking.

Some day we will join Christ in the glory of life after death. Then we will see the difference between our old selves and our new selves quite clearly. The way to prepare for that union with Christ is to use the eyes of faith to see how different we are even now and behave accordingly.

GOSPEL   Matthew 10:37–42

A reading from the holy gospel according to Matthew

Jesus said to his *apostles:*
"Whoever loves *father* or *mother* more than *me* is not *worthy*
    of me,
    and whoever loves *son* or *daughter* more than *me* is not
        worthy of me;
    and whoever does not take up his *cross*
    and *follow* after me is not *worthy* of me.
Whoever *finds* his life will *lose* it,
    and whoever *loses* his life for *my* sake will *find* it.

"Whoever receives *you* receives *me,*
    and whoever receives *me* receives the one who *sent* me.
Whoever receives a *prophet because* he is a prophet
    will receive a prophet's *reward,*
    and whoever receives a *righteous* man
    because he *is* a righteous man
    will receive a *righteous* man's reward.
And whoever gives only a cup of cold *water*
    to one of these *little* ones to drink
    because the little one is a *disciple*—
    amen, I say to you, he will surely *not* lose his *reward.*"

There is nothing threatening in these words, difficult as they may be to hear. We must hear the truth, even when it hurts. We can never say Jesus sent us forth under false pretenses.

Notice that the text is composed of a list of sayings. Let each one work its effect.

Great vocal variety will make the elements of comparison and contrast clear.

The final comforting statement is also an antidote for those of us who think the only good deeds are great deeds.

GOSPEL Today we hear the conclusion of the great missionary discourse Matthew has provided for us in the last couple of weeks. Jesus continues to instruct his disciples about the sacrifice inherent in being missionaries, the priorities that must be held and the degree of selflessness they must have to be imitators of Jesus. In other words, Jesus teaches his disciples how to be true apostles (people "sent out") by being like himself.

The second section has a great deal to say about those who receive the Good News from the missionaries charged with proclaiming it. The church has always loved its missionaries. There is something inherently noble about a life dedicated to preaching the Good News where it has not been heard before, often in situations involving deprivation. Missionaries deserve all the hospitality we can muster.

But we know that the same nobility extends to every Christian. The baptism we have received is itself a commission. It sends us forth to live in such a way that our relationship with Jesus makes us a welcome sight to all who see us. If you ever get the impression that people dread seeing you approach, make whatever adjustments are necessary! Missionaries who are begrudgingly tolerated don't do a whole lot of good. "Speak softly and carry a big stick" is not a workable slogan for Christians.

"A cup of cold water in my name" is a much-loved saying among Christians. It impresses us with the profound implications of even the smallest act of unselfish love. Its larger meaning is that our reward for such acts is ludicrously greater than our effort. It teaches us something about God's loving kindness toward us.

14TH SUNDAY IN ORDINARY TIME

Lectionary #100

READING I Zechariah 9:9–10

A reading from the book of the prophet Zechariah

The text is poetry. The tone must be bright, clear and confident. Since it begins with a call to joy, be sure you have the assembly's complete attention before you begin.

Savor the apparent contradiction of a humble king.

"He shall . . . his dominion shall . . ." Communicate the confidence here. Ephraim = EE-fray-im

Thus says the LORD:
Rejoice *heartily*, O daughter Zion,
    shout for *joy*, O daughter Jerusalem!
See, your king shall *come* to you;
    a *just* savior is he,
meek, and riding on an *ass*,
    on a *colt*, the *foal* of an ass.

He shall *banish* the *chariot* from *Ephraim*,
    and the *horse* from *Jerusalem*;
the warrior's *bow* shall be *banished*,
    and he shall proclaim *peace* to the *nations*.
His dominion shall be from *sea* to *sea*,
    and from the *River* to the ends of the *earth*.

READING I Zechariah's prophecy of a king and savior for Israel is a striking contrast to the conquering hero we see elsewhere in the Hebrew scriptures. The prophet predicts a different kind of ruler— one who will be renowned for justice and peace, who will bring an end to wars. The image of his arrival on the foal of a donkey bespeaks humility. His meekness will conquer the pride of Ephraim's chariots and destroy the war horse and the warrior's bow. His rule will extend from sea to sea. It is a lovely image, and Matthew quotes this passage from Zechariah when he describes Jesus' entry into Jerusalem, which we commemorate on Palm Sunday.

The same image is echoed strongly in Jesus' cry of jubilation in today's gospel. He praises the Father for revealing the mysteries of God's reign to the lowly rather than the highborn, and he describes himself as the meek and humble refuge for all who feel weary and burdened with life's toil. Although Zechariah had a temporal ruler in mind, it is easy to see how this reading complements the gospel passage. Jesus also ushers in a worldwide dominion of peace, although it is not the peace that the world gives.

READING II Romans 8:9, 11–13

A reading from the letter of Saint Paul to the Romans

Brothers and sisters:
You are *not* in the *flesh*;
  on the *contrary*, you are in the *spirit*,
  if only the Spirit of God *dwells* in you.
Whoever does *not* have the Spirit of Christ
    does not *belong* to him.

If the *Spirit* of the one who raised Jesus from the dead
    dwells in you,
  the one who raised Christ from the dead
  will give life to *your* mortal bodies *also*,
  through his *Spirit* that *dwells* in you.

Consequently, brothers and sisters,
  we are not *debtors* to the *flesh*,
  to *live* according to the flesh.
For if you live according to the *flesh*, you will *die*,
  but if by the *Spirit* you put to *death* the deeds of the *body*,
  you will *live*.

Strong statements open this reading. Highlight the contrast between "flesh" and "spirit."

Be deliberate throughout. The logic is Pauline, not syllogistic.

We are flesh, but we don't act like it! We are spirit; that's how we act. The power and pervasiveness of the spirit is nowhere more compellingly stated than here.

READING II Throughout its history, the church has resisted philosophies that see material things (including the human body) as tainted and the spiritual alone as good. The heresy has many names and will continue to express itself, as indeed it does today whenever we are taught to despise the earth, neglect the created world and long only for our notions of heaven. The effect is always the same: guilt, depression, intolerance and elitism. These are hardly the signs of healthy Christian life.

The whole person, the whole world, is redeemed by Christ and filled with the Holy Spirit. Everything that exists, says Paul, has been transformed and renewed by the resurrection. The Christian who is fundamentally negative about the present world will do little to prepare it for the next. Any view of human nature as essentially corrupt is a caricature of Christianity. It sees the Good News as too good to be true.

We are in debt, Paul says, but not in the sense that we are hampered or held back by the hopelessness of a physical existence that ends at death. No, we are in debt to

Christ because his resurrection has totally transformed us and the world. "The earth is filled with the goodness of Christ." We are not held ransom by an earthbound view of life. We see beyond the earth, and that is precisely why we love it, for through life in it, we approach God's new creation, in which God will make all the earth new.

GOSPEL To prepare your proclamation of this gospel passage, divide it into three parts. First, Jesus addresses himself in an exultant prayer to

Jesus' cry of exultation must ring out. The point is not that God hides anything but that mere worldly wisdom hides God.

Jesus defines his mission: to reveal the Father. The Son wants to show the Father to everyone who will listen with an open heart.

This is surely one of the most beloved texts in scripture. Read it as lovingly as Jesus said it. Experiment with different emphasis. Try emphasizing "yoke" and "learn." Then emphasize "my" and "me." Which works best?

GOSPEL   Matthew 11:25–30

A reading from the holy gospel according to Matthew

At that time Jesus *exclaimed*:
"I give *praise* to you, Father, *Lord* of heaven and *earth*,
    for although you have *hidden* these things
    from the *wise* and the *learned*
    you have *revealed* them to *little* ones.
Yes, Father, such has been your gracious *will*.

"*All* things have been *handed over* to me by my *Father*.
No one knows the *Son* except the *Father*,
    and no one knows the *Father* except the *Son*
    and anyone to whom the Son *wishes* to *reveal* him.

"*Come* to me, all you who *labor* and are *burdened*,
    and *I* will give you *rest*.
Take *my* yoke upon you and learn from *me*,
    for *I* am *meek* and *humble* of heart;
    and you will find *rest* for yourselves.
For *my* yoke is *easy*, and *my* burden *light*."

the Father, rejoicing that his ministry reveals God's special love for the poor. Then Jesus gives us a kind of definition of himself. Though we are all sons and daughters of God, Jesus is *the* Son, to whom full knowledge of the Father has been given. The Son's mission is to reveal that knowledge of the Father to us. More than his mission, revelation of the Father is the Son's very identity and being. Jesus *is* the image of God. If we want to know God we have only to look closely at Jesus.

Finally, Jesus speaks directly to the weary, the oppressed, those for whom the world seems only to be a place of suffering. Jesus offers refreshment and relief in his person. The yoke we bear upon our shoulders has been placed there by a gentle and humble master, who shares completely in our weakness. Thus the burden given and received in mutual love will seem light and easy to the beloved. William Barclay points out in his *Daily Study Bible* that the word "easy" here also implies that each yoke is custom-made, as indeed yokes were for teams of oxen. Yokes didn't hang in rows on ready-to-wear racks. Each was carefully crafted by the carpenter for the team that would bear it. It's a wonderful insight and may be the inspiration underlying the conviction that "God never places more on our shoulders than we can bear."

Jesus' experience throughout his ministry was that the humble found it easier to accept his revolutionary doctrine than did those who were full of their own self-importance. Here he not only defines himself more clearly, he also shows us the kind of people with whom he wishes to be identified.

15TH SUNDAY IN ORDINARY TIME

Lectionary #103

READING I   Isaiah 55:10–11

A reading from the book of the prophet Isaiah

Thus says the LORD:
Just as from the *heavens*
 the *rain* and *snow* come down
and do not *return* there
 till they have *watered* the earth,
 making it *fertile* and *fruitful*,
giving *seed* to the one who *sows*
 and *bread* to the one who *eats*,
so *shall* my *word* be
 that goes forth from my *mouth*;
my word shall *not* return to me *void*,
 but *shall* do my *will*,
 achieving the *end* for which I *sent* it.

Grammatically, this brief reading is one sentence. But it is a poem, and we all know about poetic license! Read the sense units and emphasize the "just as . . . so shall" structure.

Remember to emphasize the occurrences of "shall."

READING I Isaiah is the patron saint of the proclaimer. In an earlier chapter (50), Isaiah has the servant of God utter these words: "The Lord has given me a well-trained tongue, that I might announce to the weary a word that will rouse them." Some translations indicate that "well trained tongue" would be more accurately rendered "the tongue of a teacher" or "the tongue of a well-taught disciple." That defines you, the proclaimer, perfectly.

The first reading for today describes the effect of your ministry. The word that goes out from God's mouth (through you) *will* achieve the purpose for which it was sent. There is both comfort and challenge for you in these words. God's word has a life of its own. It *will* have its intended effect. It's not all up to you, the proclaimer, so you don't have to feel that the success of God's word is at the mercy of your ministry. And yet, in a way, it is. A poor proclamation hinders the word; a good proclamation assists it. Be comforted; be challenged.

The structure of this text is the clue to its meaning and the surest hint at the most effective proclamation. It is based on a simile: "just as the rain . . . so shall my word . . ." Do not be disturbed that the text is all one sentence; it is poetry, after all, and the meaning is clear. The images build upward and upward, commingling to enrich the picture, and then the resolution comes, bringing all the images to focus on the one controlling thought.

The first sentence is a courageous proclamation of hope. Let it ring out as such; the assembly needs to hear this.

This is a complex idea. The earth itself (all creation, not just humankind) is eager for the fullness of redemption. We are intimately joined with the rest of creation; the glorious freedom to come will liberate the entire universe from corruption.

The image of creation groaning for fulfillment is powerful. Only those who have given up hope stop groaning. To groan is to hope!

Emphasize the "large crowds" and the vivid image of Jesus teaching from a moored boat as the people stand on the shore. These details enable the assembly to see the scene.

READING II   Romans 8:18–23

A reading from the letter of Saint Paul to the Romans

Brothers and sisters:
I consider that the *sufferings* of this *present* time are as *nothing*
    compared with the *glory* to be *revealed* for us.
For *creation* awaits with eager *expectation*
    the *revelation* of the children of *God*;
    for *creation* was made subject to *futility*,
    not of its *own* accord but because of the one who *subjected* it,
    in hope that creation *itself*
    would be set *free* from slavery to *corruption*
    and share in the glorious *freedom* of the children of *God*.

We know that *all* creation is *groaning* in *labor* pains
        even until *now*;
    and not only *that*, but we *ourselves*,
    who have the *firstfruits* of the Spirit,
    we *also* groan within ourselves
    as we wait for *adoption*, the *redemption* of our *bodies*.

GOSPEL   Matthew 13:1–23

A reading from the holy gospel according to Matthew

On that day, *Jesus* went out of the *house* and sat down by the *sea*.
Such large *crowds* gathered around him
    that he got into a *boat* and sat *down*,
    and the whole *crowd* stood along the *shore*.

The rain and the snow are absolutely vital to life; when they fall upon the earth, life inevitably responds. The word of God is no less vital and no less predictable in achieving its purpose. The word of God is God at work. In Hebrew, the word for "word" is the same as the word for "deed."

READING II This selection from Paul's letter to the Romans is striking in its vivid portrayal of our present spiritual condition. Anyone who has felt the futility and agony of life's struggles will find

great solace in the assurance that all creation will be freed from its apparent destiny of death and decay, and will share in the glorious freedom of the children of God.

The most striking thing about this passage, however, is the enormous dignity that Paul accords hopeful believers. The Spirit, which we have as "first-fruits" (a primer, a promissory note), gives our efforts, our suffering, our weakness, the same nobility we see in the sufferings of Christ. This is not counsel to "bear up" under our sufferings

with a stiff upper lip and the stoic's resignation to pain. It is far more ennobling than that. Christ's suffering was not borne as a meaningless inevitability. Christ chose suffering for the sake of a redemptive purpose, and our suffering contributes to that purpose. We are counseled to find that purpose and allow suffering to be the noble thing it becomes when united with Christ's.

This does not mean we are to seek out suffering and inflict it upon ourselves. In the first place, seeking suffering is like seeking one's own nose. It's there and it's plain to see, unless denial has become a fine art to

Read each sentence of the parable itself with deliberate care. Each one leads up to the good soil.

And he *spoke* to them at length in *parables*, saying:
 "A *sower* went out to *sow*.
And *as* he sowed, *some* seed fell on the *path*,
 and *birds* came and ate it *up*.
Some fell on *rocky* ground, where it had little *soil*.
It sprang up at *once* because the soil was not *deep*,
 and when the *sun* rose it was *scorched*,
 and it *withered* for lack of *roots*.
Some seed fell among *thorns*, and the thorns grew *up*
 and *choked* it.
But *some* seed fell on *rich* soil, and produced *fruit*,
 a *hundred* or *sixty* or *thirtyfold*.
Whoever has *ears* ought to *hear*."

The remainder of the reading (including the long quotation from Isaiah) is an intimate dialogue between Jesus and his disciples. We should hear a change in tone from the preaching in the first two paragraphs.

The *disciples* approached him and said,
 "Why do you speak to them in *parables*?"
He said to them in *reply*,
 "Because *knowledge* of the mysteries of the kingdom
 of *heaven*
 has been granted to *you*, but to *them* it has *not* been granted.
To anyone who *has*, more will be *given* and he will grow *rich*;
 from anyone who has *not*, even what he *has* will be
 taken away.

"*This* is why I speak to them in *parables*, because
 'they *look* but do not *see* and *hear* but do not *listen*
 or *understand*.'
Isaiah's prophecy is *fulfilled* in them, which says:
 'You *shall* indeed *hear* but not *understand*,
 you *shall* indeed *look* but *never* see.
 Gross is the heart of this people,
 they will hardly *hear* with their ears,
 they have *closed* their eyes,

us. Besides, to seek suffering is far too self-centered an activity for the Christian, unless our search is for the suffering of others, which we do all we can to relieve.

The Christian does not regret the fact that we must live in hope, subject to all the miseries of the flesh. How can it be otherwise? Is it possible to hope for something we already have? We hope for what we cannot see, and we do so in patient endurance, the same patient endurance we see in Jesus. It is the Spirit dwelling within us that ennobles our hope.

GOSPEL I only rarely recommend taking the shorter option of an assigned gospel text. Today is one of those few times. The shorter form gives the parable of the sower in its original form and with its own implied but clear interpretation. The first reading demonstrated how the word of God fulfills its appointed purpose, achieving the end for which it is sent. The shorter form of the gospel restates this theme most effectively. In this case, "less is more."

The longer form includes the commentary on Jesus' reasons for teaching in parables and gives an interpretation of the

parable of the sower, which we know was added later and which alters the original meaning. The simple meaning of the original parable is that, despite all obstacles (rocky ground, for example), the word of God *will* bear fruit and will do so in amazing abundance. A hundredfold is an astronomically large yield and so makes Jesus' point. The parable clearly reflects Jesus' own experience; the obstacles to his ministry are legion, but the fruits of his labor will become bountiful beyond comprehension. The same point is clearly made in the first reading for today's

lest they *see* with their eyes
and *hear* with their ears
and *understand* with their *hearts* and be *converted*,
and I *heal* them.'

"But *blessed* are *your* eyes, because they *see*,
and your *ears*, because they *hear*.
Amen, I say to you, many *prophets* and *righteous* people
longed to see what *you* see but did *not* see it,
and to *hear* what *you* hear but did *not* hear it.

"*Hear* then the parable of the *sower*.
The seed sown on the *path* is the one
who *hears* the word of the kingdom without
understanding it,
and the *evil* one comes and *steals away*
what was sown in his heart.
The seed sown on *rocky* ground
is the one who *hears* the word and *receives* it at once with *joy*.
But he has no *root* and lasts only for a *time*.
When some *tribulation* or *persecution* comes because
of the word,
he immediately falls *away*.
The seed sown among *thorns* is the one who *hears* the word,
but then worldly *anxiety* and the lure of *riches choke* the word
and it bears no *fruit*.

"But the seed sown on *rich* soil
is the one who *hears* the word and *understands* it,
who *indeed* bears *fruit* and yields a *hundred* or *sixty*
or *thirtyfold*."

[Shorter: Matthew 13:1–9]

Mass and explains why it was chosen as a match for the gospel.

For liturgical purposes, the shorter form also seems more conducive to celebration of the kingdom of heaven and its inexorable growth, which preoccupies us during these Sundays in Ordinary Time spent with Matthew's gospel.

The longer form of the gospel includes the later addition of an interpretation that is completely different. It centers on those who receive the seed (God's word) and encounter various hardships in bringing it to fruition. It counsels perseverance in face of difficulty.

The middle section of the long form is evidence of the belief that Jesus' mission had to be conducted in relative secrecy until its validity has been proven by the resurrection. This has been called the "Messianic secret," which is a constant theme in Mark's gospel (one of Matthew's sources).

16TH SUNDAY IN ORDINARY TIME

Lectionary #106

READING I   Wisdom 12:13, 16–19

A reading from the book of Wisdom

There is *no* god besides *you* who have the *care* of *all*,
   that you need *show* you have not *unjustly* condemned.
For your *might* is the *source* of *justice*;
   your *mastery* over all things makes you *lenient* to all.
For you *show* your *might* when the *perfection* of your *power*
      is *disbelieved*;
   and in those who *know* you, you rebuke *temerity*.
But though you are master of *might*, you judge with *clemency*,
   and with much *lenience* you *govern* us;
   for *power*, whenever you will, *attends* you.

And you *taught* your people, by these *deeds*,
   that those who are *just* must be *kind*;
and you *gave* your children good ground for *hope*
   that you would permit *repentance* for their *sins*.

Like all good poetry, this reading is packed with beautifully expressed truths. Proclaim it slowly and carefully, being careful to give each image its due.

God's power is what makes God lenient! This is a striking concept! Emphasize it.

temerity = tuh-MER-uh-tee

Take a significant pause here, moving from present tense into past tense.

READING I   There are still some people who describe the God of the Old Testament as harsh and cold, preoccupied with law, and the God of the New Testament as the God of love. This is one of many passages we could refer to when we hear such a description. God has not changed, but our knowledge of God has changed dramatically over the centuries and, we believe, come to fullness with the appearance of Jesus. The scriptures are a record of how we have come to know God over a long period of time. Both testaments are equally valuable in our journey. Can you imagine Jesus proclaiming the Good News without reference to the scriptures he knew and loved so well?

This reading is a lovely poem that extols the divine qualities we long to see in leaders: care, justice, mercy, leniency. It makes the point clearly that God's leniency is in direct proportion to God's power. More than that, the text asserts that it is precisely God's power that is the source of divine leniency.

Notice, finally, that God teaches us that to be righteous and just we must be kind. Without kindness, we cannot be in right relationship with God. How long will it take us learn this fundamental truth? Our world today, marred by such horrors as ethnic cleansing and bigotry, has never needed to hear this message more than it does today.

READING II Romans 8:26–27

A reading from the letter of Saint Paul to the Romans

Brothers and sisters:
The *Spirit* comes to the *aid* of our *weakness*;
　for we do not *know* how to *pray* as we *ought*,
　but the Spirit *himself* intercedes with inexpressible *groanings*.
And the one who searches *hearts*
　knows what is the *intention* of the Spirit,
　because he *intercedes* for the *holy* ones
　according to God's *will*.

This is a lovely and comforting text. Notice that it uses the words "our" and "we," giving you, the reader, immediate identity with your hearers.

The "holy ones" here are the members of the Christian community.

GOSPEL Matthew 13:24–43

A reading from the holy gospel according to Matthew

Jesus proposed *another parable* to the crowds, saying:
"The kingdom of *heaven* may be likened to a man
　who sowed *good seed* in his *field*.
While everyone was *asleep* his *enemy* came
　and sowed *weeds* all through the *wheat*, and then went off.

"When the crop *grew* and bore *fruit*, the *weeds* appeared as well.
The *slaves* of the householder came to him and said,
　'Master, did you not sow *good* seed in your field?
Where have the *weeds* come from?'
He answered, 'An *enemy* has done this.'
His slaves said to him, 'Do you want us to go and pull them *up*?'

Parables are short stories. This one includes quite a lot of dialogue. Employ sufficient vocal variety to indicate different speakers (including Jesus, the narrator). Use effective pauses and transitions in moving from one speaker to another.

This reading complements the gospel selection for today: The householder in the parable advises against trying to separate the weeds from the wheat lest the wheat be harmed. He is tolerant, wise and lenient, for he realizes how difficult it often is to distinguish saint from sinner.

READING II We continue over several weeks to read Paul's letter to the Romans. This selection, like many others, provides a vivid picture of our personal experience. Anyone who has felt prayer to be a bumbling, awkward experience should take great comfort in these words: "The Spirit helps us in our weakness, for we do not know how to pray as we ought."

The most striking thing about this part of Romans, however, is the enormous dignity that Paul accords hopeful believers. The Spirit that has come to dwell in us gives our efforts, our suffering, our weakness, the same nobility we see in the sufferings of Christ. And that makes even the most hesitant and timid effort for good worthy of high praise.

As we noted last week, we should not regret the fact that we must live in hope, subject to all the travails of the flesh. How can it be otherwise? Is it possible to hope for something we already have? We hope for what we cannot see, and we do so with patient endurance, the same patient endurance we see in Jesus. It is the Spirit dwelling within us that ennobles our hope.

He replied, '*No*, if you pull up the *weeds*
    you might uproot the *wheat* along *with* them.
Let them grow *together* until *harvest*;
    then at *harvest* time I will say to the *harvesters*,
    "*First* collect the *weeds* and tie them in *bundles* for *burning*;
    but gather the *wheat* into my *barn*."'"

He proposed *another* parable to them.
"The kingdom of heaven is like a *mustard* seed
    that a person took and *sowed* in a *field*.
It is the *smallest* of *all* the seeds,
    yet when *full-grown* it is the *largest* of *plants*.
It becomes a large *bush*,
    and the 'birds of the *sky* come and dwell in its *branches*.'"

He spoke to them *another* parable.
"The kingdom of heaven is like *yeast*
    that a *woman* took and mixed with three measures
        of *wheat* flour
    until the *whole batch* was leavened."

All these things Jesus spoke to the crowds in *parables*.
He spoke to them *only* in parables,
    to *fulfill* what had been said through the *prophet*:
    "I will open my mouth in *parables*,
    I will announce what has lain *hidden* from the foundation
    of the *world*."

Then, *dismissing* the crowds, he went into the *house*.
His *disciples* approached him and said,
    "*Explain* to us the parable of the *weeds* in the field."
He said in reply, "He who sows *good* seed is the Son of *Man*,
    the *field* is the *world*, the *good* seed the children
        of the *kingdom*.

The reckoning will come, and the good and bad will be separated. The judging will be done by the only one who knows all, but even then the judgment will be lenient.

Pause significantly before the next parable (if you take the long form of the reading).

Take another significant pause here, even though the preceding section is brief. Like yeast, a little bit of good news goes a long way!

It is clear that a summary section begins here. A parable reveals by being laid alongside (parallel to) the reality it seeks to explain.

GOSPEL Rarely do I recommend taking the shorter option of an assigned gospel text. Today is one of those rare times. The shorter form gives the parable of the weeds and wheat in what is surely its original form, with its own implied but clear interpretation. The longer form of the reading includes two more brief parables (mustard seed and yeast) as well as the commentary on Jesus' reasons for teaching in parables.

Then comes an interpretation of the parable of the weeds and wheat, which we know was added later and changes its focus. For liturgical purposes, the shorter form seems more conducive to identification and recognition of the kingdom of heaven, which preoccupies us during these Sundays in Ordinary Time spent with Matthew's gospel.

The meaning of the original parable is that, unlike human beings, who tend to judge quickly, God is lenient and patient. (See the first reading for a description of

what it means to be just and righteous as God is.) The parable clearly reflects Jesus' own experience in the face of condemnation for associating with social outcasts. It says clearly that Jesus' notion of the reign of God on earth is a challenge to our less tolerant views. Sometimes it seems that we view leniency as weakness. If we are of a masochistic bent, we even feel a bit guilty when we are dealt with too leniently. How very different from God's nature and God's

The *weeds* are the children of the *evil* one,
  and the *enemy* who *sows* them is the *devil*.
The *harvest* is the *end* of the age, and the *harvesters* are *angels*.

"Just as *weeds* are collected and burned up with *fire*,
  so will it *be* at the end of the *age*.
The Son of Man will send his *angels*,
  and they will *collect* out of his kingdom
  all who cause *others* to *sin* and all *evildoers*.
They will throw them into the fiery *furnace*,
  where there will be *wailing* and grinding of *teeth*.
Then the *righteous* will *shine* like the *sun*
  in the kingdom of their *Father*.
Whoever has *ears* ought to *hear*."

[Shorter: Matthew 13:24–30]

The final sentence is clearly a formula and so should be set off by a pause.

view! There are many issues in our contemporary church that could be resolved if we were brave enough to exercise the radical kind of leniency we see in God.

The two additional parables (mustard seed and yeast) are an assertion of the inexorable growth of the kingdom of heaven on earth. The middle section of the long form complicates the situation further. It is an assertion of the belief that Jesus' mission had to be conducted in relative secrecy until its validity had been proven by the resurrection. From the point of view of liturgical experience, the gospel proclamation thus begins to become too complex.

17TH SUNDAY IN ORDINARY TIME

Lectionary #109

READING I   1 Kings 3:5, 7–12

A reading from the first book of Kings

First, God initiates the dialogue.

The LORD appeared to *Solomon* in a *dream* at night.
God said, "*Ask* something of me and I will *give* it to you."
Solomon *answered*:
"O LORD, my God, you have *made* me, your *servant*, *king*
    to succeed my father *David*;
    but I am a mere *youth*, not knowing at *all* how to act.
I *serve* you in the midst of the *people* whom you have *chosen*,
    a people so *vast* that it cannot be *numbered* or *counted*.

Next, Solomon makes his request with humble confidence.

"*Give* your servant, therefore, an *understanding heart*
    to *judge* your people and to distinguish *right* from *wrong*.
For who is able to *govern* this vast *people* of yours?"

The LORD was *pleased* that Solomon made this request.
So God said to him:
    "*Because* you have asked for *this*—
    not for a long *life* for yourself,
    nor for *riches*,
    nor for the life of your *enemies*,
    but for *understanding* so that you may know what is *right*—
    I *do* as you *requested*.

God grants the request and gives far more than was requested. This seems to be a habit with God!

I give you a heart so *wise* and *understanding*
    that there has never been anyone *like* you up to *now*,
    and *after* you there will come *no* one to *equal* you."

READING I   We've all heard of the wisdom of King Solomon. In this reading we see the origin of it. It comes from God as an answer to a humble prayer. We might wish fervently that all those in leadership positions would make Solomon's prayer their own. It exhibits the selflessness that should characterize the attitude and actions of anyone in a position of power and influence. It is also a model for all prayer: "O Lord, you have given me life itself. What can I ask for except the wisdom and grace to be an influence for good in the lives of all I meet."

Because it takes wisdom to see the kingdom of heaven on earth, this reading complements the gospel narrative today. Whether in positions of leadership or not, every Christian needs insight and wisdom to discern and apply Christian values to everyday life. Wisdom of this kind is not to be confused with intelligence and learning, though both can foster or hinder true wisdom. The wisdom of faith lies in the heart and comes from knowing God through Jesus Christ and the manifestation of the Spirit in the life of every human being.

The structure of this reading should be noted: God asks that Solomon make a request. Solomon does so in terms so unselfish that it is deceptively simple: He asks to know right from wrong, good from evil. God approves and grants the request. If your proclamation moves carefully from one structural unit to the next and respects the transitions between them, it will be most effective.

READING II   We have been reading from Paul's letter to the Romans for several Sundays now. You may wish to

READING II Romans 8:28–30

A reading from the letter of Saint Paul to the Romans

Brothers and sisters:
We *know* that all things work for *good* for those who love *God*,
    who are *called* according to his *purpose*.
For those he *foreknew* he also *predestined*
    to be *conformed* to the image of his *Son*,
    so that he might be the *firstborn*
    among *many* brothers and sisters.
And those he *predestined* he also *called*;
    and those he *called* he also *justified*;
    and those he *justified* he also *glorified*.

This is an exultant demonstration of the orderly way in which God brings us back into participation in divine life.

God knew us before we knew ourselves, called us into being, planned from the beginning to mold us in Christ's image, called us back from exile, justified us (put us in right relationship) and glorified us! Proclaim this marvel with energy.

GOSPEL Matthew 13:44–52

A reading from the holy gospel according to Matthew

Jesus said to his *disciples*:
"The kingdom of *heaven* is like a *treasure* buried in a *field*,
    which a person *finds* and *hides* again,
    and out of *joy* goes and sells *all* that he *has* and *buys* that field.

"*Again*, the kingdom of heaven is like a *merchant*
    searching for fine *pearls*.
When he finds a pearl of great *price*,
    he goes and *sells* all that he *has* and *buys* it.

"*Again*, the kingdom of heaven is like a *net* thrown into the *sea*,
    which collects *fish* of every *kind*.

Let the images of buried treasure, pearl and net each work its different effect. Do not rush from one to the other. Each new figure should begin with a renewed energy level.

consult earlier commentaries to get a clearer idea of the context and to see the dramatic shift in Paul's tone and topic this week. He has been writing at some length about the suffering and struggle that accompany the life of every human being. Now he moves toward a consideration of the wonders that await the faithful. Notice, however, that he emphasizes the past tense. Our final destiny, following the struggle of life, is glorious because of what God has accomplished on our behalf.

The common (and understandable) notion that our eventual glory is a reward for our patient endurance should be refined a bit. Our glory is inevitable in the plan of God, and our suffering is inevitable in the course of human life. But we would do better to see the glory and suffering as the mixture that makes up our present existence rather than see no glory until the end, when suffering is finished. Even now, we participate to some degree in the glory that is to come in fullness. Such a view is the result of prayerful insight (wisdom) and much more conducive to a fruitful Christian life. Christians who view this present life as nothing more than a time of trial are a pretty grim lot!

The guiding principle of Christian optimism is beautifully stated in the opening words of this reading. All things work together for good in those who love God— *all* things, both here and hereafter.

GOSPEL | Jesus continues to teach us about the kingdom of heaven. The three comparisons in today's gospel are quite vivid. For the last two Sundays I have recommended proclaiming the shorter version of the gospel. Today there is good reason to take the longer form, which isn't terribly

When it is *full* they haul it *ashore*
and sit down to put what is *good* into *buckets.*
What is *bad* they throw *away.*

"*Thus* it will be at the end of the *age.*
The *angels* will go out and *separate* the *wicked* from
the *righteous*
and throw them into the fiery *furnace,*
where there will be *wailing* and grinding of *teeth.*

"Do you *understand* all these things?"
They answered, "*Yes.*"
And he replied,
"Then every *scribe* who has been *instructed*
in the kingdom of *heaven*
is like the head of a *household*
who *brings* from his *storeroom* both the *new* and the *old.*"

[*Shorter: Matthew 13:44–46*]

There should be a significant pause before "Do you understand all these things?" You could direct the question to the assembly with eye contact.

Jesus' response means "Good! Now that you understand, you will be able to apply the meaning of these parables to any given situation."

long. It gives us three images that teach us a great deal about how to live as loyal subjects of the kingdom of heaven.

First, the person who buys the field with the buried treasure shows us that total investment is characteristic of those who recognize the value of the kingdom (such a person sells everything to buy the field). There is even a hint of conniving in this person. He hides the buried treasure he found and may have negotiated a price for the property that did not include the value of the treasure. We should not be squeamish at

such a parallel. Jesus would have us imitate his resourcefulness and dedication, not the deception.

The "pearl of great price" has become a colloquial standard of evaluation. Not many things are worth investing every resource we have in order to acquire it, but the kingdom of heaven is one of them. The image of the "net" introduces a different notion about the kingdom. It is indiscriminate, collecting old tires as well as big fish. It reminds us of last Sunday's gospel when the workers were told to let the wheat and weeds grow together until harvest. The separation of the

valuable from the worthless comes later. Echoed here is the notion that God's tolerance is the model for our own; given our limited knowledge and our tendency to evaluate on appearances, we simply must avoid judging others. At the same time, the horrifying punishment that awaits the "useless" is meant to inspire us to conversion.

Finally, the scribe who is learned in the kingdom of heaven is wise enough to hear, contemplate and apply the meaning of these parables to any given situation. The wisdom granted to Solomon (see the first reading) is echoed here.

18TH SUNDAY IN ORDINARY TIME

Lectionary #112

READING I   Isaiah 55:1–3

A reading from the book of the prophet Isaiah

Thus says the LORD:
All you who are *thirsty*,
    come to the *water*!
You who have no *money*,
    come, receive *grain* and *eat*;
Come, without *paying* and without *cost*,
    drink *wine* and *milk*!

Why spend your *money* for what is not *bread*;
    your *wages* for what fails to *satisfy*?
Heed me, and you shall eat *well*,
    you shall *delight* in rich *fare*.
Come to me *heedfully*,
    listen, that you may have *life*.
I will *renew* with you the *everlasting* covenant,
    the *benefits* assured to *David*.

Proceed through this series of invitations deliberately, allowing each one to soak in. Vocal variety is absolutely essential, so that each invitation has a different ring from the last one uttered.

This sentence renews the invitation: "Come! Listen!"

READING I   We heard the first part of this text as the fourth reading at the Easter Vigil. Today, as then, the passage is chosen for its banquet imagery. The scholars tell us that the author of these verses of poetry lived in a poor community. One would expect the image of a banquet to describe God's reign in such a context, along with the consoling message that no money is needed to partake in it. The sensitive prophet writes in a way his audience can understand.

The image of a sumptuous banquet is an integral part of the Jewish and Christian traditions, and other religious traditions as well. Perhaps they are less effective in a well-fed (or even overfed) society than among poorer people, who can appreciate the idea of abundance because they experience it so rarely. But certainly everyone can be encouraged by the promise that all people will share equally in the heavenly banquet, which is more a feast for the soul than for the stomach. The banquet described by Isaiah and the heavenly banquet are both clearly associated with a future time, the "end times," when God's reign will be fully visible.

The Christian belief is that those "end times" have already begun to appear. In today's gospel story we see that the reign of God has arrived in the presence and ministry of Jesus: "All those present ate their fill." And though they were only 5,000, they symbolize the world's billions, for whom the Lord has multiplied his grace, favor and provident love.

How do we share in the banquet of God's reign? Isaiah gives us the answer in

The list is not easy; the secret is to move slowly through it, making each item sound fresh and new. And each word is a rhetorical question (distress? persecution? nakedness?), calling for the answer "Of course not!"

READING II   Romans 8:35, 37–39

A reading from the letter of Saint Paul to the Romans

Brothers and sisters:
What will *separate* us from the love of *Christ*?
Will *anguish*, or *distress*, or *persecution*, or *famine*,
    or *nakedness*, or *peril*, or the *sword*?
No, in all these things we conquer *overwhelmingly*
    through him who *loved* us.

For I am *convinced* that neither *death*, nor *life*,
    nor *angels*, nor *principalities*,
    nor *present* things, nor *future* things,
    nor *powers*, nor *height*, nor *depth*,
    nor any *other* creature will be able to *separate* us
    from the love of *God* in Christ *Jesus* our *Lord*.

The transition from concentration on Jesus' lonely grief to his pity for the crowds must be slow. Pause significantly between the scenes.

GOSPEL   Matthew 14:13–21

A reading from the holy gospel according to Matthew

When *Jesus* heard of the *death* of John the *Baptist*,
    he *withdrew* in a *boat* to a *deserted* place by *himself*.
The crowds *heard* of this and *followed* him on *foot*
        from their *towns*.
When he *disembarked* and *saw* the vast crowd,
    his *heart* was moved with *pity* for them,
        and he cured their *sick*.

the Lord's words: "Come to me, listen to me. You will have life."

READING II This is Paul at his most confident. The strength of belief expressed here is the best instruction on how to read it effectively. It is almost brash in its certainty. But Paul often borders on brash, and that's one of the reasons he is both a challenge and a comfort to the proclaimer.

Notice again the power of the rhetorical question (a question that expects no response because the response is so obvious): "What will separate us from the love of

Christ?" It is precisely our conviction in faith that *nothing* will separate us that makes the question so powerful.

Paul sounds like an effective motivational speaker, arousing his audience to a fever pitch of confidence and courage. You should sound the same way while avoiding, of course, inappropriate exaggeration that would make this beautiful passage a caricature of "Onward, Christian soldiers!" The energy here is meant to encourage the disheartened, not embolden the presumptuous.

This text will be most effective when your rendition of it begins with great energy

and gradually winds down to the calm assurance of "the love of God." This does not mean that the final words are nearly inaudible, simply that the intensity declines gradually until the last sentence has a sense of quiet closure and peaceful assurance.

GOSPEL This is one of the most well-known and beloved stories from the life of Jesus, known as the "feeding of the 5,000" or the "multiplication of the loaves and fishes."

Some scripture scholars argue that the real miracle in this event is not a miraculous

A new narrative begins here.

When it was *evening*, the *disciples* approached him and said,
 "This is a *deserted* place and it is already *late*;
 dismiss the crowds so that they can go to the *villages*
 and buy *food* for themselves."
Jesus said to them, "There is no *need* for them to go away;
 give them some food *yourselves*."
But they said to him,
 "Five *loaves* and two *fish* are all we *have* here."
Then he said, "*Bring* them here to me,"
 and he ordered the *crowds* to sit down on the *grass*.

Taking the five *loaves* and the two *fish*, and looking up to *heaven*,
 he said the *blessing*, *broke* the loaves,
 and gave them to the *disciples*,
 who in *turn* gave them to the *crowds*.

**Don't throw away the leftover fragments.
This is an important point. Emphasize it.**

They *all ate* and were *satisfied*,
 and they picked up the *fragments* left *over—*
 twelve wicker *baskets* full.
Those who *ate* were about *five thousand* men,
 not counting women and children.

**The final phrase discounting the "women
and children" is unfortunate. It seems a
shame to risk distracting from the powerful
story by adding this phrase. It might be
better to end the reading with, "Those who
ate were about 5,000."**

multiplication of food, but Jesus' ability to get the crowd to share generously what little food they had and so discover that there was more than enough for all. Knowing what we do about human selfishness, this second interpretation might reveal the greater miracle!

In any event, the story again presents us with a situation of crisis to which Jesus brings resolution, showing that in his presence such problems can be resolved. In and through Jesus the world's hunger—both physical and spiritual—can be satisfied.

There is clearly something of the mystical guru in Jesus when he replies to the disciples' concern with a remark that seems like a riddle: "Give them something to eat yourselves." It is clear from this response that Jesus intends to use the situation to teach something. The meaning may well have been, "Share with them what you have brought for yourselves." We can only imagine the look on their faces if this were the case.

Jesus may have been speaking tongue-in-cheek, though you want to avoid anything that makes it sound like Jesus is playing with his disciples in some trivial way. The

most effective course is to allow the text to work on its own, with its gratifying twist.

Special attention must be paid to your reading of Jesus' ritual approach to this miraculous meal. The words "he took . . . looked up to heaven . . . blessed and broke" are so clearly related to the eucharistic formula we will hear later in the liturgy that they deserve great emphasis and intensity. Finally, the leftover fragments are a sign of the profligate providence of God. With God there is more than enough, far more than enough, infinitely more than we can imagine.

19TH SUNDAY IN ORDINARY TIME

Lectionary #115

READING I   1 Kings 19:9a, 11–13a

A reading from the first book of Kings

At the mountain of *God, Horeb,*
    Elijah came to a cave where he took *shelter.*
Then the LORD said to him,
    "Go *outside* and stand on the *mountain* before the LORD;
    the LORD will be *passing by.*"

A *strong* and heavy *wind* was *rending* the mountains
    and crushing *rocks* before the LORD—
    but the LORD was *not* in the *wind.*
After the *wind* there was an *earthquake*—
    but the LORD was *not* in the *earthquake.*
After the *earthquake* there was *fire*—
    but the LORD was *not* in the *fire.*
After the *fire* there was a tiny *whispering* sound.

When he heard *this,*
    Elijah hid his *face* in his *cloak*
    and went and *stood* at the *entrance* of the *cave.*

Horeb = HOHR-eb
Elijah = ee-LĪ-juh

Pay particular attention to the traditional device of repetition for the sake of effect: "but the Lord was not in the wind"; "but the Lord was not in the earthquake"; "but the Lord was not in the fire." Gradually build toward the "quiet" climax.

Elijah hides his face before the divine presence but stands ready to do God's bidding.

READING I   The violence of nature plays a role in all three readings today. This passage from the first book of Kings complements the gospel narrative. In both we see God at work in the context of dramatic natural phenomenon, either preceded by them, at work in the midst of them, or in control over them. Although we no longer associate wind, fire and thunder with a manifestation of the divine, we can certainly appreciate the magnitude of these natural occurrences and allow them to remind us of the greatness of creation and its creator.

Recognizing the presence of God in our lives usually occurs after the wind dies down. In stormy times, our fear and confusion can deafen us to the subtle, quiet ways in which God reveals provident love. Or we can look back at times of turmoil and see that God truly was at work in us even though our distraction kept us from noticing.

It is important throughout our lives to develop our ability to hear God's own still, small voice both within the silence of our own hearts and in the words spoken through others. It is also important to develop the insight that enables us to see God at work in the commonplace and the unspectacular. God's ways are not our own. We could all long for the special revelations granted to some of the saints. But recall that such revelations were always more for the sake of others than for the one who received them. Perhaps we want special signs because faith seems to be such hard work. But that is true only when we struggle to believe. Faith is a gift offered to all and is most effectively received in peaceful silence.

READING II   Romans 9:1–5

A reading from the letter of Saint Paul to the Romans

Brothers and sisters:
I speak the *truth* in *Christ,* I do not *lie;*
    my *conscience* joins with the Holy *Spirit*
        in bearing me *witness*
        that I have great *sorrow* and constant *anguish* in my *heart.*

For I could wish that I *myself* were *accursed*
        and cut *off* from Christ
    for the sake of my *own people,*
        my *kindred* according to the *flesh.*
They are *Israelites;*
        theirs the *adoption,* the *glory,* the *covenants,*
        the giving of the *law,* the *worship,* and the *promises;*
        theirs the *patriarchs,* and from *them,*
        according to the *flesh,* is the *Christ,*
        who is over *all,* God blessed *forever. Amen*

It is shocking to hear the extent of Paul's anguish. He can imagine nothing worse than being separated from Christ.

Read the list deliberately. It is long, but each word must be absorbed before the next one is read.

GOSPEL   Matthew 14:22–33

A reading from the holy gospel according to Matthew

After he had *fed* the people, Jesus made the *disciples*
        get into a *boat*
    and *precede* him to the other *side,*
        while *he* dismissed the *crowds.*
After *doing* so, he went up on the *mountain* by *himself* to *pray.*

The opening line is a rough transition. Consider trying something smoother: "Immediately after feeding the crowd with the five loaves and two fish . . ."

READING II Clearly, Paul experienced deep personal sorrow over the inability of some of his fellow Jews to accept his view of Jesus as the promised Messiah. His human nature is in great turmoil, like the forces of nature in the other two readings.

The degree of his turmoil is profound indeed if it causes him to consider separation from Christ. It is not unlike the feeling of those who have experienced separation from family and friends over choices in faith and religion. The cry "Is it worth it?" is not uncommon in the minds and hearts of some Christians. Perseverance and good will often lead to reconciliation, if not unity.

Paul's lament is poignant and touching. All that benefits Christians belongs to the Jews: adoption, glory, covenant, law, worship, promise, patriarchs and Jesus himself in his human origin. We should allow ourselves to be moved deeply by Paul's sorrow, and to acknowledge anew our indebtedness to our Jewish brothers and sisters. The modern reader cannot help but be reminded of Pope John's XXIII's insight: "Spiritually, we are all Semites."

GOSPEL Though we may not think of it as often as we should, take note here that Jesus insists on being alone for prayer. It seems to have been a real challenge for him to find solitude, but he manages it frequently—and very often immediately before a marvelous event. Last week, he was alone in grief over the death of John the Baptist. The miracle of the multiplication of loaves and fishes follows. Today we see him alone in prayer immediately before his unforgettable appearance walking on water.

The dramatic narrative begins here, and the tension builds until the wind abates.

When it was *evening* he was there *alone*.
Meanwhile the *boat*, already a few miles offshore,
    was being *tossed about* by the *waves*,
        for the *wind* was against it.

During the *fourth* watch of the night,
    he *came* toward them *walking* on the *sea*.
When the disciples *saw* him walking on the sea
        they were *terrified*.
"It is a *ghost*," they said, and they cried out in *fear*.
At *once* Jesus *spoke* to them, "Take *courage*, it is *I*;
        do not be *afraid*."

Peter said to him in reply,
    "*Lord*, if it is *you*, command me to *come* to you on the *water*."
He said, "*Come*."
Peter got out of the *boat* and began to *walk* on the water
        toward Jesus.
But when he saw how *strong* the *wind* was
        he became *frightened*;
    and, beginning to *sink*, he cried out, "Lord, *save* me!"

Jesus "immediately" reaches out to Peter in his terror. This deserves appropriate emphasis.

Immediately Jesus stretched out his *hand* and *caught* Peter,
    and said to him, "O you of little *faith*, why did you *doubt*?"
After they got into the *boat*, the *wind* died *down*.
Those who were in the boat did him *homage*, saying,
    "*Truly*, you *are* the Son of *God*."

This is the resolution. It should descend into quiet awe, and the acclamation should be subdued.

This wonderful story as told by Matthew is one of the most cherished narratives in the gospels. The miracle and Peter's doubt have inspired artwork through the centuries. There is a great deal more in Matthew's intent than the apparent miracle of walking on water. The acclamation of the disciples at the end of the story ("Truly you are the Son of God!") comes closer to explaining why Matthew told the story in the way he did. The real miracle here is the victory over fear and doubt, which only Jesus can conquer.

Mark's account is much less straightforward and raises complex questions about the nature of Jesus and the confusion of the disciples regarding who Jesus really is. Matthew, however, tells the story to demonstrate the kind of faith that followers of Jesus must develop. The stormy seas provide a setting in which Jesus not only shows his power over the forces of nature but tests the faith of the leader of the apostles and teaches them the degree of faith necessary if his disciples are to weather the storms that are an inevitable part of Christian life. Peter was fine as long as he trained his eyes

on Jesus and kept moving toward him. But when he looked at the adversity around him instead, he began to sink. Even then, when faith flickers in adverse times, the hand of Christ is there to catch us.

The narrative has all the elements of a vivid drama. The familiar image can be enriched in its hearing if all the details are given their due. An effective proclamation will be fresh and animated so that this familiar story will not be taken for granted.

ASSUMPTION VIGIL

Lectionary #621

READING I   1 Chronicles 15:3–4, 15–16; 16:1–2

A reading from the first book of Chronicles

"All Israel"—this is quite a throng! And it says something about the importance of the event.

Notice the progression: "David assembled . . . David called together . . . David commanded . . ."
Aaron = AYR-uhn
Levite = LEE-vı̆t

David assembled all *Israel* in *Jerusalem* to bring the *ark*
    of the LORD
    to the place that he had *prepared* for it.
David *also* called together the sons of *Aaron* and the *Levites*.

The *Levites* bore the ark of God on their *shoulders* with *poles*,
    as *Moses* had *ordained* according to the word of the LORD.

Make this list impressive.
Lyres = lı̄rz

David commanded the *chiefs* of the *Levites*
    to appoint their *kinsmen* as *chanters*,
    to play on musical *instruments, harps, lyres,* and *cymbals,*
    to make a loud *sound* of *rejoicing.*

They *brought* in the ark of God and set it within the *tent*
    which David had *pitched* for it.
Then they offered up burnt *offerings* and *peace* offerings to God.
When David had *finished* offering up the burnt offerings
    and peace offerings,
    he *blessed* the people in the *name* of the LORD.

David's blessing brings the reading to a quiet close.

READING I One of Mary's titles is "ark of the covenant," which explains why this text was chosen for the vigil of the Assumption. The comparison is fairly obvious. Since the ark contained the stone tablets of the ten commandments and symbolized God's presence among the people of Israel, so Mary carried within her body the incarnation of God in Jesus Christ. The difference is also important: no longer is the law inscribed on stone tablets; it is now flesh and blood in the person of Jesus. It is for the homilist to make the typology clear.

Clearly the scene here is one of great joy. David had prepared a special place for the ark, and now it is borne into the city amid the noisy rejoicing of the crowd. Notice the detail in the chronicler's report. The descendants of Aaron and the Levites are the priestly clan, charged by Moses in accord with God's directive to carry the ark. Their descendants provide the liturgy that accompanies this joyous occasion: harps, lyres, cymbals, singers, and so on. The scene is quite vivid, and your proclamation should take advantage of every detail to make it so.

READING II The significance of today's feast is that Mary is the first human being (besides Jesus himself, of course) in Christian tradition to experience fully that total union with God that is the final destiny of us all. God accords Mary that privilege because of her unique role in salvation history.

Paul quotes scripture to make his point about the fruits of Christ's resurrection—and a powerful and poetic text it is! Two rhetorical questions constitute one of the most popular acclamations in Christian

Take a deep breath and bring out the two
sets of contrasting words with strong
vocal inflection.
This is a strong and comforting victory cry.

READING II   1 Corinthians 15:54b–57

A reading from the first letter of Saint Paul to the Corinthians

Brothers and sisters:
When that which is *mortal* clothes itself with *immortality*,
 then the *word* that is *written* shall come *about*:
 "*Death* is swallowed up in *victory*.
 Where, O death, is your *victory*?
 Where, O death, is your *sting*?"

The sting of *death* is *sin*,
 and the *power* of sin is the *law*.
But thanks be to *God* who gives *us* the victory
 through our *Lord* Jesus *Christ*.

"But" is an important word here. It's
different for us because of Jesus.

GOSPEL   Luke 11:27–28

A reading from the holy gospel according to Luke

While *Jesus* was *speaking*,
 a *woman* from the crowd *called out* and said to him,
 "Blessed is the *womb* that *carried* you
 and the *breasts* at which you *nursed*."

He replied,
 "*Rather*, *blessed* are those
 who *hear* the word of *God* and *observe* it."

This reading will be over before the
assembly begins to listen unless you
prepare them for it with a pause after the
announcement.
The woman ecstatically praises Jesus, not
Mary. She herself would wish to have
such a son.

literature: "O death, where is thy victory? O death, where is thy sting?"

The sting of death is sin. Death comes to us through disobedience of the law. But Christ has freed us from the law and its condemnation and so has taken the sting out of death and swallowed up death itself by his own victory on the cross. Mary is the first to reap the benefits of her son's triumph.

GOSPEL | There is power in the brevity of this gospel because its few words formulate a description of the true

follower of Jesus. As with all brief proclamations, the reader must pause more than usual after the announcement of the reading and then read it with great deliberateness and care. It should not be stilted or artificial, of course, and certainly not rattled off.

It is possible that some will feel these words of Jesus about his mother are harsh and unfeeling. Does he deny that Mary was blessed because she was privileged to bear the Messiah? Jesus does not deny that she is blessed, but he clarifies what it is that makes her, and all his followers, so blessed. Perhaps the best translation here would be

"Happy are those," for that is what the word means in this context. Yes, those who hear the word and keep it have received a blessing but, more to the point, they have found the source of true happiness.

Mary is happy, no doubt, that she was chosen to be the mother of Jesus. But her greatest happiness, as we read elsewhere in scripture, comes from her obedience to the word of God. Mary is the perfect model of openness to God's will. This brief gospel text is the perfect choice for the vigil of the feast that celebrates the reward of her openness.

ASSUMPTION

Lectionary #622

READING I   Revelation 11:19a; 12:1–6a, 10ab

A reading from the book of Revelation

The text is broad in its themes and images. Let your proclamation be expansive throughout.
This is more like poetry than prose. Let the images work their magic.

God's *temple* in *heaven* was *opened*,
    and the ark of his *covenant* could be seen in the temple.

A great *sign* appeared in the sky, a *woman* clothed with the *sun*,
    with the *moon* beneath her *feet*,
    and on her *head* a crown of twelve *stars*.
She was with *child* and wailed *aloud* in *pain* as she *labored*
        to give *birth*.

Recognize the transitions: The sign appears; the labor begins; the dragon appears.

Then *another* sign appeared in the sky;
    it was a huge red *dragon*, with seven *heads* and ten *horns*,
    and on its heads were seven *diadems*.
Its *tail* swept away a third of the *stars* in the sky
    and hurled them down to the *earth*.

The scene is horrific: The dragon waits to devour the newborn.

Then the dragon *stood* before the woman about to give *birth*,
    to *devour* her *child* when she gave birth.

She gave birth to a *son*, a *male* child,
    destined to *rule* all the *nations* with an iron *rod*.

The resolution is an enormous relief.

Her child was *caught up* to *God* and his *throne*.
The woman *herself* fled into the *desert*
    where she had a place *prepared* by God.

READING I I've always loved the epitaph that Benjamin Franklin wrote for his own tomb:

The body of Benjamin Franklin, Printer (like the cover of an old book, its contents torn out and stripped of its lettering and gilding), lies here, food for worms; but the work shall not be lost, for it will (as he believed) appear once more in a new and more elegant edition, revised and corrected by the Author.

On the feast of Mary's assumption we are reminded that we are to follow her into glory, as she has followed Christ. We are reminded that what we call death is nothing more than the last thing we do in life. And it will be the best and finest thing we do, for in dying we are introduced into the presence of the one who conquered death. In Christ, death itself dies.

Mary has been taken up into heaven, body and soul. The promise brought to fulfillment in her is a promise we all share. Celebrating her triumph in Christ should give us pause, and it should give us hope as well. We pause to examine the fervor of this revolutionary belief, and we rejoice in the hope we receive from that belief.

The first reading is a classic example of apocalyptic literature in which metaphor and symbol are used to meditate on eternal truths. Mary has long been called "ark of the

Then I heard a loud *voice* in heaven say:
   "*Now* have *salvation* and *power* come,
   and the *kingdom* of our *God*
   and the *authority* of his *Anointed* One."

> **The reading ends with a triumphant cry, demanding a significant pause before proclaiming strongly, "The word of the Lord."**

READING II   1 Corinthians 15:20–27

A reading from the first letter of Saint Paul to the Corinthians

> **The gratuitous addition of "Brothers and sisters" here weakens a strong beginning. Consider beginning boldly, with rock-solid assurance: "Christ has been raised . . ."**

Brothers and sisters:
Christ has been *raised* from the *dead*,
   the *firstfruits* of those who have fallen *asleep*.
For since *death* came through man,
   the *resurrection* of the dead came *also* through man.
For just as in *Adam* all *die*,
   so too in *Christ* shall all be brought to *life*,
   but each one in proper *order*:
   Christ the *firstfruits*;
   then, at his *coming*, those who *belong* to Christ;
   then comes the *end*,
   when he *hands over* the kingdom to his God and *Father*,
   when he has *destroyed* every *sovereignty*
   and every *authority* and *power*.

> **Ending with "The last enemy to be destroyed is death" makes for a stronger conclusion, given today's feast.**

For he must *reign* until he has put all his *enemies* under his *feet*.
The *last* enemy to be destroyed is *death*,
   for "he subjected *everything* under his *feet*."

---

covenant" (see the first reading for yesterday's vigil). The woman clothed with the sun symbolizes at least three persons: the corporate person of Israel, triumphant in the fulfillment of God's promises; the church, through which the reign of God is expressed most vividly; and Mary, the mother of the Messiah, through whom the messianic promises were fulfilled and for whom a special place has been prepared.

Clearly the choice of this text for today's liturgy has the last of these three persons in mind, though not to the exclusion of the other two. The struggle between good and evil is personified in the woman and the dragon and the rescued child. Centuries of study have revealed that the various elements of this vision are taken from many sources. The drama presented here is effective on its own terms if it is read with conviction and great care.

| READING II | Today's feast deals with revolutionary beliefs, and there's nothing more revolutionary than what Paul says here: "Christ has been raised from the dead, the first fruits of those who have fallen asleep." We Christians believe in a great many revolutionary things. The challenge, of course, is to believe in them in a revolutionary way. There's nothing new about that for the Christian, but the *way* in which the Christian believes and lives is supposed to be always new.

We have Christ's promise that the world will be divided as a result of his word and his life; we should expect nothing else. We have his word that to follow him, to believe what he believes and does, will make us signs of contradiction in the world. That is

GOSPEL Luke 1:39–56

A reading from the holy gospel according to Luke

Mary set *out*
    and traveled to the *hill* country in *haste*
    to a town of *Judah*,
    where she entered the house of *Zechariah*
    and greeted *Elizabeth*.

When Elizabeth *heard* Mary's greeting,
    the *infant leaped* in her *womb*,
    and *Elizabeth*, filled with the Holy *Spirit*,
    cried out in a loud *voice* and said,
    "*Blessed* are you among *women*,
    and blessed is the *fruit* of your *womb*.
And how does this happen to *me*,
    that the mother of my *Lord* should come to me?
For at the moment the sound of your *greeting* reached my *ears*,
    the *infant* in my womb *leaped* for *joy*.
Blessed are you who *believed*
    that what was *spoken* to you by the *Lord*
    would be *fulfilled*."

And *Mary* said:
    "My *soul* proclaims the *greatness* of the Lord;
    my *spirit rejoices* in God my *Savior*
    for he has *looked* upon his lowly *servant*.
    From this *day* all *generations* will call me *blessed*:
    the *Almighty* has done great *things* for me,
    and *holy* is his *Name*.
    He has *mercy* on those who *fear* him
    in every *generation*.

The sense of urgency here should be communicated. This is the first "missionary journey" of the new age of Jesus the Messiah.

Elizabeth's cry is the cry of generations of expectant people. The baby who stirs in her womb is John the Baptist, whose cry will be, "Behold, the Lamb of God!"

The second part of the reading begins here. Pause before it.

The canticle of Mary (the Magnificat) has two parts. The first few lines are about Mary's blessedness; the larger portion is about God's saving power.

probably a good test of the fervor of our belief: How much of a sign of contradiction are we? How radically different are our Christian values? Is it obvious how different they are even to the casual observer? Perhaps you have heard the provocative question: "If you were brought to trial for being a Christian, would there be enough evidence to convict you?" It's a timely question in every age, but perhaps especially in our own.

In Christ's resurrection we see the promise of our own resurrection. In Mary's assumption we see that promise already fulfilled in one like ourselves. In Mary's triumph we see the reign of God already triumphant over every other sovereignty and power. God is putting all enemies (the dragon of the first reading) under the sovereignty of Christ.

GOSPEL It was on the feast of All Saints only 50 years ago that Pope Pius XII proclaimed to all the world that the mother of Jesus, having completed

her earthly life, was taken up into heaven body and soul. Christians have believed in Mary's assumption from the earliest times. We find it in the writings of the early church Fathers; we even find it depicted by a ninth-century artist in the subterranean basilica of St. Clement in Rome.

Our faith often turns the world upside down, presents a topsy-turvy view of things, and makes revolutionary statements about life, death, life-after-death and values in general. There's nothing any more revolutionary about what Pius XII said in 1950 than

The world is turned upside down. The powerful fall; the humble rise; the rich go hungry; the hungry are filled. Relish the revolution God's mercy brings.

"He has shown the *strength* of his *arm*,
and has *scattered* the *proud* in their *conceit*.
He has cast down the *mighty* from their *thrones*,
and has *lifted up* the *lowly*.
He has filled the *hungry* with *good* things,
and the *rich* he has sent away *empty*.
He has come to the *help* of his servant *Israel*
for he has *remembered* his promise of *mercy*,
the promise he made to our *fathers*,
to *Abraham* and his children for *ever*."

The final assertion of the song extols the fidelity of God.

The narrative detail at the end lends a gentle feeling of closure.

Mary *remained* with her about three *months*
and then *returned* to her *home*.

what Mary said a long time before: God has deposed the mighty from their thrones and raised the lowly to high places. God has given every good thing to the hungry, and sent the rich away empty.

This beloved gospel story is about women, and more than just about Mary and Elizabeth. The words and accomplishments of women from the Hebrew scriptures (Jael, Judith and Hannah) are placed in the mouth of Mary and her cousin so that Luke can demonstrate the completion of a long period of preparation for the Messiah's coming. "Leaping in the womb" is a traditional sign of recognition by the unborn of God's intervention in human history.

Mary's exultant song of praise is Israel's hymn, bursting forth in utter joy at the inauguration of the long-awaited messianic age. Notice that Mary's singular "my" becomes the plural "our" in the final words of her song. This is an obvious indication that Mary is the mouthpiece for the chosen people of all ages.

The thing to remember in proclaiming this reading is that the event described here is Luke's way of bringing a much larger reality into focus. It is the inauguration of God's reign and the fulfillment of God's promise to send us a redeemer.

20TH SUNDAY IN ORDINARY TIME

Lectionary #118

READING I   Isaiah 56:1, 6–7

A reading from the book of the prophet Isaiah

The familiar formula "Thus says the Lord" signals a solemn proclamation of special importance.

Thus says the *Lord*:
Observe what is *right*, *do* what is *just*;
    for my *salvation* is about to *come*,
      my *justice*, about to be *revealed*.

Pause here. Several verses have been omitted. The central topic is introduced: inclusion of non-Israelites. The structure of this long sentence is poetic, so focus on reading the sense lines, and let the images accumulate.

The *foreigners* who *join* themselves to the Lord,
    ministering to him,
loving the *name* of the Lord,
    and becoming his *servants*—
all who keep the *sabbath* free from *profanation*
    and hold to my *covenant*,
them I will bring to my holy *mountain*
    and make *joyful* in my house of *prayer*;
their burnt *offerings* and *sacrifices*
    will be *acceptable* on my *altar*,
for *my* house shall be called
    a house of *prayer* for *all* peoples.

Here is the point, and it is a striking announcement. Emphasize "all" in the phrase "all people."

READING I   The revealed truths we hold so dear did not come to us in one blinding flash, whole and entire. Salvation history unfolds gradually. The revelation of God's plan for the world comes through human beings in particular times and places, and is subject to all the clumsiness of human faith seeking understanding. With this in mind we can approach today's readings with greater insight and empathy.

Isaiah is dealing with the practical problem of what to do about non-Israelites, who are mingling more and more with the chosen people. What we hear in this reading is God's solution to the problem: Foreigners who abide by the essentials of the covenant will be welcome on "the holy mountain," that is, Jerusalem and the temple. Though there are certain restrictions placed on these foreigners, they are clearly part of God's saving plan. Thus we see the chosen people begin to wrestle with the notion that God offers saving mercy to all people. It was not an easy concept for them to accept, as we shall see in the second reading and gospel today, but it is a concept that steadily grows and gains more and more acceptance right up to our own day.

The radical inclusiveness taught by Jesus was revolutionary, but it has its roots in the Hebrew scriptures. Who would deny that contemporary believers are still wrestling with this problem? We see something far less than radical inclusiveness in some Christian communities. Seeing how far we have come makes it all the more urgent that we continue to grow. It is God's will: "My house shall be called a house of prayer for *all* peoples." This is a summons to far more than passive non-exclusiveness; it demands aggressive inclusiveness. We have to go out

READING II   Romans 11:13–15, 29–32

A reading from the letter of Saint Paul to the Romans

Brothers and sisters:
I am speaking to you *Gentiles*.
Inasmuch as I am the *apostle* to the Gentiles,
  I *glory* in my *ministry* in order to make my *race jealous*
  and thus *save* some of them.
For if their *rejection* is the *reconciliation* of the *world*,
  what will their *acceptance* be but *life* from the *dead*?

For the *gifts* and the call of *God* are *irrevocable*.
Just as you once *disobeyed* God
  but have now received *mercy* because of *their* disobedience,
  so *they* have now disobeyed in order that,
  by virtue of the *mercy* shown to *you*,
  they *too* may now receive mercy.
For God delivered all to *disobedience*,
  that he might have *mercy* upon all.

The point is cleverly made. If *rejection* of Jesus was part of God's plan, so also is the *redemption* and *salvation* of every nation under earth—only more so!

Once the chosen people, always the chosen people—the preferred pronunciation of "irrevocable" puts the emphasis on the second syllable, not the third.
irrevocable = eer-REV-uh-kuh-b*l

Here's the point: *All* have disobeyed; *all* will be shown mercy.

---

and find those who have been excluded and bring them back where they belong.

READING II We continue reading Paul's description of his agonized distress that Jesus is not accepted as Messiah by his fellow Jews, but this passage is also filled with hope. Though it may seem a disingenuous argument to us, Paul reasons that the faith of the Gentiles who have accepted Jesus will cause the Jews to turn to him as well—out of "jealousy," as Paul says. He presumes that the Gentiles have the Good News preached to them *because* it was rejected by the Jews. He then speaks of the irony of God's irrevocable plan: When the condemnation brought on by rejection is great, the mercy that comes with acceptance is even greater.

Whatever we think of the cogency of Paul's argument, we can admire the optimism with which he expresses it. He has every confidence that somehow his own people will be included in God's loving plan to redeem the world in love. We need to embrace and express a similar confidence, for it will expunge our natural tendency to be exclusive and selfish with our faith. The devilish need to be "right" in matters of faith is one of human nature's most insidious "wrongs." It leads to intolerance, bigotry and prejudice. Worst of all, it tries to put limits on God's love. Paul shows us here that everything is governed by the divine will. If it appears that some are disobedient, this must be God's clever way of preparing them for greater mercy and love. Maybe Paul's argument is not so disingenuous after all!

GOSPEL The crux of this reading is the Canaanite woman's faith, which crashes through every possible human

GOSPEL Matthew 15:21–28

A reading from the holy gospel according to Matthew

At that time, *Jesus withdrew* to the region of *Tyre* and *Sidon*.
And *behold*, a *Canaanite* woman of that district came
    and *called out*,
  "Have *pity* on me, *Lord*, Son of *David*!
My *daughter* is tormented by a *demon*."
But Jesus did not say a *word* in answer to her.

Jesus' *disciples* came and asked him,
  "Send her *away*, for she keeps *calling out* after us."
He said in reply,
  "*I* was sent only to the lost sheep of the house of *Israel*."

But the *woman* came and did Jesus *homage*, saying,
    "Lord, *help* me."
He said in reply,
  "It is not *right* to take the food of the *children*
  and throw it to the *dogs*."
She said, "*Please*, Lord, for even the *dogs* eat the *scraps*
  that fall from the *table* of their *masters*."

Then Jesus said to her in reply,
  "O *woman*, *great* is your *faith*!
Let it be *done* for you as you *wish*."
And the woman's *daughter* was *healed* from that *hour*.

There is no haughtiness here, only a simple statement of fact, and a hint of more to come.
The woman's second appeal is heartrending in its simplicity.

The dialogue hints at gentle banter. Both Jesus and the woman are engaged in wordplay (see the commentary).

Here we have an acclamation filled with praise and admiration.

Do not miss the matter-of-fact tone of the final sentence. Your reading of it should imply, "What else did you expect?"

---

barrier erected to exclude certain people from God's saving love. "Only believe," as the old hymn title puts it, and you will be saved.

As in all the readings today, we see the theme of universal inclusion developed in striking ways. Here the evangelist makes another point: Inclusion requires both a deep-seated desire and a recognition of our need to be included. Jesus is portrayed by Matthew as being reluctant to grant the woman's request to heal her daughter. Her first entreaty is met by Jesus with silence.

The disciples look upon her more harshly as a noisy nuisance.

How does Jesus respond to the disciples' request to send her away? Is it agreement, as in, "Yes, you're right; she has no claim on my powers." Or is it, rather, directed at the woman herself: "Your people and mine are enemies; surely you know I must care for my own first." We can't be sure, but it is clear that Jesus invites the woman to plead her case further. And she does so, kneeling and addressing Jesus as "Lord."

Most striking in this story is the metaphor that Jesus and the woman use in their exchange. When Jesus says that the food he brings for the house of Israel should not be thrown to the dogs, he uses a word that means "pets" or "puppies," not ravenous scavengers. The woman gets the point, obviously, and responds in kind: "Surely you wouldn't deny the household pets a scrap from the table." It is a charming bit of repartee, but it is also a persistent and convincing expression of faith arising out of the love the woman feels for her ailing daughter. God never refuses such humble love; neither should we.

21ST SUNDAY IN ORDINARY TIME

Lectionary #121

READING I   Isaiah 22:19–23

A reading from the book of the prophet Isaiah

The text is dark and threatening, but Shebna has grievously abused his authority and power.
Shebna = SHEB-nah

"On that day" begins a prophetic passage in poetic form. Read it with special attention to the parallelism and solemn effect of repetitive forms: "when he opens, no one shall shut, when he shuts, no one shall open."
Eliakim = ee-LĪ-uh-kim
Hilkiah = hil-KĪ-uh

Thus says the *Lord* to *Shebna*, master of the *palace*:
"I will *thrust* you from your *office*
    and pull you *down* from your *station*.
On that day I will summon my servant
    Eliakim, son of *Hilkiah*;
I will clothe *him* with your *robe*,
    and *gird* him with your *sash*,
    and give over to *him* your *authority*.
He shall be a *father* to the inhabitants of *Jerusalem*,
    and to the house of *Judah*.

"I will place the *key* of the *House* of David
        on *Eliakim's* shoulder;
    when *he* opens, *no one* shall shut
    when he *shuts*, no one shall *open*.
I will *fix* him like a *peg* in a *sure* spot,
    to be a place of *honor* for his *family*."

READING I   The compilers of the lectionary chose this reading because of the echo of the image of "keys" that occurs in the gospel. The historical situation described here shows the action of God in clearing the way for a chosen leader who is more worthy of the position assigned to him. Thus, as is so often the case, the history of God's people serves as the framework through which the inevitability of the divine will is made clear. Despite the failings of chosen leaders, despite all the obstacles that human weakness creates, God will appoint a worthy servant who will be the perfectly fitted "peg," firmly supporting the tent in which the chosen people dwell.

For the Christian, Eliakim becomes a type of the ultimate leader, the Christ, the descendant of the house of David, who wields ultimate authority: "When he opens, no one shall shut." One of the great O Antiphons sung during the week immediately preceding Christmas is *O Clavis David,* "O Key of David." This text is the origin of the title given to Christ. All the titles can be found in the fuller version of the hymn "O come, O come, Emmanuel."

Note the wonderful structure: two exclamations, two rhetorical questions and a concluding doxology.

Though most readers will want to emphasize the contrasting prepositions here, try to emphasize the pronoun instead. It makes a familiar text take on new meaning.

Caesarea Philippi = sez-uh-REE-uh fih-LIP-pī

Emphasize *"Son of Man is?"* The sentence rises from the beginning and climaxes in the final verb.

Jeremiah was a prophet, too, so it is necessary to emphasize the word "one."

READING II   Romans 11:33–36

A reading from the letter of Saint Paul to the Romans

Oh, the *depth* of the *riches* and *wisdom* and *knowledge* of *God*!
How *inscrutable* are his *judgments* and how *unsearchable*
    his *ways*!
    "For who has *known* the mind of the *Lord*
    or who has been his *counselor*?
    Or who has *given* the Lord anything
    that he may be *repaid*?"
For from *him* and through *him* and for *him* are *all* things.
To *him* be *glory* for*ever*. Amen.

GOSPEL   Matthew 16:13–20

A reading from the holy gospel according to Matthew

Jesus went into the region of *Caesarea Philippi* and
    he asked his *disciples*,
    "*Who* do people *say* that the *Son of Man is*?"
They replied, "*Some* say John the *Baptist*, others *Elijah*,
    still others *Jeremiah* or *one* of the prophets."

He said to them, "But who do *you* say that I am?"
Simon *Peter* said in reply,
    "You are the *Christ*, the Son of the living *God*."

READING II | Paul becomes rhapsodic in the final verses of the eleventh chapter of Romans. Having completed a lengthy discussion of the universality of God's loving plan, Paul must sum up his theology in the most appropriate way: a hymn of inspired praise.

Who would have thought that the saving love of the Lord would extend beyond the Christian church to include not only the Jews, our ancestors in faith, but the Gentiles

as well—those who seemed most unlikely to accept the Good News? What seems impossibly irreconcilable from our point of view is not so from God's. Thus we can rejoice with Paul and leave our bewilderment aside as we ask: "Who has known the mind of God? To God be glory forever. Amen."

GOSPEL | Here is one of the most important passages in the gospels. In Mark, the earliest of the gospels, it is the central point for which the first half

of the gospel is preparation and the second half is explanation. Matthew adds special features of his own to the account (Jeremiah, for instance, the image of a *suffering* spokesman for God), but the burden of the text is the same in both: Jesus is firmly identified by the apostles as the Messiah, the "anointed one" promised by God as savior.

The entrusting of the keys of the kingdom is an echo from Isaiah in the first reading for today's liturgy. The keys are an

Jesus said to him in reply,
"*Blessed* are you, Simon son of Jonah.
For *flesh* and *blood* has not revealed this to you,
    but my heavenly *Father*.
And so I say to *you*, *you* are *Peter*,
    and upon this *rock* I will build my *church*,
    and the gates of the *netherworld* shall not *prevail* against it.
I will *give* you the *keys* to the *kingdom* of *heaven*.
Whatever you bind on *earth* shall be bound in *heaven*;
    and whatever you *loose* on earth shall be *loosed* in heaven."
Then he strictly *ordered* his disciples
    to tell *no* one that he was the *Christ*.

Be sure that the last sentence is not thrown away. It is an assertion of "the messianic secret," which the homilist will hopefully explain.

extremely powerful symbol of the authority entrusted to the apostles. It gives them the power to lead the young church after Jesus' resurrection and return to the Father.

The role of Peter as the rock upon which the church is founded is another important feature of this text. Matthew has Jesus making a pun on the Greek words *petros* and *petra* ("rock"). In Aramaic, the language spoken by Jesus and his disciples, the word is *kepa.* Elsewhere in scripture, Peter is referred to by the name "Cephas" (pronounced SEE-fuhs). Throughout the centuries, many writers have delighted in the fact that something so great and so significant as the Christian church was founded with a pun!

22ND SUNDAY IN ORDINARY TIME

Lectionary #124

READING I   Jeremiah 20:7–9

A reading from the book of the prophet Jeremiah

You *duped* me, O LORD, and I *let* myself be *duped*;
  you were too *strong* for me, and you *triumphed*.
All the *day* I am an object of *laughter*;
  everyone *mocks* me.

Whenever I *speak*, I must cry *out*,
  violence and *outrage* is my message;
the word of the LORD has brought me
  derision and *reproach* all the *day*.

I *say* to myself, I will not *mention* him,
  I will *speak* in his name no *more*.
But *then* it becomes like *fire* burning in my *heart*,
  imprisoned in my *bones*;
I grow *weary* holding it in, I cannot *endure* it.

From the start, this text is striking. But the opening sentence about being "duped" is poetic, not literal. Acceptance of his fate is hinted at even in Jeremiah's lament. The Lord tricks no one, but it seems so at times to the one who speaks for him.

Pause and renew your tone here. It is a new section, and the point is that the call to prophecy is irresistible, even though it brings suffering.

READING I   G. K. Chesterton once said, only half in jest, that we don't know whether Christianity will work or not because it has never been tried. To the degree this is true, one reason why it hasn't been tried could be that it's so darned diffi-cult! Those who have tried it with all their might can certainly identify with Jeremiah in this reading.

The purpose of this passage is to explain what Jesus means in today's gospel when he speaks of saving our lives by los-ing them. The point is that suffering for the fervent Christian is not a likelihood; it is an inevitability, indeed a necessity.

Jeremiah's depression is real, and we should not shy away from its depths. On the other hand, notice that something else is hinted at, even as Jeremiah is at his lowest point. It is the conviction that he has no real choice in the matter. God's call to prophecy is a consuming fire, and even though obey-ing it brings suffering, obedience is not a matter of choice. Thus we see the fervor of Jeremiah's discipleship as well as the pro-fundity of his suffering. He can endure his

pain far more easily than he can resist the summons to speak on God's behalf.

The entire reading is a prayer, though Jeremiah addresses God in the third person. It has the charm of respect, indirectness, the inability to look in God's face and say these things. Few of us can use these words with sincerity. We may try to make them our own when we're feeling sorry for ourselves and a little smug about our missionary zeal at the same time. But that is clearly not the case with Jeremiah.

READING II   Romans 12:1–2

A reading from the letter of Saint Paul to the Romans

I *urge* you, brothers and sisters, by the *mercies* of *God*,
    to offer your *bodies* as a living *sacrifice*,
    holy and *pleasing* to God, your spiritual *worship*.
Do not *conform* yourselves to *this* age
    but be *transformed* by the *renewal* of your *mind*,
    that you may *discern* what is the will of *God*,
    what is *good* and *pleasing* and *perfect*.

Paul is pleading, not whining.

The implication throughout is that we ought to behave in a certain way because of what God has done for us. Therefore, the tone is positive.

GOSPEL   Matthew 16:21–27

A reading from the holy gospel according to Matthew

Jesus began to *show* his disciples
    that he must go to *Jerusalem* and suffer *greatly*
    from the *elders*, the chief *priests*, and the *scribes*,
    and be *killed* and on the *third* day be *raised*.

Then *Peter* took Jesus *aside* and began to *rebuke* him,
    "God *forbid*, Lord! No such thing shall *ever* happen to you."
He turned and said to Peter,
    "Get *behind* me, Satan! You are an *obstacle* to me.
You are thinking not as *God* does, but as *human beings* do."

This is a long compound sentence with several important elements. Proceed slowly.

This exchange is harsh, but avoid anything like an imitation of Jesus' frustration. You are proclaiming an *account* of his rebuke, not re-creating it for us.

READING II This brief section of Romans begins a new chapter. We have been reading from Romans for several weeks now. You may wish to glance at earlier commentaries to get a feel for the whole work.

The message in all three readings is consistent today. Suffering and sacrifice are integral to the Christian life when it is undertaken with sincerity. For Paul the natural state of human beings is a state of warfare, a battle between our inclinations and our aspirations. Any honest person can see the truth in this conviction.

Paul pleads with us to see things more clearly and to use our better insights to guide our behavior. Those insights are quite capable of being blinded to what is good, acceptable and perfect. The apostle begs us to see more clearly, knowing from his own experience that what he asks may not be an easy thing.

GOSPEL There are 28 chapters in Matthew's gospel. At this point we are only slightly past the middle of it. Here, Jesus begins to alter dramatically

the expectations the apostles have of him. Peter's horrified response is understandable from any point of view, but much more than bad news is involved here.

First of all there is the matter of what scholars call the "messianic secret." It is most pronounced in Mark, but appears in all the gospels. The "secret" is simply that the way Jesus will achieve our salvation will be far different from what generations of faithful Jews have expected. He will not be a conquering warrior in any traditional sense. He will not restore the kings of Israel

Clearly, a significant pause must separate this new section from the previous one. Then proclaim the list of sayings, giving each one its own space and emphasis. Do not run the sayings together.

Two rhetorical questions complete the list of sayings. Let them work their magic by giving the assembly a moment to respond silently.

Then Jesus said to his *disciples*,
   "*Whoever* wishes to come after *me* must *deny* himself,
   take up his *cross*, and *follow* me.
For whoever wishes to *save* his life will *lose* it,
   but whoever *loses* his life for *my* sake will *find* it.
What *profit* would there be for one to *gain* the whole *world*
   and forfeit his *life*?
Or what can one *give* in exchange for his *life*?

"For the Son of *Man* will come with his *angels*
      in his Father's *glory*,
   and then he will repay *all* according to his *conduct*."

and usher in the messianic age by conquering Israel's enemies. Instead, he will die for his people. He will conquer death itself, and he will do so to save all the nations.

This sounds like defeat and disgrace to Peter (and to us) without the benefit of the resurrection. Jesus can not claim to be the Messiah of Jewish expectation and then die at the hands of Gentiles. This is unthinkable. Yet Jesus presents a drastically more profound understanding of his mission. Part of that understanding comes with the instruction that immediately follows his rebuke of Peter. God's ways are at work here, not

human ways. Full understanding will not come until the apostles see the empty tomb.

Then there is the matter of Jesus' human nature confronting the awful ordeal ahead of him. How else could he respond to Peter's unwillingness to accept it when he himself will struggle mightily before he can say to the Father, "Not my will, but yours be done?" Peter is indeed acting in the role of Satan by trying to dissuade Jesus from his awful course. It is the same Satan who appeared in the desert and tempted him to renounce his mission in other ways.

This traumatic exchange between Peter and Jesus is difficult to hear, but nothing could drive home more strongly the point that suffering cannot be avoided by those who would follow Jesus. Here we have a dramatic example of the truth that God's ways are not our ways.

In the second section of this passage, Jesus expands on the meaning of genuine Christian discipleship with several oft-quoted sayings. Translated into virtues, we could tag them in this way: (1) self-denial, (2) self-sacrifice, (3) self-respect, (4) self-esteem.

23RD SUNDAY IN ORDINARY TIME

Lectionary #127

READING I   Ezekiel 33:7–9

A reading from the book of the prophet Ezekiel

This reading must be delivered boldly but not harshly. It contains some sobering directives which, though not new to us, may well be hard to hear.

Thus says the LORD:
You, son of man, I have appointed *watchman*
        for the house of *Israel*;
    when you hear me *say* anything, you shall *warn* them for me.

If I tell the *wicked*, "O *wicked* one, you shall surely *die*,"
        and you do not speak out to *dissuade* the wicked from his *way*,
    the wicked shall *die* for his *guilt*,
    but I will hold *you responsible* for his death.

This section shows us the other side of the coin, though our hearts still go out to the unrepentant sinner.

But if you *warn* the wicked,
        trying to *turn* him from his way,
    and he *refuses* to turn from his way,
    he shall *die* for his *guilt*,
    but you shall *save* yourself.

READING I — All three scripture texts today deal with the dramatic degree of responsibility we have for each other. All three have something to say about how Christians deal with their fellow human beings, whether Christian or not.

The prophet Ezekiel represents the whole people of Israel when he is told that he is responsible for the sins of the wicked if he does not try to dissuade them from their ways. We are responsible for each other, and some are chosen to exercise that responsibility in a special way. They are prophets, ministers and religious leaders, all of whom are appointed to watch over the people. Though we cannot renounce our individual responsibility for one another, it is true that we should be able to depend on those appointed by God to take on that responsibility with greater boldness and solicitude.

The duty of a watchman is to protect the city from harm. In this passage from Ezekiel, and in Jesus' words in today's gospel reading, we see that duty redefined to include watching out for individuals within the city.

We all recoil from the self-righteous person who acts like a self-appointed morals officer. That kind of misguided arrogance is not implied here. It is presumed that the prophet appointed by God speaks for God and speaks to those under his or her care with genuine humility and love for them. Nevertheless, the penalty is harsh for those who are too timid or complacent to address wrongdoing. And the reward is great for those whose best efforts seem to fail nonetheless.

READING II   Romans 13:8–10

A reading from the letter of Saint Paul to the Romans

Brothers and sisters:
Owe *nothing* to *anyone*, except to *love* one another;
    for the one who *loves* another has *fulfilled* the *law*.

The *commandments*, "You shall not commit *adultery*;
    you shall not *kill*; you shall not *steal*; you shall not *covet*,"
    and whatever *other* commandment there may be,
    are summed up in *this* saying, *namely*,
    "You shall *love* your *neighbor* as *yourself*."

Love does no *evil* to the *neighbor*;
    hence, *love* is the *fulfillment* of the *law*.

GOSPEL   Matthew 18:15–20

A reading from the holy gospel according to Matthew

Jesus said to his *disciples*:
"If your brother *sins* against you,
    go and *tell* him his fault between you and him *alone*.
If he *listens* to you, you have won *over* your brother.
If he does *not* listen,
    take one or two *others* along with you,
    so that 'every *fact* may be *established*
    on the *testimony* of two or three *witnesses*.'
If he refuses to listen to them, tell the *church*.

The first sentence is not designed to capture attention unless it is preceded by silence and delivered strongly and slowly.

*The challenge in reading a list is to give each item a slightly different emphasis and "space," so the list doesn't **sound** like a list.*

All of these words come from Jesus' mouth. Adopt a gentle yet strong and authoritative tone.

Notice the many steps taken toward reconciliation.

READING II Sometimes the apostle Paul is difficult to listen to. He is capable of ranting and raving, and at times we want to tune him out. But when we come to a passage such as this one, we listen with ease and delight. Saint Paul tells the Romans that the only thing we owe each other is love.

There is a discernible and gratifying order to Paul's argument: Love one another, because all rules can be reduced to one rule, that is, to love one another. What could be simpler when we feel the weight of many

rules and regulations? Saint Augustine said it another way: "Love, and do what you will."

We should notice, too, that Paul gets his formulation of the one law of love from the Hebrew scriptures. We should rid ourselves of any notion that the New Testament is original in its proclamation of love as the fulfillment of the law. "You shall love your neighbor as yourself" is a quote from Leviticus, the quintessential Old Testament rule book.

GOSPEL Jesus' words to his disciples are clear: "When someone treats you badly, point out the fault, but keep it between the two of you if you can. If the offender listens, you have won your enemy over." Now it might be easy to interpret the words to mean that we have a duty to point out the faults of others. But that's a shallow interpretation. Our motive for doing so is at the heart of these words. The great test we need to give ourselves is whether our motive is genuine love for the person we correct.

Note the phrase "a Gentile or tax collector." The point is not so much punishment by exclusion as recognition that such a person is beyond help. The universalism of the gospel ("even the Gentiles") is not yet clear, and a tax collector (working for Caesar against his own people) has chosen the role of traitor.

This is quite a promise, followed by an assurance. Be sure the familiarity of the text doesn't make it dull.

If he refuses to listen even to the *church*,
    then treat him as you would a *Gentile* or a *tax* collector.

"*Amen*, I say to you,
    whatever you bind on *earth* shall be bound in *heaven*,
    and whatever you *loose* on earth shall be *loosed* in heaven.
Again, *amen*, I say to you,
    if *two* of you agree on *earth*
    about *anything* for which they are to *pray*,
    it shall be *granted* to them by my heavenly *Father*.
For where *two* or *three* are gathered *together* in my *name*,
    there am *I* in the *midst* of them."

But it is even deeper than that. We are being counseled here to regard every human being as worthy of acceptance, respect and love. People, even wicked people, who are shown acceptance, respect and love have a way of becoming good people.

Imagine a world (or city, neighborhood, parish, family) in which this degree of acceptance, love and respect was the order of the day. It's a lovely picture, and it may seem terribly idealistic. But that's no reason to give up on it, especially if we really intend to give Christianity a try.

This gospel reading is ultimately about the church, and may even be considered a definition of the church. Certainly a community of believers will realize that mutual responsibility for the individual members is part of that definition and that responsibility involves correcting those who stray or exercise a bad influence on the larger group. Most important here is the clear indication that the church (the assembled community) has the power to govern itself and its membership.

In our time, large parishes of enormously diverse membership make it difficult for us to conceive of the situation described here by Jesus. Yet, unless a faith community realizes its self-governing power and its responsibility toward every member, true Christian identity will escape it.

It is encouraging to hear Jesus speak of the church as "two or three gathered" in his name. It reminds us that the church is not a structure or a hierarchy or a group of ministers but the entire community of the baptized gathered in the name of Jesus.

24TH SUNDAY IN ORDINARY TIME

Lectionary #130

READING I   Sirach 27:30—28:7

Sirach = SEER-ak

This is poetry, not prose. Use an exalted tone. Otherwise, the poetic word order and the rhetorical questions will sound ridiculous or insipid.

Pause after each rhetorical question.

These lines are beautifully structured: two couplets, each containing four elements. Feel the rhythm.

A reading from the book of Sirach

Wrath and *anger* are *hateful* things,
  yet the *sinner* hugs them *tight*.
The *vengeful* will suffer the LORD's vengeance,
  for he *remembers* their sins in *detail*.
Forgive your neighbor's *injustice*;
  then when you *pray*, your *own* sins will be forgiven.

Could anyone nourish *anger* against *another*
  and expect *healing* from the LORD?
Could anyone refuse *mercy* to another like *himself*,
  can he seek *pardon* for his *own* sins?
If one who is but *flesh* cherishes *wrath*,
  who will forgive his *sins*?

Remember your last *days*, set enmity *aside*;
  remember *death* and *decay*, and *cease* from sin!
Think of the *commandments*, hate *not* your neighbor;
  remember the Most High's *covenant*, and *overlook* faults.

READING I There's an old Arabic proverb that could sum up the exhortations in today's readings: "Write the wrongs that are done to you in sand, but engrave the good things that happen to you in marble. Let go of emotions such as resentment and retaliation, which diminish you, and hold onto emotions such as gratitude and joy, which increase you."

This first reading is from the "wisdom literature" of the Hebrew scriptures, from a book written only shortly before the Christian era. Notice how closely it resembles Jesus' teaching in the gospel narrative for today.

The wisdom writer asks a heady question: "Can we refuse mercy to others yet seek pardon for ourselves?" If we who are mere flesh and blood cherish wrath, who will forgive our sins? In the responsorial psalm we will hear, "The Lord is kind and merciful; slow to anger, and rich in compassion."

Notice too that Sirach is in poetic form. It requires an exalted and poetic delivery since it uses an economy of words to paint vivid pictures of how we should behave toward each other. The rhetorical questions are especially powerful. They expect no answer because the answer is obvious. Yet a pause after each rhetorical question prompts the hearers to answer in the silence of their minds.

The problem with hearing what we already know is that it may pass us by. None of what you proclaim in this reading is new, but it can seem fresh to your hearers if you proclaim it with conviction and great care. The content naturally appeals to every person of good will; and your presumption must be that each one who hears you is that kind of person!

READING II Romans 14:7–9

A reading from the letter of Saint Paul to the Romans

Brothers and sisters:
None of us *lives* for *oneself*, and no one *dies* for oneself.
For if we *live*, we *live* for the *Lord*,
    and if we *die*, we *die* for the Lord;
        so then, whether we *live* or *die*, we are the *Lord's*.
For this is why *Christ* died and came to *life*,
    that he might be *Lord* of both the *dead* and the *living*.

This brief reading must be read slowly and preceded by silence between the announcement ("A reading from . . .") and the text itself.
This is one of Paul's word games, and it works if you employ the right variety of vocal inflection.

GOSPEL Matthew 18:21–35

A reading from the holy gospel according to Matthew

Peter approached *Jesus* and asked him,
"*Lord*, if my brother *sins* against me,
    how *often* must I *forgive*?
As many as *seven times*?"

Jesus answered, "*I* say to you, not *seven* times
        but *seventy-seven* times.
That is why the kingdom of *heaven* may be likened to a king
    who decided to settle *accounts* with his *servants*.
When he *began* the accounting,
    a *debtor* was brought before him who *owed* him
        a *huge* amount.

Parables are short stories, complete with situation, conflict, climax and resolution. The situation is clear. The conflict is the official's unfairness. The climax is the official being called to task. The resolution comes when justice is exercised. Be sure each stage of the story is clearly separate but all of one piece.

READING II It is impossible to be a Christian and a loner at the same time. At the very least, being a Christian means acknowledging that *Jesus* is Lord, not any of us. But it also means doing so in the context of a community that is composed of good people and bad people, not-so-good people and not-so-bad people. Whatever category we fall into, we belong to the Lord, who is Lord of the strong and the weak, the living and the dead.

Our response to this knowledge should be a cry of joyous relief, for it is a terrible thing to think we are masters of our own

fates. It leads to isolation and arrogance, a kind of independence that makes us small and selfish or defensive and afraid. A wonderful irony is found here: When we acknowledge Jesus as loving master and bind ourselves to his loving community, then we are truly free.

GOSPEL The parable in this reading is unique to Matthew, and a precious story it is. Something in human nature seems to make us feel quite deserving of mercy but quite often reluctant to show it. A careful reading of this wonderful

story should show us a far better way to deal with each other.

It is a better way because it is God's way. God has dealt with us in a totally forgiving and accepting way, through no merits of our own. Only God's love and forgiveness are completely free and pure. We can imitate such grace in a life of mutual forgiveness even if we can't equal it.

In the exchange between Peter and Jesus, the number seven appears as a figure of fullness and perfection. The old law required that we forgive only three wrongdoings. Peter feels he is being generous in

Since he had no *way* of paying it *back*,
    his master ordered him to be *sold*,
    along with his *wife*, his *children*, and all his *property*,
    in *payment* of the debt.
At *that*, the servant fell *down*, did him *homage*, and said,
    'Be *patient* with me, and I will pay you back in *full*.'
Moved with *compassion* the *master* of that servant
    let him *go* and *forgave* him the loan.

"When that servant had *left*, he found one of his *fellow* servants
    who owed him a much *smaller* amount.
He *seized* him and started to *choke* him, demanding,
    'Pay *back* what you *owe*.'
Falling to his *knees*, his *fellow* servant *begged* him,
    'Be *patient* with me, and I *will* pay you back.'
But he *refused*.
Instead, he had the fellow servant put in *prison*
    until he paid back the *debt*.

"Now when his *fellow* servants saw what had *happened*,
    they were deeply *disturbed*, and went to their *master*
    and *reported* the whole *affair*.
His master *summoned* him and said to him,
    'You *wicked* servant!
I forgave *you* your entire *debt* because you *begged* me to.
Should *you* not have had *pity* on your *fellow* servant,
    as *I* had pity on *you*?'
Then in *anger* his master handed him over to the *torturers*
    until he should pay back the whole *debt*.

"So will my heavenly *Father* do to *you*,
    unless *each* of you forgives your *brother* from your *heart*."

Do not imitate different "voices" for the characters. You are telling a parable to adults, not re-creating a drama for children. Emotions are *suggested* by the reader's tone, but never mimicked.

It is the nature of parables that we know where it's going, which is all the more reason to proclaim it with high energy.

The final sentence is the moral of the story. Separate it from the narrative, and read it matter-of-factly.

---

doubling that number and adding one for good measure. Jesus responds with a number of "forgivenesses" so ludicrously huge that it means "unlimited."

In the parable, the king is like God, who has the right to demand what we have no hope of paying but in mercy forgives the entire debt. If we think we can get away with treating each other with mercy of a lesser quality, we are sadly mistaken.

The ending of today's gospel story is terrifying: "The master handed over that unforgiving servant to the torturers until he paid back all he owed. My heavenly Father will treat you in exactly the same way unless you forgive one another from your heart." That is a threat and a promise. But it's clear from the story itself that we are to forgive, not out of fear of punishment, but out of a sense of having been forgiven ourselves. We give forgiveness because we have received it.

Fear is never the Christian's real motive for doing the right thing, just as it is never God's motive. God's only motive is love. Remember John 3:16: "God loved the world so much that he gave his Son." We usually don't scare the ones we love into loving us back. Fear is more likely to inspire hate than love. Ultimately, our motive for forgiving each other in an unlimited way is our love for each other, prompted by the self-knowledge that we need unlimited forgiveness ourselves.

More precisely, our good motives arise from the knowledge that God has forgiven our sins. And why? God is good, and God has made us good, and deserving of forgiveness. That's what John 3:16 means: "We are good because God has loved us so much." So we quite naturally will treat each other as good and worthy of forgiveness.

25TH SUNDAY IN ORDINARY TIME

Lectionary #133

READING I   Isaiah 55:6–9

A reading from the book of the prophet Isaiah

Seek the LORD while he may be *found*,
    call him while he is *near*.
Let the *scoundrel forsake* his way,
    and the *wicked* his *thoughts*;
let him turn to the LORD for *mercy*;
    to our *God*, who is *generous* in forgiving.

For *my* thoughts are not *your* thoughts,
    nor are *your* ways *my* ways, says the LORD.
As high as the *heavens* are above the *earth*,
    so high are *my* ways above *your* ways
    and *my* thoughts above *your* thoughts.

The text must be proclaimed with the poetic expansiveness it clearly contains.

God pardons abundantly. We tend not to. Bring this out.

Proclaim the final sentence broadly. It makes the point of the reading in a striking way.

READING I | The prodigality of God's loving mercy and forgiveness is so often described in the scriptures that one has to wonder why so many people fret about their sins. They seem to think they must be found worthy of forgiveness. We must be aware of our need for forgiveness, and perhaps unawareness of that need is a more common problem. But any notion of having to beg or beseech or storm heaven to be forgiven is entirely misguided. God is eager to forgive us. And the breadth of God's mercy is far greater than our sins or our need. That's the nature of God.

The great abundance of God's mercy is the crux of this reading. God deals with us in ways different from our own. We cannot remind ourselves of that difference too often. God *never* withholds mercy or grace or pardon, although we often do.

Isaiah's poetry makes the point in a straightforward manner. The first sentence communicates a clear sense of urgency: "Seek the Lord while he may be found." This does not mean we have limited opportunities to do so. The Lord is always near and can always be found; we, however, may be neither. We are reminded of the adage "If you feel that God is far from you, guess who moved!"

Those who know poetry recognize this text as belonging to the *carpe diem* genre, urging the reader to seize the day, take advantage of the moment, make the most of a present opportunity, strike while the iron is hot. We see the reason for urgency in the final part of the text, when God begins speaking. Realizing the vast difference between our ways and God's makes us see that genuine conversion may take some time, so it's best to start now!

READING II Philippians 1:20c–24, 27a

A reading from the letter of Saint Paul to the Philippians

Brothers and sisters:
Christ will be *magnified* in my *body*, whether by *life* or by *death*.
For to *me life* is *Christ*, and *death* is *gain*.
If I go on living in the *flesh*,
    that means *fruitful* labor for me.
And I do not *know* which I shall *choose*.
I am *caught* between the two.
I long to *depart* this life and be with *Christ*,
    for that is far *better*.
Yet that I remain in the *flesh*
    is more *necessary* for *your* benefit.

Only, *conduct* yourselves in a way *worthy* of the *gospel* of Christ.

These are the words of a man facing death. Let the urgency be heard.

This is Paul's version of "To be, or not to be: That is the question."

This is Paul's resolution: Well, let's go on living for now, toiling productively for the gospel.

READING II We have been reading from Paul's letter to the Romans for several weeks. Now we open to the first page of his letter to the Philippians. It is clear that Paul feels a special affection and tenderness for his beloved Philippians. Every line of this letter reveals the joyful pride he feels in the authentic Christian witness of this community.

Paul is writing these words from prison. Knowing he can be martyred at any moment, Paul dwells on the tension between "now" and "then." He is eager for the peace and freedom that will come when we share the intimacy of God's life in heaven, but there is work to be done and that means there is still some "dying" to be done: dying to self and rising to a holier life in Jesus.

The rewards of the afterlife are sweet to contemplate, and we need to think about heaven more than we do. But there is more to be done than fantasize about that happiness. These are not idle or purely theoretical considerations for Paul. He is writing from a prison cell with the prospect of death before him. Knowing this can lend your proclamation of his words greater urgency and appeal.

GOSPEL Today's parable appears only in the gospel of Matthew. Both he and Luke drew much of their material from Mark's gospel, but both have elements that are unique to them, and both seem to have drawn on yet another source about which we know almost nothing. In any case, we can be immensely grateful for this story for it is a striking one, involving the hearer in a wide range of emotional responses and faith challenges.

Be sure to proclaim the parable as a good story—with great vocal variety and inflection—so that it comes alive again.

GOSPEL Matthew 20:1–16a

A reading from the holy gospel according to Matthew

Jesus told his *disciples* this *parable*:
"The kingdom of *heaven* is like a *landowner*
    who went out at *dawn* to hire *laborers* for his *vineyard*.
After *agreeing* with them for the usual daily *wage*,
    he sent them into his *vineyard*.
Going out about *nine o'clock*,
    the landowner saw *others* standing *idle* in the *marketplace*,
    and he said to them, 'You *too* go into my vineyard,
    and I will *give* you what is *just*.'
So they went off.

"And he went out *again* around *noon*,
    and around *three o'clock*, and did *likewise*.
Going out about *five* o'clock,
    the landowner found *others* standing around, and said to them,
    'Why do you stand here *idle* all day?'
They answered, 'Because no one has *hired* us.'
He said to them, 'You *too* go into my vineyard.'

"When it was *evening* the owner of the vineyard
        said to his *foreman*,
    '*Summon* the laborers and give them their *pay*,
    beginning with the *last* and *ending* with the *first*.'
When those who had started about *five* o'clock came,
    each received the *usual* daily *wage*.
So when the *first* came, *they* thought that *they* would
        receive *more*,
    but *each* of them *also* got the *usual* wage.

The effectiveness of the parable is that it imitates life, but in an exalted sense. We compare it to our own experience and note the similarities as well as the differences.

You have a lot of dialogue to proclaim. Let it sound easy and natural, not exaggerated with "character voices." Liturgical proclamation is not reenactment.

By now (or even earlier), we know what's going to happen. How and why it happens is the point.

Anything overly dramatic or exaggerated is inappropriate in the liturgical context, however. For every member of the assembly who might want a dramatic rendering, there is another who would be insulted by it, knowing that this is exalted literature, written for a purpose far beyond the story that contains it. A literal reenactment tends to concentrate on the action and draw attention away from the application. Outside the liturgical context, of course, a thoughtful dramatization can be quite effective.

The outrageous generosity of the landowner (unfair by our standards) parallels God's outrageous mercy and goodness. God pays us in coin so totally out of proportion to what we can earn that ordinary terms of barter and trade become meaningless. "An honest day's pay for an honest day's work" is completely inadequate to describe our relationship with God. Something more like "an everlasting fortune for a good-hearted attempt" is nearer the truth.

Jesus spent a lot of time with society's outcasts, those who would have been considered "last" in his culture. This parable

may have been told in response to those who objected to such preference for the poor and the sinner. Or it may refer to those who first heard the Good News but rejected it, or to those who were considered least likely to have accepted it. In any case, the point is clear. God's ways are not our ways, and we're in for some surprises on the day of reckoning unless we strive mightily to align our ways with God's.

Another way of looking at this parable comes to mind, prompted by the scripture text "Not as we see does God see, for God

The grumblers would have a good case in a human court. That's the point.

There is no injustice, but it feels unfair by human standards.

The parable actually says, "both last and first will be first." All the workers were paid the same. The saying may have been added later; the parable is stronger without the adage.

And on *receiving* it they *grumbled* against the landowner, saying,
　'These *last* ones worked only one *hour*,
　and you have made *them* equal to *us*,
　who bore the day's *burden* and the *heat.*'
He said to one of them in reply,
　'My *friend*, I am not *cheating* you.
Did you not *agree* with me for the *usual* daily *wage*?
Take what is *yours* and *go*.
What if I wish to give this *last* one the *same* as you?
Or am I not *free* to do as I *wish* with my own *money*?
Are you *envious* because I am *generous*?'

"Thus, the *last* will be *first*, and the *first* will be *last*."

looks at the heart." All the workers in this parable were eager for the job. They were idle only because they could not find employment. Consider this: Those who worked least needed the full day's wage just as much as those who worked most. Perhaps the landowner is paying what he knows his workers need, not just what they have earned. Or consider this: Those who worked the full day seem rather mean-spirited. They expect more than the amount agreed upon when they see the latecomers treated like equals. They grumble, "It's not fair!" Are

they thinking of the needs of their fellow workers or of what they feel they are owed?

It is a terrible thing to be jealous of someone's generosity. It shows just how different our ways are from God's. Why are we envious of another's good fortune? Why do we envy those who are generous with their wealth, talents, time or goodwill? Surely a moment's reflection is enough to show us that we would be happier rejoicing in their generosity, regardless of their motives. The only alternative is to become cynical about the goodness in other people, and cynicism is certain death for the human spirit.

The parable is about God's goodness. It is meant to inspire us toward enlarging our hearts, broadening our horizons, expanding our minds and spirits. In other words, it's about becoming a bit more like God.

26TH SUNDAY IN ORDINARY TIME

Lectionary #136

READING I   Ezekiel 18:25–28

A reading from the book of the prophet Ezekiel

The opening exclamation is powerful. Be sure the assembly is settled, quiet and ready to hear it.

Again, relish the power of the rhetorical question. Give the assembly a few seconds to respond silently.

Death is not the point; conversion that leads to life is the point.

Thus says the LORD:
You say, "The LORD's way is not *fair*!"
Hear *now*, house of *Israel*:
    Is it *my* way that is unfair, or *rather*, are not *your* ways unfair?

When someone *virtuous* turns *away* from virtue
        to commit *iniquity*, and *dies*,
    it is because of the *iniquity* he committed that he must die.

But if he *turns* from the wickedness he has committed,
    and does what is *right* and *just*,
    he shall *preserve* his life;
    since he has turned *away* from all the *sins*
        that he has *committed*,
    he shall surely *live*, he shall *not* die.

READING I Reading this passage might prompt the question "What's unfair about that?" When the good turn bad, they are punished. When the bad turn good, they are rewarded. What is Israel complaining about? Israel is exhibiting one of human nature's worst traits: self-righteousness. When I struggle all my life to be good and then see the wanton sinner turn away from sin late in life, I'm filled with indignation. That's not fair, I think. What am I really saying? Do I wish I could have had all the pleasures of sin, repented late, and still received

the reward of the righteous? We need to give such feelings a great deal of thought.

A constant refrain throughout our tradition is "Why do the wicked prosper?" We have to remember this saying to understand this reading. Our tendency to sit in judgment is alive and well in such questions, as is our tendency to blame others for our unhappiness. But such tendencies reveal an inadequate and underdeveloped understanding of God's nature. This reading can help.

It is not unheard of even today for certain groups to lay the blame for communal suffering at the feet of those they perceive

to be sinners. Only recently an archbishop claimed that a natural disaster in his country (which killed tens of thousands) was a sign of God's anger at corrupt political leaders. And religious groups still occasionally say that the AIDS epidemic is God's way of punishing homosexuals. This is puerile Christianity, a tit-for-tat notion that one suspects is willfully ignorant of God and woefully deaf to Christ.

Those who explain suffering so hardheartedly or resent deathbed conversions on the grounds of unfairness have yet to

The reading begins with a long and complex sentence, a series of assertions, really. But it is also exceptionally rich and beautiful. Read the sense units carefully and deliberately. A well-prepared and upbeat proclamation will give you mastery over it.

READING II   Philippians 2:1–11

A reading from the letter of Saint Paul to the Philippians

Brothers and sisters:
If there is any *encouragement* in *Christ*,
    any *solace* in *love*,
    any *participation* in the *Spirit*,
    any *compassion* and *mercy*,
    complete my joy by being of the same *mind*,
        with the same *love*,
    united in heart, thinking *one* thing.
Do *nothing* out of *selfishness* or out of *vainglory*;
    rather, humbly regard *others* as more *important*
        than *yourselves*,
    each looking out *not* for his *own* interests,
    but *also* for those of *others*.

Have in *you* the same *attitude*
    that is *also* in Christ *Jesus*,
    Who, though he was in the form of *God*,
    did not regard *equality* with God
     something to be *grasped*.
Rather, he *emptied* himself,
    taking the form of a *slave*,
    coming in *human* likeness;
    and found *human* in *appearance*,
    he *humbled* himself,
    becoming *obedient* to the point of *death*,
    even *death* on a *cross*.

understand how the grace of God operates. Ezekiel makes it clear that God's way seems unfair only to those who cannot imagine unlimited goodness.

In no way, however, does individual responsibility for individual sin diminish the communal solidarity we have as church. We are one body, and each part affects all the others. Though no one will be punished for anyone else's sins, each member of the body is in some way diminished by the sins of others, and, indeed, each benefits from the good done by others. This is because we each gain our identity as a Christian from

our membership in the body of Christ, to which we all belong.

READING II Paul loved the Philippians, and here he waxes eloquent, begging them to be the perfect reflection of a Christian community. Clearly he saw their potential for being so, and in seeing their potential and loving them deeply he empowered them to be all they could be. They were a good community, and he loved them into being a better one.

Paul's exalted prose is an appropriate preface to the great hymn that follows. In

that famous text ("he took the form of a slave") we learn what makes us one and what makes it possible to respond to Paul's exhortation to realize our potential. You are privileged to proclaim one of ancient Christianity's most moving and beautiful summaries of Christ's person and mission.

Your purpose here is to move your hearers to live lives in imitation of their noble model. But it is also to remind us of what we already are and what makes it possible for us to be united in spirit and ideals.

Most striking of all is the clear indication that the model is God. God is just as

Here the exultant hymn begins.
Pause before it, then adopt a more
expansive tone.

Because of this, God greatly *exalted* him
  and *bestowed* on him the *name*
  which is above *every* name,
  that at the name of *Jesus*
  every *knee* should *bend*,
  of those in *heaven* and on *earth* and *under* the earth,
  and every *tongue* confess that
  Jesus *Christ* is *Lord*,
  to the *glory* of God the *Father*.

[Shorter: Philippians 2:1–5]

GOSPEL Matthew 21:28–32

A reading from the holy gospel according to Matthew

Begin to build here and do not slacken
through the end.

Jesus said to the chief *priests* and *elders* of the people:
"What is *your* opinion?
A *man* had two *sons*.
He came to the *first* and said,
  'Son, go out and work in the *vineyard* today.'
He said in reply, 'I will *not*,'
  but *afterwards* changed his *mind* and *went*.
The man came to the *other* son and gave the *same* order.
He said in reply, 'Yes, sir,' but did *not* go.
Which of the two did his father's *will*?"
They answered, "The *first*."

We are in the middle of a discussion.
Jesus tells the brief story as an example
of the larger point he is making.

much God in suffering as in glory. Suffering is not merely something endured for a time because it leads to glory. Suffering and glory are the natural mix that defines Jesus and defines us as his disciples.

When we proclaim our belief "that Jesus Christ is Lord, to the glory of God the Father," we accept the apparent contradiction of a Christian life: obedience unto death, which leads to life eternal. Since Jesus is the perfect model of perfect acceptance of the paradox, every knee must bend to acknowledge and imitate that perfection.

GOSPEL One of Catholicism's claims to fame in the world of literature is a woman with the unusual name Flannery O'Connor. Her short stories are all concerned with Christian themes: redemption, forgiveness, revelation, good versus evil. Strangely enough, she writes not from an obvious Catholic perspective but from the view of a simple, fundamental, evangelical kind of Christianity that could be called "bare-bones" faith.

One of O'Connor's short stories is entitled "Revelation," and it came immediately to mind as I read today's scripture texts. The

heroine of the story thinks rather well of herself and takes great satisfaction in seeing how much better off she is than the lesser people who move through her life. Her prim superiority eventually crumbles when an ugly young girl, taunted beyond endurance, wrestles her to the floor in a doctor's office, screaming, "Go straight to hell, you old warthog!" Bewildered, angry, resentful, she goes home to pout over the grave injustice done her. And then she has a vision: multitudes of sinners, "poor white trash," all the people she scorned, dancing into heaven. The revelation, however, is not that she also

Notice the quick response of the chief priests and elders. They know the right answer but seem unable to apply it to their lives.

Jesus said to them, "*Amen*, I say to you,
    tax collectors and *prostitutes*
    are entering the kingdom of *God* before *you*.
When *John* came to you in the way of *righteousness*,
    you did not *believe* him;
    but *tax* collectors and *prostitutes* did.
Yet even when you saw *that*,
    you did not later *change* your minds and *believe* him."

sees herself, bringing up the rear; the revelation is that she is dancing, too.

Are the Lord's ways unfair? Sinners who turn from their sin will be saved. The son who refused to go to the vineyard but then relented did the will of the father. Jesus emptied himself and became a slave for our redemption. What a revelation! There is nothing tidy or neat or completely clear about this faith of ours.

The moment we feel we may have a handle on God and our fellow Christians we are in need of a revelation. The tax collectors and prostitutes and "poor white

trash" will enter first. That doesn't mean the righteous will not enter, but it does remind them of God's idea about who is first in line. If we avoid church because it is full of hypocrites, we've really missed the point. Is there a better place for them to be, where they will hear the word of God and be helped toward conversion?

We can consider this gospel parable as a warning against being slow to believe for the wrong reasons. Jesus was often criticized for consorting with the socially unacceptable, and for some that "guilt by association" was the perfect excuse for

not believing his teachings. The choice to believe may come late, or even after denial, but such a choice is infinitely better than living a lie. To say we believe and then behave as if we don't is the worst kind of hypocrisy. Likewise, to think we can easily distinguish the worthy from the unworthy is a devastating mistake. If we choose not to believe because we don't like the looks of other believers, this parable can be quite a revelation for us.

Lectionary #139

READING I   Isaiah 5:1–7

A reading from the book of the prophet Isaiah

The first sentence is a mini-prologue. The ballad begins with the second sentence. We should hear a difference.

Let me now sing of my *friend*,
  my friend's *song* concerning his *vineyard*.
My friend had a *vineyard*
  on a fertile *hillside*;

Draw the pictures carefully, letting the images create a vivid scene.

he *spaded* it, cleared it of *stones*,
  and *planted* the choicest *vines*;
within it he built a *watchtower*,
  and hewed out a *wine* press.
Then he looked for the crop of *grapes*,
  but what it *yielded* was *wild* grapes.

There is an abrupt change of mood here. Prepare for it with a pause and a change of tone.

Now, inhabitants of *Jerusalem* and people of *Judah*,
  judge between *me* and my *vineyard*:
What *more* was there to *do* for my vineyard
  that I had not *done*?
Why, when I looked for the crop of *grapes*,
  did it bring forth *wild* grapes?

After the two rhetorical questions, a new section begins.

Now, I will let you know
  what I mean to *do* with my vineyard:
take *away* its hedge, give it to *grazing*,
  break through its *wall*, let it be *trampled*!

READING I   The first reading today tells a sad story. It is all the more sad because it begins so beautifully, with a love song. When you proclaim this reading you are like a troubadour. The text is a poetic ballad, requiring you to establish a tone and mood suitable to it.

The farmer is God and the vineyard is Israel. The farmer has done everything possible to insure a good harvest. Beyond that, he has tended the vineyard with devotion. And yet, despite all his loving care, the harvest is bad, the grapes are bitter, his efforts

are all for naught. The lament turns desperate, giving us the image of inconsolable grief: "What more could I have done?"

But bitter grief slowly turns into seething resentment and anger, and, finally, to vengeful punishment. Israel, the unfaithful and unfruitful, shall be reduced to ruins, untended, uncultivated, arid and worthless. The picture is astoundingly bleak. The song that began with such heartrending love has ended in heartbreaking desolation.

Is the reading about the farmer or the vineyard, about God or about his unfaithful people? Does God punish in this wrathful

way those who do not respond to his tender care? The reading is about Israel's infidelity, and Isaiah explains their present misery by demonstrating that they have brought it on themselves. But even more important, the purpose of the ballad is to call Israel to repentance, to a return to their God. As they weep and wail over their dispersion and exile, they are reminded that a God of love made them what they are and can restore them to what they should be.

The reading was obviously chosen to complement the gospel, and it does so very effectively. Even the twist is paralleled as

Yes, I will make it a *ruin*:
  it shall not be *pruned* or *hoed*,
  but *overgrown* with *thorns* and *briers*;
I will command the *clouds*
  not to send *rain* upon it.
The *vineyard* of the LORD of *hosts* is the *house* of *Israel*,
  and the people of *Judah* are his cherished *plant*;
he looked for *judgment*, but see, *bloodshed*!
  for *justice*, but *hark*, the *outcry*!

Again, the images build to create a vivid, tragic picture.

READING II   Philippians 4:6–9

A reading from the letter of Saint Paul to the Philippians

Brothers and sisters:
Have no *anxiety* at *all*, but in *everything*,
  by *prayer* and *petition*, with *thanksgiving*,
  make your requests *known* to *God*.
Then the *peace* of God that surpasses all *understanding*
  will *guard* your hearts and minds in Christ *Jesus*.

Finally, brothers and sisters,
  whatever is *true*, whatever is *honorable*,
  whatever is *just*, whatever is *pure*,
  whatever is *lovely*, whatever is *gracious*,
  if there is any *excellence*
  and if there is anything worthy of *praise*,
  think about *these* things.
Keep on *doing* what you have *learned* and *received*
  and *heard* and *seen* in *me*.
Then the God of *peace* will be *with* you.

As with all abrupt beginnings, it is important that you have the assembly's attention before beginning. The first sentence is crucial.

God's own peace will guard us—a truly beautiful thought.

This is a list of virtues. Lists are difficult to read effectively, but each item must be given its due.

Jesus turns the tables on his audience. It should be clear to the assembly by your careful proclamation that each member needs to remember the care with which God has prepared us to lead good and holy lives. God has equipped us for doing good, and yet how often our selfishness renders that loving preparation fruitless.

READING II **As we continue to take the second reading from Paul's letter to the Philippians, you may find it** helpful to read earlier commentaries to get a feel for the overall thrust of the letter.

Nothing is more debilitating or fruitless than anxiety. It does nothing to solve our dilemma and, indeed, makes it more difficult by sapping the strength from our attempts at a solution. Anxiety is fear, but fear is useless, the Lord has told us. What is needed is trust. If we find ourselves filled with anxiety, we might do well to consider these words of Walt Whitman in *Leaves of Grass:*

  I think I could turn and live
    with animals,
    they are so placid and self-contain'd,

I stand and look at them long and long.
They do not sweat and whine about
    their condition,
They do not lie awake in the dark and
    weep for their sins,
They do not make me sick discussing
    their duty to God,
Not one is dissatisfied, not one is
    demented with the mania of
    owning things.

Paul presents us with a more constructive alternative. In presenting our needs to God in prayer and simple gratitude, we can

GOSPEL   Matthew 21:33–43

A reading from the holy gospel according to Matthew

Jesus said to the chief *priests* and the *elders* of the people:
"Hear *another* parable.
There was a *landowner* who planted a *vineyard*,
    put a *hedge* around it, dug a *wine* press in it, and built a *tower*.
Then he *leased* it to *tenants* and went on a *journey*.

"When *vintage* time drew near,
    he sent his *servants* to the tenants to obtain his *produce*.
But the *tenants seized* the servants and *one* they *beat*,
    another they *killed*, and a *third* they *stoned*.
Again he sent *other* servants, more *numerous* than the first ones,
    but they treated *them* in the same *way*.

"*Finally*, he sent his *son* to them, thinking,
    'They will *respect* my *son*.'
But when the tenants saw the *son*, they said to one another,
    'This is the *heir*.
Come, let us *kill* him and acquire his *inheritance*.'
They *seized* him, threw him *out* of the vineyard, and *killed* him.

"What will the *owner* of the vineyard *do* to those tenants
        when he *comes*?"
They answered him,
    "He will *put* those wretched *men* to a wretched *death*
    and lease his *vineyard* to *other* tenants
    who will give him the *produce* at the proper *times*."

Margin notes:

"Hear *another* parable." We've been hearing parables for the last few Sundays. The emphasis might also work this way: "Hear another *parable*."

The property owner prepared the vineyard well, just as we heard in the first reading. Jesus' audience would probably recall the Isaiah story.

The response of the tenants is shocking, even though we may have seen it coming.

Pause before Jesus asks the trick question.

Do not pause before the immediate response to the question.

assess our situation with a quiet heart and arrive at resolutions more productively.

Notice that the list of good things toward which our thoughts ought to be directed is not specifically religious and certainly not uniquely Christian. All people of goodwill embrace what is true, honest, pure, and so forth. What makes the difference for us is that these good things are sought not in order to obtain faith; they are sought because we have faith.

When Paul asks us to live according to what we have heard him say and do, he is not setting himself up as a model of virtue. Rather, he is referring to his total dedication to the gospel of Christ, reminding us that the gospel is the motivation for our pursuit of goodness. Christians are good because they are responding to the good that has been done for them by Christ. They do not "make me sick discussing their duty to God." They lighten my darkness by proclaiming God's goodness to them.

GOSPEL In the first reading we saw a lovingly tended vineyard go bad. Here we see bad tenant farmers deny the owner his due. The bottom line here, as Matthew tells the story, echoes the prologue to John's gospel: "He came unto his own and his own received him not." The parable is an indictment of those who refuse to believe and continuously mistreat the messengers of God.

The final statement is hard to hear, but tell it like it is.

Jesus said to them, "Did you never read in the *Scriptures*:
  'The *stone* that the builders *rejected*
  has become the *cornerstone*;
  by the *Lord* has this been done,
  and it is *wonderful* in our *eyes*?'
Therefore, I say to you,
  the kingdom of *God* will be taken *away* from you
  and given to a people that will *produce* its *fruit*."

Clearly the story Jesus tells is a setup, and it works. It can elicit only one response from the chief priests and elders: "He will punish those wicked tenants severely and hire his vineyard out to others." Jesus elicits from the ones who mistrust him a vindication of all the rejected prophets, including himself, and a castigation of those who refuse to accept and believe.

Without the final paragraph, which was added by the author of the gospel, the parable has an entirely different meaning. Most simply, Jesus is telling us a story that exemplifies the lengths to which people will go to get what they want. The point is that we must go to any lengths for the sake of the kingdom of God. We are not being counseled here to beat, stone or kill, or do to anything wicked at all. But we are being told that the same kind of relentless determination should characterize our efforts. This is not the only time Jesus uses an example of bad behavior to exemplify a noble degree of determination.

Like every good story, this one has more than one application. Certainly it is a reminder that we must be slow to take our status as "members of the elect" for granted. Perhaps even more important is the admonition to be on the alert for messengers of the Good News, even among those who do not measure up to our idea of a prophet. Jesus didn't measure up either.

28TH SUNDAY IN ORDINARY TIME

Lectionary #142

READING I Isaiah 25:6–10a

A reading from the book of the prophet Isaiah

The mountain referred to is Mount Zion. You may wish to begin, "On the mountain of Zion, the Lord of hosts will . . ."

On *this* mountain the LORD of hosts
    will *provide* for all *peoples*
a *feast* of rich *food* and choice *wines,*
    juicy, rich food and *pure, choice* wines.

There will no longer be a separation between God and the people.

On *this* mountain he will *destroy*
    the *veil* that *veils* all peoples,
the *web* that is woven over all *nations;*
    he will destroy *death forever.*
The Lord GOD will wipe away
    the *tears* from every *face;*
the *reproach* of his people he will *remove*
    from the whole *earth;* for the LORD has *spoken.*

The final section is filled with joy at seeing God face to face.

On *that* day it will be said:
"*Behold* our *God,* to whom we looked to *save* us!
    This is the LORD for whom we *looked;*
    let us *rejoice* and be *glad* that he has *saved* us!"
For the hand of the LORD will *rest* on this *mountain.*

READING I The use of banquet imagery to describe the fullness of life in God's presence is a constant in our tradition. For our ancestors, there was no greater sign of unity, hospitality and *shalom* than a meal taken together with one's family and friends. The worst kind of betrayal is that of a friend who has sat at one's table. In Christian faith, the eucharistic banquet brings this image to perfection, of course, in which we partake of the body and blood of Christ every Sunday.

Isaiah takes up the banquet theme with particular vividness in this reading, which is used elsewhere in the church's liturgy in the votive Mass for a happy death. What could be more appropriate, since death is the door through which we pass into the banquet hall of heaven. Isaiah is looking forward to that day when Israel will be restored to her former greatness and enjoy the blessings of happy life under the provident hand of God.

Jesus relates a parable in today's gospel centered in a banquet setting, and so this reading has been chosen to complement it (though Jesus' purpose goes beyond Isaiah's, as we shall see). But the beauty of Isaiah's description prepares us well for the lesson Jesus' parable teaches.

It is particularly important to remember that you are proclaiming poetry here. All the images of choice foods and good wines should be savored and relished. The veil or shroud that covers the people is whatever separates them from the favor of God and the comfort of the divine presence. That shroud will be destroyed, and God will wipe away all tears and remove the reproach and disgrace under which the chosen people now live. The calm assurance that these things will come to pass should be quite

READING II   Philippians 4:12–14, 19–20

A reading from the letter of Saint Paul to the Philippians

This is an expression of gratitude, but the "thank you" comes later.

Brothers and sisters:
I *know* how to *live* in *humble* circumstances;
    I know *also* how to live with *abundance.*
In *every* circumstance and in *all* things
    I have learned the *secret* of being well *fed* and of going *hungry,*
    of living in *abundance* and of being in *need.*

"It was kind of you"—direct address always adds a special immediacy to the proclamation.

I can do *all* things in him who *strengthens* me.
Still, it was *kind* of you to *share* in my *distress.*

The reading (and the letter) ends with an acclamation. A few verses of greetings follow, but the "Amen" here signals the end. Leave a distinct pause before saying "The word of the Lord."

My God will fully *supply* whatever you *need,*
    in accord with his glorious *riches* in Christ *Jesus.*
To our God and *Father,* glory for*ever* and *ever. Amen.*

apparent in the strength and confident peace of your proclamation.

READING II As we have noted in earlier commentaries, Paul wrote his letter to the church of Philippi from a prison cell. In this section of the letter he expresses his sincere gratitude for their kindness in sending gifts to provide for his basic needs. Paul cannot resist, however, using even this occasion of kindness to point out that his real strength and sustenance comes from the Lord—as indeed ours must. Though he could do without the charity of the Philippians, having learned to cope with both abundance and poverty, he is nevertheless grateful for their kindness. And he takes obvious delight in assuring them that God will reward their generosity.

Notice that a few verses have been edited from this passage (verses 15–18). It's a shame really, for Paul says something wonderful about the gift he has received from the Philippians in those verses. He says that he rejoices primarily because the gift they have given will put them in good stead with God. In other words, he appreciates their gesture of concern more because it will bring them God's favor than because it will benefit him. It's a charming and inspiring expression of thanks that shows how selflessly he loved the Philippians.

Though the match is coincidental, the imagery in this reading complements the images of banquet in the first reading and the gospel parable. God, Paul says, will supply our needs fully out of the divine abundance.

GOSPEL   Matthew 22:1–14

The longer form of the gospel contains two parables, which are not easy to relate to one another, and both stories are harsh. Pull no punches, but let the stories themselves be the admonition. Avoid sounding overbearing or condemnatory.

A reading from the holy gospel according to Matthew

Jesus again in *reply* spoke to the chief *pri*ests and *elders*
    of the people
  in *parables*, saying,
"The kingdom of *heaven* may be likened to a *king*
  who gave a *wedding* feast for his son.
He dispatched his *servants*
  to *summon* the invited guests to the *feast*,
  but they *refused* to *come*.

Pause slightly before the "but" that signals the guests' refusal.

The second summons is a genuine plea.

A *second* time he sent *other* servants, saying,
  'Tell those *invited*: "*Behold*, I have prepared my *banquet*,
  my *calves* and fattened *cattle* are *killed*,
  and everything is *ready*; come to the *feast.*"'
Some *ignored* the invitation and went *away*,
  one to his *farm*, another to his *business*.
The *rest* laid hold of his *servants*,
  mistreated them, and *killed* them.
The king was *enraged* and sent his *troops*,
  destroyed those murderers, and burned their *city*.

The fury of the king should not be overdone. It is more sad than furious.

"Then he said to his *servants*, 'The feast is *ready*,
  but those who were *invited* were not *worthy* to come.
Go out, therefore, into the main *roads*
  and *invite* to the feast whomever you *find*.'
The servants went out into the *streets*
  and gathered *all* they found, *bad* and *good alike*,
  and the hall was *filled* with guests.

From here through "filled with guests," a more upbeat tone is appropriate.

GOSPEL It would be a good idea to take the shorter form of this gospel if a more consistent treatment of the "kingdom-as-banquet" theme is to be maintained. We have here not one parable but two. They have been rather artificially stuck together in Matthew's gospel, and the author has added to the original forms of the parable as well. Not only will the proclamation make more sense if the shorter form is taken, but it will also make the homilist's job much easier!

The first parable deals with rejection of the king's invitation by those who had been invited long ago. Invitations were sent out far in advance of the actual feast, and when the banquet was prepared and ready, servants were sent out to call the invited guests together. Refusing at this point was an outrageous insult to one's host. Declining because of business concerns was rude enough. Abusing the servants was detestable.

The parable says flatly that the Jews, who were children of the covenant and heirs of God's promises, refused to accept God's reign in the person of Jesus. Because of this, the Gentiles—foreigners, outsiders and sinners, who had no expectation or hope of an invitation—would replace the Jews as the king's guests.

At this point, Matthew adds the fury of the king, who sends armies to destroy those who murdered his servant and to burn their city. It is an obvious reference to the destruction of Jerusalem in the year 70 (Matthew is writing between 80 and 90); the evangelist

Pause before this new section. The harshness appears again.

"But when the king came in to *meet* the guests,
   he saw a *man* there not *dressed* in a *wedding* garment.
The king said to him, 'My friend, how *is* it
   that you *came* in here without a *wedding* garment?'
But he was reduced to *silence*.
Then the king said to his *attendants*, 'Bind his *hands* and *feet*,
   and *cast* him into the darkness *outside*,
     where there will be *wailing* and grinding of *teeth*.'
Many are invited, but *few* are chosen."

[Shorter: Matthew 22:1–10]

sees this catastrophe as punishment of those who refused to accept Jesus as Messiah. What the Jews reject, the gospel's author argues, the non-Jews accept readily, so that the hall is filled with banquet-goers who have been called in from the street.

The second parable about the man improperly dressed for a wedding banquet is clearly distinct from the first, though as an admonition to be properly prepared for the feast it can be seen as an elaboration on it. From another point of view, however, it's not a good fit. How could the man be expected to be properly dressed when he had been hustled in off the street? The answer is simple. This story already existed in rabbinic literature, and Jesus' hearers would recognize it. Remember that the invitations were sent out long ago. Those invited had plenty of time to be prepared for the moment when the final summons came. Coming unprepared (improperly dressed) is a sign of disrespect to the host.

In the final analysis, then, the shorter version of the gospel is more accessible, unless the homilist can explain how the two parables have two different points.

29TH SUNDAY IN ORDINARY TIME

Lectionary #145

READING I   Isaiah 45:1, 4–6

A reading from the book of the prophet Isaiah

The passage is in poetic form. It must be proclaimed expansively. The long first sentence is not a problem if you read it in sense units.
Cyrus = SĪ-ruhs

Thus says the LORD to his anointed, *Cyrus*,
    whose right *hand* I grasp,
subduing *nations* before him,
    and making kings *run* in his *service*,
opening *doors* before him
    and leaving the *gates* unbarred:

This is the point: "I do these things through Cyrus *for the sake of my chosen people.*"

For the sake of *Jacob*, my *servant*,
    of *Israel*, my *chosen* one,
I have *called* you by your *name*,
    giving you a *title*, though you knew me *not*.
I am the LORD and there is no *other*,
    there is no *God* besides *me*.
It is *I* who arm you, though you know me *not*,
    so that toward the *rising* and the *setting* of the *sun*
    people may *know* that there is *none* besides *me*.

The final sentence has appeared earlier. It is the refrain and the overall message.

I am the LORD, there is no *other*.

READING I Cyrus is a unique character in the Hebrew scriptures. He is a Gentile and a pagan, yet he receives the title "the Lord's anointed." The members of the assembly who do not know this cannot possibly understand the import of this reading without the homilist's help. You, the proclaimer, can help by taking special pains with the two appearances of the assertion that God will work through Cyrus *even though he does not know the Lord.* This will not guarantee that the members of the assembly will understand, but it will prepare them to make the connection when the homilist makes the significance of the assertion explicit.

The point is that God makes use of this pagan king without Cyrus knowing it to accomplish good things for the chosen people, Israel. The text complements the gospel reading: Jesus demonstrates how to deal with Caesar, pagan king of the Romans, who occupied Jerusalem during the time of Jesus' ministry and forced the local population to pay taxes. God will achieve the work of salvation in any situation and will employ the power of nonbelievers to do so if necessary. We do not live in isolation from the non-Christian world, nor should we try. The notion that Christian faith will flourish when it breaks off contact with outside ("evil") influences is woefully misguided. One glance at Jesus' love for the outsider should convince us of that. Worse yet, such a position is by definition exclusionary. And if Christianity is not aggressively inclusive, it is unworthy of its name.

This reading repeats another lesson for emphasis: "I am the Lord and there is no other." Isaiah is at pains to refute any and all evidence that earthly kings and their gods

READING II   1 Thessalonians 1:1–5b

A reading from the first letter of Saint Paul to the Thessalonians

Paul, Silvanus, and *Timothy* to the church of the *Thessalonians*
   in God the *Father* and the Lord Jesus *Christ:*
   grace to you and *peace.*

We give *thanks* to God *always* for *all* of you,
   remembering you in our *prayers,*
      unceasingly calling to *mind* your work of *faith* and labor
         of *love*
   and endurance in *hope* of our Lord Jesus *Christ,*
   before our God and *Father,*
      knowing, brothers and sisters loved by God,
      how you were *chosen.*
For our *gospel* did not come to you in *word alone,*
   but also in *power* and in the Holy *Spirit*
      and with much *conviction.*

Be careful and deliberate with such opening greetings. They set the tone. Silvanus = sil-VAY-nuhs

The three great theological virtues are named: faith, love, hope. Emphasize them.

"Congratulations," Paul says. "You practice what I preached."

---

operate on their own. They are in the service of the one God of Israel, the only God, whether they realize it or not.

READING II Having completed our reading of Paul's letter to the Philippians, we now begin his first letter to the Christian community in Thessalonica. It begins here with congratulatory praise, but as we shall soon see, Paul has a great deal of scolding to do in this letter and in a second to the same community.

Paul congratulates the Thessalonians on the good report about them he has just received from his coworker Timothy. Paul is obviously proud of his achievement in preaching to the members of this young church, the first to be established in Europe, and they seem to have kept the faith. He explains to them that the reason for their fidelity is the fact that they received the Good News as a way of living rather than a mere code of conduct. It is an important distinction. Christianity can never be seen as a set of rules to obey. Christianity is the person of the risen Christ living and active in the world through those who bear his name. Rules keep changing; Jesus doesn't.

The message here is just as valid for the members of the assembly who will hear you proclaim it. They deserve to be congratulated for their faith and love. Though you cannot know the degree and quality of their faith, they are seated there before you to hear the Good News. And affirmation leads us to conversion more effectively than criticism does.

GOSPEL Paying taxes to the emperor of Rome was a real problem for the Pharisees and for all Jews living in a country occupied by the armies of Rome. Paying tribute to Caesar implied for the Jew

GOSPEL   Matthew 22:15–21

A reading from the holy gospel according to Matthew

The *Pharisees* went off
  and *plotted* how they might *entrap* Jesus in *speech*.
They sent their *disciples* to him, with the *Herodians*, saying,
  "*Teacher*, we know that you are a *truthful* man
  and that you teach the way of *God* in accordance
    with the *truth*.
And you are not *concerned* with anyone's *opinion*,
  for you do not *regard* a person's *status*.
Tell us, then, what is your *opinion*:
  Is it *lawful* to pay the *census* tax to *Caesar* or *not?*"

Knowing their *malice*, Jesus said,
  "Why are you *testing* me, you *hypocrites?*
Show me the *coin* that pays the *census* tax."
Then they handed him the Roman *coin*.
He said to them, "Whose *image* is this and whose *inscription?*"
They replied, "*Caesar's.*"
At that he said to them,
  "Then *repay* to *Caesar* what *belongs* to *Caesar*
  and to *God* what *belongs* to *God.*"

The beginning is awkward. Consider providing some context: "When the chief priests and Pharisees had heard the parables, they realized that Jesus was speaking about them. Then the Pharisees went off . . ."

Dialogue is more powerful than descriptive narrative. Make it come alive.

Pause before Jesus' recognition of their bad faith. Let the trick question hang for a beat or two.

Jesus' honest question should not sound petulant. Make it strong and firm.

Jesus states the simple truth. Proclaim his answer strongly but simply.

---

that there was a sovereign other than God ruling over them. In Caesar's case it was even a sovereign who claimed divinity for himself.

If Jesus had responded to the Pharisees' question with "No, you should not pay the tax," he would have been charged with sedition. Indeed, Jesus was so charged—unjustly—later on. Had he responded with a simple, "Yes, pay the tax," he would have been acknowledging a sovereignty that the entire Jewish people resented.

The response Jesus does give recognizes that the state has its place in society, but it cannot lay claim to what belongs to God. In other words, the power of the state is limited and does not supplant God's authority. As a matter of fact, Jesus implies that a ruler has no power except that which is given from above, a point Jesus makes explicitly to Pilate during his trial.

Jesus' response to his tricky interrogators is straightforward and direct, not evasive or an exercise in one-upmanship. And there is nothing new in his response. It was,

in fact, what the Pharisees already knew and believed. They had hoped for a response they could argue with, but they didn't get it. What Jesus says is true, plain and simple. It is the sanest approach to a less than ideal situation and is better than chaos.

Jesus recognizes the duplicity in the question, and he gets the better of those who taunt him. But he does so with the simple truth. "Repay to Caesar what belongs to Caesar, and to God what belongs to God."

30TH SUNDAY IN ORDINARY TIME

Lectionary #148

READING I   Exodus 22:20–26

A reading from the book of Exodus

Thus says the *Lord*:
"You shall not *molest* or *oppress* an *alien*,
    for *you* were once aliens *yourselves* in the land of *Egypt*.
You shall not *wrong* any *widow* or *orphan*.
If ever you *wrong* them and they cry *out* to me,
    I will surely *hear* their cry.
My *wrath* will flare up, and I will *kill* you with the *sword;*
    then your *own* wives will be *widows*,
        and *your* children *orphans*.

"If you lend *money* to one of your *poor* neighbors
        among my people,
    you shall not act like an *extortioner* toward him
    by demanding *interest* from him.
If you take your neighbor's *cloak* as a *pledge*,
    you shall *return it* to him before *sunset;*
    for this *cloak* of his is the only *covering* he has for his *body*.
What else has he to *sleep* in?
If he cries *out* to me, I will *hear* him; for I am *compassionate*."

Consider the following helpful introduction from the Canadian lectionary: "The Lord said to Moses: 'Thus shall you say to the Israelites, these are the ordinances that you shall set before them.'"

Though the reading centers on "you shall nots," there's no reason it should sound negative or brutal. It is persuasive in the very mercy it requires.

READING I True faith expresses itself in justice and mercy toward all, especially the downtrodden and the needy. This selection from Exodus is part of a larger treatise on social justice guided by mercy. It is chosen for today's liturgy because it makes explicit the summary of the law that Jesus offers in the gospel narrative.

The indignation of God can seem brutal. It is not easy to hear the words "I will kill you with the sword," but the very force of this threat impresses us with just how outrageous it is to mistreat the helpless. It also reminds us that widespread or politically sanctioned oppression always leads to war and bloodshed. It is not God who kills. Injustice and selfishness are the weapons that wound us mortally.

If we are sincere about doing unto others as we would have them do unto us, we will see how unthinkable it is to mistreat anyone, particularly the defenseless. The Christian should have great difficulty understanding how horrors like ethnic cleansing, "holy" wars, mass starvation and capital punishment can still exist in our world.

READING II "Heroes are those who kindle a great light in the world, who set up blazing torches in the dark streets of life for others to see by. Saints, on the other hand, are those who walk through the dark paths of the world and are themselves the light" (Felix Adler, adapted).

Paul encourages the Thessalonians to "walk through the world and be its light." He congratulates them for being a model of the faith for Macedonia and Achaia and beyond. Though young in the faith, the strength of their belief is already praised and emulated in distant lands.

READING II   1 Thessalonians 1:5c–10

A reading from the first letter of Saint Paul to the Thessalonians

Brothers and sisters:
You *know* what sort of people we *were* among you for *your* sake.
And you became *imitators* of us and of the *Lord*,
    receiving the word in great *affliction*,
        with *joy* from the Holy *Spirit*,
    so that you became a *model* for all the believers
    in *Macedonia* and in *Achaia*.
For from *you* the word of the Lord has sounded *forth*
    not only in *Macedonia* and in *Achaia*,
    but in *every* place your faith in *God* has gone *forth*,
    so that we have no *need* to say *anything*.
For they *themselves* openly *declare* about us
    what sort of *reception* we had among you,
    and how you turned to *God* from *idols*
    to serve the *living* and *true* God
    and to await his *Son* from *heaven*,
    whom he *raised* from the *dead*,
Jesus, who *delivers* us from the coming *wrath*.

These are the words of a convinced and convincing missionary.

A justifiably proud spiritual parent is speaking here.
Macedonia = mas-eh-DOH-nee-uh
Achaia = uh-KEE-uh

Sometimes the greatest compliment is the one that's presumed!

The final sentence is complex and long. Take it slowly, and concentrate on the sense units.

The importance of the Christian community in Thessalonica was great, for it was an influential city, a crossroads to other lands, and the church there was the first Christian community in Europe. From there the gospel could spread both west and east, which was all the more reason for Paul to keep the Thessalonians on the straight and narrow. They were crucial to the missionary success of the new faith.

One phrase should capture special attention here: waiting for the return of God's Son from heaven. This alerts us to the conviction held among early Christians (including Paul himself at first) that the return of Jesus and the fullness of the reign of God on earth was imminent. That is why the Thessalonians are concerned about some of their members who have died. What will happen to them? They didn't make it to the parousia, the second coming of Jesus!

Another problem crops up later, necessitating a second letter from Paul. Taking the notion of "waiting for the Lord's return" literally, some of the Thessalonians stopped working and became idle, reasoning that such efforts were pointless. These problems had to be dealt with, and Paul does so, both later in this letter and in a second missive.

GOSPEL The first thing most listeners want to know after hearing the first words of this gospel narrative is, "How did Jesus silence the Sadducees? And what was the argument about?" The lectionary arrangement and editing of the scripture readings still has a long way to go. The texts cannot be chosen and presented effectively without an ear acutely trained in

GOSPEL   Matthew 22:34–40

A reading from the holy gospel according to Matthew

When the *Pharisees* heard that *Jesus* had *silenced* the *Sadducees*,
　　they gathered *together*, and *one* of them,
　　a scholar of the *law*, *tested* him by asking,
　　"*Teacher*, which *commandment* in the law is the *greatest*?"

He said to him,
"You shall *love* the *Lord*, your *God*,
　　with *all* your *heart*,
　　with *all* your *soul*,
　　and with *all* your *mind*.
This is the greatest and the *first* commandment.

"The *second* is *like* it:
　　You shall love your *neighbor* as *yourself*.
The whole *law* and the *prophets*
　　　　depend on *these two* commandments."

See the commentary for an alternate way of beginning this narrative.

Dialogue is more vivid than straight narration. Get into it.

Notice that Jesus ignores whatever malice lies beneath the questioner's motives and answers with noble simplicity. There is no hint of rebuke.

Without being prompted, Jesus expands on his answer, pointing out that the law is not theory but practice.

their public proclamation. It would be better to begin this reading simply with a statement that the Pharisees gathered together to approach Jesus.

If you choose to keep the opening words, the homilist can explain that the argument with the Sadducees was about the resurrection of the dead, which they thought was ludicrous. To discredit him, the Sadducees present Jesus with what they think is a clever way to ridicule the idea. Jesus beats them at their own game. (See Matthew 22:23–33.)

This passage centers on Jesus' summary of the law. The fact that it is delivered to those who were attempting to trip him up makes the statement all the more memorable and a bit ironic. The charge to love your neighbor as yourself has just been broken by those who question Jesus deceitfully. Nobody likes to be dealt with falsely, so we shouldn't deal with others in such a manner.

Most striking here is Jesus' assertion of a relationship between the first and greatest commandment, and the second, which is like it. Fulfilling the law by loving God and neighbor is not an original idea to Jesus. It exists

early in the Hebrew scriptures and continues to appear throughout them. There is something unique, however, in Jesus' claim. He is saying that we can't have one without the other. Love of neighbor springs naturally from genuine love of God; love of God is demonstrated and strengthened in love of neighbor. It's the "faith versus good works" controversy again, and Jesus solves it for all time. Faith without good works is dead.

ALL SAINTS

Lectionary #667

READING I   Revelation 7:2–4, 9–14

A reading from the book of Revelation

I, *John*, saw another *angel* come up from the *East*,
  holding the *seal* of the living *God*.
He cried out in a loud *voice* to the *four* angels
  who were given power to *damage* the *land* and the *sea*,
  "Do *not* damage the *land* or the *sea* or the *trees*
  until we put the *seal* on the *foreheads* of the servants
    of our *God*."
I heard the *number* of those who had been marked with the seal,
  one *hundred* and forty-four *thousand* marked
  from every *tribe* of the *Israelites*.

After *this* I had a vision of a great *multitude*,
  which *no* one could *count*,
  from every *nation*, *race*, *people*, and *tongue*.
They stood before the *throne* and before the *Lamb*,
  wearing white *robes* and holding *palm* branches in their hands.
They cried out in a loud *voice*:
  "*Salvation* comes from our *God*,
  who is *seated* on the *throne*,
  and from the *Lamb*."

All the *angels* stood around the throne
  and around the *elders* and the four living *creatures*.
They *prostrated* themselves before the throne,
  worshiped *God*, and exclaimed:

Literature such as this must ring out expansively. Any proclamation that sounds literal or analytical is out of the question.

A new section begins here, following the missing verses. The imagery is vivid and beautiful.

READING I The observance of a day in honor of all the saints is the result of two church efforts to supplant pagan beliefs with Christian practice. In the seventh century, the Pantheon in Rome (a domed structure built in the second century to honor all the gods of Rome) was renamed in honor of Mary and all martyrs. About 200 years later, Pope Gregory IV made a day for all saints official. November 1 was probably chosen because it was one of the four great seasonal pagan festivals in the north. The Orthodox church celebrates All Saints on the Sunday after Pentecost.

Though in popular culture Halloween seems to have lost its association with All Saints, the proper name for the day is All Hallows' Eve, and "Hallows" means "Holy Ones." Here, too, a pagan observance (a final fling for ghouls and goblins before harvest) was Christianized, but in North America we seem to have returned to a non-religious observance of it for the most part.

There's no mistaking the nature of today's feast once we have heard this first reading from the apocalyptic literature of John. Taken just a bit out of context, this passage conveys the glory of heaven enjoyed by the elect, those who have survived the great ordeal and now rejoice in the presence of Jesus, the Lamb of God.

In context, the scene—a description of the terrible Day of the Lord—is actually quite horrific. Angels wreak havoc on the earth before the chosen ones are united with Christ in glory. Those chosen ones are marked with a special sign to protect them from the wrath to come. Despite the terror described here, John writes to comfort a church under persecution. He shows them that those who have survived the ordeal will ultimately triumph.

These acclamations should not be shouted. The speakers are bowed in humility before the throne.

"*Amen. Blessing* and *glory, wisdom* and *thanksgiving,*
    honor, power, and *might*
        be to our *God* for*ever* and *ever. Amen.*"

Then one of the *elders* spoke up and said to me,
    "Who *are* these wearing white *robes,* and where did they
        come from?"
I said to him, "My *lord, you* are the one who *knows.*"
He said to me,
    "*These* are the ones who have *survived* the time
        of great *distress;*
    they have *washed* their robes
    and made them *white* in the *blood* of the *Lamb.*"

Make the dialogue lively, the question real.

READING II   1 John 3:1–3

A reading from the first letter of Saint John

Beloved:
See what *love* the *Father* has *bestowed* on us
    that we may be called the *children* of God.
Yet *so* we *are.*
The reason the *world* does not *know* us
    is that it did not know *him.*

The text begins with an exclamation. Make it sound like one.

The world does not recognize us because we look so much like Jesus.

Beloved, we are God's children *now;*
    what we *shall be* has not yet been *revealed.*
We *do know* that when it is *revealed* we shall be *like* him,
    for we shall *see* him as he *is.*

Everyone who has this *hope* based on *him* makes himself *pure,*
    as *he* is pure.

To place our hope in Jesus is to become like him.

A word about the numerology here is in order. The number 144,000 is a number of absolute perfection. It is 12 times 12 multiplied by 1,000. The meaning of the number is not that there are only 144,000 chosen; rather, in its perfection, it symbolizes an unlimited number. Literalists will have to abandon any exclusionary interpretations.

An effective proclamation of apocalyptic literature will surrender to the splendor and majesty of the text, reveling in the poetic imagery.

READING II "In the evening of life we shall be judged on love alone." This is John's theme song. Here he reminds us not of something we shall become but of what we already are: children of God. It is an adoption that has happened to us because of God's immense love. Christians sometimes concentrate so much on their duty that they forget their dignity. John is out to convince us that, although we do not know what eternal life with God will be like, we do know what we are now. We are God's beloved and redeemed children, all evidence to the contrary notwithstanding.

Realizing our dignity inspires us to behave accordingly. The effect of focusing only on our duty is that we feel only obligation, a far cry from what the love of God intends for us. John seems to understand that the best way to help people be good is to point out how good they already are.

Today's feast reminds us that the destiny in store for us is glorious, and many have already achieved it. Believing in our dignity as children of God is what makes us saints, and saints are quite simply people who live now in accord with their final destiny.

GOSPEL   Matthew 5:1–12a

A reading from the holy gospel according to Matthew

When *Jesus* saw the *crowds*, he went up the *mountain*,
and after he had *sat down*, his *disciples* came to him.
He began to *teach* them, saying:
"*Blessed* are the *poor* in *spirit*,
for *theirs* is the kingdom of *heaven*.
Blessed are they who *mourn*,
for *they* will be *comforted*.

"*Blessed* are the *meek*,
for *they* will inherit the *land*.
Blessed are they who *hunger* and *thirst* for *righteousness*,
for *they* will be *satisfied*.

"*Blessed* are the *merciful*,
for *they* will be *shown* mercy.
Blessed are the clean of *heart*,
for *they* will see *God*.

"*Blessed* are the *peacemakers*,
for *they* will be called *children* of God.
Blessed are they who are *persecuted* for the sake
of *righteousness*,
for *theirs* is the kingdom of *heaven*.

"*Blessed* are *you* when they *insult* you and *persecute* you
and utter every kind of *evil* against you *falsely* because of *me*.
Rejoice and be *glad*,
for your *reward* will be *great* in *heaven*."

Like Moses, Jesus proclaims the new law from the mountaintop. Like a teacher with authority, he sits down to deliver his important doctrine.

Whether you pronounce it "blest" or "BLES-*d," be consistent and authoritative. I prefer the latter because it more effectively connotes the meaning "happy," which is the meaning here, rather than "having received a blessing."

The text is so important. Let each beatitude stand on its own. Employ vocal variation.

The list shifts from personal attributes to attributes affecting how we treat, and are treated by, others.

The final encouraging admonition is important. Suffering is seen in its true light, and the saints are proof of its value and its reward.

GOSPEL   Matthew presents Jesus as the new Moses, the teachings of Jesus as the new law, and the community Jesus gathers as the new Israel. Thus Jesus proclaims the new commandments on a mountaintop, just as Moses proclaimed the old commandments on Mount Sinai. Only the formulation and the lawgiver, however, are truly new. Every one of the so-called "beatitudes" can be found in the Hebrew scriptures that Jesus knew so well. He came, as he himself said, not to destroy the law but to bring it to perfection.

The list of beatitudes is perhaps most revealing when we apply it to Jesus himself and see that his life is an incarnation of each one. God comes to us in human form to restore the divine image within us. Jesus was poor in spirit, meek and lowly, hungry for holiness, merciful, pure in heart, a peacemaker, persecuted, insulted, slandered and sorrowful. Yet he was the most joyful person who ever lived. It is Jesus' life that gives such power to his teaching. He himself is the Good News.

And it is the life of Jesus that gives us the ability to follow him and his teaching.

The saints prove this to us, and we celebrate that proof in today's feast. Our own lives prove the power of Jesus. This need not surprise us, since we ourselves are among those who are called "saints," made so by the love and election of God.

Proclaiming the beatitudes well is not easy. You are challenged to enable the assembly to hear each one in its uniqueness. After all, it is not a list but a series of acclamations, a song of praise, a declaration of independence and a portrait of Jesus the Christ.

31ST SUNDAY IN ORDINARY TIME

Lectionary #151

READING I   Malachi 1:14b—2:2b, 8–10

Malachi = MAL-uh-kī

The opening words are strong and powerful. God is jealous of his people's welfare.

"Lay it to heart to give glory to my name" — good ministry defined!

You "have caused many to falter" — bad ministry defined!
Levi = LEE-vī

The voice changes to that of a repentant people.

A reading from the book of the prophet Malachi

A great *King* am I, says the LORD of *hosts*,
    and my *name* will be *feared* among the *nations*.

And *now*, O priests, *this* commandment is for *you*:
    If you do not *listen*,
if you do not lay it to *heart*,
    to give *glory* to my *name*, says the LORD of hosts,
I will send a *curse* upon you
    and of your *blessing* I will make a curse.

You have turned *aside* from the *way*,
    and have caused *many* to *falter* by your *instruction*;
you have made *void* the *covenant* of *Levi*,
    says the LORD of hosts.
I, therefore, have made you *contemptible*
    and *base* before all the *people*,
since you do not *keep* my ways,
    but show *partiality* in your *decisions*.

Have we not all the *one* father?
    Has not the *one* God *created* us?
Why then do we break *faith* with one another,
    violating the *covenant* of our *fathers*?

READING I   Here we see an indictment of those who have failed in their duty to teach God's law. Jesus' words in the gospel form a similar indictment of the scribes and Pharisees, who say all the right things but do not observe their own teaching. There seems to be something in human nature that tempts those charged with teaching righteousness to consider themselves above their own prescriptions.

Malachi's complaint (placed on God's lips) is that the priests have neglected their duty to preach the Torah (the law) with fidelity and good example. They thus have voided the covenant with Levi, the priestly tribe of Israel and are responsible for the erosion of faith among the people. It's a timeless complaint, and responding to it is crucially important for religious credibility.

This prophetic passage is written in verse form, and so you must be poetic in your rendering of it. Notice the parallel structures, for instance, and the exalted tone of prediction. Your proclamation must match this tone.

Notice that the last four lines shift from first person (God speaking) to second person (the priests and people lamenting). They have more than understood their sin; they have recognized its saddest effect: division and broken faith and denial of their unity under the covenant. Be sure your tone and inflection change appropriately to signal this shift.

The reading opens with a touching image. It sets the tone for what follows.

Good ministry shares its life, which is the gospel in practice.

Lengthy final sentences are difficult. Sustain this one through to the end and communicate a firm sense of closure.

READING II   1 Thessalonians 2:7b–9, 13

A reading from the first letter of Saint Paul to the Thessalonians

Brothers and sisters:
We were *gentle* among you, as a nursing *mother* cares
    for her *children*.
With such *affection* for you, we were determined
    to *share* with you
    not only the *gospel* of *God*, but our very *selves* as *well*,
    so dearly *beloved* had you *become* to us.
You *recall*, brothers and sisters, our *toil* and *drudgery*.
Working *night* and *day* in order not to *burden* any of you,
    we *proclaimed* to you the gospel of *God*.

And for *this* reason we *too* give thanks to God *unceasingly*,
    that, in *receiving* the word of God from hearing *us*,
    you received not a *human* word but, as it truly *is*,
       the word of *God*,
    which is now at *work* in you who *believe*.

READING II We have been reading from First Thessalonians for several weeks. You may wish to consult earlier commentaries to understand its overall purpose and thrust.

Paul is obviously proud of his record as an apostle to this young and influential community. We have already heard him congratulate its members on the good reports that have spread to distant lands about their practice of the faith.

Paul has a right to be proud of his work among the Thessalonians. Not only did he give them the Good News in its simplicity,

he also demonstrated the purity of his intentions. He made his own living and did not impose himself on their kindness by expecting something in return for the gospel.

Paul's combination of self-sufficiency and sincere regard for the spiritual welfare of his flock makes us see him as the ideal apostle, preaching and teaching in the most effective way imaginable. He has personal integrity and credibility because what he has received as a gift he gives as a gift. The effect is that the people of Thessalonica accept the gospel as the word of God, not as the message of a human being.

GOSPEL Matthew's account of Jesus' harsh condemnation of the religious leaders of his time must be tempered with an awareness of Matthew's situation and restraint in applying his words beyond that situation. Matthew wrote his gospel during a bitter struggle between the fledgling Christian communities and long-established Judaism. There can be no doubt that his formulation of Jesus' words about religious leaders is colored by this struggle. Warlike language is used in situations of conflict.

GOSPEL   Matthew 23:1–12

A reading from the holy gospel according to Matthew

Jesus spoke to the *crowds* and to his *disciples*, saying,
"The *scribes* and the *Pharisees*
    have taken their *seat* on the chair of *Moses*.
Therefore, *do* and *observe* all things *whatsoever* they *tell* you,
    but do *not* follow their *example*.
For they *preach* but they do not *practice*.
They tie up heavy *burdens* hard to *carry*
    and lay them on people's *shoulders*,
    but they will not lift a *finger* to *move* them.
All their *works* are performed to be *seen*.
They *widen* their *phylacteries* and *lengthen* their *tassels*.
They love places of *honor* at *banquets*,
        seats of *honor* in *synagogues*,
    greetings in marketplaces, and the salutation '*Rabbi*.'

"As for *you*, do not be *called* 'Rabbi.'
You have but *one* teacher, and you are all *brothers*.
Call *no* one on earth your *father*;
    you have but *one* Father in *heaven*.
Do *not* be called '*Master*';
    you have but *one* master, the *Christ*.
The *greatest* among *you* must be your *servant*.
Whoever *exalts* himself will be *humbled*;
    but whoever *humbles* himself will be *exalted*."

Jesus is not ranting and raving. The point is not so much the hypocrisy as the serious consequences of it.

The tone here is exasperation. To demand what we will not give is to abase ourselves as well as those we torment.

phylacteries = fih-LAK-tuh-reez
It's a pretty awful picture, but don't be squeamish. We all recognize these abuses.

Jesus is making the point that bearers of title must live up to them, as he does to the titles of "rabbi," "teacher" and "Christ."

Hindsight always shows us that we must temper the hard language of our sacred texts. Matthew mission, in part, is to show that the old Israel is being supplanted by the new Israel, that the Jews who rejected Jesus have been replaced by the Gentiles who accepted him. One can hardly expect the writer to pursue his mission without being influenced by the situation in which he presents his case.

Jesus is speaking of bad leaders and bad leadership. There is no justification here whatsoever for presuming that all the scribes and Pharisees of Jesus' time (or of Matthew's) were hypocritical. Such presumption is tempting because it is easier to be naive in our thinking than to spend time sorting things out. In fact, and this is borne out by the gospels, the vast majority of the religious leaders were good and faithful servants of God's law and God's people.

All things considered, this reading nevertheless gives us an extremely powerful and useful message about religious leadership, relevant for all time. We have wandered a long, long way from the ideal Jesus showed us by his words and deeds. Wide phylacteries and huge tassels still seem quite popular among the clergy. Places of honor seem not to make enough of them uncomfortable. Titles of reverence are often closely guarded as signs of human respect rather than as symbols of God's presence in human instruments. Such externals have enormous power, for good or ill. How that power plays out depends entirely upon the person invested with them.

32ND SUNDAY IN ORDINARY TIME

Lectionary #154

READING I   Wisdom 6:12–16

A reading from the book of Wisdom

Resplendent and *unfading* is *wisdom,*
　　and she is readily *perceived* by those who *love* her,
　　and *found* by those who *seek* her.
She *hastens* to make herself *known* in *anticipation* of their *desire;*
　　whoever *watches* for her at *dawn* shall not be *disappointed,*
　　for he shall *find* her sitting by his *gate.*

For taking *thought* of wisdom is the *perfection* of *prudence,*
　　and whoever for *her* sake keeps *vigil*
　　shall *quickly* be free from *care;*
because she makes her *own* rounds,
　　　seeking those *worthy* of her,
　　and graciously *appears* to them in the *ways,*
　　and *meets* them with all *solicitude.*

Note the poetic structure and tone. A certain expansive exaltation is the appropriate mode of proclamation.

Wisdom is almost always portrayed in feminine imagery, and positively so.

Wisdom is a personification of God, eager to be known and embraced.

Bring out the immediacy here: Even to think of wisdom is to acquire it; to seek wisdom is already to be free from care.

The solicitude of God/Wisdom is poignant here. We are being pursued lovingly!

READING I   The church's liturgical year is a seamless garment. Advent flows smoothly into the Christmas and Epiphany season; Epiphany and Baptism reveal Jesus at the beginning of his ministry; Lent brings us into the desert with Jesus early in his mission and leads inexorably to the Paschal Triduum, and the 50 days of Easter, culminating in Pentecost and the resumption of our telling of Jesus' ministry in the second part of Ordinary Time. Today the transition from Ordinary Time into Advent becomes very clear. The celebration of All Saints (November 1) is another annual clue that we are about to enter the season of "comings"—the coming of the Lord at Christmas and in glory at the end of time. Today's reading are all concerned with that final coming.

The wisdom literature of the Hebrew scriptures contains some of the most beautiful poetry in the Bible. It is calm yet sturdy, strong yet pliable, peaceful yet exhilarating. There is holiness in wisdom, and to be wise is to be near God. This is not the same as saying it is wise to be near God. That's just being smart. To be wise is to know that God is near. Wisdom is that elusive attribute that enables us to see beyond the surface of things into their depths, to see as God sees, and therefore to see God. One of the aspects of wisdom emphasized here is that she is eager to make herself known to us.

READING II 1 Thessalonians 4:13–18

A reading from the first letter of Saint Paul to the Thessalonians

The studied beginning of this section already shows us that Paul is wrestling with the problem as he writes about it. Be comforted! Your deceased loved ones will not be neglected.

We do not want you to be *unaware*, brothers and sisters,
  about those who have fallen *asleep*,
  so that you may not *grieve* like the *rest*, who have no *hope*.
For if we believe that Jesus *died* and *rose*,
  so *too* will *God*, *through* Jesus,
  bring with him those who have fallen *asleep*.
Indeed, we tell you *this*, on the word of the *Lord*,
  that we who are *alive*,
  who are *left* until the *coming* of the Lord,
  will surely not *precede* those who have fallen *asleep*.

Notice the change of tone and the visionary language.

For the Lord *himself*, with a word of *command*,
  with the *voice* of an *archangel* and with the *trumpet* of *God*,
  will come down from *heaven*,
  and the *dead* in Christ will rise *first*.
Then we who are *alive*, who are *left*,
  will be caught up *together* with them in the *clouds*
  to *meet* the *Lord* in the *air*.
Thus we shall always *be* with the *Lord*.
Therefore, *console* one another with these *words*.

[Shorter: 1 Thessalonians 4:13–14]

Speak the final line directly to the members of the assembly, looking at them. Pause, but do not break eye contact, and then proclaim, "The word of the Lord!"

The vigilant bridesmaids of today's gospel parable exemplify the wisdom described here. The sad fate of the bridesmaids who foolishly go to sleep on the job shows the consequence of failing to seek wisdom. Thus this first reading complements the gospel.

Wisdom is, after all, not elusive, though it often seems so. Unlike knowledge, which requires hard labor to acquire, wisdom is available to all who seek it. Indeed, as the reading makes clear, Lady Wisdom is eager to meet her pursuer more than halfway. Wisdom is clearly a personification of God, who is not elusive and yet must be sought. Seeking God means recognizing God's presence. Just seeking wisdom is the first step in acquiring it.

READING II This section of Paul's letter is concerned with the "end time," as are all the readings today. The conviction on the part of the earliest Christians—including those living in Thessalonica—that Jesus' return in glory would occur very soon, even in their lifetime, made it difficult for them to accept the death of their members. Paul is coming to terms with this disappointment himself as he assures the Thessalonians that Jesus is the Lord of life and death. Whether our expectations are accurate or not, Paul says, makes no difference. When Jesus does return in glory, all those who have died will be raised just as he was raised.

GOSPEL   Matthew 25:1–13

A reading from the holy gospel according to Matthew

Jesus told his *disciples* this *parable*:
"The kingdom of *heaven* will be like ten *virgins*
    who took their *lamps* and went out to meet the *bridegroom.*
Five of them were *foolish* and five were *wise.*
The *foolish* ones, when taking their lamps,
    brought no *oil* with them,
    but the *wise* brought flasks of *oil* with their lamps.
Since the bridegroom was long *delayed,*
    they all became *drowsy* and fell *asleep.*

"At *midnight,* there was a *cry,*
    '*Behold,* the *bridegroom!* Come out to *meet* him!'
Then all those *virgins* got up and *trimmed* their *lamps.*
The *foolish* ones said to the wise,
    '*Give* us some of your *oil,*
    for *our* lamps are going *out.*'
But the *wise* ones replied,
    '*No,* for there may not be *enough* for us *and* you.
Go instead to the *merchants* and *buy* some for yourselves.'
While they went off to *buy* it,
    the *bridegroom* came
    and those who were *ready* went into the *wedding feast*
        with him.
Then the *door* was *locked.*

Notice that this parable is spoken to Jesus' disciples, which may indicate a more intimate setting.

This is a short story, and a good one. Set the scene, introduce the crisis, relish the climax, and announce the moral. In other words, respect the movement from one part to the next.

Although the bridegroom is announced with a shout, do not shout. You are narrating the story, not reenacting it.

Dialogue is always stronger than straight narrative. Use appropriate inflection and pauses.

It may be difficult for us to appreciate the concerns expressed here. But that's only because we presume the return of the Lord in glory is a long way off. It might do us a lot of good to share something of the Thessalonians' (and Paul's) expectation of it!

The short form of this reading may be proclaimed if one wishes to avoid the imagery of the archangel's voice, God's trumpet and meeting the Lord in the air. This is the imagery of "the Rapture," so dear to some

Christian communities. It can be dear to us, too, if we understand its meaning correctly—namely, that eternal union with Christ is the church's ultimate destiny, offered to us by Christ's victory over death, not earned by our individual worth. It is a destiny we share as a people. We must reject any notion that some are excluded from this rapturous experience. Anyone who wants to participate will be there!

Considering the time of year we're in, the imagery of the second part of the reading is singularly appropriate and should

probably be proclaimed. The passage seems more complete when it is included.

GOSPEL   This colorful parable is the first of three we will hear as we move through these last Sundays before Advent. All three make the point that "the end time" is coming and we must be prepared for it, though we know neither the day nor the hour.

Prepare to deliver the moral of the story by pausing slightly before it.

"Afterwards the *other* virgins came and said,
  '*Lord, Lord,* open the *door* for us!'
But he said in reply,
  '*Amen*, I say to you, I do not *know* you.'
Therefore, stay *awake*,
  for you know neither the *day* nor the *hour.*"

The story of the wise and foolish virgins may be interpreted on more than one level. The simplest meaning, and probably the one most relevant to Jesus' historical situation (and Matthew's overall purpose), is that those who were open to the wisdom of God had "ears to hear" and accepted Jesus' message willingly. Those who rejected it found themselves rejected.

We have seen Matthew make this point in several parables over the past several weeks, and he clearly targets the Jews as the rightful heirs who reject their inheritance. The Gentiles, sinners and outcasts of society, who had no reasonable expectation of an invitation into the new kingdom, will supplant them.

The parable is a crystal clear warning to live lives of watchfulness and prudent preparedness. Such virtues develop in us when we are attentive to the word of God and carry it out in practice. We cannot, in other words, sleep on the job.

As with all parables or allegorical literature, we must not get bogged down in details that are beside the point. The customs surrounding matrimony that provide the setting for this story may be foreign to us, but that doesn't lessen our ability to understand and apply the story to our own time.

33RD SUNDAY IN ORDINARY TIME

Lectionary #157

READING I   Proverbs 31:10–13, 19–20, 30–31

A reading from the book of Proverbs

When one finds a worthy *wife*,
    her *value* is far beyond *pearls*.
Her *husband*, entrusting his *heart* to her,
    has an unfailing *prize*.
She brings him *good*, and not *evil*,
    all the days of her *life*.
She obtains *wool* and *flax*
    and works with loving *hands*.

She puts her hands to the *distaff*,
    and her *fingers* ply the *spindle*.
She reaches out her *hands* to the *poor*,
    and extends her *arms* to the *needy*.

Charm is *deceptive* and *beauty fleeting*;
    the woman who fears the LORD is to be *praised*.
Give her a *reward* for her *labors*,
    and let her *works praise* her at the city *gates*.

The book of Proverbs is written in verse form. Adapt your proclamation accordingly.

Do not rush through the discrete units. They are tiles in a mosaic. To appreciate the whole, we must savor the parts.

The repetition of "she" over and over demands wide vocal variation, to keep it fresh.

Here is a real proverb (charm/beauty/fear of the Lord). Proclaim it with some weight.

READING I This text is made up of several verses of a much longer passage. You may want to read the entire thirty-first chapter of Proverbs as a way to prepare.

The reading describes a woman who invests her talents wisely and reaps a bountiful return on them. She is thus an icon of the wise servant portrayed in today's gospel and the perfect foil for the timid and fawning servant who lets his talent lie fallow.

The virtue of the admirable woman depicted here is not so much her skill or ability as it is her cleverness in turning her talents to good ends. If the portrait seems stereotypical to the modern reader, consider what the writer has to say about how the woman looks: Any notion of her as a pretty object is rejected. Charm and beauty aside, she is praiseworthy because she fears the Lord. Since fear of the Lord is the beginning of wisdom, her most precious virtue is her wisdom, and for this she will be praised at the city gates and rewarded for her labors.

READING II This is the last of several Sundays on which the second reading is from First Thessalonians. You will have a clearer sense of this passage if you consult earlier commentaries.

The Thessalonians are disappointed that some of their members have died before the Lord's return, which they expected to come within their own lifetime. Paul tries to assuage their disappointment as he himself labors with his own similar expectations. He is forced to develop a theology that explains the relative insignificance of *when* the Lord will come, and he instructs the young church

READING II   1 Thessalonians 5:1–6

A reading from the first letter of Saint Paul to the Thessalonians

The beginning is abstract. Make sure you have the full attention of the assembly.

Concerning *times* and *seasons*, brothers and sisters,
   you have no need for *anything* to be *written* to you.
For you yourselves *know* very *well* that the day of the *Lord*
    will come
   like a *thief* at *night.*

Take advantage of the familiarity of "thief in the night," "children of the day," and so on.

When people are saying, "*Peace* and *security*,"
   then sudden *disaster* comes upon them,
   like *labor* pains upon a *pregnant* woman,
   and they will not *escape.*

We are different. Emphasize the contrast.

But *you*, brothers and sisters, are not in *darkness*,
   for that day to *overtake* you like a *thief.*
For all of *you* are children of the *light*
   and children of the *day.*
We are not of the *night* or of *darkness.*
Therefore, let us not *sleep* as the *rest* do,
   but let us stay *alert* and *sober.*

---

on how to live in expectation while at the same time leading industrious and profitable lives for the sake of the gospel.

The point he makes, and it is timely at any point in history, is that it is a big mistake to be mesmerized by speculations of when "the great day of the Lord" will arrive. Every age has its prophets of doom and calculators of an event that no one can possibly predict. We have this on Jesus' own authority: "No one knows the day or the hour. Not even the Son knows. This knowledge is reserved to the Father." Nevertheless, many are still led tragically astray by misguided

zealots who see signs where there are no signs and predict the unpredictable. We saw a rash of such speculations some years ago with the arrival of the year 2000.

It is our privilege and our duty to live in such a way that it makes no difference when the Lord returns. Since we are children of the daylight, as Paul says, it is impossible for us to be caught off guard by the "thief in the night." We live, then, neither in false security nor in constant dread. If we are truly eager for the Lord's return, we should take comfort in the possibility that we hasten it by making the world a better place.

"When the Son of Man returns in glory, will he find faith upon the earth?" Yes, if we do our job in the joy of peaceful confidence.

GOSPEL   The original meaning of the parable of the talents is simpler and more historically grounded than our perception of it as an allegory on industry, courage and the wise investment of our gifts and abilities. It was probably Jesus' way of pointing out the futility of "guarding" religious tradition in an overly zealous way. It is an indictment of a subtle form of idolatry, that is, valuing the inviolability of the

GOSPEL   Matthew 25:14–30

A reading from the holy gospel according to Matthew

Jesus told his *disciples* this *parable*:
"A man going on a *journey*
	called in his *servants* and entrusted his *possessions* to them.
To *one* he gave *five* talents; to another, *two*; to a third, *one*—
	to *each* according to his *ability*.
Then he went away.

"*Immediately* the one who received *five* talents
		went and *traded* with them,
	and made *another* five.
Likewise, the one who received *two* made *another* two.
But the man who received *one* went off and dug a *hole*
		in the ground
	and *buried* his master's money.

"After a long time
	the *master* of those servants came *back*
	and settled accounts with them.
The one who had received *five* talents came forward
	bringing the *additional* five.
He said, 'Master, you gave me *five talents*.
See, I have made five *more*.'
His master said to him, 'Well *done*, my *good* and *faithful* servant.
Since you were faithful in *small* matters,
	I will give you *great* responsibilities.
Come, share your master's *joy*.'

"Then the one who had received *two* talents *also* came forward
		and said,
	'Master, you gave me *two* talents.

Before the first section of the parable, consider adding some helpful introductory material from the Canadian lectionary: "Jesus said to his disciples, 'About the day and hour of the coming of the Son of Man, no one knows, neither the angels of heaven, nor the Son, but only the Father."" Then, "A man was going on a journey . . .""

The urgency of the first man's industry should be emphasized.

The industry of the second should be emphasized as well, though a bit less.

Emphasize the contrast of the third man's action.
Section two begins here. The time for settling accounts comes and a sense of foreboding is palpable.

Here begin the formulaic statements and the formulaic response of the master. They should sound like the formulas they are, though we should sense a build throughout.

---

law over inspiration, development, revelation and the future. Thus the law becomes greater than the people for whom it was formulated; it restricts and binds them rather than setting them free. Such a position is sometimes called "defending the faith."

Those who were not open to Jesus' teaching were guilty of such a mistake. If faith is seen as something that has to be defended or protected, it is probably not genuine—and it certainly will not grow if its fundamental approach is to "play it safe." "I knew you were a hard man, Master, so I decided not to take any risks. Better to hold

on tight to what I have than end up losing it." This is the position that earned the censure "You wicked, lazy servant!"

This parable is much loved by the industrious and enterprising entrepreneur, but it is more than a little threatening to the person who finds taking risks rather scary. The parable points out that life itself is a risk; ignoring that fact is a sure way of getting oneself into serious trouble. Keep in mind from the beginning of the story that the third servant, who buried his talent, had a suspicion that he was not taking the most commendable course. He knew that he was

acting out of timidity and fear but chose to continue on that course rather than risk what little he had. The monstrous irony is that he does lose everything after all. If this timid soul had acted honestly in innocence and naiveté, he surely would have been treated more sympathetically.

Taking the shorter form of this gospel story completely eviscerates both its meaning and its power to make us ponder that meaning. The short form eliminates the contrast between how people deal with their talents, which makes the industrious servant's reward meaningful. From a purely literary

See, I have made two *more*.'
His master said to him, 'Well *done*, my *good* and *faithful* servant.
Since you were faithful in *small* matters,
　I will give you *great* responsibilities.
Come, share your master's *joy*.'

"Then the one who had received the *one* talent came forward
　　and said,
　'Master, I *knew* you were a *demanding* person,
　harvesting where you did not *plant*
　and *gathering* where you did not *scatter*;
　so out of *fear* I went off and *buried* your talent in the *ground*.
Here it is *back*.'

"His master said to him in reply, 'You *wicked*, *lazy* servant!
So you *knew* that I *harvest* where I did not *plant*
　and *gather* where I did not *scatter*?
Should you not then have put my money in the *bank*
　so that I could have got it back with *interest* on my *return*?
Now then! *Take* the talent from him and *give* it to the one
　　with *ten*.
For to everyone who *has*,
　more will be *given* and he will grow *rich*;
　but from the *one* who has *not*,
　even what he *has* will be taken *away*.
And throw this *useless* servant into the darkness *outside*,
　where there will be *wailing* and *grinding* of *teeth*.'"

[Shorter: Matthew 25:14–15, 19–21]

Section three, the climax, begins here. Notice that the third man doesn't give a report. Instead, he offers a defense of his actions, which he knows even now were not wise.

Take advantage of the Master's rhetorical question. It is powerful. "You *knew* . . ."

The first man reaps the benefit of the third man's mistake. Those who have will get more.

point of view, the full version has the charm of predictability with its formulaic presentation. It arouses and allays our expectations in a steady rhythm of repeated phrases, each of which leads to a slightly different outcome. It is a masterpiece of Middle Eastern storytelling that uses devices we are familiar with in our Western tradition.

　For example, in what may seem an inappropriate comparison, consider "Goldilocks and the Three Bears" (or any of a thousand tales like it). The example has to do with literary form and style, not content. The story

progresses with gratifying familiarity as the refrains appear and reappear. "Oh, this porridge is too hot . . . this is too cold . . . this is just right." "Oh, this bed is too hard . . . this bed is too soft . . . this bed is just right."

　"To one he gave five thousand . . . to a second two thousand . . . to a third a thousand." "The first made another five . . . the second doubled his figure . . . the third dug a hole in the ground." "Master, I made five thousand more. Well done!" "Master, I doubled your money. Well done!" "Master, I buried your money; here it is back. You wicked, lazy servant!"

　I have belabored the point to demonstrate how a story like this works its effect on us. The child never tires of hearing the predictable fable she knows by heart. We never tire of hearing a parable we can predict with ease. The story works its magic through its structure and form, not through suspense. To take only part of the story is to rob it of its magic. And any number of gospel parables achieve their purpose in precisely the same way.

CHRIST THE KING

Lectionary #160

READING I Ezekiel 34:11–12, 15–17

A reading from the book of the prophet Ezekiel

Thus says the Lord G OD:
I *myself* will *look* after and *tend* my *sheep.*
As a *shepherd* tends his *flock*
  when he *finds* himself among his *scattered* sheep,
  so will *I* tend *my* sheep.
I will *rescue* them from every place where they were *scattered*
  when it was *cloudy* and *dark.*

I *myself* will pasture my sheep;
  I *myself* will give them *rest,* says the Lord G OD.
The *lost* I will seek *out,*
  the *strayed* I will bring *back,*
  the *injured* I will bind *up,*
  the *sick* I will *heal,*
  but the *sleek* and the *strong* I will *destroy,*
  shepherding them *rightly.*

As for *you,* my sheep, says the Lord G OD,
  I will *judge* between *one* sheep and *another,*
  between *rams* and *goats.*

Readings that begin "Thus says the Lord God" contain solemn and important announcements. Let your proclamation match the significance.

This is a series of promises, both touching and tender.

Lost, strayed, injured, weak, sick, sleek— do not rush through these vivid images.

READING I The feast of Christ the King is new by liturgical standards. It was added to the calendar of feasts by Pope Pius XI on December 11, 1925. The institution of the new feast was part of celebrating a Jubilee year, as was the dogmatic proclamation of the assumption of Mary in 1950 by Pius XII. The meaning and significance of hailing Christ as king of the universe is not difficult to discern. The image of the Messiah-king is everywhere in the Hebrew scriptures. And the titles Son of Man, Son of David and Son of God in the Christian scriptures make the image explicit with regard to Christ.

Though kings who exercise sovereign power in our time are few, our associations with the title reveal much about Christ. We must also remember what a special kind of king our Lord is. Christ is the shepherd-king *par excellence,* a role found often in the Hebrew scriptures.

In this first reading we hear God describe himself as a good shepherd. This is the language of the great apocalyptic writer Ezekiel. Notice that the entire reading is in the future tense. In the age to come, there will be no need to appoint shepherds, for God will assume this role. What better guarantee of full mercy and justice?

The reason underlying the choice of this reading for today's liturgy is apparent in its orientation toward the final age, especially in the final sentence. The great day of reckoning involves the separation of good from bad, those who accept the shepherd from those who reject him. Today's gospel parable dwells on the same theme.

Although this is a dense and complex
argument, careful and meticulous
preparation will make it clear.
Emphasize both "Christ" and "first."

This is a new section. Pause slightly.

This is a victory cry: "The *last* enemy to be
destroyed is *death!*"

A vision of heavenly peace ends the
reading.

READING II   1 Corinthians 15:20–26, 28

A reading from the first letter of Saint Paul to the Corinthians

Brothers and sisters:
Christ has been *raised* from the *dead*,
  the *firstfruits* of those who have fallen *asleep*.
For since *death* came through man,
  the *resurrection* of the dead came *also* through man.
For just as in *Adam* all *die*,
  so too in *Christ* shall all be brought to *life*,
  but each *one* in proper *order*:
  Christ the *firstfruits*;
  then, at his *coming*, those who *belong* to Christ;
  then comes the *end*,
  when he *hands over* the *kingdom* to his God and *Father*,
  when he has *destroyed* every *sovereignty*
  and every *authority* and *power*.
For he must *reign* until he has put all his *enemies* under his *feet*.
The *last* enemy to be destroyed is *death*.

When everything is *subjected* to him,
  then the Son *himself* will *also* be subjected
  to the one who *subjected* everything to him,
  so that *God* may be *all* in *all*.

READING II   Paul presents us with a fascinating account of how salvation history will end. The beginning of the end was the resurrection, when Christ ushered in the new age, the unending age that we now live in but do not experience fully. The day is coming, though, when death itself will be powerless and the risen Christ will hand over to the Father the harvest of his great work of redemption.

Meanwhile, the risen Christ reigns in our midst as we hasten the day of his coming in glory by living under his rule as loyal and productive subjects. We do not wait passively for the "day of the Lord." In vibrant faith and generous good works, we contribute to the glorious fulfillment of God's promises.

Paul's language in the final section of this passage is reaching to describe divine realities in human terms. When he says that Christ himself will be subjected to the Father, he seems to contradict the equality with the Father that Christ himself asserts so often. We are looking at Christ here as the obedient Son who hands over to the Father the completed task he was sent to accomplish. In that sense, Christ is subordinate to the Father; his perfect obedience to the Father's will accomplished the work the Father sent him to do.

Yes, Christ is king. And his reign over the New Kingdom covers the time from his resurrection from the dead to his return in glory—the Christian age, the life of the church from its birth to its transformation in glory. We live and worship somewhere in that "between time" and are acutely aware that the day is coming when God—Father, Son and Spirit—will be all there is, and our life will be God's life.

GOSPEL Matthew 25:31–46

A reading from the holy gospel according to Matthew

Jesus said to his *disciples*:
"When the Son of *Man* comes in his *glory*,
 and all the *angels* with him,
 he will sit upon his glorious *throne*,
 and all the *nations* will be *assembled* before him.
And he will *separate* them *one* from *another*,
 as a *shepherd* separates the *sheep* from the *goats*.
He will place the *sheep* on his *right* and the *goats* on his *left*.

"*Then* the king will say to those on his *right*,
 '*Come*, you who are *blessed* by my *Father*.
Inherit the *kingdom* prepared for you
   from the *foundation* of the *world*.
For I was *hungry* and you gave me *food*,
 I was *thirsty* and you gave me *drink*,
 a *stranger* and you *welcomed* me,
 naked and you *clothed* me,
 ill and you *cared* for me,
 in *prison* and you *visited* me.'

"Then the *righteous* will *answer* him and say,
 'Lord, when did we *see* you hungry and *feed* you,
 or *thirsty* and give you *drink*?
When did we *see* you a *stranger* and *welcome* you,
 or *naked* and *clothe* you?
When did we *see* you *ill* or in *prison*, and *visit* you?'
And the king will say to them in reply,
 '*Amen*, I say to you, *whatever* you did
 for one of the least *brothers* of mine, you did for *me*.'

The scene is majestic and awesome. Take your time describing the grandeur of it all.

Here is the Son of Man, Christ, as king, seated in a position of authority.

Be careful not to separate the assembly into sheep and goats by unwitting eye contact. I've seen it happen.

The list of needy conditions is repeated over and over. Do not sound bored with it. Keep it fresh.

The ritual structure of the interrogation is intentional. Let it work its hypnotic magic.

GOSPEL As we read Matthew's gospel during this liturgical year, we saw over and over that the parables of Jesus are concerned with the acceptance or rejection of his preaching. And we were reminded over and over that to accept or reject Jesus is to accept or reject God. Further, to accept a disciple sent by Jesus is to accept Jesus.

Today's parable offers a vision of the day when there will be a great separation of those who accept Jesus and his teaching from those who do not. This is the heart of the parable. Its great truth does not center

so much on who are sheep and who are goats as it does on the certainty that there are both and they will be separated. The image is taken from actual practice in animal husbandry. Though the sheep and goats graze together during the day, the goats must be separated at night because, unlike the sheep, they need shelter from the cold.

The image as employed here by Jesus reveals that the ultimate separation at the end of time is necessary and inevitable, and it is based on whether or not his message and his messengers have been accepted. The goats, on the left (the dishonorable

side in Jesus' culture), did not recognize or accept the messenger or the message. The sheep, on the right (the honorable side), accepted both.

Such a view presumes that Jesus is speaking of his disciples, whom he sent to preach his message, when he refers to the thirsty, naked, ill and imprisoned ones who were either cared for or neglected. This does not exclude the necessity of caring for others in need, but it does focus the parable more specifically on the disciples. It also, by the way, shows us just how closely Jesus

You now turn to the goats. Prepare for the switch.

"*Then* he will say to those on his *left*,
　　'*Depart* from me, you *accursed*,
　　into the eternal *fire* prepared for the *devil* and his *angels*.
For I was *hungry* and you gave me *no* food,
　　I was *thirsty* and you gave me *no* drink,
　　a *stranger* and you gave me *no* welcome,
　　naked and you gave me *no* clothing,
　　ill and in *prison*, and you did not *care* for me.'

This is ritual formula again. Make it just as new and fresh as the last time, even more so.

"Then they will answer and say,
　　'*Lord*, when did we *see* you *hungry* or *thirsty*
　　or a *stranger* or *naked* or *ill* or in *prison*,
　　and not *minister* to your *needs*?'
He will answer them, '*Amen*, I say to you,
　　what you did *not* do for one of these *least* ones,
　　you did *not* do for *me*.'
And *these* will go off to eternal *punishment*,
　　but the *righteous* to eternal *life*."

The overall effect of the story is invariably sobering and solemn. You cannot diminish this effect, nor should you want to. Remember, however, that we are celebrating the kingship of Christ. In this liturgical context, the sobering gospel story is balanced with many expressions of optimistic hope and joy.

identifies himself with his ambassadors: "When you did it to them, you did it to me."

We must also remember what Jesus has made clear over and over: that acceptance or rejection of him is acceptance or rejection of God who sent him. To reject Jesus the Son is to reject God the Father. To reject a disciple sent by Jesus is to reject Jesus. Christ the King will separate the sheep from the goats at the end of time on the basis of whether or not they have accepted the incarnate Word of God by accepting those he sent into the world to proclaim the Good News.

Like so many of the parables, this one is a literary masterpiece, an example of superbly crafted Middle Eastern storytelling. But it does not depend for its effect on suspense or surprise. We know what's coming at the end even as we hear the beginning. Such literature arouses our expectations in a steady rhythm of repeated phrases, each of which leads to a slightly different outcome.

As you prepare to proclaim this gospel, please look at the commentary for last Sunday's gospel, in which I have tried to demonstrate how stories like this work.

Here I simply summarize the principles governing their structure. The story progresses with gratifying familiarity as the refrains appear and reappear. As the child never tires of hearing the predictable fable she knows by heart, so we never tire of hearing a parable whose outcome we can predict with ease. The tedium we might feel at hearing the formulas repeated over and over is part of the experience. We need to stop listening for information and surrender ourselves to the story's flow, for it works its magic through its structure and form, not through new information.